Wastewater Irrigation and Health

Wastewater Irrigation and Health

Assessing and Mitigating Risk in Low-Income Countries

Edited by
Pay Drechsel, Christopher A. Scott,
Liqa Raschid-Sally, Mark Redwood
and Akiça Bahri

International Development Research Centre
Ottawa · Cairo · Dakar · Montevideo · Nairobi · New Delhi · Singapore

publishing for a sustainable future

London · Sterling, VA

First published by Earthscan with the International Development Research Centre (IDRC) and the International
Water Management Institute (IWMI) in the UK and USA in 2010

ISBN 978-1-84407-795-3 hardback
    978-1-84407-796-0 paperback

Typeset by JS Typesetting Ltd, Porthcawl, Mid Glamorgan
Cover design by Ruth Bateson

For a full list of publications please contact:

Earthscan
Dunstan House
14a St Cross Street
London EC1N 8XA, UK
Tel: +44 (0)20 7841 1930
Fax: +44 (0)20 7242 1474
Email: earthinfo@earthscan.co.uk
Web: **www.earthscan.co.uk**

22883 Quicksilver Drive, Sterling, VA 20166-2012, USA

Earthscan publishes in association with the International Institute for Environment and Development

IDRC publishes an e-book edition of this book (ISBN 978-1-55250-475-8)

For further information, please contact:
International Development Research Centre
PO Box 8500
Ottawa, ON
Canada K1G 3H9
Email: pub@idrc.ca
Web: www.idrc.ca

IDRC is a Canadian public corporation that works in close collaboration with researchers from the developing world
with the aim of building healthier, more equitable and more prosperous societies

A catalogue record for this book is available from the British Library

Library of Congress Cataloging-in-Publication Data

Wastewater irrigation and health : assessing and mitigating risk in low-income countries / edited by Pay Drechsel
… [et al.].
    p. ; cm.
  Includes bibliographical references and index.
   ISBN 978-1-84407-795-3 (hardback) – ISBN 978-1-84407-796-0 (pbk.) 1. Sewage irrigation–Developing
countries. 2. Sewage–Health aspects. 3. Public health–Developing countries. I. Drechsel, Pay.
   [DNLM: 1. Sewage. 2. Water Purification. 3. Agriculture–methods. 4. Developing Countries. 5. Risk
Assessment. WA 690 W323 2009]
   TD760.W345 2009
   363.72'84--dc22

                                2009029309

Mixed Sources
Product group from well-managed
forests and other controlled sources
www.fsc.org Cert no. SA-COC-1565
© 1996 Forest Stewardship Council

FSC

Contents

PART 5 — CONCLUSIONS AND OUTLOOK

Figures, Tables and Boxes

FIGURES

TABLES

Boxes

Foreword

Wastewater use for agricultural irrigation can have multiple benefits for almost all countries, but it is particularly beneficial and cost-effective in low-income arid and semi-arid countries. In such areas additional low-cost water resources can have a high payoff in human welfare and health, with increased possibilities for food production and increased employment opportunities for poor population groups living in the peripheries of towns and cities, which are the source of copious wastewater streams. However, in humid areas of low- and middle-income countries, wastewater flows from large urban areas are untreated and laden with the full spectrum of excreted bacterial, viral, protozoan, and helminthic pathogens endemic in the community, thus presenting a serious health risk when entering water sources used for irrigation.

Assessing and mitigating the health risks to the farmers themselves, to population groups residing in the immediate vicinity and to the public who may consume contaminated wastewater-irrigated crops is the subject of this important book. Over the past 150 years opinions have varied widely as to the benefits and health risks associated with wastewater irrigation. In the earliest period there were the idealistic conservationists such as Victor Hugo, who in 1868 enthusiastically promoted use of the sewage of Paris, which, if returned to the land, 'should suffice to nourish the world'.[1] The Royal Commission on the Sewage of Towns, 1857–65, in the United Kingdom gave its official blessing to land disposal of wastewater in order to prevent river pollution.[2] Both are worthy goals to this day. There was little thought given to any problems of disease transmission or regulations in those early days, only to the benefits.

However, this changed in the 1880s when Louis Pasteur and Robert Koch discovered pathogenic microbes and the mode of disease transmission. The industrialized and developed countries of the world took on an almost obsessive fear of disease transmission by pathogen-laden wastewater and developed strict, often irrational and, most of all, needlessly costly health guidelines and standards for use, such as those promulgated in California in 1918[3] and 1933 and made even stricter by the US Environmental Protection Agency and the US Agency for International Development in 1992.[4] These standards, copied by many countries around the world, required wastewater to essentially meet the microbial quality of drinking water for the irrigation of edible crops, despite the fact that few river waters used for irrigation could actually meet such a quality. They were aimed at being 'fail-safe' and 'zero-risk' and had little or no scientific or epidemiological basis to back them up. Meeting those standards was very expensive and required high-tech treatment processes suitable only to the economies and technical infrastructure of industrialized countries. Such overly strict and irrational standards often placed a needless barrier on wastewater use, particularly in low-income countries.

The prominent authors of this book – physical and social scientists, engineers, public-health experts and policy-makers from around the world – represent a new, pioneering school of thought in assessing the risks of wastewater use, based, for the first time, on rigorous scientific methods such as quantitative microbial risk assessment. Their chapters introduce innovative methods of risk analysis and new considerations of cost-effectiveness and social adoption, and for the first time place the recommended health guidelines for wastewater use on a rational, meticulous, scientific epidemiological basis. They have also introduced for the first time humanitarian and social considerations of the health, social welfare and environmental benefits of wastewater irrigation in balance with the associated risks, particularly in low-income settings, but applicable to all countries. The methods and strategies for control and mitigation of risks presented in this book are important and innovative, based on worldwide scientific and engineering know-how and practical experience. The World Health Organization has led the way in sponsoring much of the research on more liberal, cost-effective and innovative approaches that will support its current and future *Guidelines for the Safe Use of Wastewater, Excreta and Greywater*.

The social, economic and health values of more food, better nutrition and employment as by-products of wastewater irrigation have been incorporated in the delicate matrix of weights and balances in determining health guidelines and standards. This book represents the best modern and innovative thinking on the topic and symbolizes an important turning point in the history of wastewater use in irrigation as a major contributor to water and nutrient conservation, public health and social welfare.

Professor Hillel Shuval, DSc
Head, Department of Environmental Health Sciences,
Hadassah Academic College, and
Emeritus Professor of Environmental Sciences,
Hebrew University, Jerusalem, Israel

NOTES

1 Victor, H. (1862) 'The land impoverished by the sea', in *Les Misérables*, A. Lacroix, Verboeckhoven & Ce, Paris, vol 5, book 2, ch 1. Available at: www.online-literature. com/victor_hugo/les_miserables/323/.

2 Royal Commission on the Sewage of Towns (1865) 'Sewage of towns: Third report and appendices of the commission appointed to inquire into the best mode of distributing the sewage of towns, and applying it to beneficial and profitable uses', Her Majesty's Stationery Office, London. See also Tzanakakis, V. E., Paranychianaki, N. V. and Angelakis N. (2007) 'Soil as a wastewater treatment system: Historical development', *Water Science & Technology: Water Supply*, vol 7, no 1, pp67–75.

3 California State Board of Health (1918) 'Regulations governing use of sewage for irrigation purposes', California State Board of Health, Sacramento. See also *California Health Laws Related to Recycled Water*, *'The Purple Book'*, 2001 edition, available at: www.cdph.ca.gov/certlic/drinkingwater/Documents/Recharge/Purplebookupdate6-01.PDF.

4 *Guidelines for Water Reuse* (first edition, 1992), second edition (EPA/625/R-04/108) published in 2004 and available at www.epa.gov/ord/NRMRL/pubs/625r04108/625r04108.pdf.

Preface

This book is written for practitioners, researchers and graduate students in environmental and public health, sanitary and agricultural engineering, and wastewater irrigation management in developing countries. In particular, it should be useful for all those working to assess and mitigate health risks from the use of wastewater and faecal sludge in agriculture, under conditions where wastewater treatment is absent or inadequate to safeguard public health. In this respect, the book builds on and complements the international *Guidelines for the Safe Use of Wastewater, Excreta and Greywater* published in 2006 by the World Health Organization in collaboration with the Food and Agriculture Organization of the United Nations and the United Nations Environment Programme.

The book adds new data on the cost-effectiveness of treatment and post-treatment measures for health-risk reduction, discusses ways to facilitate behaviour-change towards safer practices and adds new dimensions to reuse-oriented governance of wastewater.

The overall sequence of sections addresses key issues concomitant with wastewater irrigation in developing countries (risk assessment, risk mitigation, wastewater use governance), while the individual chapters aim at concise information primarily on microbiological but also chemical risks. The authors link water and health to the establishment and implementation of effective, affordable and efficient options for risk reduction. Targeting developing countries, the book also tries to address situations where legislation and institutional capacities are constraints and where the availability of data for risk assessments is limited. We expect that the book will influence further applied multidisciplinary research on wastewater use related risk and its mitigation.

This volume would not have been possible without the support of the International Development Research Centre and the Google Foundation. Numerous other funding bodies supported work presented in individual chapters. Special acknowledgement is due to the Challenge Program on Water and Food of the Consultative Group on International Agricultural Research, the World Health Organization, and the Food and Agriculture Organization of the United Nations for their continued support.

The Editors

Contributors and Reviewers

CONTRIBUTORS

Priyanie Amerasinghe, International Water Management Institute (IWMI) Hyderabad, c/o ICRISAT, Patancheru – 502 324, Hyderabad, Andhra Pradesh, India. p.amerasinghe@cgiar.org

Philip Amoah, International Water Management Institute (IWMI) West Africa, PMB CT 112, Accra, Ghana. p.amoah@cgiar.org

Akiça Bahri, International Water Management Institute (IWMI) West Africa, PMB CT 112, Accra, Ghana. a.bahri@cgiar.org

Kelly Bidwell, Innovations for Poverty Action, PMB 57, OSU, Accra, Ghana. kbidwell@poverty-action.org

Robert Bos, Coordinator, Water, Sanitation, Hygiene and Health Unit (WSH), World Health Organization, Geneva, Switzerland. bosr@who.int

François Brissaud, Maison des Sciences de l'Eau, Université Montpellier II, 34095 Montpellier Cedex 05, France. brissaud@msem.univ-montp2.fr

Chris Buckley, Pollution Research Group, University of KwaZulu-Natal, Howard College Campus, 4041, Durban, South Africa. buckley@ukzn.ac.za

Richard Carr, formerly in the WSH unit, now with the Global Malaria Programme, World Health Organization, Geneva, Switzerland. carrr@who.int

Olufunke O. Cofie, International Water Management Institute (IWMI) West Africa, PMB CT 112, Accra, Ghana. o.cofie@cgiar.org

Pay Drechsel, International Water Management Institute (IWMI), 127 Sunil Mawatha, Pelawatte, Battaramulla, Sri Lanka. p.drechsel@cgiar.org

Alexandra E. V. Evans, International Water Management Institute (IWMI), 127 Sunil Mawatha, Pelawatte, Battaramulla, Sri Lanka. a.evans@cgiar.org

Andrew J. Hamilton, Department of Resource Management and Geography, Melbourne School of Land and Environment, University of Melbourne, 500 Yarra Boulevard, Richmond, Victoria 3121, Australia. andrewjh@unimelb.edu.au

Frans Huibers, Wageningen University and Research Centre, Wageningen, The Netherlands. frans.huibers@wur.nl

Sanja Ilic, Food Animal Health Research Program, Ohio Agricultural Research and Development Center, Ohio State University, 1680 Madison Ave., Wooster, OH 44691, USA. ilic.2@osu.edu

Regina Jeitler, Wageningen University and Research Centre, Wageningen, The Netherlands. regina.jeitler@hotmail.com

Blanca Jiménez Cisneros, Instituto de Ingeniería, Universidad Nacional Autónoma de México, Ciudad Universitaria, Apdo Postal 70472, 04510 Coyoacan, Mexico, DF. bjimenezc@iingen.unam.mx

Natalie Karavarsamis, Department of Mathematics and Statistics, Faculty of Science, University of Melbourne, Parkville, Victoria 3052, Australia. nkarav@unimelb.edu.au

Hanna Karg, Department of Physical Geography, University of Freiburg, Werthmannstrasse 4, 79085 Freiburg, Germany. hanna.karg@gmx.de

Bernard Keraita, International Water Management Institute (IWMI) West Africa, PMB CT 112, Accra, Ghana, and Department of International Health, University of Copenhagen, Denmark. b.keraita@cgiar.org

Doulaye Koné, Department of Water and Sanitation in Developing Countries / Swiss Federal Institute of Aquatic Science and Technology (EAWAG/SANDEC), P.O. Box 611, 8600 Dübendorf, Switzerland. doulaye.kone@eawag.ch

Flemming Konradsen, Copenhagen School of Global Health, University of Copenhagen, Øster Farimagsgade 5, DK-1014 Copenhagen, Denmark. flko@sund. ku.dk

Jeffrey T. LeJeune, Food Animal Health Research Program, Ohio Agricultural Research and Development Center, Ohio State University, 1680 Madison Ave., Wooster, OH 44691, USA. lejeune.3@osu.edu

Duncan Mara, School of Civil Engineering, University of Leeds, Leeds LS2 9JT, UK. d.d.mara@leeds.ac.uk

Christine Moe, Center for Global Safe Water, Hubert Department of Global Health, Rollins School of Public Health, Emory University, 1518 Clifton Rd N.E., Atlanta, GA 30322, USA. clmoe@sph.emory.edu

Ashley Murray, Energy and Resources Group, University of California, Berkeley, CA 94720–1710, USA. murray.ash@gmail.com

Clare A. Narrod, International Food Policy Research Institute (IFPRI), 2033 K St. N.W., Washington, DC, USA. c.narrod@cgiar.org

Inés Navarro, Universidad Nacional Autónoma de Mexico, Av. Universidad 3000, Coyoacán 04510, DF, Mexico. ing@pumas.iingen.unam.mx

Kara Nelson, Civil and Environmental Engineering, University of California, Berkeley, CA 94720–1710, USA. nelson@ce.berkeley.edu

Manzoor Qadir, International Center for Agricultural Research in the Dry Areas (ICARDA) and International Water Management Institute (IWMI), P.O. Box 5466, Aleppo, Syria. m.qadir@cgiar.org

Liqa Raschid-Sally, International Water Management Institute (IWMI) West Africa, PMB CT 112, Accra, Ghana. l.raschid@cgiar.org

Mark Redwood, Urban Poverty and Environment Program, International Development Research Centre (IDRC), P.O. Box 8500, Ottawa, Ontario, Canada. mredwood@idrc.ca

Christopher A. Scott, Udall Center for Studies in Public Policy and School of Geography and Regional Development, University of Arizona, Tucson, AZ, USA. cascott@email.arizona.edu

Razak Seidu, Department of Mathematical Sciences and Technology, Norwegian University Life Sciences, Postboks 5003, N–1432 As, Norway. razak.seidu@umb.no

Hillel Shuval, Department of Environmental Health Sciences, Hadassah Academic College, P.O. Box 7456, Jerusalem, 94265 Israel. hshuval@vms.huji.ac.il

Robert Simmons, Department of Natural Resources, Cranfield University, Cranfield, Bedfordshire MK43 0AL, UK. r.w.simmons@cranfield.ac.uk

Andrew Sleigh, School of Civil Engineering, University of Leeds, Leeds LS2 9JT, UK. p.a.sleigh@leeds.ac.uk

Peter Teunis, Center for Global Safe Water, Rollins School of Public Health, Emory University, 1518 Clifton Rd, N.E., Atlanta, GA 30307, USA. peter. teunis@emory.edu

Marites M. Tiongco, International Food Policy Research Institute (IFPRI), 2033 K St. N.W., Washington, DC, USA. m.tiongco@cgiar.org

REVIEWERS

Andrew Bradford, University of Sheffield, UK

Stephanie Buechler, University of Arizona, USA

Samuel Godfrey, UNICEF, Mozambique

George Frisvold, University of Arizona, USA

Sasha Koo-Oshima, Food and Agriculture Organization of the United Nations, Italy

Kerri Jean Ormerod, University of Arizona, USA

Tauhidur Rahman, University of Arizona, USA

Lisa Roma, Cranfield University, UK

Bahman Sheikh, San Francisco, USA

Martin Strauss, Department of Water and Sanitation in Developing Countries / Swiss Federal Institute of Aquatic Science and Technology, Switzerland

Thor-Axel Stenström, Swedish Institute for Infectious Disease Control, Sweden

Wim van der Hoek, University of Copenhagen, Denmark

Gwen Woods, University of Arizona, USA

Abbreviations

ADI	acceptable daily intake
APT	advanced primary treatment
BOD	biochemical oxygen demand
CEA	cost-effectiveness analysis
CEC	cation exchange capacity
CEPT	chemically enhanced primary treatment
CER	cost-effectiveness ratio
CGIAR	Consultative Group on International Agricultural Research
CI	confidence interval
COD	chemical oxygen demand
CSSRI	Central Soil Salinity Research Institute
DALYs	disability-adjusted life years
DFID	Department for International Development
DFS	Design for Service
EC	electrical conductivity
ES	effective size
EU	European Union
FAO	Food and Agriculture Organization of the United Nations
FILTER	Filtration and Irrigated Cropping for Land Treatment and Effluent Reuse
FS	faecal sludge
FSO	food-safety objectives
HACCP	hazard analysis and critical control point
HO	helminth ova
HRT	hyaraulic retention time
ICER	incremental cost-effectiveness ratio
IR	ingestion rates
IWMI	International Water Management Institute
KAPP	knowledge, attitude, perception and practices
KTR	King Talal Reservoir
LCA	life-cycle analysis

MCS	Monte Carlo simulation
MPAP	Multi-Stakeholder Participatory Action Planning
NV	norovirus
PAP	Participatory Action Planning
PCP	personal care product
POP	persistent organic pollutant
pppy	per person per year
QCRA	quantitative chemical risk assessment
QMRA	quantitative microbial risk assessment
RSC	Residual Sodium Carbonate
RUAF	Resource Centres on Urban Agriculture and Food Security
SAR	Sodium Adsorption Ratio
SAT	soil-aquifer treatment
SLF	Sustainable Livelihood Framework
SS	suspended solids
SW	solid waste
SWITCH	Sustainable Water Management Improves Tomorrow's Cities' Health
TDI	tolerable daily intake
TDS	total dissolved solids
TN	total nitrogen
TP	total phosphorous
TS	total solids
TVS	total volatile solids
UASB	upflow anaerobic sludge-blanket
UC	uniformity coefficient
UD	urine-diverting
UN	United Nations
UNEP	United Nations Environment Programme
UNHSP	United Nations Human Settlements Programme (UN-Habitat)
UNIDO	United Nations Industrial Development Organization
USEPA	United States Environmental Protection Agency
VIP	ventilated improved pit latrine
VSS	volatile suspended solids
WASPA	Wastewater Agriculture and Sanitation for Poverty Alleviation
WHO	World Health Organization
WSP	waste stabilization ponds
WSTR	wastewater storage and treatment reservoirs
WTP	willingness to pay
WWTP	wastewater treatment plant

Part 1

Setting the Stage

1

Wastewater, Sludge and Excreta Use in Developing Countries: An Overview

Blanca Jiménez, Pay Drechsel, Doulaye Koné, Akiça Bahri, Liqa Raschid-Sally and Manzoor Qadir

ABSTRACT

After introducing terms and terminology of wastewater, sludge and excreta use, the chapter highlights their global drivers and significance using examples from different parts of the developing world. It is useful in the discussion to differentiate between unplanned use of wastewater resulting from poor sanitation, and planned use which tries to address matters such as economic or physical water scarcity. Both types of wastewater use can have significant socio-economic benefits but also institutional challenges and risks which require different management approaches and, ideally, different guidelines. This diversity makes the current WHO Guidelines, which try to be global in nature, complex to understand and apply. Whilst planned reuse will remain the norm in countries that can afford treatment, most countries in the developing world are likely to continue to use non- or only partially treated wastewater, for as long as sanitation and waste disposal are unable to keep pace with urban population growth. However, there are options to link urban faecal sludge and wastewater management with urban food demands or other forms of resource recovery that provide opportunities to safely close the nutrient and water loops.

BOX 1.1 DEFINITIONS

The term 'wastewater' as used in this book covers wastewater of different qualities, ranging from raw to diluted, generated by various urban activities:

- Urban wastewater is usually a combination of one or more of the following which makes it polluted water:
  - Domestic effluent consisting of blackwater (excreta, urine and faecal sludge, i.e. toilet wastewater) and greywater (kitchen and bathing wastewater)
  - Water from commercial establishments and institutions, including hospitals
  - Industrial effluent where present
  - Stormwater and other urban run-off.
- Treated wastewater is wastewater that has been processed through a wastewater treatment plant up to certain standards in order to reduce its pollution or health hazard; if this is not fulfilled; the wastewater is considered at best as partially treated.
- Reclaimed (waste)water or recycled water is treated wastewater that can officially be used under controlled conditions for beneficial purposes such as irrigation.
- Faecal sludge is the general term for the undigested or partially digested slurry or solid that results from the storage or treatment of blackwater in so-called on-site sanitation systems such as septic tanks, latrines, toilet pits, dry toilets, unsewered public toilets and aqua privies.
- Biosolids are treated sludge or the treated by-products of domestic and commercial sewage, wastewater and faecal sludge treatment that can be beneficially utilized as soil amendment and fertilizer. These residuals are treated to reduce their organic matter content, volume and/or mass, the pathogens and the vector attraction potential.

Source: Raschid-Sally and Jayakody (2008), modified

INTRODUCTION

Describing the present use of polluted water, excreta and sludge in the agricultural practices of developing countries is not an easy task. On the one hand, there is a lack of reliable and sufficient information and, on the other, the available information does not use uniform terms and units to describe these practices, making it difficult to compare data or establish global inventories. The common lack of data is in part due to the informal character of the practice or even, in some cases, to the intention not to disclose data. This may be done because either farmers fear difficulties when trading their produce or governments do not want to acknowledge what appears to be a malpractice. For these reasons, this chapter will firstly introduce some definitions of terms that will be used throughout the entire book and will secondly analyse existing information from different sources using, for the given reasons, non-standardized methods of reporting. Despite these limitations, the descriptions presented are useful to provide an idea of the extent of the use of wastewater, excreta and sludge for agricultural practices in low- and middle-income countries.

BACKGROUND

Land application of wastewater, sludge and excreta is a widespread practice with a long tradition in many countries around the world. For centuries, farmers in China used human and animal excrements as fertilizers. Wastewater and sewage sludge, just as manure, have also been used by the northern European and Mediterranean civilizations; for instance, wastewater was reused in the 14th and 15th centuries in the Milanese Marcites and in the Valencian huertas, respectively (Soulié and Tréméa, 1991). In many European and North American cities, wastewater was disposed of in agricultural fields before the introduction of wastewater treatment technologies to prevent pollution of water bodies. In Paris, for instance, the use of partially treated wastewater was common until the second part of the 1900s (Asano et al., 2007). In developing countries like China, Mexico, Peru, Egypt, Lebanon, Morocco, India and Vietnam, wastewater has been used as a source of crop nutrients over many decades (AATSE, 2004; Jiménez and Asano, 2008). Therefore, agricultural use of untreated wastewater has been associated with land application and crop production for centuries (Keraita et al., 2008). However, over the years, it has become less popular in developed countries with the improvement of treatment technologies and increased awareness of the environmental and health issues associated with the practice; by contrast, in developing countries, due to a variety of factors described later, farmers use it extensively, even drawing advantages to improve their livelihoods.

The oldest references to the use of excreta come from some Asian countries, where it was used to increase fish production through aquaculture (World Health Organization (WHO), 2006). Sludge management has only recently become an issue, even for developed countries, because the densely populated areas are producing such large amounts of sludge and excreta that natural assimilation into the environment is not possible, while space for stockpiling is limited (United Nations Human Settlements Programme (UNHSP), 2008). Moreover, management is complex and there is a lack of social support: people prefer to ignore what happens to excreta after it is disposed of into latrines – and they are uncomfortable if it is brought to their attention, be it in developed or developing countries (Snyman, 2008).

This chapter attempts to give an overview of the use of wastewater, excreta and faecal sludge in agriculture; to characterize their use, the benefits derived and the costs involved, particularly regarding health consequences; and to provide perceptions around such uses and perspectives for the future. It is to be noted that

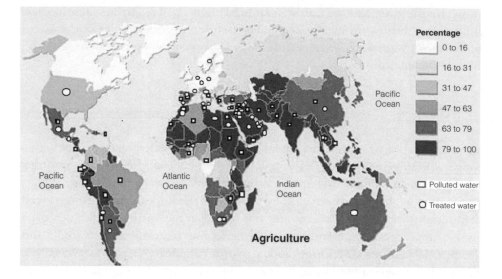

Figure 1.1 *Freshwater withdrawals for agricultural use in the year 2000 and countries reporting the use of wastewater or polluted water for irrigation*

Source: World Resources Institute (2000), adding information from Jiménez and Asano (2008); Keraita et al. (2008) and UNHSP (2008)

whilst mention will be made of reclaimed or recycled water, where relevant, the main thrust will be on non-treated wastewater.

EXTENT OF THE USE OF WASTEWATER, EXCRETA AND SLUDGE

In spite of the data limitations mentioned above, an attempt is made, in the following sections, to produce a broad picture of the extent of use of wastewater, sludge and excreta around the world using the best available information.

Table 1.1 *Some characteristics of countries using wastewater for irrigation*

Use of wastewater for irrigation	Total number of countries	GDP per capita for 50% of the countries (in US$)	Sanitation coverage for 50% of the countries (in %)
Untreated	23	880–4800	15–65
Treated and untreated	20	1170–7800	41–91
Treated	20	4313–19800	87–100

Wastewater

In the literature, there is no comprehensive global inventory of the extent of non-treated wastewater used for irrigation; actually, none exists even for treated wastewater. Based on information from the countries providing data on irrigated areas, it is estimated that more than 4–6 million hectares (ha) are irrigated with wastewater or polluted water (Jiménez and Asano, 2008; Keraita et al., 2008, UNHSP, 2008). A separate estimate indicates 20 million ha globally, an area that is nearly equivalent to 7 per cent of the total irrigated land in the world (WHO, 2006). In contrast, the area reported to be irrigated with treated wastewater amounts to only 10 per cent of this value. In practice, due to the under-reporting of areas irrigated with polluted water, the difference may be much higher. Two decades ago, WHO (1989) estimated that the area using raw wastewater or polluted water was 3 million ha; recent data suggest an area six times larger. It cannot be determined whether this difference refers to a de facto increase in the area or only in available data, but both might be the case, given the increasing amounts of wastewater generated as well as urban food needs.

The resulting agricultural activities are indeed most common in and around cities (Drechsel et al., 2006), but can also be seen in rural communities located downstream of where cities discharge, unless treatment or self-purification processes take place. Much of this use is not intentional and is the consequence of water sources being polluted due to poor sanitation and waste-disposal practices in cities. Raschid-Sally and Jayakody (2008) suggest from a survey across the developing world that wastewater without any significant treatment is used for irrigation purposes in four out of five cities.

In terms of volume of wastewater used for various purposes, the quantity varies considerably from one country to another. The majority of this is reported to be used in developing countries, where 75 per cent of the world's irrigated land is located (United Nations (UN), 2003), with a small amount, even if not expected, being used in some developed countries (Jiménez and Asano, 2008). In a new review integrating data from Jiménez and Asano (2008) and the UNHSP (2008), 46 countries report the use of polluted water for irrigation purposes (Figure 1.1). Table 1.1 shows a clear increase in GDP and the percentage of improved sanitation from countries using untreated to treated wastewater. Countries with middle income are those using both types of water, indicating a transition between unplanned and uncontrolled reuse to planned and controlled reuse. Countries using only treated water for irrigation purposes have sanitation coverage of at least 87 per cent.

Few studies have quantified the aggregate contribution of wastewater to food supply. In Pakistan, about 26 per cent of national vegetable production is irrigated with wastewater (Ensink et al., 2004), while in Hanoi, Vietnam, which is much wetter than Pakistan, about 80 per cent of vegetable production is from urban and peri-urban areas irrigated with diluted wastewater (Lai, 2002). Across major cities in West Africa, between 50 and 90 per cent of vegetables consumed by urban dwellers are produced within or close to the city (Drechsel et al., 2006) where much of the water used for irrigation is polluted.

The use of greywater exclusively has not been extensively documented, partly because it tends to be mixed together with blackwater. In cases where it is used as such, it is commonly an in-house practice, which makes it difficult to assess, but it is being popularized in the Middle East for irrigation purposes. In some States in the USA, greywater use is permitted for household irrigation and state legislation and guidelines exist. Australia, which has major scarcity problems, commissioned studies on greywater reuse but no comprehensive information is available. In countries where this is permitted, there are instances of greywater use for toilet flushing after treatment. Low- and middle-income countries such as India, Mali, Jordan, Palestine, South Africa, Nepal, Sri Lanka, Costa Rica and Malaysia are using greywater for gardening and irrigation of non-edible crops (such as fodder and olive trees) (Morel and Diener, 2006).

In most cities of sub-Saharan Africa, greywater is channelled into drains where it often gets mixed with stormwater, solid waste and excreta from open defecation before it enters natural water bodies. As these drains or streams are often used for irrigation, it is difficult to distinguish between greywater and wastewater use (Cornish and Lawrence, 2001; Drechsel et al., 2006; Qadir et al., 2007). A recent survey in two Ghanaian cities showed that greywater use for backyard irrigation is very low (International Water Management Institute (IWMI), 2008), despite the fact that greywater and blackwater have separate networks, and the proper use of greywater could be promoted. The situation can be different in drier areas where tap water is precious and natural water sources rare. Jordan is piloting projects with a view to upscaling greywater use as, for example, in the Jerash Refugee Camp, where greywater is separated and discharged from all houses into the environment through small ditches and open canals that serve farmers producing crops (WHO-IDRC, 2006). India is also using partially treated greywater for kitchen-garden irrigation and sanitation (Godfrey et al., 2007) and it seems that this practice is beginning to be widely applied in several regions.

Faecal sludge, excreta and biosolids

The problem of faecal sludge management is compounded by the large number of on-site sanitation systems, such as latrines, unsewered public toilets or septic tanks, used by the majority of the population for disposal of blackwater in densely populated cities. Faecal sludge collected from on-site sanitation installations is sometimes transported to treatment ponds but is more often dumped in depressions, streams or the ocean, or reused untreated on farmland, discharged in lakes or fish ponds or disposed of within the household compound. Assuming a per capita faecal sludge production of 1 litre/day (Strauss et al., 1997), a truck-load of 5m^3 dumped indiscriminately is equivalent to 5000 open defecations (Koné et al., 2007a).

These practices represent a significant risk to public health and have a high disease impact on workers emptying the tanks and trucks, their families, the households living in the immediate area and on vulnerable populations in latrine-based cities (WHO, 2006). In Ghana, Mali and Benin, farmers are known to bribe septic truck drivers to dump the faecal matter in their fields. Fortunately, the practice poses little health risk to consumers where there is sufficient exposure to sun and a long dry season which result in pathogen die-off, or where the crops grown are cereals (Asare et al., 2003; Cofie et al., 2003, 2005). Systems where the faecal sludge is first dried and then mixed with solid waste for co-composting have been reported from experimental stations in Ghana and Nigeria. Settled sludge from sludge treatment ponds has also been used to 'blend' compost from solid waste, as observed in Accra, Ghana (Drechsel et al., 2004; Koné et al. 2007a).

Use of excreta is seldom made public, but is known to have been practised for centuries in Asia (WHO, 2006), in particular in China (UNHSP, 2008) and Vietnam (Jensen et al., 2005; Phuc et al., 2006) in both agriculture and aquaculture. In China, use of excreta in agriculture continues to be common and this practice has led to a strong economic linkage of urban dwellers and urban farmers. Thus, vegetables grown on excreta-conditioned soils yield higher sales prices. With increasing efforts to introduce urine-separating toilets, the first data on urine reuse has emerged.[1]

In both developed and developing countries, sludge disposal is an issue growing in line with the increase in the volume of wastewater treated. Historically, sewage sludge has been considered to be waste that is to be disposed of at the least possible cost (UNHSP, 2008). As a result, it has traditionally been dumped in landfills, holes, any unoccupied surface and drainage systems (Jiménez et al., 2004). However, faecal sludge, excreta and biosolids are increasingly being applied on land in low- and middle-income countries due to the high cost of modern landfills that meet all environmental requirements, the difficulty of finding suitable sites for landfills (even in developed countries) and the benefit of recycling plant nutrients and enhancing soil characteristics. Their main use worldwide (greater than 60 per cent) is to fertilize agricultural fields or green areas. This practice solves a problem for municipalities, helps farmers to decrease their organic and mineral fertilizer costs and preserves or improves soil fertility. Another important use of sludge is to improve degraded soils at mining sites, construction sites and other disturbed areas (UNHSP, 2008).

DRIVERS OF WASTEWATER USE

In developing countries, the limited financial and physical resources to treat water, the socio-economic situation and the context of urbanization create the conditions for unplanned and uncontrolled wastewater use. A study commissioned by the Comprehensive Assessment of Water Management in Agriculture showed that across 53 cities in the developing world the main drivers of wastewater use in irrigated agriculture are a combination of the following aspects (Raschid-Sally and Jayakody, 2008):

- limited capacities of cities to treat their wastewater, causing pollution of soils, water bodies and traditional irrigation water sources;
- lack of alternative (cheaper, similarly reliable, available or safer) water sources in the physical environment;
- urban food demand and market incentives favouring food production in the proximity of cities, where water sources are usually polluted.

In addition, Jiménez (2006) pointed to the influence of socio-economic factors at the household level, like poverty and low education in developing countries, where lack of job opportunities and a limited awareness for health risks coexist. In such circumstances, wastewater reuse can represent a promising opportunity for cash crop production or to improve food supply. Once wastewater reuse is in place and its advantages have been gauged by the population, it is difficult to alter behaviour especially if changes have an associated cost or are linked to historical water rights. This may be compounded by reduced availability of freshwater resources, be it for economic or physical reasons. The nutrient value of (raw) wastewater and sludge is inherently recognized by farmers, which is also a factor driving their use.

In contrast, in more developed countries, water reuse and recycling are increasingly seen as a means to respond to physical water scarcity (including climate change and drought management), water reallocations from agriculture to other uses and also as an economic response to costly inter-basin transfers. An additional factor influencing recycling is the stringent environmental standards, which make land application of wastewater and sludge both unavoidable and economically feasible.

Drivers of agricultural reuse of sludge and excreta are linked more to disposal issues than to the intention to reclaim components of them. However, many farmers consider them to be a valuable resource similar to farmyard manure. This beneficial use is increasingly gaining momentum, driven by the intention of closing nutrient loops to ensure that nutrients are returned to agricultural land to improve soil fertility. One of the main differences observed between the use of wastewater and that of sludge and excreta is a greater acceptance of wastewater use, as sludge and excreta have been historically considered, in most cultures, to be not only noxious but also an object of shame (UNHSP, 2008).

TYPOLOGY OF WATER USE

Various authors have attempted to provide typologies for wastewater recycling and use (e.g. van der Hoek, 2004), but none of these has been taken up universally or been standardized. However, in describing wastewater reuse, the terms direct, indirect, planned and unplanned recur frequently. These are explained here with examples:

- Direct use of untreated wastewater refers to the use of raw wastewater from a sewage outlet, directly disposed of on land where it is used for crop production.
- Indirect use of untreated wastewater refers to the abstraction of usually diluted wastewater (or polluted stream water) for irrigation. This is common downstream of urban centres where treatment facilities are limited. Farmers might or might not be aware of the water-quality challenge.
- Direct use of treated wastewater refers to the use of reclaimed water that has been transported from the point of treatment or production to the point of use without an intervening discharge to waters.
- Planned water reuse refers to the conscious and controlled use of wastewater either raw (direct) or diluted (indirect). However, most indirect use happens without planning, at least initially, for using low quality water.

Direct use often takes place in dry climates where water sources are scarce. Treated, untreated or partially treated wastewater is used directly for irrigation without being mixed or diluted. Direct use of treated wastewater is most common as a planned process in developed countries including some larger parts of the Middle East and North African region, but can also take place unplanned, for example in dry seasons, when streams only carry wastewater, as is the case for the Musi River in Hyderabad, India.

However, the use of diluted wastewater for irrigation (indirect use) is significantly more frequent than direct use and occurs even more in wetter climates. In this situation, untreated or partially/insufficiently treated wastewater from urban areas is discharged into drains, small streams and other tributaries of larger water bodies where it is usually mixed with stormwater and freshwater, resulting in diluted wastewater (or polluted surface water). It is then used by farmers, most of whom are traditional users of these water sources. Lack of adequate sanitation and waste-disposal infrastructure in cities is one of the direct causes of such pollution and use (Jiménez and Asano, 2008, Raschid-Sally and Jayakody, 2008).

This situation is not limited to low-income countries that have no capacity to collect and treat wastewater comprehensively, but occurs also in fast-growing economies like China, Brazil, and some countries of the Middle East and North Africa region. For example, despite massive investments in wastewater treatment, the city of Beijing is only able to treat about half of the wastewater generated and untreated wastewater is discharged into waterways used downstream by farmers (Yang and Abbaspour, 2007). Also, in Lebanon and Palestine most of the wastewater collected from sewered localities is discharged into nearby rivers, *wadis*, and the sea, and on open land from where it infiltrates the ground with little or no treatment (Post et al., 2006). In spite of strict European Union (EU) regulations, untreated wastewater is discharged into rivers which are used for irrigation in some countries such as Spain, Italy and Portugal, especially in summer when there is little or no river flow (Juanico and Salgot, 2008). However, this practice is being reduced due to efforts made by countries to increase the level of wastewater treatment to meet EU legislation. In Turkey, an enormous amount of domestic wastewater is discharged into rivers and used for irrigation because of insufficient sewerage facilities and lack of satisfactory treatment (Juanico et al., 2008).

In some areas, irrigation infrastructure originally built to transport freshwater, surface or groundwater, is now used for wastewater during certain periods. Wastewater is pumped into irrigation canals to supplement fresh irrigation water. For instance, in Vietnam, wastewater from Hanoi and other cities along the Red River Delta is pumped into irrigation canals at certain times of the year to supplement irrigation water (Trang et al., 2007a and b). However, at the tail end of irrigation systems or throughout in the dry season, wastewater may be the only water flowing in the canals in areas such as Haroonabad in Pakistan and Hyderabad in India (Ensink et al., 2004; Ensink, 2006).

In Jordan, the As-Samra wastewater treatment plant mainly treats the domestic wastewater of the capital Amman. On its course to the Jordan Valley, the reclaimed water is mixed with surface run-off from *wadis* before it is temporarily stored in the country's largest reservoir, the King Talal Reservoir (KTR) (which has a storage capacity of 75 million cubic metres). The detention time of the water in the reservoir, which used to be about ten months, has been reduced to a few months with the increase of the wastewater flow. About 20km downstream from the KTR outlet, Zarqa Carriers divert part of the KTR water directly to fields in the Jordan Valley. The rest of the reclaimed water is finally released into the King Abdullah Canal which brings freshwater in the north to the Jordan Valley.

ADVANTAGES AND DISADVANTAGES OF REUSING WASTEWATER, SLUDGE, AND EXCRETA

While the drivers for the use of wastewater, sludge and excreta in agriculture differ between regions, their use – be it directly, indirectly, diluted or not – has a number of advantages alongside the well-known risks (WHO, 1989, 2006; Scott et al., 2004).

Advantages

As a consequence of the high global food demand, it is not surprising that, worldwide, the biggest user of wastewater (treated or not) is agriculture (Jiménez and Asano, 2008). An important factor which makes wastewater valuable is that it is a reliable source of water, as it is available all year round, unlike pluvial precipitation or seasonal streams. Consequently, it permits higher crop yields, year-round production, and increases the range of crops that can be irrigated, particularly in (but not limited to) arid and semi-arid areas (Keraita et al., 2008). Studies conducted in Hubli-Dharwad showed that wastewater allowed farming to be done in the dry season when farmers could sell their produce at three to five times the kharif (monsoon) season prices (Huibers et al., 2004). Wastewater reliability also allows for multiple cultivation cycles and flexibility of crops planted (Raschid-Sally et al., 2005). Similar situations have been reported for Haroonabad, Pakistan; Accra, Ghana; and Dakar, Senegal (Gaye and Niang, 2002; van der Hoek et al., 2002; Koottatep et al., 2006). The increased productivity and related income/food supply gains allow farmers a more reliable livelihood with indirect benefits of using the income for education and improving health conditions.

Where vegetables are the main commodity produced with wastewater, there can be a significant aggregate benefit for the society in terms of a more balanced diet. In the case of Accra, for example, more than 200,000 people eat vegetables produced with wastewater every day (Amoah et al., 2007). On the other hand, this is also the group potentially at risk as the possible adverse health effects to farmers and consumers are well established (WHO, 2006).

As part of the urban food-production systems, urban livestock contributes to cities' food security by providing meat and dairy products (Bonfoh et al., 2003; Wolf et al., 2003). In semi-arid countries, livestock production relies mainly on natural pasture, which is often limited or decreasing due to low precipitation. In Sahelian countries (i.e. Burkina Faso, Mali, Senegal), forage biodiversity has decreased over time and plant species with lower nutritive value and palatability are becoming predominant (Bonfoh et al., 2003 and 2006; Food and Agriculture Organization of the United Nations (FAO), 2006; Sanon et al., 2007; Toutain et al., 2006). At the same time, however, the demand for dairy in cities is increasing with urbanization and changing diets. For example in Asian countries, the demand for dairy products is growing by a factor of 3.5 per year (Moran, 2005). Reusing wastewater or faecal sludge for fodder production appears an important and comparatively low-risk avenue which can contribute to enhancing the resilience to climate changes and food insecurity especially of small and middle-sized cities in developing countries (Koné, in press).

Another well-established advantage of wastewater and sludge reuse is their nutrient content. Even when treated, wastewater recycles organic matter and a larger diversity of nutrients than any commercial fertilizer can provide. Biosolids, sludge and excreta in particular, provide numerous micronutrients such as cobalt, copper, iron, manganese, molybdenum and zinc, which are essential for optimal plant growth. It is estimated that 1000 cubic metres of municipal wastewater used to irrigate one hectare can contribute 16–62kg total nitrogen, 4–24kg phosphorus, 2–69kg potassium, 18–208kg calcium, 9–110kg magnesium, and 27–182kg sodium (Qadir et al., 2007). It therefore can reduce the demand for chemical fertilizers especially where the wastewater is not diluted, i.e. make crop nutrients more accessible to poor farmers. In the light of the global phosphorus crisis, excreta and wastewater can be critical sources of phosphorus (Rosemarin, 2004). On the other hand, excessive concentrations of nitrogen in wastewater can lead to over-fertilization and cause excessive vegetative growth, delayed or uneven crop maturity and reduced quality (Jiménez, 2006; Qadir et al., 2007). Excessive concentrations of some trace elements may also cause plant toxicity and sometimes become a health risk for crop consumers.

Few studies have quantified the economic gains from nutrients in wastewater under actual field conditions. In Guanajuato, Mexico, the estimated saving arising from using wastewater to supply the required nitrogen and phosphorus for crops was US$135 per hectare (Keraita et al., 2008). A study comparing vegetable production using freshwater and untreated wastewater in Haroonabad, Pakistan, found that the gross margins were significantly higher for wastewater (US$150 per hectare), because farmers spent less on chemical fertilizer and achieved higher yields (van der Hoek et al., 2002).

In a cost–benefit analysis of greywater reuse systems constructed in residential schools in India, the internal and external benefits far outweighed the costs (Godfrey et al., 2009). Although studies conducted to quantify economic returns are still few and lack a uniform methodological approach, they consistently report significant gains among farmers with access to wastewater. The annual income reported in such studies performed in India, Ghana, Senegal, Kenya and Mexico varied from US$420 to $2800 per hectare per year (Keraita et al., 2008). According to studies in Ghana, the greatest factor influencing farmers' profits is not so much the yield obtained, but the ability to produce crops that are in high demand and low supply, at the right time, the result being that they can be consistently sold at above average prices (Cornish et al., 2001). The profitability of the business is also reflected in farmers' decisions to pay more for (especially nutrient-rich) wastewater than normal water. In the Mezquital Valley, Mexico, the availability of wastewater instead of freshwater as irrigation water caused land rents to increase from US$170 to $350–950 per year (Jiménez, 2005). In Quetta, Pakistan, farmers paid 2.5 times more for wastewater than for freshwater (Ensink et al., 2004).

While farmers and their families are direct beneficiaries, there are also indirect beneficiaries along the supply chain including farm labourers, transporters, vendors, processors, input suppliers and consumers (Buechler et al., 2002). With low investments and quick returns, this practice is lucrative and enables many farmers to leap over the poverty line (Danso et al., 2002). In many West African countries, it is especially attractive to poor migrants looking for jobs in the city (Faruqui et al., 2004).

BOX 1.2 DISEASES COMMONLY ASSOCIATED
WITH WASTEWATER AND EXCRETA

The most common diseases associated with wastewater and excreta are the diarrheic ones. Examples include several kinds of helminthiases that are caused by intestinal infestation of parasitic worms. Helminthiases are common where poverty and poor sanitary conditions prevail; under these conditions they can affect up to 90 per cent of the population (Bratton and Nesse, 1993). Ascariasis (produced by *Ascaris* worms) is the most common one and is endemic in Africa, Latin America, and the Far East. It is estimated that 133 million people suffer from high-intensity ascariasis infections, which often lead to severe consequences, such as cognitive impairment, severe dysentery or anaemia. Even though helminthiases have a low mortality rate (for ascariasis nearly 10,000 persons per year), most of the people affected are children under 15 years old with problems of faltering growth and/or impaired fitness. Approximately 1.5 million of these children never attain expected growth, even if treated (Silva et al., 1997). Another common helminthiasis is Schistosomiasis that affects approximately 246 million people worldwide (United Nations, 2003). It causes tens of thousands of deaths every year, mainly in sub-Saharan Africa. It is strongly related to unsanitary excreta disposal and the absence of nearby sources of safe water.

Another important disease is cholera, caused by bacteria named *Vibrio cholerae*. These bacteria cause not only epidemics but are responsible for several pandemics. Cholera is strongly related to the use of polluted water for irrigation or to unsafe disposal of sludge and excreta. Major risks occur where there are large concentrations of people and hygiene is poor (as in refugee camps and urban slums).

Other diarrheic diseases related to unsafe agricultural practices are salmonellosis, typhoid, shigellosis, gastric ulcers (caused by *Helicobacter pylori*), giardiasis and amoebiasis (Blumenthal and Peasey, 2002). In addition, skin diseases associated with contact with untreated water have been reported. Nail problems (koilonychias) characterized by spoon-formed nails have also been reported and are associated with the anaemia produced by hookworm infections which cause iron deficiency (van der Hoek et al., 2002). However, it must be kept in mind that in developing countries with various disease exposure pathways, the comparative risk contribution from wastewater irrigation and contaminated crops has never been comprehensively studied. Quantitative microbial risk assessment (QMRA) methodologies can and should be used effectively for this purpose, in order to have a realistic perspective of the situation.

The land application of wastewater, sludge and excreta for agricultural use constitutes a low-cost disposal method and a land-treatment system that uses the soil to attenuate contaminants. If carried out under controlled conditions, it can also be safe. Wastewater use can also recharge aquifers through infiltration or reduce the impact on surface-water bodies, as wastewater is 'treated' in the vadose before reaching them (Jiménez, 2006). Several wastewater constituents are subject to processes that remove them or significantly reduce their concentration. Reduced costs to society are also noteworthy, in view of reducing the use of fossil fuels to produce fertilizer.

Disadvantages

Among the disadvantages of using untreated or partially treated wastewater, sludge or excreta, the most obvious are the health risks from pathogens. These have been discussed extensively elsewhere (WHO, 2006) and are also the subject of several chapters in this book. Some references will be provided here in order to give an idea of the magnitude of the problem. Firstly, it should be stated that diseases are linked to the nature of the pathogen in the wastewater and thus vary locally following the local public-health pattern. Secondly, risks are not limited to farmers, but can be observed in four groups: agricultural workers and their families; crop handlers; consumers of crops or meat and milk coming from cattle grazing on polluted fields; and those living on or near the areas where wastewater, sludge or excreta is used. Within these groups the most vulnerable sections of the population are children and the elderly. Thirdly, observed responses may vary considerably between developing and developed countries. This is because pathogen distributions and concentrations, to which these groups are exposed, are very different, as are the living conditions and the level of resistance to disease between developing and developed countries (Jiménez, 2007; Jiménez and Wang, 2006). Furthermore, the statistics on food safety are unreliable because laboratory standards are so low in most developing countries.

Pathogens contaminate crops mainly via direct contact, though some cases of uptake by plants have been recorded (Hamilton et al., 2007). Beside pathogens, wastewater and sludge can also be a source of high levels of heavy metals and organic toxic compounds (Abaidoo et al., 2009; Hamilton et al., 2007). Contamination can occur, in the case of metals and some organic chemicals, through absorption from the soil, which strongly depends on the location (possible contamination sources), the environmental conditions (particularly the soil), bio-availability (in the case of some contaminants), type of plant and agricultural practices (quantity of water applied and irrigation method) (Jiménez, 2006).

There is relatively good knowledge concerning the allowable amounts of heavy metals that crops and soil can be exposed to when wastewater, sludge or biosolids are applied to soil (Page and Chang, 1994; UNHSP, 2008; WHO, 2006). Moreover, for both developed and developing countries, the content of heavy metals in wastewater, excreta and sludge from domestic sources is generally low enough to allow their use for crop fertilization (Jiménez and Wang, 2006; UNHSP, 2008; WHO, 2006). However, there are always cases where care has to be taken, for example, close to tanneries or mining areas (Abaidoo et al., 2009). The risk from organic components derived via wastewater is in general much lower than via direct pesticide application. In comparison with pathogenic health risks, pesticide levels on vegetables, even if elevated, were considered to be of secondary importance in the context of a developing country (Amoah et al., 2006).

As described above, the use of wastewater, biosolids and excreta implies benefits but also risks. Frequently, experts recommend simply banning this unsafe practice and 'properly' treating wastewater, sludge and excreta. Such recommendations, besides being nearly impossible to implement in most developing countries for both economic and social reasons, would also result in the removal of components from these 'waste' products that are not acting as pollutants but, conversely, are beneficial. Therefore, in practice, there has to be a trade-off between the advantages and disadvantages and the best solution for each situation should be sought, even if this is considered unconventional, especially from a developed country perspective. From a technical point of view, the solution will basically consist of finding a way to supply soils and crops with water, nutrients and organic matter. This should take advantage of the assimilation capacity of the soil, so that pathogens or heavy metals do not cause harm, while putting in place additional measures to deliver safe food to consumers. These and other alternative options for health-risk reduction are supported by the Guidelines of WHO (2006) where conventional wastewater treatment fails for whatever reason (see Chapters 10 to 12 of this book).

OFFICIAL PERCEPTION AND POLICY GUIDANCE

Wastewater and excreta

Policies to control the unplanned reuse of wastewater where it is an ongoing practice are not only hard to implement but are even difficult to develop (Drechsel et al., 2002) because governments are faced with the trade-off between public-health protection and the ethical question of whether to prevent wastewater farmers from cultivating with the only source of water that is accessible to them (Jiménez and Garduño, 2001). The WHO, to assist in this decision-making process, has in recent years been giving consideration both to the limitations faced by developing countries in providing sufficient wastewater treatment to meet water-quality standards and the increasingly important livelihood dimension of wastewater use. This is reflected in the 2006 Guidelines.

If a government concludes that the practice must be stopped, then it has to put in place a complex process for control, with few successful examples in practice. In almost all countries legislation exists, dating back several years or decades and referring directly or indirectly to the use of polluted water or wastewater for irrigation, which is always forbidden. Many countries have irrigation water-quality guidelines, but they do not always consider microbiological standards, and where wastewater use is permitted, the legislation requires that certain quality conditions are met. Such conditions usually follow the previous WHO Guidelines (1989) which recommended water-quality thresholds. (This approach has now been revised: see the following chapter.) Such regulations are not followed in practice for the many reasons mentioned above. A further factor is that wastewater irrigation usually takes place outside the officially recognized formal irrigation sector. As a result, most governments ignore the situation or have no other means than to adopt a laissez-faire attitude (Drechsel et al., 2006).

Joint efforts by WHO, FAO and United Nations Environment Programme (UNEP) to respond to this global situation, and to encourage resource recovery, resulted in an enforceable and achievable regulatory framework to support worldwide the reuse of wastewater, greywater and excreta in agriculture and aquaculture (Jiménez and Asano, 2008; WHO, 2006). These new Guidelines build on previous ones but are in their 2006 version much more supportive of the difficult sanitation conditions in most developing countries and have suggested a multiple-barrier approach for the long-term achievement of a universal health-based target. Furthermore, WHO suggests local adaptation of the Guidelines with incremental achievements towards this target. This flexibility means that authorities require support to understand and apply the new approach. The previous WHO Guidelines (1989) are often considered more straightforward, especially for countries that already have comprehensive wastewater collection and treatment in place.

The resulting bias towards countries at the lower part of the sanitation ladder caused discomfort among those countries further up which have few problems in enforcing and monitoring crop or water-quality thresholds. These countries prefer to use, for example, standards similar to the California Title 22 (State of California, 2001). Such fixed standards are indeed most useful where they can actually be met by treatment, and wastewater use is a planned and controlled activity. However, they are difficult to apply where treatment is rudimentary or lacking and when thousands of farmers already use polluted water sources because they have no alternative. Here, different strategies for health-risk reduction are needed. Similar regulations based on local needs and capabilities had been developed before the 2006 WHO Guidelines were released, e.g. in Australia (AATSE, 2004) and in Mexico in 1996 (Jiménez, 2005). The advantage of the WHO Guidelines is that all the developing countries that have ignored previous guidelines, because the water-quality thresholds were too high, are now challenged to control the health risks as far as possible, rather than continuing to disregard the problem. The same applies to excreta management which the WHO (2006) is also addressing.

Treated and untreated sludge

Sludge management is mostly an issue for developed countries where wastewater treatment facilities allow sludge generation, separation, storage, transport and reuse. Considerable experience concerning the development of policies and regulations to promote the beneficial use of municipal sludge and biosolids in soil exists in the EU and the USA. These regions have comprehensively analysed the risks and benefits of the different use and disposal options. Many other countries have built their understanding and policies from this foundation of knowledge and experience, but integrate local needs and conditions into their policies, laws and regulations.

In general, the USA has adopted the concept of risk assessment in their environmental regulations contained in the 40 CFR Part 503 sludge regulation dating from the early 1990s. The approach takes maximum advantage of the soil's capacity to assimilate, attenuate and detoxify pollutants. Land application guidelines based on this approach set the maximum permissible pollutant loading and provide users with the flexibility to develop suitable management practices for using sewage sludge (Chang et al., 2002). In contrast, the EU has adopted a precautionary or a no-net-degradation approach (UNHSP, 2008). This approach prevents pollutant accumulation into biosolids-receiving soils. As a result of this, the EU is well ahead of the USA in researching and phasing out chemicals of concern in personal care and commercial products, resulting in more costly control programmes. Both approaches address pathogen reduction, the potential for accumulation of persistent pollutants in soils (heavy metals and persistent chemicals) and the application of appropriate amounts of nutrients. One notable difference is that the EU Directive has stringent upper limits for pollutants and generally limits rates of applications of biosolids to lower amounts than are allowed in the USA. The cost of implementation of the Directive is also higher, as wastewater treatment plants need to employ advanced wastewater treatment technologies to minimize the pollutant levels in the reclaimed wastewater and sewage sludge.

Regulatory structures in other countries that may not have the same level of resources available for wastewater sludge management are less precautionary. Balancing the need for strong regulations and enforcement with what is practical and achievable is the challenge. Snyman (2008), for example, has pointed out that in South Africa an initial set of biosolids management regulations that were consistent with some of the stricter regulations in Europe made management of wastewater sludge nearly impossible. Newer, more appropriate regulations are now helping move the country's wastewater sludge management programmes towards higher levels of recycling and greater sustainability.

Examples of sludge management policies implemented in developing countries are still rare as the existence of properly functioning wastewater treatment plants is still an evolving phenomenon. One notable example occurs in the state of Paraná in Brazil where practical, successful, full-scale programmes can be found (Andreoli et al., 2008). In Tunisia, standards have been established for maximum allowable concentrations of chemical and biological components in soil and sewage sludge. Pollutant concentration limits for land application of sewage sludge were derived from the existing regulations, while specific management practices for land application and disposal of sewage sludge have been included in the national standards.

Perspectives and conclusions

With an increasing world population and improved living standards, domestic water use will increase and so will the production of wastewater, excreta and biosolids. Similarly, the share of the urban population using on-site sanitation

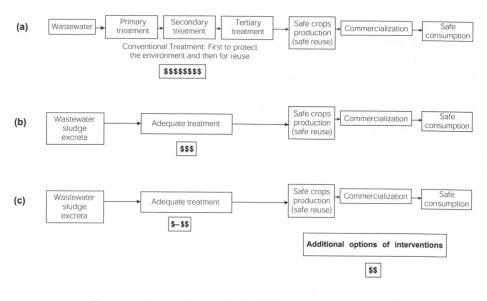

Figure 1.2 *Options to deal with the reuse of wastewater for agricultural purposes*

systems (currently 40 per cent or 1.1 billion world urban dwellers) will increase with efforts to improve sanitation coverage. Hence, a huge quantity of faecal sludge will have to be dealt with in the future (Koné et al., 2007b).

Simultaneously, there are many regions facing severe freshwater shortages which are responding increasingly with unplanned or planned wastewater use. Water scarcity will thus continue to be a key driver for recycling wastewater next to poor sanitation and widespread water pollution. Reuse will be supported by economic and environmental perspectives to substitute for some uses that do not need potable water quality and will contribute to nutrient recovery (Mekala et al., 2007). Whilst planned reuse (of treated wastewater) will be the norm in countries that can afford treatment, the vast majority of low-income countries are, however, likely to continue to use non- or only partially treated wastewater, as long as sanitation and waste disposal do not keep pace with population growth in cities.

In the case of wastewater, there are three possible scenarios that future policy needs to address:

- Continue to promote wastewater reuse in the traditional way (Figure 1.2a), using conventional treatment methods developed first to protect the environment and then to reuse water. As a result, norms are very stringent and treatment methods are based on adding steps to conventional wastewater treatment systems to further improve quality. This will lead to higher costs, more fragile systems with probably lower viability in developing countries and the removal of nutrients from water which does not favour agricultural reuse (Jiménez and Garduño, 2001).

- Look for appropriate treatment alternatives (Figure 1.2b) that adequately target health protection and enhance reclamation of water and nutrients (Jiménez and Garduño, 2001; Koné, in press). For example, linking wastewater or faecal sludge treatment to forage production can generate additional income for operation and maintenance and support local dairy production systems. In this option, as the treatment of wastewater is designed from the outset to reuse wastewater, it can be performed at a lower cost than the first option, but differs from the third option in that health risks should be controlled solely with treatment; no other interventions are considered.
- Apply an integrated approach (Figure 1.2c) combining a locally adequate treatment process, which in combination with ('non-treatment') interventions applied at different entry points along the production and consumption chain, will achieve the health target required.

The last two options are similar, varying only in the type of additional intervention methods considered and can also be applied to sludge and excreta. The third option is in line with the current WHO Guidelines (2006).

With regard to excreta management, a more sensitive approach is needed which respects cultural perceptions. The long-term goal is to move from the ignorance of what happens to people's wastewater and excreta after they are discarded, towards educating people on what is done – and what could be done – with their waste as a valuable resource (UNHSP, 2008).

The global fertilizer and energy crises call for the development of alternative solutions for producing affordable nutrients which can sustain agricultural food production. A new paradigm in waste processing is needed. Population growth, urbanization and improved quality of life are accompanied by an increase in demand for food and water, leading to the generation of large concentrations of waste products originating from urban centres. In addition, there are the expected impacts of climate change, which will reduce water availability, and a growing awareness of environmental water needs.

Under these conditions, resource recovery of biosolids, water and nutrients becomes essential. The most appropriate options for water and excreta reuse are offered by the agricultural sector which uses on average around 80 per cent of total water consumption in developing countries; moreover, agriculture accepts a lower water quality compared to other uses (Jiménez and Garduño, 2001). In fact, water and nutrient recovery is happening extensively already but the practice at present is not free from risks. To move forward, a strategy that accommodates the needs of the users while fulfilling the public health and environment requirements is essential. This strategy should be developed locally, based on local options and needs, and can contribute to financing treatment facilities. A related concept (Design for Service) is described in Chapter 15.

In the case of sludge, biosolids and excreta, it is expected that the decreasing availability especially of natural phosphorous reserves will increasingly shift the attention to ecological sanitation in its broad sense and the need for nutrient recovery.

There is clearly an opportunity for urban planners and policy-makers to reinvent the role of excreta and wastewater treatment infrastructure by linking them to city development and food security agendas. It is a considerable matter of concern that the present rate of economic growth and the probable impact of climate change are already overshooting the carrying capacity of the earth's ecosystems to produce the required resources and to absorb the pollution caused by human activities. The impact of the expected doubling of the human population by the middle of the next century, most of which will take place in developing countries, calls for the definition of a clear environmental sustainability strategy for renewable resources management.

Linking urban faecal sludge and wastewater treatment and management infrastructure to the agenda of food production and food security can draw financial resources for building infrastructure and securing operation and maintenance costs, as city planners and utilities might see the direct economic benefits. It is also an opportunity to close the nutrient and water loops through resource-oriented urban excreta and wastewater management.

NOTES

1   See http://conference2005.ecosan.org.
2   The hectare base is used for standardization; farmers' fields might be much smaller.

REFERENCES

AATSE-Australian Academy of Technological Sciences and Engineering (2004) *Water Recycling in Australia*, AATSE, Victoria, Australia

Abaidoo, R., Keraita, B., Drechsel, P., Dissanayake, P. and Maxwell, A. (2009) 'Soil and crop contamination through wastewater irrigation and options for risk reduction in developing countries', in P. Dion (ed) *Soil Biology and Agriculture in the Tropics*, Springer Verlag, Heidelberg

Amoah, P., Drechsel, P., Abaidoo, R. C. and Henseler, M. (2007) 'Irrigated urban vegetable production in Ghana: Microbiological contamination in farms and markets and associated consumer risk groups', *Journal of Water and Health*, vol 5, no 3, pp455–66

Amoah, P., Drechsel, P., Abaidoo, R. C. and Ntow, W. J. (2006) 'Pesticide and pathogen contamination of vegetables in Ghana's urban markets', *Archives of Environmental Contamination and Toxicology*, vol 50, no 1, pp1–6

Andreoli, C., Garbossa, L., Lupatini, G. and Pegorini, S. (2008) 'A Brazilian approach in United Nations Human Settlements Programme', in R. LeBlanc, P. Matthews and P. Roland (eds) *Global Atlas of Excreta, Wastewater Sludge, and Biosolids Management:*

www.earthscan.co.uk

IWMI
International
Water Management
Institute

This complimentary copy of *Wastewater Irriga*
and Health is sent with best wishes from Cana
International Development Research Centre a
the International Water Management Institut

Moving Forward the Sustainable and Welcome Uses of a Global Resource, UN-Habitat, Nairobi, pp131–46

Asano, T., Burton, H., Leverenz, H., Tsuchihashi, R. and Tchobanoglous, G. (2007) *Water Reuse: Issues, Technologies, and Applications*, McGraw-Hill Professional, New York, p1570

Asare, I., Kranjac-Berisavljevic, G. and Cofie, O. (2003) 'Faecal sludge application for agriculture in Tamale', *Urban Agriculture Magazine*, vol 10, pp31-3

Blumenthal, U. J. and Peasey, A. (2002) 'Critical review of epidemiological evidence of the health effects of wastewater and excreta use in agriculture', unpublished document prepared for World Health Organization, Geneva, www.who.int/water_sanitation_health/wastewater/whocriticalrev.pdf

Bonfoh, B., Ankers, P., Sall, A., Diabaté, M., Tembely, S., Farah, Z., Alfaroukh, O. I. and Zinsstag, J. (2006) 'Operational plan for small scale milk producers in peri-urban of Bamako (Mali)', *Journal of Sahelian Studies and Research*, vol 12, nos 7–25

Bonfoh, B., Sall, A., Diabaté, M., Diarra, A., Netoyo, L., Mbaye, Y., Simbé, C. F., Alfaroukh, O. I., Farah, Z. and Zinsstag, J. (2003) 'Viabilité technico-économique du système extensif de production et de collecte de lait à Bamako', *Revue Etudes et Recherches Sahéliennes*, vols 8–9, pp173–84

Bratton, R. and Nesse, R. (1993) 'Ascariasis: An infection to watch for in immigrants', *Postgraduate Medicine*, vol 93, pp171–8

Buechler, S., Devi, G. and Raschid-Sally, L. (2002) 'Livelihoods and wastewater irrigated agriculture along the Musi River in Hyderabad City, Andhra Pradesh, India', *Urban Agriculture Magazine*, vol 8, pp14–17

Chang, A. C., Pan, G., Page, A. L. and Asano, T. (2002) 'Developing human health-related chemical guidelines for reclaimed wastewater and sewage sludge applications in agriculture', report submitted to World Health Organization, Geneva

Cofie, O., Kranjac-Berisavljevic, G., Drechsel, P. (2005) 'The use of human waste for peri-agriculture in northern Ghana', *Renewable Agriculture and Food Systems*, vol 20, no 2, pp73–80

Cofie, O., Strauss, M., Montangero, A., Zurbrugg, C. and Drescher, S. (2003) 'Co-composting of faecal sludge and municipal organic waste for urban and peri-urban agriculture in Kumasi, Ghana', Final Project Report submitted to PSEau, IWMI, Ghana, p123

Cornish, G. and Lawrence, P. (2001) 'Informal irrigation in peri-urban areas: A summary of findings and recommendations', Report OD/TN 144, Nov 2001, HR Wallingford Ltd, Wallingford, UK

Danso, G., Drechsel, P., Wiafe-Antwi, T. and Gyiele, L. (2002) 'Income of farming systems around Kumasi', *Urban Agriculture Magazine*, vol 7, pp5–6

Drechsel, P., Blumenthal, U. J. and Keraita, B. (2002) 'Balancing health and livelihoods: Adjusting wastewater irrigation guidelines for resource-poor countries', *Urban Agriculture Magazine*, vol 8, pp7–9

Drechsel, P., Cofie, O., Fink, M., Danso, G., Zakari, F. M. and Vasquez, R. (2004) 'Closing the rural-urban nutrient cycle. options for municipal waste composting in Ghana', Final Scientific Report submitted to IDRC (project 100376), IWMI, Ghana

Drechsel, P., Graefe, S., Sonou, M. and Cofie, O. (2006) 'Informal irrigation in urban West Africa: An overview', *Research Report 102*, International Water Management Institute, Colombo, Sri Lanka

Ensink, J. (2006) 'Water quality and the risk of hookworm infection in Pakistani and Indian sewage farmers', PhD thesis, London School of Hygiene and Tropical Medicine, University of London, London

Ensink, J., Mahmood, T., van der Hoek, W., Raschid-Sally, L. and Amerasinghe, F. (2004) 'A nation-wide assessment of wastewater use in Pakistan: An obscure activity or a vitally important one?', *Water Policy*, vol 6, pp197–206

FAO (2006) 'Country pasture/forage resource profiles – Burkina Faso', FAO, Rome, www.fao.org

Faruqui, N., Niang, S. and Redwood, M. (2004) 'Untreated wastewater reuse in market gardens: A case study of Dakar, Senegal', in C. Scott, N. Faruqui and L. Raschid-Sally (eds) *Wastewater Use in Irrigated Agriculture: Confronting the Livelihood and Environmental Realities*, CABI Publishing, Wallingford, UK, pp113–25

Gaye, M. and Niang, S. (2002) *Epuration des eaux usées et l'agriculture urbaine*, *Etudes et Recherches*, ENDA-TM, Dakar, Senegal

Godfrey, S., Labhasetwar, P., Swami, A., Wate, S. R., Parihar, G. and Dwivedi, H. (2007) 'Water safety plans for grey water in tribal schools', *Water Lines*, vol 5, no 3, pp8–10

Godfrey, S., Labhasetwar, P. and Wate, S. (2009) 'Greywater reuse in residential schools in Madhya Pradesh India – a case study of cost benefit analysis', *Resources, Conservation and Recycling*, vol 53, pp287–93

Hamilton, A. J., Stagnitti, F., Xiong, X., Kreidl, S. L., Benke, K. K. and Maher, P. (2007) 'Wastewater irrigation: The state of play', *Vadose Zone Journal*, vol 6, no 4, pp 823–40

Hoek, W. van der (2004) 'A framework for a global assessment of the extent of wastewater irrigation: The need for a common wastewater typology', in C. A. Scott, N. I. Faruqui and L. Raschid-Sally (eds) *Wastewater Use in Irrigated Agriculture: Confronting the Livelihood and Environmental Realities*, CABI Publishing, Wallingford, UK, pp11–24

Hoek, W. van der, Ul Hassan, M., Ensink, J., Feenstra, S., Raschid-Sally, L. and Munir, S. (2002) 'Urban wastewater: A valuable resource for agriculture', *International Water Management Institute Research Report*, vol 63, Colombo

Huibers, F., Moscoso, O., Duran, A. and van Lier, J. (2004) 'The use of wastewater in Cochobamba, Bolivia: A degrading environment', in C. Scott, N. Faruqui and L. Raschid-Sally (eds) *Wastewater Use in Irrigated Agriculture: Confronting the Livelihood and Environmental Realities*, CABI Publishing, Wallingford, UK, pp135–44

IWMI (2008) 'Household survey on the role of backyard gardens for food security and food supply in Kumasi and Accra, Ghana', report, International Water Management Institute, Africa office, Accra

Jensen, P. K., Phuc, P. D., Dalsgaard, A. and Konradsen, F. (2005) 'Successful sanitation promotion must recognize the use of latrine wastes in agriculture – the example of Vietnam', *WHO Bulletin*, vol 83, pp273–4

Jiménez, B. (2005) 'Treatment technology and standards for agricultural wastewater reuse', *Irrigation and Drainage*, vol 54, no 1, pp 22–33

Jiménez, B. (2006) 'Irrigation in developing countries using wastewater', *International Review for Environmental Strategies*, vol 6, no 2, pp229–50

Jiménez, B. (2007) 'Helminth ova control in sludge: A review', *Water Science and Technology*, vol 56, no 9, pp147–55

Jiménez, B. and Asano, T. (2008) 'Water reclamation and reuse around the world', in B. Jiménez and T. Asano (eds) *Water Reuse: An International Survey of Current Practice, Issues and Needs*, IWA Publishing, London, p648

Jiménez, B., Barrios, J., Mendez, J. and Diaz, J. (2004) 'Sustainable management of sludge in developing countries', *Water Science and Technology*, vol 49, no 10, pp251–8

Jiménez, B. and Garduño, G. (2001) 'Social, political and scientific dilemmas for massive wastewater reuse in the world', in C. Davis and R. McGinn (eds) *Navigating Rough Waters: Ethical Issues in the Water Industry*, American Water Works Association, Denver, CO

Jiménez, B. and Wang, L. (2006) 'Sludge treatment and management', in Z. Ujang and M. Henze (eds) *Developing Countries: Principles and Engineering*, IWA Publishing, London, pp237–92

Juanico, M. and Salgot, M. (2008) 'Northern Mediterranean world', in B. Jiménez and T. Asano (eds) *Water Reuse: An International Survey of Current Practice, Issues and Needs*, IWA Publishing, London, p648

Keraita, B., Jiménez, B. and Drechsel, P. (2008) 'Extent and implications of agricultural reuse of untreated, partly treated and diluted wastewater in developing countries', *Agriculture, Veterinary Science, Nutrition and Natural Resources*, vol 3, no 58, p15

Koné, D. (in press) 'Making Urban Excreta and Wastewater Management Contributes to Cities' Economic Development. A Paradigm Shift', *Water Policy*

Koné, D., Cofie, O., Zurbrugg, C., Gallizzi, K., Moser, D., Drescher, S. and Strauss, M. (2007a) 'Helminth eggs inactivation efficiency by faecal sludge dewatering and co-composting in tropical climates', *Water Research*, vol 41, no 19, pp4397–402

Koné, D., Strauss, M. and Saywell, D. (2007b) 'Towards an improved Faecal Sludge Management (FSM)', *Proceedings of the 1st International Symposium and Workshop on Faecal Sludge Management (FSM) Policy, final report, Dakar, 9–12 May 2006*, Die Eidgenössische Anstalt für Wasserversorgung, Dübendorf, Switzerland

Koottatep, T., Polprasert, C. and Hadsoi, S. (2006) 'Integrated faecal sludge treatment and recycling through constructed wetlands and sunflower plant irrigation', *Water Science and Technology*, vol 54, pp155–64

Lai, T. (2002) 'Perspectives of peri-urban vegetable production in Hanoi', background paper prepared for the Action Planning Workshop of the CGIAR Strategic Initiative for Urban and Peri-urban Agriculture (SIUPA), Hanoi, 6–9 June, convened by International Potato Center (CIP), Lima, Peru

Mekala, G. D., Davidson, B. A. and Boland, A. (2007) 'Multiple uses of wastewater: A methodology for cost-effective recycling', in S. J. Khan, R. M. Stuetz and J. M. Anderson (eds) *Water Reuse and Recycling*, University of New South Wales (UNSW) Publishing and Printing Services, Sydney, Australia, pp335-43

Moran, J. (2005) *Tropical Dairy Farming: Feeding Management for Small Holder Dairy Farmers in the Humid Tropics*, Land Links, Collingwood, Australia

Morel, A. and Diener, S. (2006) *Greywater Management in Low and Middle-Income Countries. Review of Different Treatment Systems for Households or Neighbourhoods*, Swiss Federal Institute of Aquatic Science and Technology (EAWAG), Dübendorf, Switzerland

Page, A. L. and Chang, A. C. (1994) 'Trace elements of environmental concern in terrestrial ecosystems: An overview', in *Transactions of the 15th World Congress of Soil Science*, vol 3a, pp568–85. Commission II: Symposia, Acapulco, Mexico, 10–16 July, 1994

Phuc, P. D., Konradsen, F., Phuong, P. T., Cam, P. D. and Dalsgaard, A. (2006) 'Use of human excreta as fertilizer in agriculture in Nghe An province, Viet Nam', *Southeast Asian Journal of Tropical Medicine and Public Health*, vol 37, pp222–9

Post, J. (2006) 'Wastewater treatment and reuse in eastern Mediterranean region', *Water 2*, pp36–41

Qadir, M., Wichelns, D., Raschid-Sally, L., Minhas, P. S., Drechsel, P., Bahri, A. and McCornick, P. (2007) 'Agricultural use of marginal-quality water – opportunities and challenges', in D. Molden (ed) *Water for Food, Water for Life. A Comprehensive Assessment of Water Management in Agriculture*, Earthscan, London, and International Water Management Institute, Colombo, pp425–57

Raschid-Sally, L., Carr, R. and Buechler, S. (2005) 'Managing wastewater agriculture to improve livelihoods and environmental quality in poor countries', *Irrigation and Drainage,* vol 54, no 1, pp11–22

Raschid-Sally, L. and Jayakody, P. (2008) 'Drivers and characteristics of wastewater agriculture in developing countries: Results from a global assessment, Colombo, Sri Lanka', *IWMI Research Report 127*, International Water Management Institute, Colombo

Rosemarin, A. (2004) 'The precarious geopolitics of phosphorous', *Down to Earth*, 30 June, pp27–34

Sanon, H. O., Kaboré-Zoungrana. C. and Ledin, I. (2007) 'Behaviour of goats, sheep and cattle and their selection of browse species on natural pasture in a Sahelian area', *Small Ruminant Research*, vol 67, no 1, pp64–74

Scott, C. A., Faruqui, N. I. and Raschid-Sally, L. (eds) (2004) *Wastewater Use in Irrigated Agriculture: Confronting the Livelihood and Environmental Realities*, CABI Publishing, Wallingford, UK

Silva, N., Chan, M. and Bundy, A. (1997) 'Morbidity and mortality due to ascariasis: re-estimation and sensitivity analysis of global numbers at risk', *Tropical Medicine and International Health*, vol 2, no 6, pp19–28

Snyman, H. (2008) 'South Africa', in R. LeBlanc, P. Matthews and P. Roland (eds) *Global Atlas of Excreta, Wastewater Sludge, and Biosolids Management: Moving Forward the Sustainable and Welcome Uses of a Global Resource*, UN-Habitat, Nairobi, pp514–25

Soulié, M. and Tréméa, L. (1991) 'Technologie pour le traitement et la réutilisation des eaux usées dans le bassin méditerranéen', in *Proceedings of the 3rd Meeting of the Regional Agency for Environment, Provence – Alpes – Côte d'Azur*, pp171–255

State of California (2001) 'Wastewater recycling criteria', an excerpt from the *California Code of Regulations*, Title 22, Division 4, Environmental Health, Dept. of Health Services, Sacramento, California, June 2001 edition

Strauss, M., Larmie, S. A. and Heinss, U. (1997) 'Treatment of sludges from on-site sanitation – Low-cost options', *Water Science and Technology*, vol 6, no 35, pp129–36

Toutain B., Guervilly T., Le Masson, A. and Roberge, G. (2006) 'Leçons de quelques essais de régénération des parcours en région sahélienne', *Sécheresse*, vol 17, no 1–2, pp72–5

Trang, D., Hien, B., Mølbak, K., Cam, P. and Dalsgaard, A. (2007a) 'Epidemiology and aetiology of diarrhoeal diseases in adults engaged in wastewater-fed agriculture and aquaculture in Hanoi, Vietnam', *Tropical Medicine and International Health*, vol 12, no 2, pp23–33

Trang, D., Hien, B., Mølbak, K., Cam, P. and Dalsgaard, A. (2007b) 'Helminth infections among people using wastewater and human excreta in peri-urban agriculture and aquaculture in Hanoi, Vietnam', *Tropical Medicine and International Health*, vol 12, no 2, pp82–90

United Nations (2003) *UN World Water Development Report: Water for People, Water for Life*, UNESCO and Berghahn Books, Paris, New York and Oxford

United Nations Human Settlements Programme (2008), in R. LeBlanc, P. Matthews and P. Roland (eds) *Global Atlas of Excreta, Wastewater Sludge, and Biosolids Management: Moving Forward the Sustainable and Welcome Uses of a Global Resource*, UN-Habitat, Nairobi, p632

WHO (1989) *Guidelines for the Safe Use of Wastewater in Agriculture*, WHO, Geneva

WHO (2006) *Guidelines for the Safe Use of Wastewater, Excreta and Greywater, Volume 2: Wastewater Use in Agriculture*, World Health Organization, Geneva

WHO-IDRC (2006) 'Report of the first consultative workshop on the WHO/IDRC project. Non-treatment options for safe wastewater use in poor urban communities', WHO/SDE/WSH/07.03, www.who.int/water_sanitation_health/wastewater/accraworkshop_wsh0703.pdf

Wolf, J., van Wijk, M. S., Cheng, X., Hu, Y., van Diepen, C. A., Jongbloed, A. W., van Keulen, H., Lu, C. H. and Roetter, R. (2003) 'Urban and peri-urban agricultural production in Beijing municipality and its impact on water quality', *Environment and Urbanization*, vol 15, no 2, pp141–56

World Resources Institute (2000) *World Resources 2000–2001, People and Ecosystems: The Fraying Web of Life*, WRI, Washington, DC, http://maps.grida.no/go/graphic/freshwater_withdrawal_in_agriculture_industry_and_domestic_use/

Yang, H. and Abbaspour, K. (2007) 'Analysis of wastewater reuse potential in Beijing', *Desalination*, vol 212, pp 238–50

2

Assessing and Mitigating Wastewater-Related Health Risks in Low-Income Countries: An Introduction

Robert Bos, Richard Carr and Bernard Keraita[1]

Abstract

In and around urban areas pollution of natural water bodies is on the rise. As a result, wastewater irrigation is an increasingly common reality around most cities in the developing world. For reasons of technical capacity or economics, effective treatment may not be available for years to come; therefore, international guidelines to safeguard farmers and consumers must be practical and offer feasible risk-management options. This chapter provides an introduction to microbiological hazards. These can be addressed best in a step-wise risk assessment and management approach starting with wastewater treatment where possible, and supported by different pathogen barriers from farm to fork. A major change in the most recent WHO Guidelines for the safe use of wastewater, excreta and greywater in agriculture and aquaculture (WHO, 2006) agriculture is the focus on a holistic approach to achieving health-based targets, instead of prescribing irrigation water-quality threshold levels that are often unattainable. The health-based targets should not be read as absolute values but as goals to be attained in the short, medium or long term depending on the country's technical capacity and institutional or economic conditions. Local standards and actual implementation should progressively develop as the country moves up the sanitation ladder. While health-risk assessments are recommended to identify entry points for risk reduction and health-based targets, the Guidelines also offer shortcuts in situations where research capacities and data are constrained.

INTRODUCTION

The agricultural use of treated, partially treated or untreated wastewater[2] or surface water contaminated with wastewater is common. An estimated 20 million hectares worldwide are irrigated with wastewater, more of it with untreated than treated wastewater (Jiménez and Asano, 2008; Scott et al., 2004). This misbalance in favour of untreated wastewater will continue to increase as long as the pollution of streams, by effluents from growing urban populations is not matched by treatment facilities. The increasing global scarcity of good-quality water will turn wastewater irrigation from an undesirable phenomenon into a necessity wherever agricultural water demand is not met by supply. This is not only the case in drier regions, but anywhere where farmers seek land and water to address market demand. Common examples are urban and peri-urban areas in most developing countries where clean water sources are hardly sufficient even to meet domestic demand.

The use of untreated wastewater, or polluted water in general, poses risks to human health since it may contain excreta-related pathogens (viruses, bacteria, protozoan and multicellular parasites), skin irritants and toxic chemicals like heavy metals, pesticides and pesticide residues. When wastewater is used in agriculture, pathogens and certain chemicals are the primary hazards to human health by exposure through different routes (see Table 2.1). These exposure routes are mainly contact with wastewater (farmers, field workers and nearby communities) and consumption of wastewater-grown produce (consumers). In addition, contamination may be due to poor post-harvest handling that can also lead to cross-contamination of farm produce.

This chapter and most other sections of this book target microbiological hazards, while chemical hazards are addressed in Chapter 6 and Chapter 11.

EXPOSURE ROUTES FOR HEALTH HAZARDS FROM WASTEWATER IRRIGATION

The causative agents of excreta-associated infections are released from infected persons (or animals in some cases) in their excreta. They include pathogenic viruses, bacteria, protozoa and helminths of which are released from the bodies of infected persons (or animals in some cases) in their excreta (faeces or urine). The pathogens eventually reach other people and enter either via the mouth (the faecal-oral pathway, e.g. when contaminated crops are eaten) or via the skin (contact with infective larvae, e.g. hookworm infection and schistosomiasis).

Table 2.1 *Examples of different kinds of hazards associated with wastewater use in agriculture in developing countries*

Hazard	Exposure route	Relative importance
Excreta-related pathogens		
Bacteria (for example *E. coli*, Vibrio cholerae, *Salmonella* spp. *Shigella* spp.)	Contact; Consumption	Low–high
Helminths (parasitic worms)		
• Soil-transmitted (*Ascaris*, hookworms, *Taenia* spp.)	Contact; Consumption	Low–high
• *Schistosoma* spp.	Contact	Nil–high
Protozoa (*Giardia intestinalis*, *Cryptosporidium*, *Entamoeba* spp.)	Contact; Consumption	Low–medium
Viruses (for example hepatitis A virus, hepatitis E virus, adenovirus, rotavirus, norovirus)	Contact; Consumption	Low–high
Skin irritants and infections	Contact	Medium–high
Vector-borne pathogens (*Filaria* spp., Japanese encephalitis virus, *Plasmodium* spp.)	Vector contact	Nil–medium
Chemicals		
Heavy metals (for example arsenic, cadmium, lead, mercury)	Consumption	Generally low
Halogenated hydrocarbons (dioxins, furans, PCBs)	Consumption	Low
Pesticides (aldrin, DDT)	Contact; Consumption	Low

Source: Adapted from WHO (2006)

Occupational exposure

The most affected groups are farm workers due to the duration and intensity of their contact with wastewater and contaminated soils (Blumenthal and Peasey, 2002; WHO, 2006). For instance, in Haroonabad, Pakistan, prevalence rates for hookworm infection as high as 80 per cent have been reported for farmers (mainly male adults) using untreated wastewater (van der Hoek et al., 2002). Epidemiological studies of farmer groups using wastewater have produced overwhelming evidence of the high risk of helminth infections. This has resulted in the strict WHO guideline value of ≤1 egg per litre of irrigation water (WHO, 2006). Nevertheless, recent epidemiological studies conducted among rice farmers in Vietnam using wastewater found significantly more evidence for increased diarrhoea and skin problems than for the risk of helminth infections (Trang et al., 2007a, b).

Contradictions may occur between actual risks and perceived ones. Wastewater farmers themselves seldom associate infections and diseases with their irrigation practice (Rutkowski et al., 2007), which may jeopardize efforts towards their adoption of risk reduction measures by them (see Chapter 17). It also highlights the need to educate farmers about the risks they face when using wastewater for irrigation. There are arguments based on economic impact studies as well, that the financial gains from agricultural production using wastewater irrigation can allow farmers to pay for medication to treat helminth infections (Bayrau et al., 2009). More on integrating economic impacts into risk analysis is presented in Chapter 7.

Other than helminth infections, recent studies from Vietnam and Cambodia have attributed skin diseases such as dermatitis (eczema) to contact with untreated wastewater (van der Hoek et al., 2005; Trang et al., 2007c). A study conducted in the Kathmandu Valley, Nepal, showed that more than half of 110 farmers interviewed using wastewater had experienced skin problems (Rutkowski et al., 2007). The reported skin problems included itching and blistering on the hands and feet. Similar problems were reported by rice farmers along the Musi River in Hyderabad, India, and urban vegetable farmers using wastewater in Ghana (Buechler et al., 2002; Obuobie et al., 2006). Nail problems such as koilonychias (spoon-formed nails) have also been reported but this is specifically associated with hookworm infections which cause iron deficiency (anaemia) damaging the formation of nails (van der Hoek et al., 2002). Studies conducted in Vietnam did not find an association between the risk of eye ailments (conjunctivitis or trachoma) and wastewater-related exposure but recommended more studies to determine if there is a link between skin infections and particular water pollutants (Trang et al., 2007c).

Consumption of irrigated produce

In relation to consumption-associated health risks, the primary concern is about vegetables eaten uncooked e.g. in raw salad dishes (Harris et al., 2003). Several studies including a prospective cohort study (Peasey, 2000), an analytical descriptive study (Cifuentes, 1998) and several descriptive studies including one done in Jerusalem (Shuval et al., 1984) have shown higher *Ascaris* infections for both adults and children consuming uncooked vegetables irrigated with wastewater. Studies on the impact related to diarrhoeal diseases from consumption of contaminated vegetables have been published and reviewed extensively (Beuchat, 1998; Harris et al., 2003).

The *Escherichia coli* strain enterotoxigenic *E. coli* (ETEC) is often associated with diarrhoea (travellers' diarrhoea) in developing countries (Gupta et al., 2007). In addition, viral enteritis (especially norovirus and rotavirus) and hepatitis A are the most commonly reported viral infections from vegetable consumption (Lindesmith et al., 2003; Seymour and Appleton, 2001). Several diarrhoeal outbreaks have been associated with wastewater-irrigated vegetables (Shuval et al., 1984; WHO, 2006). However, in developing countries it is often a challenge to attribute diarrhoeal outbreaks to specific exposure routes due to other contributing factors including poor hygiene, sanitation and reduced access to safe drinking water.

DISEASES ASSOCIATED WITH WASTEWATER USE IN AGRICULTURE

Not every hazard will end up causing illness and different hazards and exposure pathways will result in different disease burdens. The relative importance of health hazards in causing illness depends on a number of factors. The ability of infectious agents to cause disease relates to their persistence in the environment, minimum infective dose, ability to induce human immunity, virulence and tency periods (Shuval et al., 1986). Thus, pathogens with long persistence in the environment and low minimal infective doses that elicit little or no human immunity and having long latency periods (for example helminths) have a higher probability of causing infections than others. According to this, helminth infections, where endemic, pose the greatest risks associated with wastewater irrigation. Risks from most chemicals are thought to be low, except in localized areas with large industrial wastewater generation. Diseases associated with exposure to chemicals (aside from acute symptoms such as skin rashes, etc.), such as cancer, are harder to attribute to wastewater use in agriculture. This is because workers may be exposed to complex mixtures of chemicals in the wastewater and long latency periods before the disease symptoms appear, making it difficult to attribute the disease to any one specific exposure route or causal factor.

The diseases of most relevance differ from area to area depending on the local status of sanitation and hygiene and the level to which wastewater is treated prior to use in agriculture. Table 2.2 provides examples of the burden of some diseases of potential relevance to wastewater use in agriculture. Most of these excreta-related illnesses occur in children living in poor countries. The disease burden is measured in disability-adjusted life years (DALYs),[3] which is increasingly becoming an essential unit in comparing disease outcomes from different exposures. More details on the use of DALYs are given in the following chapters. Overall, the WHO estimates that diarrhoea alone is responsible for nearly 3 per cent of all deaths and 3.9 per cent of DALYs worldwide (Prüss-Ustün and Corvalan, 2006). Diarrhoea is indeed a disease which can be largely attributed to environmental factors (88 per cent, WHO, 2009), such as unsafe drinking water, poor hygiene and sanitation, and the consumption of pathogen-contaminated crops.

The question of how much of the disease burden can be attributed to poor sanitation, unsafe drinking water, poor hygiene and, in particular, to the consumption of wastewater-irrigated vegetables remains a challenging one. There are not many comparative studies and those that exist only look at either waterborne or foodborne pathways. Wastewater-irrigated food links both categories, but more importantly, many factors are interwoven and not mutually exclusive. The large number of confounding factors makes any specific attribution to wastewater use difficult. One way to address the challenge is via microbiological risk assessment considering location-specific exposures.

Table 2.2 *Global mortality and DALYs due to some diseases of relevance to wastewater use in agriculture*

Disease	Mortality (deaths/year)	Burden of disease (DALYs)	Comments
Diarrhoea	1,682,000	57,966,000	99.7% of deaths occur in developing countries; 90% of deaths occur in children; 94% can be attributed to environmental factors.
Typhoid	600,000	N/A	Estimated 16,000,000 cases per year.
Ascariasis	3000	1,817,000	Estimated 1.45 billion infections, of which 350 million suffer adverse health effects.
Hookworm disease	3000	59,000	Estimated 1.3 billion infections, of which 150 million suffer adverse health effects.
Lymphatic filariasis	0	3,791,000	Mosquito vectors of filariasis (*Culex* spp.) breed in contaminated water. Does not cause death but leads to severe disability.
Hepatitis A	N/A	N/A	Estimated 1.4 million cases per year worldwide. Serological evidence of prior infection ranges from 15% to nearly 100%.

N/A = not available.
Source: Prüss-Üstün and Corvalan (2006); WHO (2006)

TOOLS FOR RISK ASSESSMENT

Assessment of risks mainly relies on data from microbiological analysis, epidemiological studies and/or quantitative microbial risk assessment (QMRA), the latter being a prospective assessment rather than extrapolation from evaluations. Traditionally, microbial analysis and epidemiological studies have been extensively used in evaluating risks in wastewater-irrigated agriculture, especially among affected farmers. A number of epidemiological studies in this area have shown higher prevalence of infections in the exposed population compared to unexposed populations. The studies have also clearly associated levels of pathogens in irrigation water to infection levels (Blumenthal and Peasey, 2002). Nevertheless, from the perspective of possible risk to society or planned agricultural wastewater irrigation, the epidemiological approach has limitations in that it is relatively expensive and it does not meet the need of the public, governments and other stakeholders to obtain health-risk estimates before the commissioning of projects. QMRA is increasingly used for this purpose, giving a prospective risk assessment for the wastewater irrigation situation at hand (Hamilton et al., 2007). Contributions and limitations of the main assessment tools are shown in Table 2.3. Detailed

Table 2.3 *Data used for the assessment of health risks*

Type of study	Contributions	Limitations
Microbial analysis	• Determines concentrations of different excreted organisms in wastewater or on products. • Provides data on pathogen die-off rates. • Can help to identify sources of pathogens. • Used to link pathogen to infection/disease.	• Expensive unless indicators are used. • Collection of samples may be time-consuming. • Needs trained staff and laboratory facilities. • Obtaining laboratory results takes time. • Lack of standardized procedures for the detection of some pathogens or their recovery from food products. • Recovery percentages may show high variability. • Some methods do not determine viability.
Epidemiological studies	• Measure actual disease in an exposed population. • Can be used to test different exposure hypotheses. • Can be applied to chemical risk assessments.	• Expensive. • Bias can affect results. • Large sample sizes needed. • Ethical clearance needed. • Need for balance between power of study and its sensitivity.
QMRA	• Can estimate very low levels of risk of infection/disease. • Low-cost method of predicting risk of infection/disease. • Facilitates comparisons of different exposure routes. • Principles can also be applied to chemical risk assessments.	• Exposure scenarios can vary significantly and are difficult to model. • Validated data inputs are not available for every exposure scenario. • Predicts risks from exposure to one type of pathogen at a time.

Source: Adapted from WHO (2006)

descriptions on microbiological risk analysis and risk analysis tools are presented in the following chapters in this volume.

GUIDELINES FOR WASTEWATER IRRIGATION IN DEVELOPING COUNTRIES

While some countries, especially more developed ones, have national guidelines addressing wastewater use in agriculture, the best known international guidelines are those produced by the UN, in particular the WHO. To protect public health and facilitate the rational use of wastewater and excreta in agriculture and aquaculture, WHO developed the document *Reuse of Effluents: Methods of Wastewater Treatment and Public Health Safeguards* in the early 1970s. This first normative document from the WHO in the field of wastewater use was developed in the absence of good epidemiological studies and borrowed essentially a low-risk approach from the USA (Carr, 2005). In 1976, it was complemented by the FAO's Irrigation and Drainage Paper 29 which addressed the water-quality challenges of salinity and specific ion toxicity (FAO, 1976). The WHO publication relied on water thresholds, i.e. critical pathogen levels in the irrigation water (100 coliforms 100ml⁻¹) which should not be exceeded, and gave best practice recommendations on how to treat the water to achieve this quality standard (Havelaar et al., 2001).

In the two decades following the publication of these documents, the use of wastewater in agriculture expanded in many arid and semi-arid countries. This trend and the health and safety questions concerning this practice became driving forces for conducting a number of epidemiological studies. (A thorough review of epidemiological studies was prepared by Shuval et al., 1986.) As epidemiological evidence was compiled it became clear that the initial WHO publication needed to be revised and the following additional issues needed to be considered (Carr, 2005):

- Overly strict water-quality standards were impossible to achieve in many situations and were therefore often ignored, rendering the Guidelines useless.
- Guidelines needed to include risk-management approaches that would complement available treatment processes or could be used in the absence of wastewater treatment to reduce health risks.

Based on these considerations a second edition of the WHO Guidelines was published in 1989 (Mara and Cairncross, 1989). The FAO's Irrigation and Drainage Paper 47 followed in 1992, building on the 1989 Guidelines while also addressing issues specific to irrigation such as managing salinity (FAO, 1992). Both guidelines have been very influential and many countries have adopted them, in some cases with adaptations. In view of pathogenic threats, both reports emphasized the need for appropriate wastewater treatment before use and for water-quality criteria that are easy to monitor.

In 1997, the FAO's 'Water Report no. 10' challenged the application potential of the WHO water-quality standards, as adequate treatment facilities sufficient to help meet these standards could well be a decade or more away (FAO, 1997). This publication stressed the need for additional, interim measures, in particular crop restrictions. With increasing knowledge about and tools for risk assessments (such as QMRA), the development of the DALY concept and the increasing emphasis on critical control points to achieve food safety, the WHO joined forces with the FAO and started another historic revision of the WHO Guidelines. The revised edition was to include more information about how to define tolerable risks to society based upon the actual disease situation in any given country, with a stronger emphasis on local opportunities but also limitations to achieve risk reduction (Carr, 2005).

A major change was the shift from critical levels of microbial contamination of irrigation water to health-based targets (WHO, 2006). In addition to the challenge of achieving water quality-based targets (especially in those countries where the burden of associated illness is highest), another weakness was that water quality-based thresholds hardly helped to address food contamination taking place from sources other than irrigation. The suggested alternative was to reduce the risk, especially for consumers of wastewater-irrigated crops, wherever there is an opportunity along the production and marketing chain. This can be wastewater treatment, safer irrigation practices, only growing crops that are eaten fully cooked and washing crops as part of food preparation. Using a combination of these preventive measures, it will be possible to approach the health target values which are set at the end of the chain, i.e. at the point of consumption, similar to the concept of food-safety objectives (CAC, 2004). This target is calculated based on the pathogen reduction from the initial crop contamination level and can be expressed in DALYs averted. The emphasis on 'targets' means that these values should not be read as absolute values but as goals to be attained in the short, medium or long term depending on the country's technological, institutional or financial conditions (Sperling and Fattal, 2001).

In order to better package the Guidelines for appropriate audiences it was decided to present them in separate volumes:

- Volume 1: Policy and regulatory aspects;
- Volume 2: Wastewater use in agriculture;
- Volume 3: Wastewater and excreta use in aquaculture;
- Volume 4: Excreta and greywater use in agriculture.

The Guidelines can be downloaded from www.who.int/water_sanitation_health/ wastewater/gsuww/en/index.html. Shorter, related fact sheets and policy briefs for different stakeholder groups can be found at www.who.int/water_sanitation_ health/wastewater/usinghumanwaste/en/index.html.

APPROACHES FOR MITIGATING RISKS FROM WASTEWATER IRRIGATION

Conventional options and their limitations in developing countries

Wastewater treatment in designed plants or pond systems has long been considered the ultimate solution for reducing risks in wastewater-irrigated agriculture.

Wastewater treatment as a risk-mitigation measure has therefore been widely studied and documented in both developed and developing countries (Hammer and Hammer, 2008; Mara, 2004; Metcalf and Eddy, 2002; Patwardhan, 2008). Questions are being raised, however, about the effectiveness of conventional treatment systems in removing pathogens that are of particular concern in many developing countries and also about some emerging organic chemical compounds, such as pesticides and their residues, pharmaceutically active compounds and endocrine disrupting substances. Indeed, most conventional systems have two treatment systems: primary treatment where suspended solids and organic matter are removed; and secondary treatment for removing biodegradable organics. Tertiary level treatment may also be available, but the aim of tertiary treatment is removal of nutrients and toxic compounds (Metcalf and Eddy, 2002). So, conventional treatment systems are designed mainly to address environmental concerns and not human health risks. This was further shown by a review of more than 20 studies conducted for the WHO for the third edition of its Guidelines. The review showed wide variations in the effectiveness of log unit removals of various pathogens by different conventional treatment processes (WHO, 2006).

The processes involved in several conventional treatment systems, except stabilization ponds, are difficult and costly to operate in developing-country contexts as they have high energy requirements, need skilled labour and also have high installation, operation and maintenance costs (Carr and Strauss, 2001). This perhaps explains the high number of dysfunctional treatment plants and low general levels of wastewater treatment in developing countries of less than 1 per cent in sub-Saharan Africa, about 35 per cent in Asia and 14 per cent in South America (WHO and UNICEF, 2000). A survey in Ghana, for example, reported that only 10 per cent of the reported 70 treatment plants and faecal sludge stabilization ponds are still operating as planned, most of them belonging to larger hotels (IWMI, 2009).

Innovative changes are therefore necessary for conventional wastewater treatment to continue to be seen as a realistic health-risk mitigation option in developing countries. In recent years, some of these changes have included research towards re-engineering conventional wastewater treatment systems to make them more appropriate for irrigation, by optimizing the water and nutrient contents in treated wastewater effluents, as discussed in Chapters 14 and 15. Studies have also focused on developing systems which are more efficient in pathogen removal and nutrient conservation. Here, a focus on systems that use low-rate biological processes, such as pond systems, has been promoted, as discussed in Chapters 8 and 9. There is also a growing research emphasis on biosolids, especially developing risk-mitigation measures for faecal sludge use in agriculture, as well as on outsourcing treatment to the farm level (see Chapter 10).

Non-conventional options and the multiple-barrier approach

Considering the apparent limitations of implementing conventional wastewater treatment systems in many developing countries at present, the third edition of the WHO Guidelines recommends the use of the 'multiple-barrier approach'. The approach draws from the Hazard Analysis Critical Control Point (HACCP) concept promoted by the *Codex Alimentarius* initiative and is based on targeted interventions at key control points along the food chain to achieve a food-safety objective (CAC, 2004). Critical control points (which can be important pathogen barriers) can be found along the whole chain of events from wastewater generation to the preparation of the vegetables served for consumption. The approach therefore covers both conventional and non-conventional wastewater treatment methods as well as other health-protection measures to meet health targets, be it for the farmer or consumer. Non-conventional wastewater treatment methods include the use of low-cost systems such as on-farm ponds, sedimentation traps and biosand-filters while health-protection measures include improved irrigation methods, like drip irrigation, cessation of irrigation before harvesting and produce-washing (Keraita et al., 2008). In some parts of the 2006 edition of the Guidelines, these different options are grouped as 'treatment' and 'non-treatment' options with 'treatment' covering all conventional wastewater treatment systems (see Chapters 8 and 9) and 'non-treatment' options including all other possible practices and measures, especially on farm and in the post-harvest sector (see Chapters 10 to 12). Table 2.4 provides an overview of different health-protection measures and where they can be applied in the food-production chain.

Strengths and weaknesses of different approaches for risk reduction

All critical control points or possible 'barriers' have strengths and weaknesses. A key factor of the main groups of 'treatment' and 'non-treatment' (also known as 'post-treatment') options is that they require particular settings to work. Wastewater treatment has a marginal impact in many developing countries due to limited coverage, under-resourced institutions, limited human capacities and severe financial challenges. Post-treatment options, on the other hand, require farmers, traders or food caterers to adopt safer practices, often without any obvious or direct personal or business benefit. In the context of low-income countries with limited public education and awareness of food-safety issues, non-treatment options are thus not the panacea where wastewater treatment is missing or fails, and actually require particular efforts in terms of awareness creation, incentives and regulations as described in Chapters 16 and 17.

Post-harvest treatment and handling of fresh produce often cannot eliminate pathogens without compromising the attractiveness and physical quality of the

Table 2.4 *Overview of health-protection measures*

Health-protection measures	Location	Examples	Protected groups	Chapters in this book
Treatment options	Pre-farm	Municipal wastewater treatment plants (e.g., waste stabilization ponds, constructed wetlands)	Farming communities and consumers	8, 9
Post-treatment (or non-treatment) options	On farm	On-farm treatment systems (e.g., sedimentation traps or tanks, simple ponds, sand-filters)		10, 17 (microbiological control measures) 11 (chemical control measures)
		Protective clothing, including gloves, and footwear	Farming communities only	
		Safer collection and application of wastewater (e.g. low-cost drip irrigation, splash reduction, reduced helminth egg uptake from sediments)	Farming communities and consumers	
		Imposing a minimum period of no irrigation immediately prior to harvest (to promote pathogen die-off)	Consumers only	
		Crop restrictions (to exclude e.g. crops eaten uncooked or grow only non-edible crops)		
	Off farm (post-harvest sector)	Produce-washing, disinfection, peeling and/or cooking		12, 16

produce (Beuchat, 1998) unless the product is always consumed after cooking. Thus, it appears most feasible not to rely on only one barrier or option but to combine different barriers from wastewater treatment to on-farm and off-farm measures (see Chapters 10 and 12).

So far, the use of the multiple-barrier approach in wastewater-irrigated agriculture has not been systematically studied in a variety of different settings. However, a review conducted for WHO based on some limited studies shows that this approach appears to be feasible (Table 2.5). For example, in the WHO Guidelines, a pathogen reduction of 6–7 log units is used as the performance target for unrestricted irrigation to achieve the tolerable disease burden of $\leq 10^{-6}$ DALYs per person per year. For monitoring purposes, log unit pathogen reductions are

Table 2.5 *Pathogen reductions achievable by selected health-protection measures*

Control Measure	Reduction (log units)	Comments
Wastewater treatment (primary + secondary)	1–4	Reduction usually achieved by wastewater treatment depending on the type and functionality of the treatment system.
Drip irrigation used for:		
Low-growing crops	2	Root crops and crops such as lettuce that grow just above, but partially in contact with, the soil.
High-growing crops	4	Crops, such as tomatoes, fruit trees, the harvested parts of which are not in contact with the soil.
Pathogen die-off	0.5–2 per day	Die-off on crop surfaces that occurs between last irrigation and consumption. The log unit reduction achieved depends on climate (temperature, sunlight intensity, humidity), time, crop type, etc.
Produce-washing with water	1	Washing salad crops, vegetables and fruit with clean water.
Produce disinfection	2–3	Washing salad crops, vegetables and fruit with a weak, often chlorine-based disinfectant solution and rinsing with clean water.
Produce peeling	1–2	Fruits, cabbage, root crops.
Produce cooking	6–7	Immersion in boiling or close-to-boiling water until the food is cooked ensures pathogen destruction.

Source: Adapted and modified from WHO (2006)

not measured via actual pathogen numbers, but by the reduction in numbers of a pathogen indicator organism, which is in most cases *E. coli*. As Table 2.5 demonstrates, combining minimal wastewater treatment, drip irrigation and washing vegetables after harvesting can easily achieve a 6 log unit reduction.

ACTUAL FIELD ASSESSMENTS OF RISK-REDUCTION OPTIONS

The increased complexity of the 2006 WHO Guidelines means that they are sometimes perceived as less user-friendly. The concerns relate to the more complex health-based targets and the need to perform risk assessments, including the DALY concept. Although the Guidelines ask for a certain sequence of steps to be followed, their application should not be limited to situations where all steps can be taken. Where a risk assessment, like QMRA, is not possible for reasons of missing data or research capacity and a local performance target for irrigation cannot be calculated, it is recommended to combine options as shown in Table 2.5 aiming at a cumulative pathogen reduction of 6–7 log units where the irrigation water is likely to be contaminated with pathogens and used on crops to be eaten raw (see also Chapters 3 and 5). In countries where achieving this log reduction in the local socio-economic context is not feasible, alternative national health-based targets can be established, under the condition that their implementation procedures are strictly monitored and the targets are incrementally improved towards the globally recommended one. Lower log reductions can also be targeted where crop restrictions are possible (see Chapter 3).

Another limitation of studies conducted so far on non-conventional or 'non-treatment' options, and in particular the multiple-barrier approach, is their restricted geographical extent (WHO, 2006). Even where research has progressed over the years, as in Ghana, it is still another step to implement the research (IWMI, 2009). In Ghana, the studies have focused on the adaptation of known but also on locally developed farm-based and off-farm measures. These include the cessation of irrigation before harvesting, safer water collection and application, safe irrigation methods, sand-filters, on-farm sedimentation ponds and post-harvest measures such as various indigenous vegetable-washing methods (see Chapters 10 and 12). These studies showed that low-cost measures have the potential to reduce pathogens, especially if they are developed with the user and can be used in combination so as to have a cumulative effect (Drechsel et al., 2008). However, their success depends largely on the adoption rate which requires an appropriate analysis of possible economic and social incentives (see Chapter 16).

Figure 2.1 shows a number of combination scenarios that were discussed in the studies of farm-based options in Kumasi, Ghana (Keraita, 2008). Scenario

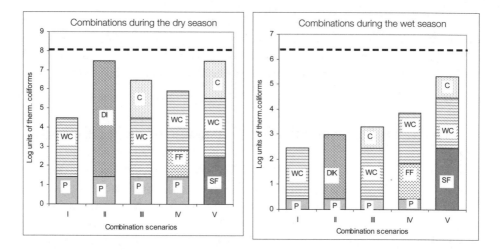

P = sedimentation ponds, WC = improved use of watering cans, SF = sand filter, FF = fabric filter, DI = Drip kits; C = cessation, ------- usual contamination levels on vegetables in Kumasi

Figure 2.1 *Feasible combinations of farm-based interventions and achievable reduction of thermotolerant coliforms on lettuce leaves in Kumasi, Ghana*

Source: Keraita (2008)

I reflects the most farmer-friendly option as it only entailed modifications of existing technologies. Although this option gives the lowest aggregate reduction in contamination levels, it is still a significant one for both the dry (4.5 log units) and wet (2.5 log units) seasons, if other barriers are available. Generally, the suggested combined intervention measures show very good performance during the dry season, but not in the wet season due to rainfall, shorter duration of sunshine and generally lower temperatures. As this was a location-specific study, similar trials elsewhere are encouraged.

CONCLUSIONS

In and around four out of five cities in the developing world, wastewater in treated, raw or diluted form is used in irrigated agriculture. Even if the areas are small, these farms are often specialized in producing highly perishable cash crops with a significant market share (Raschid-Sally and Jayakody, 2008). It is important to recognize that in many situations where wastewater is used in agriculture, effective treatment of wastewater may not be available for many years to come. International guidelines must therefore be practical and offer feasible risk-management solutions that will maximize health protection and facilitate the beneficial use of scarce resources. To achieve the greatest benefits to health, the third edition of the WHO Guidelines provides tools, methods and procedures to set health-based targets that can be achieved with different pathogen barriers from the wastewater source to the consumption of wastewater-irrigated food. This multiple-barrier approach should be implemented with other health measures such as health education, hygiene promotion and the provision of access to safe drinking water and adequate sanitation.

There are still many open questions for research and application, some of which are outlined in the last chapter of this volume. In order to properly interpret and apply the guidelines in a manner appropriate to local conditions, a broad-based policy approach is required that will include legislation as well as positive and negative incentives to support the adoption of good non-treatment or post-treatment practices. Efforts to expand the treatment of wastewater are important and need to accelerate. The current WHO Guidelines can support local, national and international standard-setting bodies in their efforts to develop their own procedures and protocols on how to achieve the recommended health-based targets. The procedures will differ between and within regions according to differences in technological, institutional and financial conditions. While the health-based targets will remain a given in any specific context, local standards and actual implementation should progressively develop as the country moves up the sanitation ladder.

NOTES

1   The opinions expressed in this chapter are those of the authors only and do not necessarily reflect the policies and positions of the World Health Organization.
2   The term 'wastewater' as used in this book covers wastewater of different qualities, ranging from raw to diluted, generated by various urban activities (see Chapter 1).
3   The DALY concept allows one to quantify the contribution to the 'burden of disease' from mortality, disability, impairment, illness and injury. One DALY can be thought of as one lost year of healthy life and is calculated as a combination of (1) years of life lost (YLL) as a result of premature mortality and (2) equivalent healthy years of life lost as a result of disability (YLD). The burden of disease therefore measures the gap between current health status and an ideal situation in which every one lives into old age free of disease and disability. See http://en.wikipedia.org/wiki/Disability-adjusted_life_year and www.who.int/healthinfo/global_burden_disease/en/index.html.

REFERENCES

Bayrau, A., Boelee, E., Drechsel, P. and Dabbert, S. (2009) 'Wastewater Use in Crop Production in Peri-urban Areas of Addis Ababa: Impacts on health in farm household', *Environment and Development Economics* (in press)

Beuchat, L. R. (1998) *Surface Decontamination of Fruits and Vegetables Eaten Raw: A Review*, Food Safety Unit, World Health Organization, WHO/FSF/98.2, available at www.who.int/foodsafety/publications/fs_management/en/surface_decon.pdf

Blumenthal, U. J. and Peasey, A. (2002) 'Critical review of epidemiological evidence of the health effects of wastewater and excreta use in agriculture', unpublished document prepared for World Health Organization, Geneva, www.who.int/water_sanitation_health/wastewater/whocriticalrev.pdf

Buechler, S., Devi, G. and Raschid-Sally, L. (2002) 'Livelihoods and wastewater irrigated agriculture along the Musi River in Hyderabad City, Andhra Pradesh, India', *Urban Agriculture Magazine*, vol 8, pp14–17

CAC (Codex Alimentarius Commission) (2004) 'Report of the twentieth session of the Codex Committee on General Principles, Paris, France, 3–7 May 2004', ALINORM 04/27/33A, Appendix II, pp37–38. ftp://ftp.fao.org/codex/alinorm04/al0433ae.pdf

Carr, R. (2005) 'WHO guidelines for safe wastewater use – more than just numbers', *Irrigation and Drainage*, no 54, ppS103–11

Carr, R. and Strauss, M. (2001) 'Excreta-related infections and the role of sanitation in the control of transmission', in L. Fewtrell and J. Bartram (eds) *Water Quality: Guidelines, Standards and Health; Assessment of Risk and Risk Management for Water-Related Infectious Disease*, International Water Association (IWA) on behalf on the World Health Organization, London, pp89–113

Cifuentes, E. (1998) 'The epidemiology of enteric infections in agricultural communities exposed to wastewater irrigation: perspectives for risk control', *International Journal of Environmental Health Research,* no 8, pp203–13

Drechsel, P., Keraita, B., Amoah, P., Abaidoo, R., Raschid-Sally, L. and Bahri, A. (2008) 'Reducing health risks from wastewater use in urban and peri-urban sub-Saharan

Africa: Applying the 2006 WHO Guidelines', *Water Science and Technology*, vol 57, no 9, pp1461–6

FAO (1976) *Water Quality for Agriculture*, R. S. Ayers and D. W. Westcot Irrigation and Drainage Paper 29, FAO, Rome, www.fao.org/DOCREP/003/T0234E/T0234E00.htm

FAO (1992) *Wastewater Treatment and Use in Agriculture*, M. B. Pescod (ed), Irrigation and Drainage Paper 47, FAO, Rome

FAO (1997) 'Quality control of wastewater for irrigated crop production', D. W. Westcot, *Water Report no 10*, FAO, Rome, www.fao.org/docrep/w5367e/w5367e00.htm

Gupta, S. K., Keck, J., Ram, P. K., Crump, J. A., Miller, M. A. and Mintz, E. D. (2007) 'Analysis of data gaps pertaining to enterotoxigenic *Escherichia coli* infections in low and medium human development index countries, 1984–2005', Part 3, *Epidemiological Infections*, 9 Aug 2007, pp1–18

Hamilton, A. J., Stagnitti, F., Xiong, X., Kreidl, S. L., Benke, K. K. and Maher, P. (2007) 'Wastewater irrigation: The state of play', *Vadose Zone Journal*, vol 6, no 4, pp823–40

Hammer Sr, M. J. and Hammer Jr, M. J. (2008) *Water and Wastewater Technology*, 6th edition, Eastern Economic Edition, Prentice Hall of India, New Delhi

Harris, L. J., Farber, J. M., Beuchat, L. R., Parish, M. E., Suslow, T.V., Garrett, E. H. and Busta, F. F. (2003) 'Outbreaks associated with fresh produce: incidence, growth, and survival of pathogens in fresh and fresh-cut produce', *Comprehensive Reviews in Food Science and Food Safety*, no 2, pp78–141

Havelaar, A., Blumenthal, J., Strauss, M., Kay, D. and Bartram, J. (2001) 'Guidelines: The current position', in L. Fewtrell and J. Bartram (eds) *Water Quality: Guidelines, Standards and Health; Assessment of Risk and Risk Management for Water-related Infectious Disease*, International Water Association (IWA) on behalf on the World Health Organization, London, pp17–42

Hoek, W. van der, Tuan Anh, V., Cam, P. D., Vicheth, C. and Dalsgaard, A. (2005) 'Skin diseases among people using urban wastewater in Phnom Penh', *Urban Agriculture Magazine*, no 14, pp30–31

Hoek, W. van der, Ul Hassan, M., Ensink, J. H. J., Feenstra, S., Raschid-Sally, L., Munir, S. et al. (2002) 'Urban wastewater: A valuable resource for agriculture', *International Water Management Institute Research Report*, no 63, Colombo

IWMI (2009) 'Wastewater irrigation and public health: From research to impact – A road map for Ghana', a report for Google.org prepared by IWMI, Accra, Ghana

Jiménez, B. and Asano, T. (2008) 'Water reclamation and reuse around the world', in B. Jiménez and T. Asano (eds) (2008) *Water Reuse: An International Survey of Current Practice, Issues and Needs*, IWA Publishing, London, p648

Keraita, B. (2008) 'Low-cost measures for reducing health risks in wastewater irrigated urban vegetable farming in Ghana', PhD thesis, Faculty of Health Sciences, University of Copenhagen

Keraita, B., Jiménez, B. and Drechsel, P. (2008) 'Extent and implications of agricultural reuse of untreated, partly treated and diluted wastewater in developing countries', *CAB Reviews: Perspectives in Agriculture, Veterinary Science, Nutrition and Natural Resources* vol 3, no 58, pp1–15

Lindesmith, L., Moe, C., Marionneau, S., Ruvoen, N., Jiang, X., Lindblad, L., Stewart, P., LePendu, J. and Baric, R. (2003) 'Human susceptibility and resistance to Norwalk virus infection', *Nature Medicine*, vol 9, pp548–53

Mara, D. D. (2004) *Domestic Wastewater Treatment in Developing Countries*, Earthscan, London

Mara, D. and Cairncross, S. (1989) *Guidelines of the Safe Use of Wastewater and Excreta in Agriculture and Aquaculture*, World Health Organization, Geneva

Metcalf and Eddy, Inc. (2002) *Wastewater Engineering: Treatment and Reuse*, 4th Edition, McGraw-Hill Science Engineering / Tata McGraw-Hill, New Delhi

Obuobie, E., Keraita. B., Danso, G., Amoah, P., Cofie, O., Raschid-Sally, L. and Drechsel, P. (2006) *Irrigated Urban Vegetable Production in Ghana: Characteristics, Benefits and Risks*, IWMI-RUAF-CPWF, IWMI, Accra, Ghana

Patwardhan, A. D. (2008) *Industrial Wastewater Treatment*, Prentice Hall of India, New Delhi

Peasey, A. (2000) 'Human exposure to *Ascaris* infection through wastewater reuse in irrigation and its public health significance', PhD thesis, University of London, London

Prüss-Üstün, A. and Corvalan, C. (2006) *Preventing Disease Through Healthy Environments, Towards an Estimate of the Environmental Burden of Disease*, WHO, Geneva

Raschid-Sally, L. and Jayakody, P. (2008) 'Drivers and characteristics of wastewater agriculture in developing countries: Results from a global assessment, Colombo, Sri Lanka', *IWMI Research Report 127*, International Water Management Institute, Colombo, p35

Rutkowski, T., Raschid-Sally, L. and Buechler, S. (2007) 'Wastewater irrigation in the developing world – Two case studies from Katmandu Valley in Nepal', *Agricultural Water Management*, no 88, pp83–91

Scott, C. A, Faruqui, N. I. and Raschid-Sally, L. (2004) 'Wastewater use in irrigated agriculture: Management challenges in developing countries', in C. A. Scott, N. I. Faruqui, L. Raschid-Sally (eds) *Wastewater Use in Irrigated Agriculture: Confronting the Livelihood and Environmental Realities*, CABI Publishing, Wallingford, UK, pp1–10

Seymour, I. J. and Appleton, H. (2001) 'Food-borne viruses and fresh produce', *Journal of Applied Microbiology*, no 91, pp759–73

Shuval, H. I., Adin, A., Fattal, B., Rawitz, E. and Yekutiel, P. (1986) *Wastewater Irrigation in Developing Countries: Health Effects and Technical Solutions*, World Bank Technical Paper no 51, World Bank, Washington, DC

Shuval, H. I., Yekutiel, P. and Fattal, B. (1984) 'Epidemiological evidence for helminth and cholera transmission by vegetables irrigated with wastewater: Jerusalem, a case study', *Water Science and Technology*, no 17, pp433–42

Sperling, M. von and Fattal, B. (2001) 'Implementation of guidelines: Some practical aspects', in L. Fewtrell and J. Bartram (eds) *Water Quality: Guidelines, Standards and Health; Assessment of Risk and Risk Management for Water-Related Infectious Disease*, International Water Association (IWA) on behalf of the World Health Organization, London, pp361–76

Trang, D. T., Hien, B. T. T., Mølbak, K., Cam, P. D. and Dalsgaard, A. (2007a) 'Epidemiology and aetiology of diarrhoeal diseases in adults engaged in wastewater-fed agriculture and aquaculture in Hanoi, Vietnam', *Tropical Medicine and International Health*, vol 12, no 2, pp 23–33

Trang, D. T., Mølbak, K., Cam, P. D. and Dalsgaard, A. (2007b) 'Helminth infections among people using wastewater and human excreta in peri-urban agriculture and aquaculture in Hanoi, Vietnam', *Tropical Medicine and International Health*, vol 12, no 2, pp82–90

Trang, D. T., van der Hoek, W., Tuan, N. D., Cam, P. C., Viet, V. H., Luu, D. D., Konradsen, F. and Dalsgaard, A. (2007c) 'Skin disease among farmers using wastewater in rice cultivation in Nam Dinh, Vietnam', *Tropical Medicine and International Health*, vol 12, no 2, pp51–8

WHO (1973) *Reuse of Effluents: Methods of Wastewater Treatment and Public Health Safeguards. Report of a WHO Meeting of Experts*, Technical Report Series, no 517, World Health Organization, Geneva

WHO (2006) *Guidelines for the Safe Use of Wastewater, Excreta and Greywater, Volume 2: Wastewater Use in Agriculture*, World Health Organization, Geneva

WHO (2009) 'Quantifying environmental health impacts', available at www.who.int/quantifying_ehimpacts/global/globalwater/en/index.htm

WHO and UNICEF (2000) 'Global water supply and sanitation assessment 2000 report', WHO/UNICEF Joint Monitoring Program for Water and Sanitation, New York

Part 2

Risks and Risk Assessment

3

Risk Analysis and Epidemiology: The 2006 WHO Guidelines for the Safe Use of Wastewater in Agriculture

Duncan Mara and Robert Bos[1]

ABSTRACT

This chapter reviews the required pathogen reductions recommended in the 2006 WHO *Guidelines for the Safe Use of Wastewater, Excreta and Greywater* in agriculture, which are based on a tolerable additional burden of disease of $\leq 10^{-6}$ Disability-Adjusted Life Year (DALY) loss per person per year. The quantitative microbial risk-analysis technique, combined with 10,000-trial Monte Carlo risk simulations, is detailed here and the resulting estimates of median risk for various levels of pathogen reduction for exposure via restricted and unrestricted irrigation are also presented. This enables the selection of suitable combinations of pathogen reduction measures (wastewater treatment and post-treatment health-protection measures) to be selected, so that the resulting additional burden of disease does not exceed 10^{-6} DALY loss per person per year.

INTRODUCTION

The World Health Organization published the third edition of its Guidelines for the safe use of wastewater in agriculture in September 2006 (WHO, 2006). These differed from the second edition of the Guidelines (WHO, 1989) principally as follows:

- The use of a risk-based approach to estimate the required reductions of viral, bacterial and protozoan pathogens.
- To protect the health of those working, or otherwise exposed, in wastewater-irrigated fields (i.e. restricted irrigation), the required pathogen reductions are to be achieved only by wastewater treatment.
- To protect the health of those consuming wastewater-irrigated food crops (i.e. unrestricted irrigation), the required pathogen reductions can be achieved by a suitable combination of wastewater treatment (commonly to the level required for restricted irrigation) and post-treatment health-protection control measures such as outlined below.

The 2006 Guidelines are essentially a code of good management practices to ensure that, when wastewater is used in agriculture (mainly for irrigating crops, including food crops that are or may be eaten uncooked), it is used safely and with minimal risks to health. They are therefore much more than a set of guideline values. However, in practice wastewater treatment and reuse engineers need to know how to use the recommendations in the Guidelines to design wastewater reuse systems that do not adversely affect public health. This means that they have to understand in detail the basis of the Guidelines so that the wastewater reuse systems they design are safe.

There are two broad groups of wastewater-related diseases relevant in the agricultural use of wastewater (Table 3.1) that are considered in the Guidelines and in this chapter:

- viral, bacterial and protozoan diseases, for which the health risks are determined by quantitative microbial risk assessment (QMRA);
- helminthic diseases, for which the Guidelines set a guideline value on the basis of epidemiological studies.

The basis of human health protection in the Guidelines is that the additional disease burden due to viral, bacterial and protozoan diseases which results from working in wastewater-irrigated fields or consuming wastewater-irrigated crops should not exceed 10^{-6} DALY loss per person per year (see Box 3.1). This level of health protection was used by WHO in its 2004 Guidelines on drinking-water quality (WHO, 2004) and thus the health risks resulting from wastewater use in agriculture are the same as those from drinking fully treated drinking water – this is basically what consumers want as they expect the food they eat to be as safe as the water they drink.

For the viral, bacterial and protozoan diseases this tolerable additional disease burden of 10^{-6} DALY loss pppy is 'translated' into tolerable disease and infection risks as follows:

Table 3.1 *Classification of diseases relevant in wastewater-irrigated agriculture*

Category	Environmental transmission features	Major examples of infection	Exposure groups in urban agriculture and relative infection risks
Non-bacterial faeco-oral diseases	Non-latent[a] Low to medium persistence[b] Unable to multiply High infectivity	Viral: Hepatitis A and E Rotavirus diarrhoea Norovirus diarrhoea Protozoan: Amoebiasis Crystosporidiasis Giardiasis Cyclosporiasis	Fieldworkers: +[c] Consumers: +++
Bacterial faeco-oral diseases	Non-latent Medium to high persistence Able to multiply Medium to low infectivity	Campylobacteriosis Cholera Pathogenic *Escherichia coli* infection Salmonellosis Shigellosis	Fieldworkers: + Consumers: +++
Geohelminthiases	Latent Very persistent Unable to multiply Very high infectivity	Ascariasis Hookworm infection Trichuriasis	Fieldworkers: +++ Consumers: +++

+++ high risk; ++ medium risk; + low risk (These risks refer to the use of untreated wastewaters; treatment and post-treatment health-protection control measures can reduce these risks to the tolerable level of ≤10^{-3} per person per year, as discussed below.)
[a]Latency is the length of time outside a human host required for the pathogen to become infective.
[b]Persistence is the length of time that the pathogen can survive in the environment outside a human host.
[c]Note that fieldworkers are commonly also consumers.
Source: Feachem et al. (1983)

$$\text{Tolerable disease risk pppy} = \frac{\text{Tolerable DALY loss pppy (i.e., } 10^{-6})}{\text{DALY loss per case of disease}} \qquad 3.1$$

$$\text{Tolerable infection risk pppy} = \frac{\text{Tolerable disease risk pppy}}{\text{Disease/infection ratio}} \qquad 3.2$$

Three 'index' pathogens were selected: rotavirus, viral pathogen; *Campylobacter*, a bacterial pathogen; and *Cryptosporidium*, a protozoan pathogen. Table 3.2 gives the DALY losses per case of rotavirus diarrhoea, campylobacteriosis and cryptosporidiosis and the corresponding disease/infection ratios. (A better index viral pathogen would now be norovirus, for which dose-response data have recently become available. See Chapter 5.)

Box 3.1 DISABILITY-ADJUSTED LIFE YEARS (DALYS)

DALYs are a measure of the health of a population or burden of disease due to a specific disease or risk factor. DALYs attempt to measure the time lost because of disability or death from a disease compared with a long life free of disability in the absence of the disease. DALYs are calculated by adding the years of life lost to premature death (YLL) to the years lived with a disability (YLD). Years of life lost are calculated from age-specific mortality rates and the standard life expectancies of a given population. YLD are calculated from the number of cases multiplied by the average duration of the disease and a severity factor ranging from 1 (death) to 0 (perfect health) based on the disease (e.g. watery diarrhoea has a severity factor from 0.09 to 0.12 depending on the age group) (Murray and Lopez, 1996; Prüss and Havelaar, 2001).

DALYs are an important tool for comparing health outcomes because they account for not only acute health effects but also for delayed and chronic effects, including morbidity and mortality (Bartram et al., 2001). Thus, when risk is described in DALYs, different health outcomes (e.g., stomach cancer and giardiasis) can be compared and risk-management decisions prioritized. Thus the DALY loss per case of campylobacteriosis in Table 3.1 includes the appropriate allowance for the occurrence of Guillain-Barré syndrome (which is an inflammatory disorder of the peripheral nerves, which may lead to paralysis, and which occurs in around 1 in 1000 cases of campylobacteriosis).

The tolerable additional disease burden of 10^{-6} DALY loss adopted in the Guidelines means that a city of 1 million people collectively suffers the loss of one DALY per year. The highest DALY loss per case of diarrhoeal disease in Table 3.2 is 2.6×10^{-2}, for rotavirus disease in developing countries. Assuming that the recommendations in the Guidelines are completely followed, this means that the tolerable number of cases of rotavirus disease, caused by the consumption of wastewater-irrigated food, in this city of 1 million people in a developing country is:

$$\frac{1 \text{ DALY loss per year}}{2.6 \times 10^{-2} \text{ DALY loss per case}} = 38 \text{ cases per year} \qquad 3.3$$

The chance of an individual living in this city becoming ill with rotavirus diarrhoea in any one year is (38×10^{-6}) – i.e., 3.8×10^{-5}, which is the tolerable rotavirus disease risk per person per year in developing countries, as determined in Table 3.2.

From the data in Table 3.2 a 'design' value of 10^{-4} pppy was chosen for the tolerable risk of rotavirus disease and 10^{-3} pppy for the corresponding tolerable rotavirus infection risk. The former is extremely safe as it is three to four orders of magnitude lower than the actual incidence of diarrhoeal disease in the world (Table 3.3).

QUANTITATIVE MICROBIAL RISK ASSESSMENT

The Guidelines adopted a standard QMRA approach (Haas et al., 1999) to risk analysis combined with 10,000-iteration Monte Carlo simulations (Mara et al., 2007). The basic equations are:

Table 3.2 *DALY losses, disease risks, disease/infection ratios and tolerable infection risks for rotavirus,* Campylobacter *and* Cryptosporidium

Pathogen	DALY loss per case of disease	Tolerable disease risk pppy equivalent to 10^{-6} DALY loss pppy[a]	Disease/ infection ratio	Tolerable infection risk pppy[b]
Rotavirus: (1) IC[c]	1.4×10^{-2}	7.1×10^{-5}	0.05^d	1.4×10^{-3}
Rotavirus: (2) DC[c]	2.6×10^{-2}	3.8×10^{-5}	0.05^d	7.7×10^{-4}
Campylobacter	4.6×10^{-3}	2.2×10^{-4}	0.7	3.1×10^{-4}
Cryptosporidium	1.5×10^{-3}	6.7×10^{-4}	0.3	2.2×10^{-3}

[a]Tolerable disease risk = 10^{-6} DALY loss per person per year (pppy) ÷ DALY loss per case of disease.
[b]Tolerable infection risk = disease risk ÷ disease/infection ratio.
[c]IC, industrialized countries; DC, developing countries.
[d]For developing counties the DALY loss per rotavirus death was reduced by 95 per cent to discount deaths occurring in children under the age of two who are not exposed to wastewater-irrigated foods. The disease/infection ratio for rotavirus is low as immunity is mostly developed by the age of three.
Source: DALY values from Havelaar and Melse (2003)

Table 3.3 *Diarrhoeal disease (DD) incidence pppy in 2000 by region and age*

Region	DD incidence in all ages	DD incidence in 0–4 year olds	DD incidence in 5–80+ year olds
Industrialized countries	0.2	0.2–1.7	0.1–0.2
Developing countries	0.8–1.3	2.4–5.2	0.4–0.6
Global average	0.7	3.7	0.4

Source: Mathers et al. (2002)

Exponential dose-response model (for *Cryptosporidium*):

$$P_I(d) = 1 - \exp(-rd) \qquad\qquad 3.4$$

Beta-Poisson dose-response model (for rotavirus and *Campylobacter*):

$$P_I(d) = 1 - [1 + (d/N_{50})(2^{1/\alpha} - 1)]^{-\alpha} \qquad\qquad 3.5$$

Annual risk of infection:

$$P_{I(A)}(d) = 1 - [1 - P_I(d)]^n \qquad\qquad 3.6$$

$P_I(d)$ is the risk of infection in an individual exposed to a single pathogen dose d – i.e., the number of pathogens ingested on any one occasion; $P_{I(A)}(d)$ is the annual risk of infection in an individual from n exposures per year to the single pathogen dose d; N_{50} is the median infective dose; and α and r are pathogen 'infectivity constants' – for rotavirus $N_{50} = 6.17$ and $\alpha = 0.253$, for *Campylobacter* $N_{50} = 896$ and $\alpha = 0.145$ and for *Cryptosporidium* $r = 0.0042$ (Haas et al., 1999).

In practice Equations 3.4, 3.5 and 3.6 are used as follows:

- $P_{I(A)}(d)$ in Equation 3.4 is set equal to 10^{-3} pppy (the tolerable rotavirus infection risk).
- The number of days of exposure (n in Equation 3.6) is determined (or selected) – e.g. for lettuce consumption on alternate days $n = 365/2$.
- $P_I(d)$ is then calculated from Equation 3.6 (e.g. for $n = 365/2$, $P_I(d) = 5.5 \times 10^{-6}$ per person per exposure).
- For this value of $P_I(d)$ d is calculated from either Equation 3.4 or Equation 3.5.
- This dose d is the number of pathogens ingested with the lettuce (or other crop) and is assumed to be in whatever volume of treated wastewater that remains on the lettuce (or other crop) after irrigation – for example, Shuval et al. (1997) found 11ml to remain on 100g of lettuce.
- This pathogen count (e.g. d per 11ml) is expressed per litre and, knowing the pathogen count per litre of untreated wastewater, the required log reduction (actually the required $\log_{10}$ reduction) of the pathogen is determined.

This required log pathogen reduction is achieved by a combination of wastewater treatment and the post-treatment health-protection control measures detailed in Table 3.4.

Table 3.4 *Post-treatment health-protection control measures and associated pathogen reductions*

Control measure	Pathogen reduction (log units)	Notes
Drip irrigation	2–4	2 log unit reduction for low-growing crops, and 4 log unit reduction for high-growing crops.
Pathogen die-off	0.5–2 per day	Die-off after last irrigation before harvest (value depends on climate, crop type, etc.).
Produce-washing	1	Washing salad crops, vegetables and fruit with clean water.
Produce disinfection	3	Washing salad crops, vegetables and fruit with a weak disinfectant solution and rinsing with clean water.
Produce peeling	2	Fruits, root crops.

Source: Produce disinfection reduction figure from Amoah et al. (2007)

Monte Carlo risk simulations

There is commonly some degree of uncertainty about the values of the parameters used to determine required log pathogen reductions – for example, it is unlikely that exactly 11ml of wastewater is always left on 100g of lettuce after irrigation. Therefore, in order to take this uncertainty into account, it is better to assign a range of values to each parameter (e.g., 10–15ml of wastewater remaining on 100g of lettuce after irrigation), rather than a single 'fixed' value (e.g. exactly 11ml), although a fixed value can be assigned to any parameter if so wished. A computer program then selects at random a value for each parameter from the range of values specified for it and determines the resulting risk.[2] The program repeats this process a large number of times (commonly for a total of 10,000 times) and then determines the median annual infection risk. The large number of repetitions removes some of the uncertainty associated with the parameter values and makes the results generated by multi-trial Monte Carlo simulations much more robust, although of course they are only as good as the assumptions made. Chapter 5 describes an improved method of determining annual risks of infection.

RESTRICTED IRRIGATION

The exposure scenario developed in the Guidelines for restricted irrigation is the involuntary ingestion of soil particles by those working, or by young children playing, in wastewater-irrigated fields. This is a likely scenario as wastewater-saturated soil would contaminate the workers' or children's fingers and so some pathogens could be transmitted to their mouths and hence ingested. The quantity of soil involuntarily ingested in this way has been reported (but not specifically for this restricted-irrigation scenario) as up to 100mg per person per day of exposure (Haas et al., 1999; WHO 2001). Two sub-scenarios were investigated: (a) highly mechanized agriculture and (b) labour-intensive agriculture. The former represents exposure in industrialized countries where farm workers typically plough, sow and harvest using tractors and associated equipment and can be expected to wear gloves and be generally hygiene-conscious when working in wastewater-irrigated fields. The latter represents farming practices in developing countries in situations where tractors are not used and gloves (and often footwear) are not worn, and where hygiene is commonly not promoted.

Labour-intensive agriculture

The results of the Monte Carlo-QMRA risk simulations are given in Table 3.5 for various wastewater qualities (expressed as single log ranges of *E. coli* numbers per 100ml) and for 300 days' exposure per year (the footnote to Table 3.5 gives the range of values assigned to each parameter). It can be seen that the median

Table 3.5 *Restricted irrigation: median infection risks from ingestion of wastewater-contaminated soil in labour-intensive agriculture with exposure for 300 days per year[a]*

Soil quality	Median infection risk pppy		
(*E. coli* per 100g)[b]	Rotavirus	*Campylobacter*	*Cryptosporidium*
10^7–10^8	0.99	0.50	1.4×10^{-2}
10^6–10^7	0.88	6.7×10^{-2}	1.4×10^{-3}
10^5–10^6	0.19	7.3×10^{-3}	1.4×10^{-4}
10^4–10^5	2.0×10^{-2}	7.0×10^{-4}	1.3×10^{-5}
10^3–10^4	1.8×10^{-3}	6.1×10^{-5}	1.4×10^{-6}
100–1000	1.9×10^{-4}	5.6×10^{-6}	1.4×10^{-7}

[a]Estimated by 10,000 Monte Carlo simulations. Assumptions: 10–100mg soil ingested per person per day for 300 days per year; 0.1–1 rotavirus and *Campylobacter*, and 0.01–0.1 *Cryptosporidium* oocyst, per 10^5 *E. coli*; $N_{50} = 6.7 \pm 25\%$ and $\alpha = 0.253 \pm 25\%$ for rotavirus; $N_{50} = 896 \pm 25\%$ and $\alpha = 0.145 \pm 25\%$ for *Campylobacter*; $r = 0.0042 \pm 25\%$ for *Cryptosporidium*. No pathogen die-off (taken as a worst case scenario).
[b]The wastewater quality is taken to be the same as the soil quality – i.e. the soil is assumed, as a worst case scenario, to be saturated with the wastewater.

rotavirus infection risk is 10^{-3} pppy for a wastewater quality of 10^3–10^4 *E. coli* per 100ml. Thus, the tolerable rotavirus infection risk of 10^{-3} pppy is achieved by a 4 log unit reduction – i.e. from 10^7–10^8 to 10^3–10^4 *E. coli* per 100ml. The table also shows that the *Campylobacter* and *Cryptosporidium* infection risks are all lower than those for rotavirus.

Highly mechanized agriculture

The simulated risks for various wastewater qualities and for 100 days' exposure per year are given in Table 3.6, which shows that a 3 log unit reduction, from 10^7–10^8 to 10^4–10^5 *E. coli* per 100ml, is required to achieve the tolerable rotavirus infection risk of 10^{-3} pppy.

UNRESTRICTED IRRIGATION

The exposure scenarios used in the Guidelines for unrestricted irrigation are the consumption of wastewater-irrigated lettuce (Shuval et al., 1997) and the consumption of wastewater-irrigated onions (a leaf and a root vegetable, respectively).

Risk simulations

For unrestricted irrigation a slightly different approach was adopted. The QMRA-Monte Carlo program determined the required log rotavirus reductions for various

Table 3.6 *Restricted irrigation: median infection risks from ingestion of wastewater-contaminated soil in highly mechanized agriculture with exposure for 100 days per year[a]*

Soil quality (E. coli per 100g)[b]	Median infection risk pppy		
	Rotavirus	Campylobacter	Cryptosporidium
10^6–10^7	6.8×10^{-2}	1.9×10^{-3}	4.7×10^{-5}
10^5–10^6	6.7×10^{-3}	1.9×10^{-4}	4.6×10^{-6}
10^4–10^5	6.5×10^{-4}	2.3×10^{-5}	4.6×10^{-7}
10^3–10^4	6.8×10^{-5}	2.4×10^{-6}	5.0×10^{-8}
100–1000	6.3×10^{-6}	2.2×10^{-7}	$\leq 1 \times 10^{-8}$

[a]Estimated by 10,000 Monte Carlo simulations. Assumptions: 1–10 mg soil ingested per person per day for 100 days per year; 0.1–1 rotavirus and *Campylobacter*, and 0.01–0.1 *Cryptosporidium* oocyst, per 10^5 *E. coli*; $N_{50} = 6.7 \pm 25\%$ and $\alpha = 0.253 \pm 25\%$ for rotavirus; $N_{50} = 896 \pm 25\%$ and $\alpha = 0.145 \pm 25\%$ for *Campylobacter*; $r = 0.0042 \pm 25\%$ for *Cryptosporidium*. No pathogen die-off (taken as a worst case scenario).
[b]The wastewater quality is taken to be the same as the soil quality – i.e., the soil is assumed, as a worst case scenario, to be saturated with the wastewater.

Table 3.7 *Unrestricted irrigation: required pathogen reductions for various levels of tolerable risk of rotavirus infection from the consumption of wastewater-irrigated lettuce and onions[a]*

Tolerable level of rotavirus infection risk (pppy)	Corresponding required level of rotavirus reduction (log units)	
	Lettuce	Onions
10^{-2}	5	6
10^{-3}	6	7
10^{-4}	7	8

[a]Estimated by 10,000 Monte Carlo simulations. Assumptions: 100g lettuce and onions eaten per person per two days; 10–15ml and 1–5ml wastewater remaining after irrigation on lettuce and onions, respectively; 0.1–1 and rotavirus per 10^5 *E. coli*; $N_{50} = 6.17 \pm 25\%$ and $\alpha = 0.253 \pm 25\%$. No pathogen die-off.

levels of tolerable rotavirus annual infection risk. The results, given in Table 3.7, show that, for the tolerable rotavirus infection risk of 10^{-3} pppy, the required pathogen reductions are 6 log units for non-root crops and 7 log units for root crops. The table also shows that the consumption of root crops requires a 1 log unit pathogen reduction greater than the consumption of non-root crops and that the required pathogen reductions change by an order of magnitude with each order-of-magnitude change in tolerable risk.

This 6–7 log unit reduction for unrestricted irrigation is best achieved by a 3–4 log unit reduction by wastewater treatment, as required for restricted irrigation, supplemented by a 2–4 log unit reduction from post-treatment health-protection control measures (Table 3.4). These post-treatment health-protection control measures are extremely reliable: in essence they always occur.

EPIDEMIOLOGICAL VERIFICATION OF THE QMRA APPROACH

Mara et al. (2007) used the field data reported by Blumenthal et al. (2003) on diarrhoeal disease incidences amongst fieldworkers and consumers in Mezquital Valley, Mexico, to obtain QMRA estimates of rotavirus infection risks in the five-month dry season. It was found that, provided the assumptions used in the QMRA-Monte Carlo risk simulations closely reflected field conditions, the agreement between the observed incidences of diarrhoeal disease and the simulated rotavirus infection risk was very close for both fieldworkers and consumers (Table 3.8).

HELMINTH EGGS

The recommendation in the Guidelines is that wastewater used in agriculture should contain ≤1 helminth egg per litre. The helminths referred to here are the human intestinal nematodes: *Ascaris lumbricoides* (the human roundworm), *Trichuris trichiura* (the human whipworm), and *Ancylostoma duodenale* and *Necator americanus* (the human hookworms); details of the diseases they cause and their life cycles are given in Feachem et al. (1983).

This recommendation is the same as was made in the 1989 Guidelines (WHO, 1989), but with two important differences: it is now based on epidemiological evidence which shows that ≤1 egg per litre protects adults but not children under 15 (Blumenthal et al., 2000); and when children under the age of 15 are exposed, additional control measures are needed, such as regular deworming (by their parents or at school).

Chapter 5 details a QMRA-Monte Carlo method for estimating *Ascaris* infection risks.

Table 3.8 *Comparison between observed incidences of diarrhoeal disease and estimated rotavirus infection risks in Mezquital Valley, Mexico*

Irrigation scenario	Wastewater quality (*E. coli* per 100ml)	Observed diarrhoeal disease incidence per person per 5 months	Estimated median rotavirus infection risk per person per 5 months
Restricted irrigation	10^3–10^5	0.37	0.33[a]
Unrestricted irrigation	10^3–10^5	0.38	0.39[b]

[a]Assumptions: soil quality per 100g taken as wastewater quality per 100ml; 10–100mg soil ingested per person per day for 65 days in five months; 0.1–1 rotavirus per 10^5 *E. coli*; ID_{50} = 6.7 ± 25% and α = 0.253 ± 25%. No pathogen die-off.
[b]Assumptions: 100g of onions consumed per person per week for five months; 1–5ml wastewater remaining on 100g onions after irrigation; 0.1–1 rotavirus per 10^5 *E. coli*; 0–1 log unit rotavirus die-off between harvest and consumption; ID_{50} = 6.7 ± 25% and α = 0.253 ± 25%.
Source: Mara et al. (2007)

SUMMARY OF RECOMMENDATIONS IN THE GUIDELINES

The 2006 WHO Guidelines make the following recommendations, either explicitly or implicitly:

- To protect the health of those working in wastewater-irrigated fields against excessive risks of viral, bacterial and protozoan infections, there should be a 3–4 log unit pathogen reduction, which is to be achieved by wastewater treatment.
- To protect the health of those consuming wastewater-irrigated food crops against excessive risks of viral, bacterial and protozoan infections, there should be a 6–7 log unit pathogen reduction, which is to be achieved by wastewater treatment (a 3–4 log unit reduction, as for restricted irrigation) supplemented by post-treatment health-protection control measures providing together a further 2–4 log unit pathogen reduction.
- To protect the health of those working in wastewater-irrigated fields and those consuming wastewater-irrigated food crops against excessive risks of helminthic infections, the treated wastewater should contain ≤1 human intestinal nematode egg per litre.

These Guidelines are reviewed, and recommendations made for their updating, in Chapter 5.

NOTES

1 The opinions expressed in this chapter are those of the authors and do not necessarily reflect the views or policies of the World Health Organization.
2 The QMRA-Monte Carlo computer programs used for the 2006 Guidelines are available at: www.personal.leeds.ac.uk/~cen6ddm/QMRA.html.

REFERENCES

Amoah, P., Drechsel, P., Abaidoo, R. and Klutse, A. (2007) 'Effectiveness of common and improved sanitary washing methods in selected cities of West Africa for the reduction of coliform bacteria and helminth eggs on vegetables', *Tropical Medicine and International Health*, no 12 (s2), pp40–50

Bartram, J., Fewtrell, L. and Stenström, T.-A. (2001) 'Harmonised assessment of risk and risk management for water-related infectious disease: An overview', in L. Fewtrell and J. Bartram (eds) *Water Quality: Guidelines, Standards and Health; Assessment of Risk and Risk Management for Water-Related Infectious Disease*, International Water Association (IWA) on behalf on the World Health Organization, London, pp2–16

Blumenthal, U. J., Mara, D. D., Peasey, A., Ruiz-Palacios, G. and Stott, R. (2000) 'Guidelines for the microbiological quality of treated wastewater used in agriculture: Recommendations for revising WHO guidelines', *Bulletin of the World Health Organization*, vol 78, no 9, pp1104–16

Blumenthal, U. J., Peasey, A., Quigley, M. and Ruiz-Palacios, G. (2003) *Risk of Enteric Infections through Consumption of Vegetables with Contaminated River Water*, London School of Hygiene and Tropical Medicine, London

Feachem, R. G., Bradley, D. J., Garelick, H. and Mara, D. D. (1983) *Sanitation and Disease: Health Aspects of Wastewater and Excreta Management*, John Wiley & Sons, Chichester

Haas, C. N., Rose, J. B. and Gerba, C. P. (1999) *Quantitative Microbial Risk Assessment*, John Wiley & Sons, New York

Havelaar, A. H. and Melse, J. M. (2003) *Quantifying Public Health Risk in the WHO Guidelines for Drinking-Water Quality: A Burden of Disease Approach*, RIVM Report no 734301022/2003, Rijksinstituut voor Volksgezondheid en Milieu, Bilthoven, The Netherlands

Mara, D. D., Sleigh, P.A., Blumenthal, U. J. and Carr, R. M. (2007) 'Health risks in wastewater irrigation: Comparing estimates from quantitative microbial risk analyses and epidemiological studies', *Journal of Water and Health*, vol 5, no 1, pp39–50

Mathers, C. D., Stein, C., Ma Fat, D., Rao, C., Inoue, M., Tomijima, N. et al. (2002) *Global Burden of Disease 2000, Version 2: Methods and Results*, World Health Organization, Geneva

Murray, C. J. L. and Lopez, A. D. (1996) *The Global Burden of Disease, Volume 1: A Comprehensive Assessment of Mortality and Disability from Diseases, Injuries, and Risk Factors in 1990 and Projected to 2020*, Harvard University Press, Cambridge, MA

Prüss, A. and Havelaar, A. (2001) 'The Global Burden of Disease study and applications in water, sanitation, and hygiene', in L. Fewtrell and J. Bartram (eds) *Water Quality: Guidelines, Standards and Health; Assessment of Risk and Risk Management for Water-related Infectious Disease*, International Water Association (IWA) on behalf on the World Health Organization, London, pp43–59

Shuval, H. I., Lampert, Y. and Fattal, B. (1997) 'Development of a risk assessment approach for evaluating wastewater reuse standards for agriculture', *Water Science and Technology*, vol 35, nos 11–12, pp15–20

WHO (1989) *Health Guidelines for the Use of Wastewater in Agriculture and Aquaculture*, Technical Report Series no 778, World Health Organization, Geneva

WHO (2001) 'Depleted uranium: sources, exposure and health effects' (Report no WHO/SDE/PHE/01.1), World Health Organization, Geneva

WHO (2004) *Guidelines for Drinking-Water Quality*, 3rd ed., World Health Organization, Geneva

WHO (2006) *Guidelines for the Safe Use of Wastewater, Excreta and Greywater, Volume 2: Wastewater Use in Agriculture*, World Health Organization, Geneva

4

Approaches to Evaluate and Develop Health Risk-Based Standards Using Available Data

Inés Navarro, Peter Teunis, Christine Moe and Blanca Jiménez

ABSTRACT

Information on the dose-response relationship of waterborne and foodborne enteric pathogens is an important component in any consideration of the health risks that may be associated with wastewater, sludge or excreta reuse for food-crop production. The three main sources of information on dose-response relationships are: human challenge studies, animal studies and outbreak investigations. Dose-response information on four representative enteric pathogens (Norwalk virus, *E. coli* O157:H7, *Giardia lamblia* and *Ascaris lumbricoides*) is presented as examples. In addition to dose-response information, the application of quantitative microbial risk assessment to examine the potential health risks associated with the consumption of food crops irrigated with wastewater or fertilized with biosolids requires information on several factors. These are transmission pathways, occurrence (frequency and concentration) of pathogens in wastewater and biosolids, persistence of pathogen viability or infectivity in the environment and on the food crops, and crop consumption (amount and frequency). Assessments of the risks of *Giardia* and *Ascaris* infection associated with food crops in several scenarios are presented and illustrate how WHO Guidelines and pathogen reduction measures (such as produce-washing) may have a significant or negligible impact on reducing the risks of infection associated with food crops irrigated or fertilized with wastewater and biosolids.

INTRODUCTION

The WHO *Guidelines for the Safe Use of Wastewater, Excreta and Greywater* (WHO, 2006) are based on the development and use of health-based targets, with the goal of attaining a certain level of health protection in an exposed population. This level of health protection can then be achieved by using a combination of risk-management approaches (e.g. crop restriction, safer application techniques, human-exposure control) (WHO, 2006). In some situations it is not possible to fully implement the desired level of protection at a given time. For this reason, the WHO Guidelines suggest designing regulations that allow progressive implementation. This can be attained over time in an ordered manner, depending on the circumstances and resources of each individual country or region. In order to achieve this, each country should try to develop a risk-management plan based on local context. For example, in the WHO Guidelines, a general pathogen reduction of 6–7 log units is used as a safe performance target for unrestricted irrigation (see Chapter 2).

In order to adjust the target to locally relevant pathogens and ways of wastewater application, quantitative microbial risk assessment (QMRA) can be used as one possible tool. The quality of the QMRA analysis depends largely on the availability of dose-response information. This information indicates the relationship between exposure to specific doses of a pathogen and the probability of developing infection and/or symptoms in the exposed host. Dose-response relationships depend on virulence characteristics of the pathogen as well as host susceptibility factors. For prediction of risk it is necessary to estimate the probability of infection, conditional on exposure, and the probability of (acute) illness, conditional to infection. Without exposure, infection cannot occur and, similarly, without infection, a person cannot become ill. This apparently trivial statement has important consequences for quantitative risk assessment: if exposure assessment indicates that the probability of exposure is smaller than a certain level, the probabilities of infection, as well as illness, generally cannot exceed that level of risk. Some micro-organisms are highly infectious, such as the Norwalk virus example described later in this chapter. Exposure to even low doses of highly infectious agents may be associated with significant risk of infection and illness.

Information on the dose-response relationship of waterborne and foodborne pathogens is an important component in any consideration of health risks that may be associated with wastewater, sludge and excreta irrigation or reuse for crop production. The available information on dose-response for enteric pathogens comes from three main sources: human challenge studies, animal challenge studies and outbreak investigations. This chapter will examine these sources of information and considerations for their use for risk assessment, taking into account different types of micro-organisms of concern. Dose-response information on four representative enteric pathogens will be presented as examples. The application of the WHO (2006) procedure to develop recommendations to reduce the risks of pathogen exposure is the same regardless of the type of pathogen, therefore in this chapter only its application to helminth (*Ascaris*) eggs is described.

HUMAN CHALLENGE STUDIES

Perhaps the most reliable dose-response information comes from human challenge studies where both the exposure and response can be well characterized. In these studies, exposure (i.e. dose) is controlled by administering various dilutions of a pathogen suspension. This inoculum must undergo rigorous safety-testing to ensure that it only contains the target pathogen and no other harmful substance. Also, the suspension needs to be titrated – by culture (for bacteria and some viruses) and polymerase chain reaction (for some viruses), or by microscopic counts or particle counts of cysts, oocysts or ova (for parasites and helminths). However, the exact number of the target pathogen that is ingested (or inhaled, for airborne exposure) in each dose is not known but must be estimated from information on the titre of the suspension and the dilution. For that reason, the estimation of exposure is part of the dose-response assessment.

The exponential and beta-Poisson models (see below) are two dose-response relationships that can be developed from biologically plausible assumptions about the infection process. Best-fit dose-response parameters for these models for a number of human pathogens were summarized by Haas and Eisenberg (2001).

The use of human volunteers limits the range of pathogens in human challenge studies to relatively mild pathogens that cause mild symptoms that are either self-limited or resolved by treatment and are not associated with any long-term adverse health effects. These studies are therefore subjected to careful review by ethical boards to ensure that the health, privacy and human rights of the volunteers are fully protected. For ethical reasons, these studies usually only involve healthy adult subjects who are able to understand the study protocol and give informed consent to participate in the study. All candidate volunteers are screened for good health and immune competence before being enrolled into the study in order to ensure that the experiments have no serious consequences for those involved. The volunteers who receive the pathogen inoculum are usually admitted into a clinical research unit so that their symptoms can be carefully monitored and recorded and so that they can receive appropriate medical care if needed. Specimens of stool, sera, whole blood, saliva, vomitus and, sometimes, intestinal biopsies are collected on a routine basis before and after, to test for infection indicators. Infection may be characterized by excretion of the challenge pathogen as detected in stool and vomitus specimens or by immune response, for example, a rise in pathogen-specific serum or salivary antibodies, or evidence of a cellular immune response.

Role of immunity

One factor that must be considered in both quantitative microbial risk assessment and the information from dose-response studies of infectious agents is the role of previous exposure and possibly protective immunity in human challenge studies. For common enteric pathogens, such as norovirus and *Cryptosporidium*, it is likely that many candidate volunteers may have had previous infections with these pathogens and that this previous exposure/infection may have an impact on the host response to challenge. In studies of norovirus infectivity, the presence of norovirus-specific antibodies in sera appeared to be a marker of susceptibility to norovirus infection and did not seem to provide protection (Lindesmith et al., 2003). In studies of *Cryptosporidium* infectivity, those volunteers who were serologically naive for *Cryptosporidium* were significantly more likely to develop infection after the challenge than volunteers who had higher measurable titres of serum antibodies against *Cryptosporidium* (Teunis et al., 2002b).

The challenge of protective immunity limits the transfer of dose-response models from industrialized to developing countries if the specific pathogen exposure is significantly different. One example of this is hepatitis A virus where results based on external dose-response models are likely to overestimate the risk for large parts of the local population who may have had hepatitis A infection during childhood and are no longer susceptible to infection. The QMRA can address this challenge in its calculations.

Heterogeneity in strain virulence and host susceptibility

The variation in infectivity among different isolates from (genetically) the same pathogen species has been shown to be considerable, at least as large as differences between different species (Chen et al., 2006; Teunis et al., 2002a). Similarly, variation in susceptibility to infection and illness among human hosts can be large (Teunis et al., 2002b, 2005). In a Norwalk virus challenge study, volunteers with blood group O were significantly more susceptible to infection than other blood types, and blood group A appeared to be less susceptible to infection. In addition, a group of volunteers that was completely resistant to Norwalk virus infection and illness was observed, and this resistance was attributed to genetic factors that may code for the virus binding site (Lindesmith et al., 2003). Finally, it is useful to note that most pathogens are initially identified in outbreaks of disease, where the most virulent strains tend to be detected and the most susceptible hosts tend to become ill. However, in human challenge studies, the hosts are screened and selected for their health and the challenge organisms tend to be less virulent in terms of illness. Thus, data from outbreaks and human challenge studies – that unfortunately are mostly performed in developed countries – tend to represent opposite ends of the dose-response continuum.

ALTERNATE SOURCES OF DOSE-RESPONSE INFORMATION

The problems associated with finding appropriate dose-response data, even for dangerous pathogens, have led risk assessors to consider surrogate data: surrogate pathogens, hosts or both.

Animal challenge studies

A human pathogen may often be adapted to its host, rendering its response in a surrogate host species distinctly different from its 'normal' behaviour (Teunis et al., 2004). Keeping in mind that quantitative risk assessment not only connects causes and consequences but even attempts to quantify the relation between exposure and health effects, animal challenge studies are not particularly well suited to provide information on dose-response in humans. Furthermore, in a few instances where there are both animal and human infectivity data, there does not seem to be agreement. For example, data from immuno-deficient mice and human volunteers for *Cryptosporidium* showed surprising similarities (Teunis et al., 2002b; Yang et al., 2000), while data from rabbits and human outbreaks of pathogenic *E. coli* showed very little agreement (Haas et al., 2000; Teunis et al., 2004).

Information from outbreak investigations

Recent studies have attempted to use outbreak investigations as a source of dose-response information (DuPont et al., 1995; Navarro et al., 2009). Not many outbreaks have been documented sufficiently well to support such analysis, because not only must the exposed and affected (ill, infected) population be known, but also there has to be some knowledge of exposure. For a small subset of all reported outbreaks, this information is available, and a novel form of meta-analysis can be done. Even a single outbreak may provide useful information (Teunis et al., 2004, 2005). A dose-response assessment using several different outbreaks needs to take into account additional levels of variation between outbreaks (Takumi et al., 2009; Teunis et al., 2008). A multi-level dose-response model is best suited for describing such data and can account for differences in exposure conditions and differences in the intrinsic properties of pathogens and hosts.

EXAMPLES OF DOSE-RESPONSE INFORMATION
ON SELECTED ENTERIC PATHOGENS

Norovirus

Noroviruses are probably the most common cause of epidemic non-bacterial acute gastroenteritis and can be transmitted by faecal-contaminated food, water, surfaces and hands. Noroviruses are pathogens of particular concern for produce quality. Several multi-country outbreaks of norovirus associated with raspberries from China or Eastern Europe that were irrigated with contaminated agricultural waters have been described (Hjertqvist et al., 2006). Many norovirus outbreaks have been associated with salads and cut fruits (Gallimore et al., 2005; Herwaldt et al., 1994). Most of these outbreaks have been attributed to produce contamination from contact with infected food-handlers, but it is possible that some of these outbreaks may also have been due to produce that became contaminated in the field or during harvest and transport. Evidence from outbreaks suggests that these viruses are quite persistent in the environment and highly infectious.

The infectivity of Norwalk virus, a prototype norovirus, was examined in a series of human challenge studies (Teunis et al., 2008a). Data from these studies were used to construct a dose-response model (Figure 4.1). A single hit model for microbial infection was adjusted for virus aggregation by performing a joint analysis of challenge studies with aggregated and disaggregated virus inocula. The model parameters (alpha, beta) describe a beta distribution of the single unit (virion) infectivity and indicate that Norwalk virus is the most infectious agent ever described. The median infectious dose was estimated to be 18 virus genome copies (as measured by quantitative real-time reverse transcription-polymerase chain reaction), and the virus was highly infectious at low doses (average probability of infection of about 50 per cent for a single virus genome), which is especially relevant for environmental contamination of produce. In addition, these challenge studies revealed differences in host susceptibility and possible protective immunity through a mucosal immune response (Lindesmith et al., 2003). At the highest doses tested, the infection rate seemed to level off at about 75 per cent (Figures 4.1a and 4.1b), suggesting that some proportion of the population may be protected from infection.

E. coli O157:H7

E. coli O157:H7 has also been associated with a number of outbreaks from contaminated produce. In 2006, a large, multi-state outbreak of E. coli O157: H7 in the USA was linked to the consumption of fresh spinach and involved over 200 laboratory-confirmed cases (Wendel et al., 2009). The dose-response model for E. coli O157:H7 (Figure 4.2) shows that the infectivity of this pathogen shows considerable variation between outbreaks, but it is likely to be high (about 1 per cent probability of infection for a single colony-forming unit). Exposure to even low doses of E. coli O157:H7 is associated with unacceptably high risks of infection and acute diarrhoeal illness (Teunis et al., 2008b). Since such infection also may lead to severe sequelae, such as hemolytic uremic syndrome (HUS), especially in children, the presence of this pathogen must be considered a serious risk at all times.

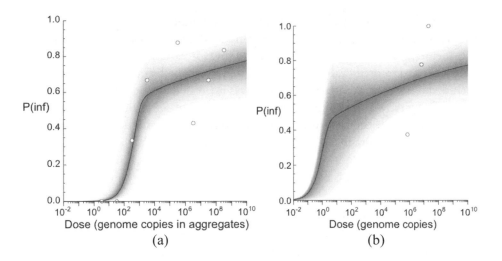

Figure 4.1 *Dose-response relation for infection by Norwalk virus in human challenge study. Model jointly fitted to (a) aggregate primary inoculum and (b) dispersed secondary inoculum, obtained from a volunteer infected with the primary inoculum. Graphs show observed fractions infected, best-fitting dose-response relation and uncertainty in predicted infection probabilities 'P(inf)', as density*

Source: Teunis et al. (2008b)

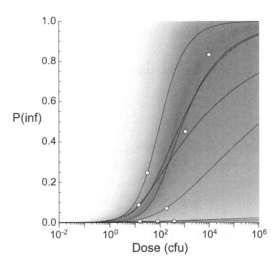

Figure 4.2 *Dose-response relation for* E. coli *O157:H7 based on eight different outbreaks, using a two-level dose-response model, allowing for variation between outbreaks*

Source: Teunis et al. (2008b)

A single hit model for microbial infection was adjusted for uncertainty due to heterogeneity in the exposure encountered in the outbreaks. The model was analysed in a hierarchical (two-level) framework to allow for variation within and between outbreaks and to predict the infectivity of this pathogen by generalizing among all included outbreaks. Predicted infectivity was expressed as a beta-distributed single unit infectivity, with parameters (alpha, beta). Figure 4.2 indicates the observed fractions infected; the best-fitting dose-response relations for each outbreak; and the uncertainty in predicted infection probabilities (as density).

Protozoa

Examples of infection models for *Giardia* and *Cryptosporidium* that have been applied in industrialized countries may be found in Rose et al. (1991) and Teunis et al. (2002a, 2002b). The prevalence of giardiasis typically ranges between 2 and 5 per cent of people in industrialized nations (Farthing, 1993). In developing countries, giardiasis prevalence can be as high as 20–30 per cent (Medicine Health, 2009) and few studies have been performed to quantify its risks, particularly compared to *Cryptosporidium*. Thus, considering the importance of *Giardia* in public health for developing nations, QMRA applications are illustrated, taking into account that: the health response in each country may be different as some infections may be endemic, and people can develop immunity; and exposure to pathogens can vary considerably at a local level, therefore exposure may be notably different between industrialized and developing countries (Jiménez, 2003; Jiménez and Wang, 2006).

Protozoa risks and reuse practice

Both *Cryptosporidium* and *Giardia* are frequently reported in association with waterborne diseases and have caused many outbreaks around the world, because of their high infectivity (Isaac-Renton et al., 1994) and resistance to chemical disinfection (Finch et al., 1994; Rennecker et al., 1999). Conventional wastewater treatment is known to reduce the numbers of *Cryptosporidium* oocysts and *Giardia* cysts by an average of 99.950 per cent (3.17 log reduction) and 99.993 per cent (4.14 log reduction), respectively (Rose et al., 1996). Even so, these protozoan parasites are often detected in tertiary-treated effluents (Gennaccaro et al., 2003; Quintero-Betancourt et al., 2003; Ryu, 2003). This is the reason why risk assessment focuses on evaluating the occurrence of *Giardia* and *Cryptosporidium* in source waters, in order to determine the appropriate treatment needed to obtain specific safety levels for drinking water. In addition, both pathogens are commonly recognized causes of recreational waterborne disease (Slifko et al., 2000). Most recreational water outbreaks are the result of faecal accidents or cross-connections in swimming pools. However, the contamination of natural recreational waters with animal wastes is not well documented or recognized (Gerba and Gerba, 1995). Outbreaks of foodborne giardiasis and *Cryptosporidium* have also been reported (Insulander et al., 2008; Rose and Slifko, 1999).

Historically, reclaimed water has been used for agricultural applications, such as pasture irrigation or non-food crop irrigation, and has often been perceived as a method of wastewater disposal. The trend has now shifted towards unconventional reclaimed water uses, such as urban horticultural irrigation, toilet and urinal flushing, commercial and industrial uses, and indirect potable reuse (United States Environmental Protection Agency (USEPA), 2004). However, concerns about the microbial quality of reclaimed water and the potential associated health risks limit its widespread use.

A review of health risks for different groups associated with the use of wastewater in irrigation indicated that no direct evidence of disease transmission was found for exposed groups of consumers, although there was evidence of the occurrence of protozoa on wastewater-irrigated vegetable surfaces (Carr et al., 2004). For farm workers and their families, the risk of *Giardia intestinalis* infection was found to be insignificant for contact with both untreated and treated wastewater, but an increased risk of amoebiasis was associated with contact with untreated wastewater. For nearby communities, there was no data on the transmission of protozoan infections from sprinkler irrigation with wastewater, and the risk could not be evaluated (Armon et al., 2002; Blumenthal et al., 2000; Blumenthal and Peasey, 2002).

Risks of infection with *Giardia* spp. and *Cryptosporidium parvum* in indus-trialized countries have been associated with drinking water, but never with the use of recycled water (Asano, 1998). However, problems with wastewater reuse have been reported in developing countries where there is evidence of increased risk of *Giardia* infection, for example, in an agricultural population in Mexico (Cifuentes et al., 2000), in the Jordan Valley (Mutaz, 2007) and in Asnara, Eritrea (Srikanth and Naik, 2004).

The occurrence of *Cryptosporidium* oocysts and *Giardia* cysts in reclaimed water and assessment of the risks associated with these protozoan parasites have not been well documented (Gennaccaro et al., 2003; Jolis et al., 1999; Quintero-Betancourt et al., 2003). While substantial efforts are ongoing to improve risk assessment for *Cryptosporidium*, due to the well-established hazards for immuno-compromised subjects, little risk assessment data are available for *Giardia* (Zmirou-Navier et al., 2006).

Dose-response model for *Giardia lamblia*

Data on infectious doses shows a considerable difference reported by different authors for the same type of micro-organisms. For *Giardia lamblia*, Feachem et al. (1983) reported 19 cysts, and Kadlec and Knight (1996) later reported between 25 and 100 cysts. However, *Giardia* species/strains are known to have a low infectious dose (Cooper and Olivieri, 1998). Studies on human volunteers performed 40 years ago revealed a dose-response relationship between the probability of infection (as measured by faecal excretion) and the ingested dose of *Giardia lamblia* (Rendtorff, 1954). The minimum ingestion dose found to be capable of initiating infection in two volunteers (100 per cent) was only ten cysts, but neither of the infected volunteers developed gastrointestinal symptoms.

The dose-response model for assessing the probability of infection from ingestion of *Giardia lamblia* cysts is an exponential equation (Rose et al., 1991) based on experimental data developed by Rendtorff (1954):

$$P = 1 - \exp(-rN) \hspace{4cm} 4.1$$

P is the individual daily probability of infection, r is an organism-specific infectivity parameter, and N is the daily ingested dose of parasites. The best-fit r value for *Giardia* is 0.0199 (95 per cent CI (confidence interval): 0.0044–0.0566) (Rose et al., 1991). The same exponential model applies for *Cryptosporidium parvum* with r = 0.0042 (DuPont et al., 1995) using data from a human challenge study.

Quantitative microbial risk assessment examples for *Giardia lamblia*

The most common application of the exponential dose-response model for *Giardia* has been for QMRA for drinking water, to define the water treatment needed to reduce the risk of waterborne giardiasis (Regli et al., 1991; Teunis et al., 1997; Zmirou-Navier et al., 2006). Fewer applications may be found for risks of giardiasis from wastewater, sludge or faecal excreta reuse (Schönning et al., 2007). Most of these were performed in industrialized rather than developing countries. One example is an epidemiology and microbial risk assessment study (Zmirou-Navier et al., 2006), carried out in southeast France, where the dose-response function derived from epidemiological data was consistent with estimates of infectious risks predicted by the dose-response curve established by Rendtorff (1954). Another study (Regli et al., 1991) gives a detailed description of how risk assessment can be used as an approach for determining what level of water treatment and *Giardia* reduction is necessary to ensure that the risk of *Giardia* from treated drinking water is less than 1 infection per 10,000 people per year.

Another example that details efforts to improve risk assessment for *Giardia* infection is the research of Teunis et al. (1997). Each of the factors contributing to quantitative risk assessment for *Giardia lamblia* was treated as a stochastic variable, for which a suitable distribution was proposed to analyse the uncertainty in the risk of infection estimations. It was found that the major contributing factors are: the concentration of cysts in raw water; the recovery efficiency of the detection method;

the viability of recovered cysts; the removal of organisms in the treatment process; and the daily consumption of unboiled tap water. In this study, the calculation of the risk of infection due to exposure to *Giardia* cysts in drinking water from a surface-water supply in The Netherlands showed that the uncertainty in the estimated removal efficiency of the treatment process dominates the uncertainties due to other contributing factors.

A further example is the work of a Canadian research programme (Saint Lawrence Vision, 2000), which quantified the risk of waterborne *Giardia* (and also *Cryptosporidium*) in 45 drinking-water treatment plants. A Monte Carlo model was developed (Barbeau et al., 2000) using a distribution of r parameter values, that was constructed using 1000 bootstrap replications of the original data from Rendtorff et al. (1954), as described elsewhere (Haas et al., 1996, 1999).

The potential risk of *Giardia* associated with the use of reclaimed wastewater was assessed by Ryu et al. (2007) for three exposure scenarios: landscape irrigation for golf courses; playgrounds; and recreational compounds. In this study, a relatively low risk of *Giardia* infection was estimated from exposure to the tertiary-treated effluents from seven reclaimed water treatment plants, located in the southwestern USA, where dual disinfection practices – chlorination and ultraviolet disinfection – demonstrated better reduction of this parasite.

An example of QMRA and hazard analysis and critical control points (HACCP) was applied to a wastewater tertiary treatment plant in the city of Hässleholm, Sweden (see Westrell et al., 2004). Here, primary and biological sludge (dewatered and anaerobically digested) is stored outside the wastewater treatment plant before its reuse on agricultural land. The risk of infection from *Giardia,* as part of a wider list of pathogens selected for control purposes, was estimated. The human exposure scenarios considered were during treatment, handling, soil application and raw crop consumption, and via water at a wetland area and recreational swimming. It was found that the consumption of vegetables grown in sludge-amended soil presented a lower risk and resulted in a lower number of yearly infections (2×10^{-3} median risk per year) than expected. However, the authors pointed out that a significantly higher risk would result if the organisms occurred in higher concentrations in lumps of sludge rather than being homogeneously distributed as assumed. It must also be taken into consideration that current Swedish regulations require a ten-month interval between sludge fertilization and harvesting of crops for raw consumption. However, in this study, a worst case scenario assuming only a one-month interval was applied.

Issues regarding dose-response

The *Giardia* dose-response relationship defined by Rendtorff (1954) has been applied in many risk-assessment studies since 1990. These studies used the exponential dose-response model to estimate risks of giardiasis from a variety of different exposure routes and reveal the breadth of experience gained from its application for risk assessment.

One concern is about the ratio of asymptomatic to symptomatic *Giardia* infections, because in Rendtorff's experiments positive response was measured by cyst excretion, but illness was not determined. Infection with *Giardia* is usually asymptomatic in humans (Benenson, 1990; Farthing, 1994), with around 39 per cent of the *Giardia* infections in children less than five years of age and 76 per cent of the *Giardia* infections in adults having no symptoms. Symptomatic infections, however, have been reported at a rate of 50–67 per cent and as high as 91 per cent, while chronic giardiasis may also develop in as much as 58 per cent of the population infected (Rose et al., 1991). Moreover, there is evidence that there may be some degree of population immunity, associated with exposure to *Giardia* cysts in drinking water (Roxstrom-Lindquist et al., 2006). Thus, the illness to infection ratio is highly variable (Nash et al., 1987) and risk estimates based on infection as an endpoint may overestimate the number of cases of illness.

Another important issue regarding the dose-response curve based on the Rendtorff data is uncertainty about differences in infectivity due to strain variation and the immune response to infection by different populations. The Rendtorff data are derived from a single *Giardia lamblia* strain and a relatively small sample population of adults. Hence, variability related to infectivity of different strains and to the immune response of hosts cannot be addressed (Zmirou-Navier et al., 2006). The confidence interval for the probability of infection at a specific dose does not take these uncertainties into account when using the model as a predictive tool. Thus, these limitations must be taken into account in risk-assessment studies (Rose et al., 1991).

Assuming the dose-response relationship derived from the Rendtorff data is representative, we may be overestimating giardiasis risks if we assume that all *Giardia* cysts detected in water are viable and are species that infect humans (Rose et al., 1991). To date, there are no data on the viability of *Giardia* cysts detected in reclaimed water (Ryu et al., 2007). On the other hand, the underestimation of risk may be of greater concern due to underestimation of exposure by the inefficiencies of the methods to concentrate and detect *Giardia* cysts in water. In spite of its limitations, the dose-response model for *Giardia* can be helpful for interpreting data from waterborne disease outbreaks and disease surveillance data associated with various exposure routes (Rose et al., 1991).

The current dose-response information for *Giardia* is based on healthy adult hosts. From a public-health perspective, this is not the most important group. Compared to newborns, elderly persons and other risk groups, the estimated risks of infection using these data may be an underestimation for some subgroups of the population (Teunis et al., 1997). Other factors, such as nutritional status, predisposing illness and previous exposure will also play a role in determining susceptibility to infection and the outcome of an infection (Flannagan, 1992).

Helminth eggs

As described in Chapter 2, helminthiases diseases are frequently linked to the use of wastewater, sludge or excreta in agriculture. Helminthiases are transmitted through the ingestion of helminth eggs which are the ova of a wide variety of pathogenic worms (Jiménez, 2009) and are considered to be the most resistant biological particles in the field of environmental engineering. The occurrence of helminth eggs in wastewater and sludge in developing countries differs considerably from that of industrialized countries because of the much lower prevalence of these infections in the latter (Jiménez, 2009). The presence of helminth eggs in wastewater or sludge cannot be inferred from the presence or concentration of faecal coliforms that are just bacterial indicators of faecal contamination. Additionally, faecal coliforms behave differently than helminth ova in conventional disinfection systems. For example, helminth eggs cannot be inactivated with chlorine, UV light or ozone (Jiménez, 2007). Differences in health conditions (Table 4.1) mean that the helminth ova (HO) content in wastewater and sludge can be 7–80 times greater in developing countries relative to developed ones.

WHO (2006) has set a limit surveillance criterion of ≤ 1 HO per litre for wastewater used for irrigation. In faecal sludge, WHO suggests a limit of 1 HO g^{-1} TS (TS: total solids). These values were established based on epidemiological evidence and not by using risk-assessment approaches (Navarro et al., 2009). Unfortunately, considering the high initial helminth egg concentrations present in wastewater and sludge in many developing countries, these criteria require very high efficiencies in treatment methods (< 99 per cent) that are often unaffordable. Thus, there is a need to determine whether these values are really necessary to protect human health and also how efficient other intervention methods, such as washing produce, are. For all these reasons, it is important to estimate the risk, and to achieve this, a dose-infection curve is needed.

Examples of dose-response and QMRAs applied to helminth eggs

In developing countries, it is difficult to obtain outbreak data. This is due to the endemic nature of helminth infections, such as Ascariasis, Trichuriasis and Schistosomiasis, the number of sources of infection and the delays observed between exposure to the pathogen and symptomatic response. Despite these limitations, a QMRA analysis was performed using a dose-response curve developed by Navarro et al. (2009), with information available from three previous studies. The first was an epidemiological study establishing the prevalence of *Ascaris lumbricoides* in the Mezquital Valley, Mexico (Blumenthal et al., 1996; Cifuentes et al., 1991, 1993). The second source of data was a wastewater-quality study assessing the occurrence of *A. lumbricoides* in the wastewater used to irrigate the valley (Jiménez et al.,

Table 4.1 *Helminth ova (HO) content in wastewater and sludge from different countries*

Country or region	Municipal wastewater HO l⁻¹	Sludge HO g⁻¹ TS
Developing countries	70–3000	70–735
Brazil	166–202	75
Egypt	No data	Mean: 67; maximum: 735
Ghana	No data	76
Jordan	300	No data
Mexico	6–98 in cities	73–177
	Up to 330 in rural and peri-urban areas	
Morocco	840	No data
Ukraine	60	No data
France	9	5–7
Germany	No data	< 1
Great Britain	No data	< 6
United States	1–8	2–13

Source: Jiménez (2009)

1992). The third study consisted of experimental research on the occurrence of *A. lumbricoides* in crops grown in biosolids-enriched soil (Jiménez et al., 2006).

Ascaris lumbricoides dose-response

The data from these studies was used to develop a dose-response relationship for exposure to *A. lumbricoides* through ingestion of raw crops irrigated with wastewater. The population of concern was children of less than 15 years of age from different communities in the Mezquital Valley (3,346 population sample size). This is the most vulnerable group in the valley, with the highest annual *A. lumbricoides* prevalence rate of between 10 and 17 per cent (Blumenthal et al., 1996; Cifuentes et al., 1991, 1993). This group is exposed to different helminth ova concentrations on crops because the quality of the wastewater used for irrigation varies through the valley as a consequence of sedimentation in several reservoirs. This variation (33 to 73 *A. lumbricoides* ova/5 litres of wastewater) was characterized from data measured across the irrigation channels in the valley, taking into account the variation in the viability of the ova (52–93 per cent). In addition, some assumptions were made in estimating the exposure dose; it was assumed that 10ml of wastewater remains (Shuval et al., 1997) in each 100g of produce eaten raw such that the *Ascaris* levels on crops varied from 0.42 to 1.15 *Ascaris* per 100ml of water in the crop. Ingestion of 100g of raw crops per week during a year was assumed as a reasonable mean consumption for a child.

The best-fit dose-response relationship for the epidemiological data, following the procedure of Haas et al. (1999), was a beta-Poisson model (alpha = 0.104 beta

= 1.096) to estimate risk of *A. lumbricoides* infection for a child who consumes raw crops once per week during a year. A detailed description of the estimates may be found in Navarro et al. (2009).

$$P(d) = 1 - \left(1 + \frac{d}{1.1}\right)^{-0.104}$$ 4.2

This dose-response relationship focuses on infection prevalence rather than on illness or disease. It applies only for *A. lumbricoides* infection in a typical Mexican wastewater irrigation scenario, but may not be representative for other common helminthiases in developing countries with different infectivity and severity of illness (Jiménez, 2007). Thus, this method should be replicated in other developing countries to fit the dose-response relationship to their local scenarios. Recognizing that there are several sources of uncertainty in the model proposed, some improvements may be considered depending on the availability of data. For example, appropriate data for the specific study region regarding types of crops, ranges of pathogen levels in wastewater, estimates of the amount of wastewater remaining on the crop, range of typical crop consumption and frequency, are needed to reduce uncertainties; furthermore, the use of probability distributions to describe model variables will improve the confidence of infection predictions.

QMRA for *Ascaris lumbricoides*

The results of a QMRA for *A. lumbricoides*, based on the dose-response developed in the above equation, are presented to analyse the potential risks from agricultural wastewater and sludge reuse in developing countries, and to develop feasible, risk-based limits on helminth ova on wastewater and sludge rather than criteria based on limited epidemiological data and efficiencies of treatment processes. Two scenarios were considered to illustrate how safety criteria may be estimated applying QMRA: consumption of raw spinach irrigated with untreated wastewater; and consumption of raw spinach and carrots grown in biosolids-amended soil.

The available data on the quality of wastewater used for irrigation, the quantity of wastewater remaining in crops, as well as the population of concern (children under 15 years of age) and the exposure frequency (once per week during a year) used for the development of the dose-response were considered. Additionally, data on child ingestion rates (IR) for each vegetable (IR_{carrot}, $IR_{spinach}$) available in an international database (USEPA, 1997 and 2002) were assumed for QMRA, rather than a point estimation of 100g/d that was used previously. These new data sources and assumptions improve the risk estimation and allow analysis of the exposure variability. A detailed description of the exposure dose estimations and risk calculations may be found in Navarro et al. (2009) and in Jiménez and Navarro (2009).

Infection risk from eating raw vegetables irrigated with untreated wastewater

The annual expected risk of *A. lumbricoides* infection associated with a single week of exposure to wastewater-irrigated spinach eaten raw after harvesting, estimated with the beta-Poisson model, varied from 5×10^{-2} to 9×10^{-1} per child per year. This estimate implies an infection rate of 5 per cent to 89 per cent in the exposed population after one year and illustrates a worst case scenario where no hygiene measures were assumed.

If a washing procedure is added after harvesting (for example, with weak detergent solution and rising thoroughly with safe drinking water) and reduces the *Ascaris* ova concentration by 1 $\log_{10}$ (WHO, 2006), the risk estimates for *Ascaris* infection are reduced by two orders of magnitude (between 5×10^{-3} to 2.5 $\times 10^{-1}$ per child per year). The expected infection rate would be less than 17 per cent per year, except for when the maximum values for *Ascaris* levels in irrigation wastewater (115 *Ascaris* ova/5 litres) and for consumption (270g/d) are assumed (Figure 4.3).

Infection incidence of less than 3 per cent might occur if efficiencies of the washing procedure were further improved resulting in a 2 log reduction in *Ascaris* exposure (between 6×10^{-4} to 2.7×10^{-2} per child per year).

These results show that risk of *Ascaris* infection depends on the concentration of the pathogen in the wastewater and the application rate on the crops ($C_{Ascaris}$), as well as the quantity of potentially contaminated crops that are consumed ($IR_{spinach}$). We demonstrate how the risk of infection could be reduced if improved washing of the harvested produce is practised.

Thus, considering those factors that influence the health-risk estimates, even though the overall risk of infection may be greater than 10^{-4} (6×10^{-4} to 3×10^{-2} per child per year), a less risky and feasible application of wastewater for irrigation in the region may be achieved if $C_{Ascaris} \leq 115$ *Ascaris lumbricoides* ova/5 litres (equivalent to 23 viable *Ascaris* ova per litre) is used for irrigation. This level of health protection may well be reinforced with intervention methods that include sanitary campaigns to improve harvesting and both commercial and consumers' washing procedures, among other practices.

Infection risk from eating raw vegetables grown in biosolids-amended soil

In order to estimate the risk of eating raw vegetables grown in soil fertilized with biosolids (0.25, 1, 4 and 37 HO/gTS), the results from an experimental study were used to estimate the number of pathogens on the crop, assuming that *A. lumbricoides* accounted for 90 per cent of the total helminth ova (HO/g) content in spinach (6.5–305 *Ascaris*/100g) and carrots (0.3–49 *Ascaris*/100g). A detailed description of the data is published elsewhere (Jiménez et al., 2006).

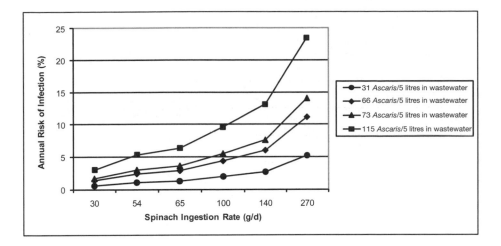

Figure 4.3 *Risk estimate from annual exposure to spinach irrigated with four different* Ascaris *concentrations in wastewater for several consumption rates*

Source: Based on Jiménez and Navarro (2009)

The annual risk of consuming uncooked spinach grown on biosolids-amended soil, after harvesting, without any intervention method, was estimated to be 1 infection per child per year. In this case, unlike the estimated risks associated with wastewater irrigation, the estimated infection rates were similar to the ascariasis incidence rate observed in the region (< 17 per cent) – assuming the USEPA (1993) criterion of HO/4gTS equivalent to 0.25 HO/gTS for the biosolids and a washing procedure that provides a 2 $\log_{10}$ reduction in *A. lumbricoides* ova concentration on the spinach (Figure 4.4). This applies to a spinach consumption rate by children of ≤ 65g/d once per week during a year. The 0.25 HO/gTS criterion for biosolids is a restrictive limit for developing countries where it is difficult to reduce the typically high HO content in sludge to such low levels.

A comparative QMRA for spinach and carrots grown on biosolids-amended soil (Navarro et al., 2009) illustrates that the health risk is also a function of the type of crop. These results indicated that the annual risk (4.5×10^{-3} to 9.6×10^{-1} *Ascaris* infections per child per year) from raw carrot ingestion is less than the annual risk associated with spinach consumption. In fact, an initial limit for the region, with annual infection rates expected < 22 per cent, may be set at 4 HO/gTS content in biosolids for a reasonable carrot mean consumption rate ≤ 100g/d once per week during a year (Figure 4.5). This situation, although not ideal, would turn out to be an acceptable safety limit with gradual reductions that progressively improve local health, social and economic conditions, since this limit is feasible in developing countries.

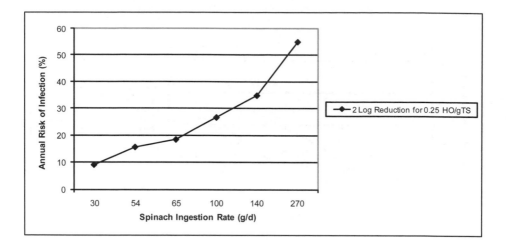

Figure 4.4 *Estimated annual risk of* Ascaris *infection associated with exposure to spinach grown on biosolids-amended soil*

Source: Based on Navarro et al. (2009)

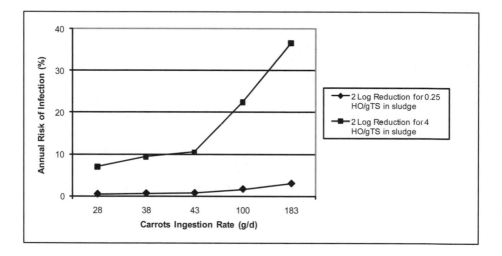

Figure 4.5 *Estimated annual risk of* Ascaris *infection associated with exposure to carrots grown on biosolids-amended soil*

Source: Based on Navarro et al. (2009)

These real scenarios illustrate a QMRA approach for examining the risks of *Ascaris* infection associated with crops that are either irrigated with wastewater or grown in soil that has been amended with faecal sludge. These analyses indicate that differences in the level of exposure to pathogenic organisms may arise from variations in HO concentrations in vegetables and in consumption patterns. To improve confidence in the estimated risks predicted by these analyses, those factors contributing to increased variability need to be better characterized in order to develop safe and feasible HO limits for wastewater and biosolids that are applied in food-crop production in developing countries. Other factors influencing HO concentrations in vegetables include irrigation practices, differences between ova accumulation on root or non-root crops, excreta application rates and efficacy of ova reduction during produce-washing. Therefore, the actual occurrence and concentration of *A. lumbricoides* in food crops will improve confidence in the risk estimation.

HELMINTH OVA STANDARDS FOR DEVELOPING COUNTRIES

The analyses presented above suggest that WHO guideline limits for wastewater and sludge reuse in agricultural production may be too restrictive for developing countries. These findings illustrate that recommended thresholds for HO concentrations in wastewater and biosolids could be raised by an order of magnitude for some settings and would not significantly increase the risk of *Ascaris* infection above current endemic rates. Although higher *Ascaris* infection rates would be predicted by a change in the thresholds and the risk estimates are greater than 10^{-4} per child per year, changing the HO standards to those that predict infection rates that are still less than the local endemic prevalence may induce a gradual improvement in population health conditions. Finally, limits on pathogen concentrations in wastewater and biosolids used for irrigation or fertilization should be implemented in an integrated framework for risk management where other sources of helminth exposure and the impact of additional health-protection measures, such as improvements in the washing of produce, may be considered.

CONCLUSIONS

Application of microbial risk assessment approaches

As presented here, it is feasible to examine the potential risks of infection associated with the consumption of food crops that are irrigated with wastewater or fertilized with biosolids using a QMRA approach. The application of QMRA to this situation requires information on pathogen dose-infection relationships, transmission pathways, occurrence (frequency and concentration) of pathogens in wastewater and biosolids, persistence of pathogen viability or infectivity in the environment and on the food crops and crop consumption (amount and frequency). This approach allows the exploration of various 'what if' scenarios that can include interventions to reduce exposure – such as treatment of the wastewater or biosolids or washing the produce.

However, assessment of the risks associated with ingestion of food crops irrigated or fertilized with wastewater, biosolids or faecal sludge should consider the local context of likely exposure routes, pathogen occurrence and concentration in wastewater and biosolids, and endemic disease rates. The availability of local data for these inputs into the risk-assessment model may be very limited or non-existent, especially in developing countries.

Estimating exposure

Pathogens are rarely measured in environmental samples (wastewater, biosolids, faecal sludge, soils and crops) because of the laboratory resources required for these analyses. Data from microbial indicator organisms (such as *E. coli* or coliphage) may be easier to collect in developing countries and may provide some indication of the magnitude of pathogen concentrations in wastewater or biosolids or on produce (Salgot et al., 2006). Similarly, the measurement of microbial indicator organisms may also provide information on the magnitude of microbial reduction that occurs from specific interventions, such as washing produce or changing irrigation methods. The use and choice of microbial indicators for waterborne pathogens has been extensively reviewed by the National Research Council (2004). However, for helminths there is no alternative indicator.

Estimating dose-response

Dose-response information is a critical component of microbial risk assessment. As described in this chapter, dose-response data are not available for all the pathogens of interest and there are several sources of uncertainty in existing dose-response data. Dose-response information often comes from studies conducted on healthy adults in industrialized countries and may not reflect the response of vulnerable subgroups in the population (young children and the elderly) or populations in developing countries where there may be greater local immunity to specific infections that are endemic. Dose-response data from outbreaks in developing countries is also rare because of the lack of resources for investigations. So, it may not be possible to use this as a source for estimating the dose-response relationship in a developing-country setting. In some settings, data on paediatric diarrhoea or helminth infections may be available from government surveillance systems, government or private health clinics, national demographic and health surveys or from specific research studies. Using QMRA, it may be possible to test the potential appropriateness of different dose-response functions by validating with outbreak data (Haas and Eisenberg, 2001) or comparing predicted risk to actual disease rates reported in surveillance systems or research studies.

Guidelines for safe use of wastewater, biosolids and faecal sludge for food crops

Microbial risk assessment can be a tool to test the usefulness of international guidelines and standards for acceptable levels of pathogens in wastewater, biosolids and faecal sludge used in the production of food crops in a defined context that takes into account local exposure routes, local immunity and alternate health risks. QMRA can be used to develop safe, appropriate local guidelines that can be adjusted as agricultural production becomes more advanced and the health and quality of life in the community improves.

REFERENCES

Armon, R., Gold, D., Brodsky, M. and Oron, G. (2002) 'Surface and subsurface irrigation with effluents of different qualities and presence of *Cryptosporidium* oocysts in soil and crops', *Water Science and Technology*, vol 46, no 3, pp 115–22

Asano, T. (1998) *Wastewater Reclamation and Reuse*, Water Quality Management Library vol 10, Technomic Publishing Inc., Lancaster, PA

Barbeau, B., Payment, P., Coallier, J, Clement, B. and Prévost, M. (2000) 'Evaluating the risk of infection from the presence of *Giardia* and *Cryptosporidium* in drinking water', *Quantitative Microbiology*, vol 2, pp 37–54

Benenson, A. S. (ed) (1990) *Control of Communicable Diseases in Man*, American Public Health Association, Washington, DC

Blumenthal, U. J., Duncan, M., Ayres, R. M., Cifuentes, E., Peasey, A., Stott, R., Lee, D. L. and Ruiz-Palacios, G. (1996) 'Evaluation of the WHO nematode egg guidelines for restricted and unrestricted irrigation', *Water Science and Technology*, vol 33, nos 10–11, pp277–83

Blumenthal, U. J., Mara, D. D., Peasey, A., Ruiz-Palacios, G. and Stott, R. (2000) 'Guidelines for the microbiological quality of treated wastewater used in agriculture: Recommendations for revising WHO guidelines', *Bulletin of the World Health Organization*, vol 78, no 9, pp1104–16

Blumenthal, U. J. and Peasey, A. (2002) 'Critical review of epidemiological evidence of the health effects of wastewater and excreta use in agriculture', unpublished document prepared for World Health Organization, Geneva, www.who.int/water_sanitation_health/wastewater/whocriticalrev.pdf

Carr, R. M., Blumenthal, U. J. and Mara, D. D. (2004) 'Guidelines for the safe use of wastewater in agriculture: Revisiting WHO guidelines', *Water Science and Technology*, vol 50, no 2, pp31–8

Chen, L., Geys, H., Cawthraw, S., Havelaar, A. H. and Teunis, P. (2006) 'Dose response for infectivity of several strains of *Campylobacter jejuni* in chickens', *Risk Analysis*, vol 26, no 6, pp1613–21

Cifuentes, E., Blumenthal, U., Ruiz-Palacios, G. and Bennett, S. (1991) 'Health impact evaluation of wastewater use in Mexico', *Public Health Review*, vol 92, no 19, pp243–50

Cifuentes, E., Blumenthal, U., Ruiz-Palacios, G., Bennett, S., Quigley, M. and Romero-Alvarez, H. (1993) 'Problemas de salud asociados al riego agrícola con agua residual en Mexico', *Salud Pública de Mexico*, vol 35, no 6, pp614–19 (in Spanish)

Cifuentes, E., Gomez, M., Blumenthal, U., Tellez-Rojo, M. M., Romieu, I., Ruiz-Palacios, G. and Ruiz-Velazco, S. (2000) 'Risk factors for *Giardia intestinalis* infection in agricultural villages practicing wastewater irrigation in Mexico', *American Journal of Tropical Medicine Hygiene,* vol 62, no 3, pp388–92

Cooper, R. C. and Olivieri, A.W. (1998) 'Infectious disease concerns in wastewater reuse', in T. Asano (ed) *Wastewater Reclamation and Reuse*, Technomic Publishing Co., Lancaster, PA, pp489–520

DuPont, H. L., Chappel, C. L., Sterling, C. R., Okhuysen, P. C., Rose, J. B. and Jakubowski, W. (1995) 'The infectivity of *Cryptosporidium parvum* in healthy volunteers', *New England Journal of Medicine*, vol 332, no 13, pp855–9

Farthing, M. J. G. (1993) 'Diarroeal disease: Current concepts and future challenges, pathogenesis of giardiasis', *Transactions of the Royal Society of Tropical Medicine and Hygiene*, vol 87, pp17–21

Farthing, M. J. G. (1994) 'Giardiasis as a disease', in R. C. A. Thompson, J. A. Reynoldson and A. J. Lymbery (eds) Giardia: *From Molecules to Disease*, CABI International, Wallingford, UK, pp15–37

Feachem, R., Bradley, D., Garelick, H. and Mara, D. (1983) *Sanitation and Disease: Health Aspects of Excreta and Wastewater Management*, John Wiley and Sons, New York

Finch, G. R., Black, E. K., Gyuèreck, L. and Belosevic, M. (1994) *Ozone Disinfection of* Giardia *and* Cryptosporidium, American Water Works Association, Denver, CO

Flannagan, P. A. (1992) '*Giardia* diagnosis, clinical course and epidemiology – A review', *Epidemiology and Infection*, vol 109, pp1–22

Gallimore, C. I., Pipkin, C., Shrimpton, H., Green, A. D., Pickford, Y., McCartney, C., Sutherland, G., Brown, D. W. and Gray, J. J. (2005) 'Detection of multiple enteric virus strains within a foodborne outbreak of gastroenteritis: An indication of the source of contamination', *Epidemiology Infections,* vol 133, no 1, pp41–7

Gennaccaro, A. L., McLaughlin, M. R., Quintero-Betancourt, W., Huffman, D. E. and Rose, J. B. (2003) 'Infectious *Cryptosporidium parvum* oocysts in final reclaimed effluent', *Applied Environmental Microbiology*, vol 69, no 8, pp4983–4

Gerba, C. P. and Gerba, P. (1995) 'Outbreaks caused by *Giardia* and *Cryptosporidium* associated with swimming pools', *Journal of Swimming Pool and Spa Industry*, vol 1, pp9–18

Haas, C. N., Crockett, C. S., Rose, J. B., Gerba, C. P. and Fazil, A. M. (1996) 'Assessing the risk posed by (oo)cysts in drinking water', *Journal of the American Works Association*, vol 88, no 9, p131

Haas, C. and Eisenberg, J. N. S. (2001) 'Risk assessment', in L. Fewtrell and J. Bartram (eds) *Water Quality: Guidelines, Standards and Health; Assessment of Risk and Risk Management for Water-Related Infectious Disease*, International Water Association (IWA) on behalf of the World Health Organization, London, pp161–83

Haas, C. N., Rose, J. B. and Gerba, C. P. (1999) *Quantitative Microbial Risk Assessment*, John Wiley and Sons, New York, p464

Haas, C. N., Thayyar-Madabusi, A., Rose, J. B. and Gerba, C. P. (2000) 'Development of a dose-response relationship for *Escherichia coli* O157:H7', *International Journal of Food Microbiology*, vol 57, pp153–9

Herwaldt, B. L., Lew, J. F., Moe, C. F., Lewis, D. C., Humphrey, C. D., Monroe, S. S., Pon, E. W. and Glass, R. I. (1994) 'Characterization of a variant strain of Norwalk virus from a foodborne outbreak of gastroenteritis on a cruise ship in Hawaii', *Journal of Clinic Microbiology*, vol 32, no 4, pp861–6

Hjertqvist, M., Johansson, A., Svensson, N., Åbom, P. E., Magnusson, C., Olsson, M., Hedlund, K. O. and Andersson, Y. (2006) 'Four outbreaks of norovirus gastroenteritis after consuming raspberries, Sweden', *Eurosurveillance*, vol 11, no 7, p9

Insulander, M., de Jong, B. and Svenungsson, B. (2008) 'A foodborne outbreak of cryptosporidiosis among guests and staff at a hotel restaurant in Stockholm county, Sweden, September 2008', *Eurosurveillance*, vol 13, no 51, www.eurosurveillance.org/ViewArticle.aspx?ArticleId=19071

Isaac-Renton, J. L., Lewis, L. F., Ong, C. S. L. and Nulsen, M. F. (1994) 'A second community outbreak of waterborne giardiasis in Canada and serological investigation of patients', *Transactions of the Royal Society of Tropical Medicine and Hygiene*, vol 88, no 4, pp395–9

Jiménez, B. (2003) 'Health risks in aquifer recharge with recycle water', in R. Aertgeerts and A. Angelakis (eds) *State of the Art Report Health Risk in Aquifer Recharge using Reclaimed Water*, WHO Regional Office for Europe, Rome

Jiménez, B. (2007) 'Helminth ova control in sludge: A review', *Water Science and Technology*, vol 56, no 9, pp147–55

Jiménez, B. (2009) 'Helminth ova control in wastewater and sludge for agricultural reuse', in W.O.K. Grabow (ed) *Encyclopaedia of Biological, Physiological and Health Sciences, Water and Health*, vol 2, EOLSS Publishers Co Ltd, Oxford, and UNESCO, Paris, pp429–49

Jiménez, B., Austin, A., Cloete, E. and Phasha, C. (2006) 'Using Ecosan sludge for crop production', *Water Sciences and Technology*, vol 5, no 54, pp169–77

Jiménez, B., Chávez, A. and Maya, C. (1992) 'Characterization of the water and wastewater used to irrigate the Mezquital Valley', Internal Report No 2345, Engineering Institute, UNAM, Mexico. Unpublished manuscript (in Spanish), available upon request

Jiménez, B. and Navarro, I. (2009) 'Methodology to set regulations for safe reuse of wastewater and sludge for agriculture in developing countries based on a scientific approach and following the new WHO Guidelines', in Dr Ashish Dwivedi (ed) *Handbook of Research on Information Technology Management and Clinical Data Administration in Healthcare*, vol 1, IGI Global, Hershey, New York, pp1027

Jiménez, B. and Wang, L. (2006) 'Sludge treatment and management', in Z. Ujang and M. Henze (eds) *Municipal Wastewater Management in Developing Countries: Principles and Engineering*, IWA Publishing, London, pp237–92

Jolis, D., Pitt, P. and Hirano, R. (1999) 'Risk assessment for *Cryptospridium parvum* in reclaimed water', *Water Research*, vol 33, no 13, pp3051–5

Kadlec, R. and Knight, R. (1996) *Treatment Wetlands*, CRC Press, Boca Raton, FL, p893

Lindesmith, L., Moe, C., Marionneau, S., Ruvoen, N., Jiang, X., Lindblad, J., Stewart, P., LePendu, J. and Baric, R. (2003) 'Human susceptibility and resistance to Norwalk virus infection', *Nature Medicine*, vol 9, no 5, pp548–53

Medicine Health (2009), www.emedicinehealth.com/giardiasis/article_em.htm

Mutaz, Al-Alawi (2007) 'Health assessment of wastewater reuse in Jordan', in *Wastewater Reuse – Risk Assessment, Decision-Making and Environmental Security,* NATO Security through Science Series, Springer, The Netherlands, pp385–92

Nash, T. E., Herrington, D. A., Losonsky, G. A., Levine, M. and Nash, T. (1987) 'Experimental human infections with *Giardia intestinalis*', *Journal of Infectious Diseases,* vol 156, pp 974–84

National Research Council (2004) *Indicators for Waterborne Pathogens,* National Academies Press, Washington, DC, www.nap.edu/catalog.php?record_id=11010#toc

Navarro, I., Jiménez, B., Cifuentes, E. and Lucario, S. (2009) 'Application of helminth ova infection dose curve to estimate the risks associated with biosolid application on soil', *Journal of Water and Health,* vol 7, no 1, pp31–44

Quintero-Betancourt, W., Gennaccaro, A. L., Scott, T. M. and Rose, J. B. (2003) 'Assessment of methods for detection of infectious *Cryptosporidium* oocysts and *Giardia* cysts in reclaimed effluents', *Applied Environmental Microbiology,* vol 69, no 9, pp5380–88

Regli, S., Rose, J. B. and Haas, C. N. (1991) 'Modelling the risk from *Giardia* and viruses in drinking water', *American Water Works Association,* vol 83, no 11, pp 76–84

Rendtorff, R. C. (1954) 'The experimental transmission of human intestinal protozoan parasites, 1. *Giardia* cysts given in capsules', *American Journal of Hygiene,* vol 59, pp209

Rennecker, J. L., Marinas, B. J., Owens, J. H. and Rice, E. W. (1999) 'Inactivation of *Cryptosporidium parvum* (oo)cysts with ozone', *Water Research,* vol 33, p2481

Rose, J. B., Dickson, L. J., Farrah, S. R. and Carnahan, R. P. (1996) 'Removal of pathogenic and indicator microorganisms by a full-scale water reclamation facility', *Water Research,* vol 30, no 11, pp2785–97

Rose, J. B., Haas, C. N. and Regli, S. (1991) 'Risk assessment and control of waterborne giardiasis', *American Journal of Public Health,* vol 81, no 6, pp709–13

Rose, J.B. and Slifko, T.R. (1999) '*Giardia, Cyclospora,* and *Cryptosporidium* and their impact on foods: A review', *Journal of Food Protection,* vol 62, pp1059–70

Roxstrom-Lindquist, K., Palm, D., Reiner, D., Ringqvist, E. and Svard, S. G. (2006) '*Giardia* immunity – An update', *Trends in Parasitology,* vol 2, no 1, pp26–31

Ryu, H. (2003) 'Microbial quality and risk assessment in various water cycles in the southwestern United States', PhD dissertation, Department of Civil and Environmental Engineering, Arizona State University, Tempe, AZ

Ryu, H., Alum, A., Mena, K. D. and Abbaszadegan, M. (2007) 'Assessment of the risk of infection by *Cryptosporidium* and *Giardia* in non-potable reclaimed water', *Water Science and Technology,* vol 55, nos 1–2, pp283–90

Saint Lawrence Vision (2000) 'Consumption of drinking water', http://slv2000.qc.ca/bibliotheque/centre_docum/bilan_sante/eau_potable/micro_organis_a.htm

Salgot, M., Huertas, E., Weber, S., Dott, W. and Hollender, J. (2006) 'Wastewater reuse and risk: Definition of key objectives', *Desalination,* no 187, pp29–40

Schönning, C., Westrell, T., Stenström, T.-A., Arnbjerg-Nielsen, K., Hasling, A. B., Hoibye, L. and Carlsen, A. (2007) 'Microbial risk assessment of local handling and use of human faeces', *Journal of Water and Health,* vol 5, no 1, pp117–28

Shuval, H., Lampert, Y. and Fattal, B. (1997) 'Development of a risk assessment approach for evaluating wastewater reuse standards for agriculture', *Water Science and Technology*, vol 35, nos 11–12, pp15–20

Slifko, T. R., Smith, H. V. and Rose, J. B. (2000) 'Emerging parasite zoonoses associated with water and food', *International Journal for Parasitology*, vol 30, pp1379–93

Srikanth, R. and Naik, D. (2004) 'Prevalence of giardiasis due to wastewater reuse for agriculture in the suburbs of Asmara City, Eritrea', *International Journal of Environmental Health Research*, vol 14, no 1, pp43–52

Takumi, K., Teunis, P., Fonville, M., Vallee, I., Boireau, P., Nöckler, K. and van der Giessen, J. (2009) 'Transmission risk of human trichinellosis', *Veterinary Parasitology*, vol 159, nos 3–4, pp324–7

Teunis, P., Chappell, C. and Okhuysen, P. (2002a) '*Cryptosporidium* dose response studies: Variation between isolates', *Risk Analysis*, vol 22, no 1, pp175–83

Teunis, P., Chappell, C. and Okhuysen, P. (2002b) '*Cryptosporidium* dose response studies: Variation between hosts', *Risk Analysis*, vol 22, no 3, pp475–85

Teunis, P. F. M., Medema, G. J., Kruidenier, L. and Havelaar, A. H. (1997) 'Assessment of the risk of infection by *Cryptosporidium* or *Giardia* in drinking water from a surface water source', *Water Research,* vol 31, no 6, pp1333–46

Teunis, P. F. M., Moe, C. L., Liu, P., Miller, S., Lindesmith, L., Baric, R. S., LePendu, J. and Calderon, R. L. (2008a) 'Norwalk virus: How infectious is it?', *Journal of Medical Virology*, vol 80, no 8, pp1468–76

Teunis, P., Ogden, I. and Strachan, N. (2008b) 'Hierarchical dose response of *E. coli* O157: H7 from human outbreaks incorporating heterogeneity in exposure', *Epidemiology and Infection*, vol 36, no 6, pp761–70

Teunis, P., Takumi, K. and Shinagawa, K. (2004) 'Dose response for infection by *Escherichia coli* O157:H7 from outbreak data', *Risk Analysis*, vol 24, no 2, pp 401–7

Teunis, P., van den Brandhof, W., Nauta, M., Wagenaar, J., van den Kerkhof, H. and van Pelt, W. (2005) 'A reconsideration of the *Campylobacter* dose-response relation', *Epidemiology and Infection*, vol 133, no 4, pp583–92

USEPA (1993) 40 Code of Federal Regulations, Part 503, Fed. Regist. 58(32), 9248–9415

USEPA (1997) *Exposure Factors Handbook, Vol II Food Ingestion Factors*, National Centre for Environmental Assessment, Washington, DC

USEPA (2002) *Child-Specific Factors Handbook*, EPA/600/P-00/002B, National Centre for Environmental Assessment, Washington, DC

Wendel, A. M., Johnson, D. H., Sharapov, U., Grant, J., Archer, J. R., Monson, C., Koschmann, T. and Davis, J. P. (2009) 'Multistate outbreak of *Escherichia coli* O157: H7 infection associated with consumption of packaged spinach, August–September 2006: The Wisconsin investigation', *Clinical Infection Diseases*, vol 48, pp1079–86

Westrell, T., Schönning, C., Stenström, T.-A. and Ashbolt, N. J. (2004) 'QMRA (Quantitative Microbial Risk Assessment) and HACCP (Hazard Analysis and Critical Control Points) for management of pathogens in wastewater and sewage sludge treatment and reuse', *Water Science and Technology*, vol 50, no 2, pp23–30

WHO (2006) *Guidelines for the Safe Use of Wastewater, Excreta and Greywater*, World Health Organization, Geneva

Yang, S., Benson, S. K., Du, C. and Healey, M. C. (2000) 'Infection of immunosuppressed C57BL/6N adult mice with a single oocyst of *Cryptosporidium parvum*', *Journal of Parasitology*, vol 86, no 4, pp884–7

Zmirou-Navier, D., Gofti-Laroche, L. and Hartemann, P. (2006) 'Waterborne microbial risk assessment: A population-based dose-response function for *Giardia* spp', *BMC Public Health*, vol 6, p122, www.biomedcentral.com/1471-2458/6/122

5

Tools for Risk Analysis: Updating the 2006 WHO Guidelines

Duncan Mara, Andrew J. Hamilton, Andrew Sleigh,
Natalie Karavarsamis and Razak Seidu

ABSTRACT

This chapter reviews developments since the WHO Guidelines for the safe use of wastewater in agriculture were published in 2006. The six main developments are: the recognition that the tolerable additional disease burden may be too stringent for many developing countries; the benefits of focusing on single-event infection risks as a measure of outbreak potential when evaluating risk acceptability; a more rigorous method for estimating annual risks; the availability of dose-response data for norovirus; the use of QMRA to estimate *Ascaris* infection risks; and a detailed evaluation of pathogen reductions achieved by produce-washing and disinfection. Application of the developments results in more realistic estimates of the pathogen reductions required for the safe use of wastewater in agriculture and consequently permits the use of simpler wastewater treatment processes.

INTRODUCTION

Since the publication of the 2006 WHO Guidelines for the safe use of treated wastewater in agriculture (WHO, 2006) there have been several pertinent developments in risk analysis techniques and the interpretation of the resulting risks. These include:

- Recognition that a tolerable additional disease burden of $\leq 10^{-6}$ Disability-Adjusted Life Year (DALY) loss per person per year (pppy) may be too stringent in many developing-country settings and that a DALY loss of $\leq 10^{-5}$ or even $\leq 10^{-4}$ pppy may be sufficiently protective of human health (WHO, 2007).
- A persuasive argument for focusing on single-event infection risks as a measure of 'outbreak potential', rather than annual risks alone, when evaluating risk acceptability (Signor and Ashbolt, 2009).
- A more rigorous method for estimating annual risks (Karavarsamis and Hamilton, 2009; see also Benke and Hamilton, 2008).
- The availability of dose-response data for norovirus (Teunis et al., 2008).
- Application of QMRA to estimate *Ascaris* infection risks (Navarro et al., 2009).
- Evaluation of pathogen reductions achieved by produce-washing and disinfection (Amoah et al., 2007).

LESS STRINGENT TOLERABLE BURDEN OF DISEASE

In *Levels of Protection*, one of the documents in the rolling revision of its drinking-water quality guidelines, WHO (2007) states that, 'in locations or situations where the overall burden of disease from microbial, chemical or radiological exposures by all exposure routes is very high, setting a 10^{-6} DALY [loss] per person per year annual risk from waterborne exposure will have little impact on the overall disease burden. Therefore, setting a less stringent level of acceptable risk, such as 10^{-5} or 10^{-4} DALY [loss] per person per year, from waterborne exposure may be more realistic, yet still consistent with the goal of providing high-quality, safer water and encouraging incremental improvement of water quality.' Following the principles of the Stockholm Framework (Fewtrell and Bartram, 2001), this can be adapted and applied to wastewater use in agriculture.

Thus, for communities with high levels of diarrhoeal disease it is probably unrealistic to set a tolerable additional burden of disease of $\leq 10^{-6}$ DALY loss pppy; a more realistic level might be $\leq 10^{-5}$ DALY loss pppy for consumers of wastewater-irrigated food crops eaten uncooked and $\leq 10^{-4}$ DALY loss pppy for those who work (or play) in wastewater-irrigated fields. A less stringent level could be set for the latter if they are given the option to make an informed choice regarding their working conditions and thus their occupational health risks (they are a readily identifiable group of people who can be easily given treatment when necessary, for example, oral rehydration salts and anti-helminthic drugs).

Fieldworkers would therefore be protected, at least partially, by wastewater treatment that achieves a pathogen reduction of two orders of magnitude lower than that for $\leq 10^{-6}$ DALY loss pppy, which is a reduction of only 1–2 log units. Similarly, consumers would be protected by a total pathogen reduction one order of magnitude lower than that for $\leq 10^{-6}$ DALY loss pppy, which is a reduction of only 1–2 log units by wastewater treatment supplemented by 4–5 log units achieved by post-treatment health-protection control measures. This is discussed further in this book.

SINGLE-EVENT INFECTION RISKS AS A MEASURE OF 'OUTBREAK POTENTIAL'

The probability of infection used as a benchmark for acceptability is typically the annualized probability of infection, where independent exposure events throughout the year are used to estimate the annual risk (as presented in the section below). However, the instantaneous level of infection risk to the exposed population fluctuates throughout the year, with disease outbreaks typically associated with shorter-duration periods of heightened risk. Signor and Ashbolt (2009) present a case for the widespread adoption of shorter-duration reference periods (i.e. per exposure or per day) for infection probability targets with which to assess, report and benchmark risks. They argue that doing so may provide opportunities for improved water-related disease risk management, with an incentive to reduce the occurrence and impact of event-driven peaks. Signor and Ashbolt suggest that for a design or operational target of annual disease risk of 10^{-4} per person, a daily or single-exposure disease probability of 10^{-6} per person would meet the aims of the original target, as well as promote the undertaking of measures to control the extent of short-term adverse risk fluctuations. This could be generalized to a single-exposure disease risk of $10^{-(x+y)}$ pppy for an acceptable annual disease risk of 10^{-x} per person, where the value of y depends on the frequency of exposure. The corresponding infection risks would, of course, be lower.

MORE RIGOROUS METHOD TO ESTIMATE ANNUAL RISKS

Karavarsamis and Hamilton (2009) recommend a superior method of estimating annual infection risks from QMRA-Monte Carlo simulations. This method is described in detail in Box 5.1 as Approach A. In brief, it appropriately represents daily variation in infection risk in the determination of annual risk, in contrast to the common practice (Approach B) of extrapolating an imprecise estimate of annual risk from infection risk for any one day of exposure (as in the procedure used by Mara et al., 2007, and in the 2006 WHO Guidelines). Karavarsamis and Hamilton point out that repeated calculation through simulation does not solve the shortcomings of the latter approach: it merely generates a distribution of imprecise estimates. Risk estimates resulting from the application of both methods to five wastewater irrigation scenarios, presented in Table 5.1, show that, while the median risks from the two methods are similar, the Karavarsamis and Hamilton method yields 95-percentile risks, which are sometimes used as conservative estimates of annual risk, up to an order of magnitude lower than the WHO (2006) method.

Box 5.1 Improved representation of uncertainty in annual infection risk modelling

The earliest QMRA methods for wastewater irrigation tended to use straightforward deterministic models, where model parameters are represented by single values (point-estimates) (e.g. Asano et al., 1992; Shuval et al., 1997). More recently, modelling techniques such as Monte Carlo simulation (MCS) have been employed and encouraged in an effort to account for uncertainty (WHO, 2006). However, proper and effective use of these tools involves more than just substituting probability distributions for point-estimates: it demands careful attention to model structure, assumptions and computation.[1]

Having used exposure and dose-response models to determine the infection risk, p, per exposure event, the total probability of infection over n exposures, $P_{\Sigma j}$, is given as:

$$P_{\Sigma j} = 1 - \prod_{k=1}^{n}\left(1 - p_k^j\right) \qquad\qquad 5.1$$

where p_k^j is the infection probability for the kth iteration of an exposure event in the jth simulation, and where events are assumed to be independent.

Clearly, if one exposure event is assumed to occur each day of the year, then p_k^j represents a daily risk (i.e. $n = 365$) and $P_{\Sigma j}$ is an annual risk. MCS can be used to draw realizations of dose, λ_k^j s, from an exposure model, which can then be fed through a dose-response model to yield p_k^j, and this can be done n times and Equation 5.1 used to give a single estimate of total risk, P_{Σ} (Figure 5.1). This entire process can then be repeated m times to obtain a simulated distribution of $P_{\Sigma j}$, to obtain a variance of the annual risk estimate. Thus, this approach involves simulations labelled j ($j = 1, 2, ... m$) which comprise iterations labelled k ($k = 1, 2, ... n$).

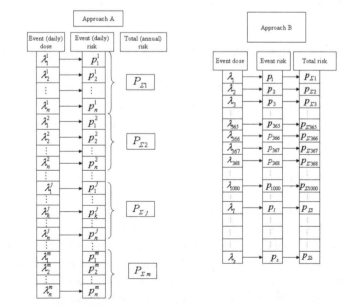

Figure 5.1 *Schematic of recommended (Approach A) and not recommended (Approach B) methods for determining annual infection risk*

If each exposure event is assumed to result in the same (i.e., constant) probability of infection, p, then Equation 5.1 reduces to:

$$p_{\Sigma\,l} = 1 - (1 - p_l)^n \qquad\qquad 5.2$$

for a given simulation, l. Equation 5.2 is clearly appropriate for a simple deterministic risk assessment, where the infection probability is described by a single constant value, p, for every exposure event. Often there is only one dose value available and this is then run through a dose-response model to yield a single probability of infection. Equation 5.1 is simply not an option in such circumstances. There are limitations associated with representing dose and consequently infection probability with a single value (Benke and Hamilton, 2008), nevertheless Equation 5.2 is a logical way of determining total risk under the assumption of constant infection probability per exposure event.

However, problems arise when this constant event infection probability assumption is violated. This has mostly occurred in the context of stochastic QMRAs that have used Equation 5.2 with MCS in an attempt to account for uncertainty in the dose distribution (e.g., van Ginneken and Oron, 2000; Hamilton et al., 2006; Mara et al., 2007; Seidu et al., 2008; WHO, 2006). This method is represented schematically in Figure 5.1 as Approach B. For a given simulation, l, a dose, λ_l, is drawn and, following implementation of the dose-response model, this gives rise to an event infection probability, p_l. Note that for this approach an iteration is equivalent to a simulation. Next, in an invalid attempt to determine an estimate of total risk, this process is then repeated s times. The key error in this approach is that the constant event infection probability assumption of Equation 5.1 is not met. Plainly $p_l (l = 1, 2, \ldots s)$ is not constant for each and every event of n. Iterating Equation 5.1 thousands of times with a different 'constant' value is simply pseudoreplication as reproducing a component of total risk many times over is not the same as simulating replications of the annual risk itself. The intent of the MCS to characterize uncertainty in total risk estimation is therefore not achieved in Approach B, and consequently Approach A is now recommended.

Table 5.1 *Comparison of the Karavarsamis and Hamilton (2009) and WHO (2006) methods for determining annual rotavirus infection risks pppy from the consumption of wastewater-irrigated lettuce[a]*

Wastewater quality (E. coli per 100ml)	Rotavirus infection risk per person per year			
	WHO (2006)		Karavarsamis & Hamilton (2009)	
	Median	95-percentile	Median	95-percentile
10^7–10^8	1	1	1	1
10^3–10^4	0.29	0.70	0.36	0.39
100–1000	3.4×10^{-2}	0.11	4.5×10^{-2}	4.9×10^{-2}
10–100	3.5×10^{-3}	1.3×10^{-2}	4.6×10^{-3}	5.1×10^{-3}
1–10	3.4×10^{-4}	1.2×10^{-3}	4.6×10^{-4}	5.1×10^{-4}

[a]Estimated by 10,000 Monte Carlo simulations. Assumptions: 100g lettuce eaten per person per two days; 10–15ml wastewater remaining on 100g lettuce after irrigation; 0.1–1 rotavirus per 10^5 E. coli; no pathogen die-off; $N_{50} = 6.7 \pm 25\%$ and $\alpha = 0.253 \pm 25\%$.

ESTIMATES OF NOROVIRUS INFECTION RISKS

The 'index' viral pathogen used in the 2006 Guidelines was rotavirus. However, a better index virus is norovirus (NV), which is a very common, if not the commonest, cause of gastroenteritis and certainly the commonest viral cause of gastroenteritis, affecting all age groups (Widdowson et al., 2005) – whereas rotavirus mainly affects children under the age of three – and for which dose-response data are now available (Teunis et al., 2008).

The tolerable NV disease and infection risks corresponding to a tolerable DALY loss of 10^{-5} pppy were determined using a DALY loss of 9×10^{-4} per case of NV disease (Kemmeren et al., 2006) and an NV disease/infection ratio of 0.8 (Moe, 2009) as follows:

$$\text{Tolerable NV disease risk} = \frac{\text{Tolerable DALY loss ppy}}{\text{DALY loss per case of NV disease}} = \frac{10^{-5}}{9 \times 10^{-4}} = 1.1 \times 10^{-2} \text{ pppy} \qquad 5.3$$

$$\text{Tolerable NV infection risk} = \frac{\text{Tolerable NV disease risk pppy}}{\text{NV disease/infection ratio}} = \frac{1.1 \times 10^{-2}}{0.8} = 1.4 \times 10^{-2} \text{ pppy} \qquad 5.4$$

The NV dose-response dataset of Teunis et al. (2008) was used in place of the beta-Poisson equation in the QMRA-MC computer program developed to determine median NV infection risks pppy (Teunis and Havelaar, 2000); the program was based on the Karavarsamis and Hamilton method described in this section. The resulting estimates of median risk obtained are given in Table 5.2, together with the assumptions on which they are based (which are the same as those used in the 2006 Guidelines but without pathogen die-off) (Mara and Sleigh, 2009a). This shows that a reduction of 5 log units results in an NV infection risk of 2.9×10^{-2} pppy, which is only marginally higher than the tolerable NV infection risk of 1.4×10^{-2} pppy determined above.

ESTIMATES OF *ASCARIS* INFECTION RISKS

The 2006 WHO Guidelines for the safe use of wastewater in agriculture (WHO 2006) make the same recommendation for helminth eggs as was made in the 1989 Guidelines (WHO 1989): ≤1 human intestinal nematode egg per litre of treated wastewater. The human intestinal nematodes of importance here are *Ascaris lumbricoides* (the human roundworm), *Trichuris trichiura* (the human whipworm), and *Ancylostoma duodenale* and *Necator americanus* (the human hookworms). However, epidemiological studies in Mexico have shown that, while this guideline value protects adults, it does not protect children under the age of 15 (Blumenthal et al., 1996). Blumenthal et al. (2000) therefore recommended lowering the

Table 5.2 *Median norovirus infection risks per person per year from the consumption of 100g of wastewater-irrigated lettuce every two days*[a]

Wastewater quality (*E. coli* per 100ml)	Median norovirus infection risk pppy
10^7–10^8	1
10^6–10^7	1
10^5–10^6	1
10^4–10^5	0.94
10^3–10^4	0.25
100–1000	2.9×10^{-2}
10–100	2.9×10^{-3}
1–10	2.9×10^{-4}

[a]Estimated by 10,000 Monte Carlo simulations. Assumptions: 10–15ml wastewater remaining on 100g lettuce after irrigation; 0.1–1 norovirus per 10^5 *E. coli*; no die-off between last irrigation and consumption.
Source: Mara and Sleigh (2009a)

guideline value to ≤0.1 egg per litre wherever children under 15 are exposed and the soil conditions are favourable to egg survival, but this recommendation was not accepted by the international group of experts who participated in the development and review of the Guidelines at a meeting held in Geneva in June 2005, on the grounds that it was too difficult to measure an egg concentration as low as 0.1 per litre. However, if the wastewater is treated in waste stabilization ponds (WSP), which are generally the best wastewater-treatment process in developing countries (Mara, 2004), the egg concentration in the effluent can be simply determined from the egg concentration in the untreated wastewater (which is relatively easy to measure) by using the design equation for egg removal in WSP given by Ayres et al. (1992).

Since the 2006 WHO Guidelines do not protect the health of children under 15 against intestinal nematode disease (unless, additionally, they are dewormed at home or at school), QMRA can be used to determine how best children under 15 can be protected against *Ascaris* infection, now that *Ascaris* dose-response data are available (for details see Chapter 4).

For a tolerable DALY loss of 10^{-5} pppy, a DALY loss per case of ascariasis of 8.25×10^{-3} (Chan, 1997) and, as a worst case scenario, an *Ascaris* disease/infection ratio of 1 (i.e. all those infected with *Ascaris* develop ascariasis), the tolerable *Ascaris* infection risk is given by:

$$\frac{\text{Tolerable DALY loss ppy}}{\text{DALY loss per case of ascariasis}} = \frac{10^{-5}}{8.25 \times 10^{-3}} = 1.2 \times 10^{-3} \text{ pppy} \qquad 5.5$$

Median *Ascaris* infection risks pppy from the consumption by children under 15 of raw carrots irrigated with wastewaters containing specified numbers of *Ascaris* eggs were determined by a QMRA-Monte Carlo computer program based on the Karavarsamis and Hamilton method described in this chapter. The resulting estimates of median *Ascaris* infection risk obtained, and the assumptions on which they are based, are given in Table 5.3 (Mara and Sleigh, 2009b). This shows that one egg per litre results in an *Ascaris* infection risk of 6×10^{-3} pppy and 0.1 egg per litre in one of 6×10^{-4} pppy; these risks are higher and lower, respectively, than the tolerable *Ascaris* infection risk of 10^{-3} pppy determined above. This could be taken to confirm the finding of Blumenthal et al. (1996) that ≤1 egg per litre is not protective of children under 15, and thus reinforce the recommendation of Blumenthal et al. (2000) that, when children under 15 are exposed, the guideline value should be ≤0.1 egg per litre. However, as noted in the 2006 WHO Guidelines (and in Chapter 3), post-treatment health-protection control measures (Table 5.4) achieve significant pathogen reductions, so that wastewater treatment does not have to achieve the total pathogen reduction required to protect consumer health. This is discussed further below.

PATHOGEN REDUCTION ACHIEVED BY PRODUCE-WASHING AND DISINFECTION

The 2006 Guidelines allocate a 1 log unit pathogen reduction to washing wastewater-irrigated food crops in clean water, a 2 log unit reduction to produce

Table 5.3 *Median* Ascaris *infection risks for children under 15 from the consumption of raw wastewater-irrigated carrots[a]*

Number of Ascaris eggs per litre of wastewater	Median Ascaris infection risk pppy	Notes
100–1000	0.86	Raw wastewaters in hyperendemic areas.
10–100	0.24	Raw wastewaters in endemic areas.
1–10	2.9×10^{-2}	Treated wastewaters.
1	5.5×10^{-3}	Wastewater quality required to comply with the 1989 and 2006 WHO Guidelines.
0.1–1	3.0×10^{-3}	Highly treated wastewaters.
0.1	5.5×10^{-4}	Wastewater quality recommended by Blumenthal et al. (2000).
0.01–0.1	3.0×10^{-4}	Treated wastewaters in non-endemic areas.

[a]Estimated by 10,000 Monte Carlo simulations. Assumptions: 30–50g raw carrots consumed per child per week (Navarro et al., 2009); 3–5ml wastewater remaining on 100g carrots after irrigation (Mara et al., 2007); $N_{50} = 859 \pm 25\%$ and $\alpha = 0.104 \pm 25\%$; no *Ascaris* die-off between final irrigation and consumption.
Source: Mara and Sleigh (2009b)

disinfection and also a 2 log unit reduction to produce peeling. Amoah et al. (2007) investigated 'common and improved sanitary washing methods for the reduction of coliform bacteria and helminth eggs on vegetables' in urban West Africa, where 56–90 per cent of the households and 80–100 per cent of the restaurants were found to use some kind of disinfectant for washing leafy vegetables to be eaten raw, with the rest using only water. In laboratory studies produce disinfection with Eau de Javel® (a chlorine solution commonly used for salad washing in francophone West Africa) achieved a 3-log unit reduction of faecal coliforms on lettuce after a contact time of ten minutes and subsequent rinsing in clean water. Helminth eggs were most effectively removed from lettuce by washing with water under an open tap; this achieved a reduction from nine eggs per 100g to one egg per 100g. More details on this are in Chapter 12.

APPLICATION TO URBAN AGRICULTURE IN DEVELOPING COUNTRIES

Exposure varies due to differences in consumption patterns which need to be accounted for in the risk calculations. For example, Seidu et al. (2008) reported that people in urban Ghana commonly consume 10–12g of lettuce in 'fast food' on each of four days per week. This refers to a specific situation in one developing country and this may or may not be representative of what happens elsewhere, but it is much less than the 100g of lettuce consumed on alternate days used by Shuval et al. (1997) to reflect the situation in Israel. Infection risks for this Ghanaian consumption of lettuce were simulated by a QMRA-Monte Carlo computer program based on the Karavarsamis and Hamilton method described in this chapter. The resulting risks, together with the assumptions on which they are based, are given in Table 5.4, which shows that a reduction of 4 log units results in a norovirus infection risk of 3.6×10^{-2} pppy, which is only marginally higher than the tolerable norovirus infection risk determined in the section for a tolerable DALY loss of 10^{-5} pppy. (Of course, if a larger quantity of lettuce were to be consumed, then the risk of infection would be correspondingly higher.) The required 4 log unit reduction (Table 5.4) could be achieved by, for example, a 1 log unit reduction by wastewater treatment and a 3 log unit reduction by produce disinfection (or, if disinfection is not routinely or reliably practised, a 2 log unit reduction through die-off and a 1 log unit reduction by produce-washing in clean water).

Implications for wastewater treatment

In the above example wastewater treatment is required to produce only a single log unit pathogen reduction. This can be readily achieved by very simple treatment processes, such as an anaerobic pond, a three-tank or three-pond system and

Table 5.4 *Median norovirus infection risks pppy from the consumption of 10–12g of wastewater-irrigated lettuce on four occasions per week*[a]

Wastewater quality (E. coli per 100ml)	Median norovirus infection risk pppy
10^7–10^8	1
10^6–10^7	1
10^5–10^6	0.97
10^4–10^5	0.30
10^3–10^4	3.6×10^{-2}
100–1000	3.6×10^{-3}
10–100	3.6×10^{-4}
1–10	3.6×10^{-5}

[a]Estimated by 10,000 Monte Carlo simulations. Assumptions: 10–15ml wastewater remaining on 100g lettuce after irrigation; 0.1–1 norovirus per 10^5 E. coli; no die-off between last irrigation and consumption.

overnight settling. The three-tank or three-pond system is operated as a sequential batch-fed process: on any one day one tank or pond is filled with wastewater, the contents of another are settling and the contents of the third are used for irrigation. This is a very reliable, almost foolproof system. In small-scale urban agriculture, as opposed to large-farm agriculture, a single tank is generally sufficient (and more affordable): on any day in the morning the tank contents are used for crop watering, and the tank is then refilled and its contents allowed to settle until the following morning.

For helminth eggs, if it is assumed that in areas where ascariasis is endemic untreated wastewater contains 100 *Ascaris* eggs per litre, a 3 log unit egg reduction is required to achieve 0.1 egg per litre. For root vegetables eaten raw and assuming that a 2 log unit reduction occurs through produce peeling prior to consumption (WHO, 2006), wastewater treatment is required to effect a reduction of 1 log unit from 100 to 10 eggs per litre. This reduction can also be achieved by any of the three methods described above. In hyperendemic areas (1000 eggs per litre of untreated wastewater) a further log unit reduction is required; this could be achieved by rinsing the peeled produce in a weak detergent solution and rinsing with clean water.

NOTE

1 The QMRA-Monte Carlo computer programs used in the preparation of this chapter are available at www.personal.leeds.ac.uk/~cen6ddm/QMRA.html. All these programs, with the exception of the one for *Ascaris*, use a range of pathogen-to-*E. coli* numbers – for example, 0.1–1 pathogen per 10^5 *E. coli*. This approach was taken by Shuval et al. (1997) and adopted in the 2006 WHO Guidelines, as there are very few, and in many situations no, data on pathogen numbers in developing-country wastewaters,

whereas *E. coli* numbers are available or, if not available, are easy to obtain. However, setting the range of pathogen numbers to 10^5–10^5 per 10^5 *E. coli* in the QMRA-MC programs (i.e., equating pathogen and *E. coli* numbers) means that the programs determine the pathogen risks directly, so that the first column in Tables 5.1, 5.2 and 5.4 would express the wastewater quality in terms of a range of pathogen numbers per 100ml (or any other desired unit volume), rather than as a range of *E. coli* numbers per 100ml.

REFERENCES

Amoah, P., Drechsel, P., Abaidoo, R. C. and Klutse, A. (2007) 'Effectiveness of common and improved sanitary washing methods in selected cities of West Africa for the reduction of coliform bacteria and helminth eggs on vegetables', *Tropical Medicine and International Health*, vol 12 (s2), pp40–50

Asano, T., Leong, L. Y. C., Rigby, M. G. and Sakaji, R. H. (1992) 'Evaluation of the California wastewater reclamation criteria using enteric virus monitoring data', *Water Science and Technology*, vol 26, nos 7–8, pp1513–24

Ayres, R. M., Alabaster, G. P., Mara, D. D. and Lee, D. L. (1992) 'A design equation for human intestinal nematode egg removal in waste stabilization ponds', *Water Research*, vol 26, no 6, pp863–5

Benke, K. K. and Hamilton, A. J. (2008) 'Quantitative microbial risk assessment: Uncertainty and measures of central tendency for skewed distributions', *Stochastic Environmental Research and Risk Assessment*, vol 22, no 4, pp533–9

Blumenthal, U. J., Mara, D. D., Ayres, R. M. et al. (1996) 'Evaluation of the WHO nematode egg guidelines for restricted and unrestricted irrigation', *Water Science and Technology*, vol 33, nos 10–11, pp277–83

Blumenthal, U. J., Mara, D. D., Peasey, A., Ruiz-Palacios, G. and Stott, R. (2000) 'Guidelines for the microbiological quality of treated wastewater used in agriculture: Recommendations for revising the WHO Guidelines', *Bulletin of the World Health Organization*, vol 78, no 9, pp1104–16

Chan, M.-S. (1997) 'The global burden of intestinal nematode infections – fifty years on', *Parasitology Today*, vol 13, no 11, pp438–43

Fewtrell, L. and Bartram, J. (2001) *Water Quality: Guidelines, Standards and Health; Assessment of Risk and Risk Management for Water-Related Infectious Disease*, International Water Association (IWA) on behalf on the World Health Organization, London

Ginneken, M. van and Oron, G. (2000) 'Risk assessment of consuming agricultural products irrigated with reclaimed wastewater: An exposure model', *Water Resources Research*, vol 36, no 9, pp2691–9

Hamilton, A. J., Stagnitti, F., Premier, R., Boland, A. M. and Hale, G. (2006) 'Quantitative microbial risk assessment models for consumption of raw vegetables irrigated with reclaimed water', *Applied and Environmental Microbiology*, vol 72, no 5, pp3284–90

Karavarsamis, N. and Hamilton, A. J. (2009) 'Estimators of annual infection risk', *Journal of Water and Health* (in press)

Kemmeren, J. M., Mangen, M. J. J., van Duynhoven, Y. T. H. P. and Havelaar, A. H. (2006) *Priority Setting of Foodborne Pathogens: Disease Burden and Costs of Selected*

Enteric Pathogens (RIVM Report 330080001/2006), National Institute for Public Health and the Environment (RIVM), Bilthoven, The Netherlands

Mara, D. D. (2004) *Domestic Wastewater Treatment in Developing Countries*, Earthscan, London

Mara, D. D. and Sleigh, P. A. (2009a) 'Estimation of norovirus infection risks to consumers of wastewater-irrigated food crops eaten raw', *Journal of Water and Health* (in press)

Mara, D. D. and Sleigh, P. A. (2009b) 'Estimation of *Ascaris* infection risks in children under 15 from the consumption of wastewater-irrigated carrots', *Journal of Water and Health* (in press)

Mara, D. D., Sleigh, P. A., Blumenthal, U. J. and Carr, R. M. (2007) 'Health risks in wastewater irrigation: Comparing estimates from quantitative microbial risk analyses and epidemiological studies', *Journal of Water and Health*, vol 5, no 1, pp39–50

Moe, C. L. (2009) 'Preventing norovirus transmission: How should we handle food handlers?', *Clinical Infectious Diseases*, vol 48, no 1, pp38–40

Navarro, I., Jiménez, B., Cifuentes, E. and Lucario, S. (2009) 'Application of helminth ova infection dose curve to estimate the risks associated with biosolids application on soil', *Journal of Water and Health*, vol 7, no 1, pp31–44

Seidu, R., Heistad, A., Amoah, P., Drechsel, P., Jensen, P. D. and Stenström, T. A. (2008) 'Quantification of the health risk associated with wastewater reuse in Accra, Ghana: A contribution toward local guidelines', *Journal of Water and Health*, vol 6, no 4, pp641–71

Shuval, H. I., Lampert, Y. and Fattal, B. (1997) 'Development of a risk assessment approach for evaluating wastewater reuse standards for agriculture', *Water Science and Technology*, vol 35, nos 11–12, pp15–20

Signor, R. S. and Ashbolt, N. J. (2009) 'Comparing probabilistic microbial risk assessments for drinking-water against daily rather than annualised infection probability targets', *Journal of Water and Health* (in press)

Teunis, P. F. M. and Havelaar, A. H. (2000) 'The beta-Poisson dose-response model is not a single-hit model', *Risk Analysis*, vol 20, no 4, pp513–20

Teunis, P. F. M., Moe, C. L., Liu, P., Miller, S. E., Lindesmith, L., Baric, R. S., Le Pendu, J. and Calderon, R. L. (2008) 'Norwalk virus: How infectious is it?', *Journal of Medical Virology*, vol 80, no 8, pp1468–76

WHO (1989) *Health Guidelines for the Use of Wastewater in Agriculture and Aquaculture* Technical Report Series no 778, World Health Organization, Geneva

WHO (2006) *Guidelines for the Safe Use of Wastewater, Excreta and Greywater, Volume 2: Wastewater Use in Agriculture*, World Health Organization, Geneva

WHO (2007) *Levels of Protection*, World Health Organization, Geneva, available at www. who.int/water_sanitation_health/gdwqrevision/levelsofprotection/en/index.html (accessed 28 March 2009)

Widdowson, M.-A., Sulka, A., Bulens, S. N., Beard, R. S., Chaves, S. S., Hammond, R., Salehi, E. D., Swanson, E., Totarc, J., Woron, R., Mead, P. S., Bresee, J. S., Monroe, S. S. and Glass, R. I. (2005) 'Norovirus and foodborne disease, United States, 1991–2000', *Emerging Infectious Diseases*, vol 11, no 1, pp95–102

6

Non-Pathogenic Trade-Offs of Wastewater Irrigation

Manzoor Qadir and Christopher A. Scott

ABSTRACT

The volume and extent of urban wastewater generated by domestic, industrial and commercial water use has increased with population, urbanization, industrialization, improved living conditions and economic development. Most developing-country governments do not have sufficient resources to treat wastewater. Therefore, despite official restrictions and potential health implications, farmers in many developing countries use wastewater in diluted, untreated or partly treated forms with a large range of associated benefits. Aside from microbiological hazards, the practice can pose a variety of other potential risks: excessive and often imbalanced addition of nutrients to the soil; build-up of salts in the soils (depending on the source water, especially sodium salts); increased concentrations of metals and metalloids (particularly where industries are present) reaching phytotoxic levels over the long term; and accumulation of emerging contaminants, like residual pharmaceuticals. As these possible trade-offs of wastewater use vary significantly between sites and regions, it is necessary to carefully monitor wastewater quality, its sources and use for location-specific risk assessment and risk reduction.

INTRODUCTION

Increased population, urbanization, improved living conditions and economic development have driven the generation of increased volumes of wastewater by the domestic, industrial and commercial sectors (Asano et al., 2007; Lazarova and

Bahri, 2005; Qadir et al., 2009). In most developing countries, urban drainage and disposal systems are such that domestic wastewater is mixed with industrial wastewater. Although water-quality management is reported to be a high priority and a major concern of developing-country governments, most do not have sufficient resources to treat wastewater. In India, only 24 per cent of wastewater generated by households and industry is treated before its use in agriculture or disposal to rivers (Minhas and Samra, 2003). In Pakistan, only 2 per cent of wastewater is treated (IWMI, 2003). Similar challenges are found in other parts of Asia, Africa and Latin America (Scott et al., 2004). Wastewater treatment plants in most cities in developing countries are non-existent or function inadequately (Qadir et al., 2007). Therefore, wastewater in partially treated, diluted or untreated form is diverted and used by urban and peri-urban farmers to grow a range of crops (Ensink et al., 2002; Murtaza et al., 2009).

Contrary to the situation of wastewater management in most developing countries, the use of recycled (treated) wastewater has been on the increase in recent years in several countries in the Middle East and North Africa, the Mediterranean, and parts of the USA, Latin America and Australia (Qadir et al., 2007; USEPA, 2004).

Despite official restrictions and potential health implications, farmers in many developing countries use diluted, untreated or partly treated wastewater because:

- Wastewater is a reliable or often the only water source available for irrigation throughout the year.
- Wastewater irrigation often reduces the need for fertilizer application as it is a source of nutrients.
- Wastewater use involves less energy even when pumping, if the alternative clean water source is from deep groundwater, which reduces costs.
- Wastewater generates additional benefits including greater income from cultivation and marketing of high-value crops such as vegetables, which create year-round employment opportunities (Buechler and Mekala, 2005; IWMI, 2003; Keraita and Drechsel, 2004; Keraita et al., 2008; Lazarova and Bahri, 2005).

Research and decision-making on wastewater irrigation have tended to focus on the impacts on the health of food consumers and producers, economic implications for producers' livelihoods, and food diversity, quality and prices. However, the biophysical implications (both positive and negative) of wastewater use and management in agricultural ecosystems have received relatively little attention (Asano et al., 2007; Lazarova and Bahri, 2005; Pescod, 1992; Pettygrove and Asano, 1985; Qadir et al., 2009).

This chapter addresses environmental quality in wastewater source and use areas, including natural water bodies that receive wastewater, through conceptual and empirical case-study consideration of the following constituents and processes: macro- and micronutrient levels; concentrations of total salts and specific ion species; levels of heavy metals; and presence and intensity of organic constituents. Environmental quality, and the positive and negative trade-offs of these constituents and processes (Table 6.1) are the focus of this chapter. Pathogenic risks (viruses, bacteria, protozoa, helminth eggs and faecal coliforms) are addressed in Chapters 3, 4 and 5.

WASTEWATER SOURCES AND THEIR POSSIBLE IMPLICATIONS

Wastewater is a generic term used for any water that has been adversely affected in quality by anthropogenic activities. Urban wastewater may be a combination of some or all domestic effluent, water from commercial establishments, industrial effluent and stormwater that does not infiltrate into soil and other urban run-off. Wastewater contains a broad spectrum of contaminants resulting from different sources, warranting suitable treatment to remove such substances before it should be used in agriculture to grow a range of crops.

Greywater comprises 50–80 per cent of residential wastewater. It is a specific term that refers to water generated from domestic processes such as dishwashing, laundry and bathing, but does not include wastewater from toilets, which is termed blackwater. Greywater is distinct from blackwater in the amount and composition of its chemical and biological contaminants. It gets its name from its cloudy appearance and from its status as being neither freshwater nor heavily polluted.

Wastewater contains different types and levels of undesirable constituents, depending on the source from which it is generated and the level of its treatment. In general, industrial wastewater contains higher levels of contaminants – metals and metalloids, and volatiles and semi-volatiles – than domestic wastewater and needs greater treatment before disposal or use. In contrast, domestic wastewater contains higher levels of pathogens. Because of the presence of residues of detergents and soaps, domestic wastewater is usually alkaline (pH > 7) unless it gets mixed with some acidic industrial constituents. In the case of mixed domestic-industrial wastewater, a common situation in developing countries, the composition of raw wastewater depends on the types and numbers of industrial units and the characteristics of the residual constituents. Table 6.1 provides an overview of different constituents of wastewater and their possible implications for agriculture, ecosystems and human health, as well as importance regionally.

POSITIVE TRADE-OFFS

Reliable irrigation supply

In general, a reliable supply of water for irrigation and essential nutrients are critical inputs to crop-production systems; to a large extent, wastewater irrigation fulfils

Table 6.1 *Constituents of wastewater and their possible implications*

Constituent	Implications: Positive	Implications: Negative	Geographical occurrence
Macronutrients: Nitrogen (N), phosphorous (P) and potassium (K)	• No or minimal need for chemical N, P and K fertilizers • N supplied through wastewater helps in crop establishment in early growth stages by mitigating the negative effects of excess salts if added through wastewater irrigation or present in pre-irrigation soil • P added to the wastewater-irrigated soil helps in crop establishment throughout the growth period • Optimal level of K helps in crop maturity and quality, and in mitigating the negative effects of excess salts (particularly sodium) applied through wastewater irrigation or present in pre-irrigation soil	• Excess N applied through wastewater may lead to excessive vegetative growth (green biomass), delay in crop maturity, lodging and low economic yield • Excess N and P in wastewater can cause eutrophication of natural water bodies and in irrigation systems, undesirable growth of algae, periphyton attached algae and weeds • Leaching of N can cause groundwater pollution and methaemoglobinemia (generally in infants) in case of drinking N-rich groundwater (particularly high levels of nitrates, NO_3) • P can accumulate in the soil where it is immobile	• Particularly in developing countries where wastewater has high organic content (from domestic, residential, food-processing sources) and is used in untreated, partly treated and diluted forms
Total dissolved solids (TDS) and major ionic elements: sodium (Na), calcium (Ca), magnesium (Mg), chloride (Cl) and boron (B)	• Ca supplied through wastewater improves soil structure and counterbalances the negative effects of accompanying high concentrations of Na and Mg • High electrolyte concentration, particularly resulting from Ca salts, improves hydraulic properties of low-permeability soils	• Excess Na and Mg can cause deterioration of soil structure and undesirable effects on hydraulic properties such as infiltration rate and hydraulic conductivity • Excess salts impact plant growth through osmotic effects • Specific ion effects from Cl, B and Na possible, including phytotoxicity • Deterioration of water quality of natural surface-water bodies receiving wastewater or drainage from wastewater-irrigated land • Salt leaching into groundwater	• Particularly in arid and semi-arid areas with high primary salinity where large-scale wastewater irrigation is practised and agricultural drainage is either non-existent or non-functional, or where saline drainage water is reused in irrigation

Table 6.1 *(Continued)*

Constituent	Implications: Positive	Implications: Negative	Geographical occurrence
Metals and metalloids: cadmium (Cd), chromium (Cr), nickel (Ni), zinc (Zn), lead (Pb), arsenic (As), selenium (Se), mercury (Hg), copper (Cu), manganese (Mn)	• No or minimal need for micronutrient fertilizers supplying essential metals ions such as Cu, Zn, Fe, and Mn	• Excess levels in irrigated soils and the environment may reach phytotoxic levels • Systemic uptake by crops, particularly those consumed by humans and animals • Possible toxicity in humans and animals • Possible contamination of groundwater under highly permeable and shallow water table conditions	• Particularly in rapidly industrializing regions, like south and southeast Asia, where industrial waste is often mixed with domestic wastewater. • In Africa more localized e.g. near mining areas or tanneries
High organic matter content, suspended solids and algal particles	• Organic matter added through wastewater improves soil structure; can enhance cation exchange capacity and bind, and gradually releases essential nutrients for crop growth • Organic matter may also hold some undesirable metal ions rendering them in less available form for plants • Can contain nutrients	• Plugging of micro irrigation systems such as drippers and sprinklers • Hypoxic conditions due to depletion of dissolved oxygen in water • Possible occurrence of septic conditions • Possibility of increased mortality in fish and other aquatic species	• Particularly in developing countries where wastewater that is high in food, industrial and/or organic content is used in untreated or partly treated forms
Emerging contaminants (residual pharmaceuticals, endocrine disruptor compounds, active residues of personal care products)	• Only limited evidence of possible uptake by crops and the food chain, especially in developing countries where use of pharmaceuticals and personal care products is lower than in developed countries	• Possible contamination of groundwater with emerging contaminants and other contaminants, particularly under highly permeable and shallow water table conditions	• Particularly in developed countries or where industries release residual pharmaceuticals, endocrine disrupting compounds and active residues of personal care products into wastewater without treatment
Pathogens: viruses, bacteria, protozoa, helminth eggs, faecal coliforms	• None	• Can cause a range of communicable diseases for farmers, traders and food consumers, such as diarrhoea, typhoid, dysentery, cholera, gastroenteritis, ascariasis, hepatitis, ulcer, food-poisoning	• Particularly in low-income countries in tropical regions where sanitation is poor and endemic disease burden is high, like in sub-Saharan Africa

both. This is particularly important in situations where wastewater is the only source of irrigation water available throughout the year. Estimates show that at least 20 million hectares are irrigated globally with different forms of wastewater – treated, untreated, partly treated and diluted (Jiménez and Asano, 2008; Raschid-Sally and Jayakody, 2008). In terms of irrigation potential in countries producing large volumes of wastewater, Minhas and Samra (2004) estimated that wastewater generated from large urban settings in India alone can irrigate 1.5 million ha. The supply of this water is continuous and independent of the rainfall, although it is still subject to scarcity resulting from drought, canal irrigation systems and availability of electricity. Although the land holdings in wastewater-irrigated areas are often small, irrigation allows for year-round farming, which may help smallholders escape from poverty.

Nutrient availability

The nutrient potential of wastewater stems from its composition, which in turn depends on the source of generation, dilution and treatment aspects. This is illustrated in Table 6.2, which shows concentrations of macronutrients (nitrogen, N; phosphorous, P; and potassium, K) in wastewater generated from some cities in India. The concentrations of these nutrient elements are highly variable: N (11–98mg per litre), P (1–30mg per litre) and K (16–500mg per litre).

The concentrations of nutrients vary widely in wastewater. Although the nutrient-supplying capacity is considered to be a major driver for untreated wastewater use in agriculture, managing the nutrient availability in wastewater is a challenge. Treatment is generally considered to remove most nutrients, implying that farmers favour untreated over treated wastewater as an irrigation source. Comparative evaluation of macronutrient concentrations in untreated and treated wastewater from Haryana, India (Figure 6.1) suggests otherwise, revealing that treated wastewater contained sufficient levels of these nutrients (Yadav et al., 2002). The concentration of N in untreated wastewater (40.1mg per litre) decreased to 29.7mg per litre in treated wastewater, indicating 74 per cent of N was retained. The percentages of P and K retained in treated wastewater were 79 per cent and 57 per cent, respectively.

Table 6.2 *Concentrations of macronutrients (N, P and K) in wastewater generated from some cities in India*

Location	N (mg l^{-1})	P (mg l^{-1})	K (mg l^{-1})	Reference
Nagpur	55–68	9–11	31–37	Kaul et al. (2002)
Calcutta	14–17	1–2	16	Mitra and Gupta (1999)
Haryana	32–70	15–30	250–500	Gupta et al. (1998)
Haryana	25–98	4–13	28–152	Baddesha et al. (1986)
Indore	11–64	1	20–54	CSSRI (2004)

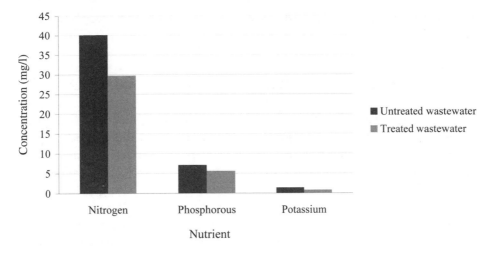

Figure 6.1 *Comparative evaluation of macronutrient concentrations in untreated and treated wastewater from Haryana, India*

Source: Based on the data from Yadav et al. (2002)

Table 6.3 *Concentrations of micronutrients (Fe, Zn and Mn) in wastewater generated from some cities in India*

Location	Fe (mg l^{-1})	Zn (mg l^{-1})	Mn (mg l^{-1})	Reference
Nagpur	1.41–1.57	0.9–1.2	0.14–0.20	Kaul et al. (2002)
Calcutta	449–656	0.3–0.4	0.65–0.66	Mitra and Gupta (1999)
Haryana	6–25	1.6–28.0	0.8–2.8	Gupta et al. (1998)
Haryana	0.6–21.8	0.13–0.90	0.25–0.60	Baddesha et al. (1986)
Indore	0.14–0.21	0.01–0.11	0.19–2.14	CSSRI (2004)

In addition to macronutrients, wastewater irrigation also adds a range of micronutrients such as iron (Fe), zinc (Zn), manganese (Mn) and copper (Cu). Table 6.3 provides information on the concentrations of micronutrients in wastewater generated from some cities in India.

Although the fertilizer value of wastewater is of great importance, periodic monitoring is required to estimate the nutrient loads in wastewater and adjust fertilizer applications (Lazarova and Bahri, 2005). Excessive nutrients can cause nutrient imbalances, undesirable vegetative growth and delayed or uneven maturity, and can also reduce crop quality and pollute groundwater and surface water. However, an optimal supply of macro- and micronutrients through treated wastewater eliminates or minimizes the need for the application of costly chemical fertilizers.

ORGANIC MATTER AND ORGANIC CARBON

Like the supply of nutrients through wastewater irrigation, the presence of organic matter in wastewater may have positive or negative implications depending on the nature of the organic materials. In terms of positive effects, organic matter added through wastewater improves soil structure, acts as a storehouse of essential nutrients for crop growth and enhances charge characteristics of irrigated soils, such as cation exchange capacity (CEC), which may hold undesirable metal ions on the cation exchange sites rendering them in less available form for plants. Since heavy metals in ionic form are positively charged cations, an increase in CEC results in greater chances of cations being adsorbed on the soil's exchange sites.

Studies undertaken in India on the long-term effects of wastewater irrigation on the physical properties of soil reveal an increase in aggregate stability, water-holding capacity, hydraulic conductivity and total porosity (Jayaraman et al., 1983; Minhas and Samra, 2004). There was almost a consistent increase in these soil parameters with wastewater-irrigation duration. For example, the hydraulic conductivity of the freshwater-irrigated soil was 19.1cm h^{-1}, which increased to 23.6cm h^{-1} after 15 years of wastewater irrigation; a 24 per cent increase in soil hydraulic conductivity. It further increased to 26.6cm h^{-1} after 25 years of wastewater irrigation; a 39 per cent increase over freshwater-irrigated soil (Table 6.4). The data on gradual increase in soil hydraulic conductivity in wastewater-irrigated soils suggest an increase of about 1.5 per cent per year. Soil hydraulic conductivity is a crucial soil physical parameter that indicates the ease of water movement through the soil profile. The increase in other soil physical parameters, such as aggregate stability, water-holding capacity and total porosity, contributes to water storage in the soil, thereby increasing water-use efficiency and productivity. This is particularly important under conditions in which water resources for agriculture are scarce.

In addition to the beneficial effects of soil organic matter on soil physical parameters, the organic carbon status of wastewater-irrigated soils increases irrespective of soil and agro-climatic conditions. Baddesha et al. (1997) observed an increase in the organic carbon level of the upper 0.3m soil depth with the application of wastewater for irrigation in India. Minhas and Samra (2004) reported that sandy loam soils irrigated with wastewater had higher organic carbon levels than those irrigated with groundwater. Studies on the long-term effects of wastewater irrigation reveal an increase in soil organic carbon of 80 per cent after 15 years of wastewater irrigation (Jayaraman et al., 1983; Minhas and Samra, 2004). The soil organic carbon level in freshwater-irrigated soil was 1.42 per cent, which increased to 2.56 per cent (Figure 6.2). As depicted by the organic carbon status

Table 6.4 *Effects of 15 and 25 years of wastewater irrigation on selected soil physical properties*

Soil physical parameter	Freshwater	Wastewater (15 years)	Wastewater (25 years)
Aggregate stability (%)	72.4	84.4 (17)[a]	83.5 (15)
Water-holding capacity (%)	33.2	49.7 (50)	59.8 (79)
Hydraulic conductivity (cm h⁻¹)	19.1	23.6 (24)	26.6 (39)
Total porosity (%)	36.2	49.7 (37)	59.8 (65)

[a]Figures in parenthesis in the last two columns indicate percentage increase in the selected parameters in wastewater-irrigated soil over the soil irrigated with freshwater.
Source: Modified from Jayaraman et al. (1983); Minhas and Samra (2004)

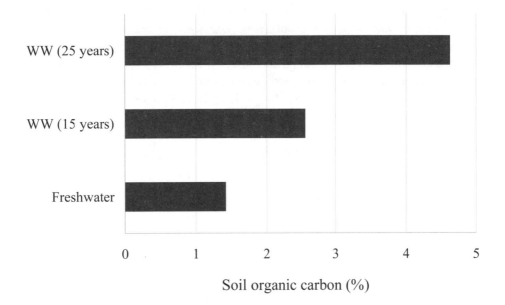

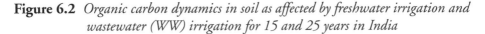

Soil organic carbon (%)

Figure 6.2 *Organic carbon dynamics in soil as affected by freshwater irrigation and wastewater (WW) irrigation for 15 and 25 years in India*

Source: Based on the data from Jayaraman et al. (1983)

of soil irrigated with wastewater for 25 years, this trend continued as the organic carbon percentage increased to 4.63 per cent, indicating a 226 per cent increase over the freshwater-irrigated soil and an 81 per cent increase over the soil irrigated with wastewater for 15 years.

Although soils of arid and semi-arid regions have low levels of organic carbon (Lal, 2001), this soil carbon pool is not only important for the soil to perform its productivity and environmental functions, but also plays a vital role in the global carbon cycle (Lal, 2004). In addition to providing essential nutrients and improving soil physical properties, wastewater irrigation contributes to mitigating the accelerated greenhouse effects by increasing soil organic carbon, which is a crucial soil quality parameter.

SOLUBLE SALTS AND CALCIUM

The high dissolved solids concentrations of most wastewater may in general have negative consequences for its use in irrigation as indicated in Table 6.1. However, for some sodic and saline-sodic soils with low permeability (low infiltration rate and low hydraulic conductivity), the presence of inorganic electrolytes in wastewater, particularly resulting from Ca salts, improves hydraulic properties. These soils are characterized by the occurrence of excess sodium (Na^+) at levels that can adversely affect soil structure. Structural problems in these soils created by certain physical processes (slaking, swelling and dispersion of clay minerals) and specific conditions (surface crusting and hard-setting) may affect water and air movement, run-off and erosion, sowing operations, seedling emergence, root penetration and crop development (Qadir and Schubert, 2002). Therefore, high-electrolyte wastewater containing an adequate proportion of divalent cations such as Ca^{2+} can be used for sodic and saline-sodic soil amelioration without the need to apply a calcium-supplying amendment (see Chapter 11).

NEGATIVE TRADE-OFFS

Excessive levels of nutrients

Maintaining adequate levels of nutrients in wastewater is a challenging task because of the possible negative impacts of their excessive addition to the wastewater-irrigated soils. In the case of macronutrients such as N and P, there are three possible impact pathways:

- Excess N applied through wastewater may lead to excessive vegetative growth (green biomass), delay in maturity, lodging and low economic yield.
- Excess N and P in wastewater can cause eutrophication of natural water bodies and in irrigation systems, undesirable growth of algae, periphyton attached algae and weeds.
- Leaching of N can cause groundwater pollution and methaemoglobinemia (decreased ability of blood to carry vital oxygen around the body, generally in infants) in case of drinking N-rich groundwater (particularly high levels of nitrates, NO_3).

Nitrates are highly soluble and can easily be moved through wastewater-irrigated soils. The implication of the retention of nutrients and other wastewater

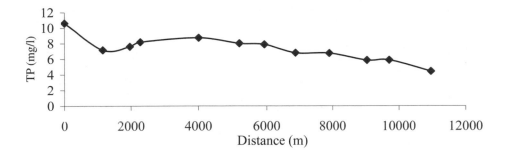

Figure 6.3 *Total phosphorous (TP) with distance downstream of discharge point, Rio Guanajuato, Mexico, 1998*

Source: Scott et al. (2000)

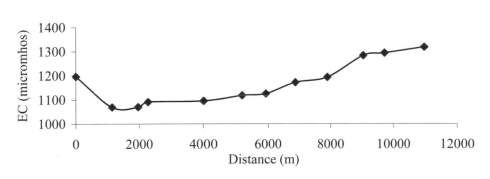

Figure 6.4 *Electrical conductivity (EC) with distance downstream of discharge point, Rio Guanajuato, Mexico, 1998*

Source: Scott et al. (2000)

contaminants in soil is that they do not reach water bodies into which wastewater would otherwise be disposed.

Nevertheless, the impact of wastewater discharge on receiving waters poses a significant challenge. Particularly in arid and semi-arid regions, irrigation withdrawal of wastewater-dominated river flows and the return flow of drainage result in two biophysical processes that have been observed in different contexts worldwide. First, high nutrient concentrations tend to be ameliorated through land application of wastewater and the retention of both P and N in agricultural produce. Fodder grass is especially well suited to wastewater irrigation (with relatively continuous year-round flow) and acts to retain N and P applied in wastewater. Figure 6.3 presents illustrative results of total phosphorous (TP) concentration in river flow in Mexico with the distance downstream of the wastewater discharge point (Scott et al., 2000).

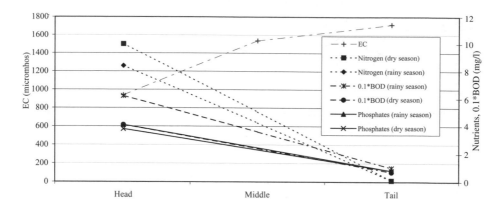

Figure 6.5 *Head–tail water quality, Tula Irrigation District, Mexico, 1997–98*

The second process is salt concentration in receiving waters both as a result of high total dissolved solids (TDS) in wastewater and due to the high irrigation applications of wastewater, whether for leaching requirements or available supplies. Successive reuse of wastewater along the river course builds up TDS, while the biochemical oxygen demand (BOD) and nutrient levels decrease, as shown in Figures 6.4 and 6.5 for wastewater-dominated rivers in two separate locations in Mexico. Similar results have been reported for Hyderabad, India, by McCartney et al. (2008).

EXCESSIVE LEVELS OF SALTS AND SODIUM

As noted above, wastewater is more saline than freshwater because salts are added to it from different sources (Qadir and Minhas, 2008). There are no economically viable means to remove the salts once they enter wastewater because the techniques are prohibitively expensive, such as cation exchange resins or reverse osmosis membranes, which are only used to produce high-quality recycled water (Toze, 2006a). Saline wastewater contains excess levels of soluble salts while sodic water is characterized by excess levels of Na^+. In many cases, both salts and Na^+ are present in excess concentrations, resulting in saline-sodic wastewater (Qadir et al., 2007).

Salts and other inorganic contaminants in wastewater originate from two broad categories of industries. The first category includes those industries that generate wastes with high salt concentrations. Examples are rayon plants and the chemical manufacturing industry (caustic soda, soap and detergents), among others. The second category consists of industries that generate varying levels of toxic wastes; for example, pesticides, fertilizers, pharmaceuticals and chromium-rich waste (Minhas and Samra, 2004). The amount and type of salts used in an industry and the relevant treatment affect its wastewater quality. In addition, the implications are complex when industrial or commercial brine waste streams are not discharged into separate waste sewers, but into main urban sewers that convey wastewater to the treatment plants or to disposal channels leading to farmers' fields. There are no restrictions on salt concentrations in industrial wastewater to be discharged into urban sewers (Lazarova and Bahri, 2005). Therefore, salinity and sodicity levels in mixed domestic-industrial wastewater largely depend on salt concentrations and the relative volume of industrial wastewater to domestic wastewater.

Salinity and sodicity related characteristics in wastewater generated in different areas of the Indian subcontinent are given in Table 6.5. Salinity (EC) levels ranged from 1.9 to 4.0 dS m^{-1} while sodicity (SAR) levels were between 3.2 and 20.8. In terms of salt accumulation in irrigated soils in Faisalabad, Pakistan, Simmons et al. (2009) found salinity (EC) and sodicity (SAR) levels in wastewater-irrigated soils to be 51 per cent and 63 per cent higher than freshwater-irrigated fields. In addition, soil alkalinity increased marginally under wastewater irrigation (pH 8.92) compared to canal-water irrigation (pH 8.75).

Excess salts added via wastewater irrigation result in negative effects on crops, soils and groundwater. Plant growth is affected by the osmotic and ion-specific effects, and by ionic imbalance. Osmotic effects depress the external water potential, making water less available to the plants. Excess levels of certain ions, such as Na$^+$ and chloride (Cl$^-$), cause ion-specific effects leading to toxicity or deficiency of certain nutrients in plants (Grattan and Grieve, 1999). In the case of sodic wastewater irrigation, the excess levels of Na$^+$ and bicarbonate (HCO$_3^-$) result in the gradual development of sodicity problem in soils, thereby exhibiting structural problems created by certain physical processes (Qadir and Minhas, 2008). Irrigation with saline and/or sodic wastewater may impact groundwater quality. In well-drained soils, there is the possibility of movement of salts and other contaminants through the soil profile into unconfined aquifers (Bond, 1998). The quality of wastewater, soil characteristics and the initial quality of the receiving groundwater are the important factors that determine the extent to which salts in wastewater impact groundwater quality.

Table 6.5 *Average salinity and sodicity related characteristics in wastewater generated in the Indian subcontinent*

Location	EC (dS m^{-1})[a]	SAR	RSC (mmol$_c$ l^{-1})	Reference
Faisalabad	3.1	16.0	4.2	Qadir and Minhas (2008)
Karnailwala	2.3	12.6	2.3	Hussain (2000)
Judgewala	4.0	20.8	6.2	Hussain (2000)
Marzipura	3.0	16.7	5.2	Hussain (2000)
Haryana	1.9	3.2	4.5	Qadir and Minhas (2008)

[a]As a salinity parameter, EC refers to electrical conductivity; sodicity parameters consist of Sodium Adsorption Ratio (SAR) and Residual Sodium Carbonate (RSC).

METAL AND METALLOIDS

Some metals and metalloids are essentially required for adequate plant growth, but are toxic at elevated concentrations; for example, copper (Cu), molybdenum (Mo), nickel (Ni), selenium (Se) and zinc (Zn). Most of the industries in developing countries discharge untreated effluent containing variable concentrations of metals and metalloids. Since there is no separation of industrial and domestic wastewater, the wastewater channels carry a blend of industrial and domestic wastewater. The exact metals discharged and their concentrations vary with the type of industry. Several studies in Pakistan reveal that industrial effluents discharged in major cities of Pakistan have had higher concentrations of chromium (Cr), lead (Pb) and cadmium (Cd) than their permissible limits in irrigation water (Hussain, 2000; Khan et al., 2007; Murtaza et al., 2008). The United Nations Industrial Development Organization (UNIDO, 2000) reported that the textile, tanning, paint and cement industries in Karachi (Pakistan) discharge raw effluent with lead (Pb) concentrations above the threshold limit at the industry outlet. Also in Africa, where larger industries are most often only along the coast, streams polluted with chromium were found close to tanneries (Binns et al., 2003). Threshold levels of metals and metalloids are given in Table 6.6. For threshold levels in soils see Chang et al. (2002).

Several studies have been carried out to evaluate the implications of wastewater irrigation on the concentrations of metals and metalloids in soils and crops (Bahri, 2009; Hamilton et al., 2007; Lazarova and Bahri, 2005; Minhas and Samra, 2004; Qadir et al., 2000; Simmons et al., 2009). In a comprehensive sampling programme undertaken in two peri-urban areas of Faisalabad, Pakistan, Simmons et al. (2009) quantified the impacts of long-term untreated wastewater irrigation on soil quality and the yield and quality of grain and straw of three wheat varieties. Wheat straw is used as a fodder in the area. In terms of heavy metal contamination and potential risks through the fodder–milk–human food chain, they did not find significant differences in aqua regia-digested soil's Cd and Zn concentrations between freshwater- and wastewater-irrigated plots. The metal ion concentrations in soils remained below the European Commission Maximum Permissible Levels for Cd, Pb, and Zn in sludge-amended soils. In all wheat varieties subject to wastewater irrigation, Cd and Pb concentrations remained below the European Commission Maximum Permissible Levels for these metals in feed materials (Table 6.7).

Based on a survey study carried out along the Musi River in India, Minhas and Samra (2004) detected transfer of metal ions from wastewater to cows' milk via grass grown on wastewater-irrigated soil and fed to the animals. The proportion of samples showing excessive amounts of pollutants in grass ranged from 4 per cent for Cd to 100 per cent for Pb. Milk samples were highly contaminated with both metal ions ranging from 1.2 to 40 times higher than the permissible limits. Qadir et al. (2000) found that in the case of irrigation with untreated wastewater, leafy vegetables accumulated certain metals such as Cd in greater

Table 6.6 *Recommended maximum concentrations (RMC)[a] of selected metals and metalloids in irrigation water*

Element	RMC mg l^{-1}	Remarks
Aluminium	5.00	Can cause non-productivity in acid soils (pH < 5.5), but more alkaline soils at pH > 7.0 will precipitate the ion and eliminate any toxicity.
Arsenic	0.10	Toxicity to plants varies widely, ranging from 12mg per litre for Sudan grass to less than 0.05mg per litre for rice.
Beryllium	0.10	Toxicity to plants varies widely, ranging from 5mg per litre for kale to 0.5mg per litre for bush beans.
Cadmium	0.01	Toxic at concentrations as low as 0.1mg per litre in nutrient solution for beans, beets and turnips. Conservative limits recommended.
Chromium	0.10	Not generally recognized as an essential plant growth element. Conservative limits recommended.
Cobalt	0.05	Toxic to tomato plants at 0.1mg per litre in nutrient solution. It tends to be inactivated by neutral and alkaline soils.
Copper	0.20	Toxic to a number of plants at 0.1 to 1.0mg per litre in nutrient solution.
Iron	5.00	Non-toxic to plants in aerated soils, but can contribute to soil acidification and loss of availability of phosphorus and molybdenum.
Lithium	2.50	Tolerated by most crops up to 5mg per litre. Mobile in soil. Toxic to citrus at low concentrations with recommended limit of < 0.075mg per litre.
Manganese	0.20	Toxic to a number of crops at a few-tenths to a few mg per litre in acidic soils.
Molybdenum	0.01	Non-toxic to plants at normal concentrations in soil and water. Can be toxic to livestock if forage is grown in soils with high concentrations of available molybdenum.
Nickel	0.20	Toxic to a number of plants at 0.5 to 1.0mg per litre; reduced toxicity at neutral or alkaline pH.
Lead	5.00	Can inhibit plant cell growth at very high concentrations.
Selenium	0.02	Toxic to plants at low concentrations and toxic to livestock if forage is grown in soils with relatively high levels of selenium.
Zinc	2.00	Toxic to many plants at widely varying concentrations; reduced toxicity at pH ≥ 6.0 and in fine textured or organic soils.

[a]The maximum concentration is based on a water application rate which is consistent with good irrigation practices (10,000 m^3 ha^{-1} yr^{-1}). If the water application rate greatly exceeds this, the maximum concentrations should be adjusted downward accordingly. No adjustment should be made for application rates less than 10,000 m^3 ha^{-1} yr^{-1}. The values given are for water used on a long-term basis at one site.
Source: Ayers and Westcot (1985); Pescod (1992)

amounts than non-leafy species. Sharma et al. (2007) concluded that wastewater irrigation increased contamination of edible parts of vegetables with Cd, Pb and Ni, resulting in potential health risks in the long term. Similar findings have been documented from a study conducted in Harare, Zimbabwe where farmers used wastewater for irrigating leafy vegetables (Mapanda et al., 2005). Generally, metal ion concentrations in plant tissue increase with concentrations in irrigation water. Concentrations in the roots are usually higher than in the leaves.

Table 6.7 *Differences in average metal ion (Zn, Cd and Pb) concentrations in straw of three wheat varieties and aqua regia-digested concentrations in soil samples under canal-water and wastewater-irrigated areas*

Irrigation	Metal ion concentration in wheat straw (mg kg^{-1})			Metal ion concentration in soil (mg kg^{-1})		
	Zn	Cd	Pb	Zn	Cd	Pb
Canal water	8.66	0.064	0.353	55.8	1.56	9.79
	(±1.33)[a]	(±0.036)	(±0.204)	(±2.69)	(±0.147)	(±0.204)
Wastewater	10.5	0.173	1.280	58.7	1.66	8.62
	(±1.89)	(± 0.133)	(±0.628)	(±6.79)	(±0.160)	(±1.33)
MPL[b]	–[c]	< 1.0	< 10.0	< 300	< 3.0	< 300

[a]Values in parentheses indicate ± standard deviation.
[b]Maximum permissible levels (MPL) based on the European Commission Directive 2002/32/EC for Pb and Cd in feed materials and Directive 2002/32/EC for sludge-amended soils.
[c]Not available.
Source: Based on Simmons et al. (2009)

While reviewing the use of reclaimed water in the Australian horticultural production industry, Hamilton et al. (2005) classified potentially phytotoxic metals in wastewater (reclaimed water) into four groups based on their retention in soil, translocation in plants, phytotoxicity and potential risk to the food chain. They classified Cd, Co, Mo and Se in Group 4, posing the greatest risk to human and animal health even though they may appear in wastewater-irrigated crops at concentrations that are not generally phytotoxic. This is supported by the WHO, which lists boron and cadmium to be of particular concern because of their high level of toxicity and bioaccumulation in crops (WHO, 2006a).

Uncontrolled metal and metalloid inputs to soils via wastewater irrigation are undesirable because, once accumulated, it is extremely difficult to remove them. This situation may subsequently lead to toxicity to plants grown on contaminated soils; absorption by crops, resulting in metal and metalloid levels in plant tissues which may be harmful to the health of humans or animals consuming the crops; and transport from soils to groundwater or surface water, thereby rendering the water hazardous for other uses (Murtaza et al., 2009).

The potential hazard of metals and metalloids can be determined by estimating their cumulative total loading in the soils. Table 6.8 provides information on the length of time for wastewater-irrigated soils (cation exchange capacity, CEC 5–15 cmol$_c$ kg^{-1}) to reach loading limits of some metals and metalloids. The data used represent calcareous, alluvial soils from three locations in Pakistan: Faisalabad, Peshawar and Haroonabad. The time required for Cd to reach its loading limit varied between 13 years for the heavily industrialized city of Faisalabad to 67 years for the less industrialized, small city of Haroonabad. The estimates of metal and metalloid loading suggest that their accumulation is a slow process even in cases of untreated wastewater irrigation. However, it would be extremely difficult to

Table 6.8 *Estimated length of time for wastewater-irrigated agricultural soils to reach metal limits in three locations in Pakistan[a]*

Location	Metal	Concentration (mg L^{-1})	Annual input (kg ha^{-1})[b]	Loading limit (kg ha^{-1})[c]	Estimated time (years)
Faisalabad	Cd	0.05	0.75	10	13
Peshawar	Cd	0.04	0.60	10	17
Haroonabad	Cd	0.01	0.15	10	67
Faisalabad	Cu	0.17	2.54	250	99
Peshawar	Cu	0.26	3.88	250	65
Haroonabad	Cu	0.35	5.22	250	48
Faisalabad	Ni	0.38	5.67	250	44
Peshawar	Ni	1.25	18.64	250	13
Haroonabad	Ni	0.14	2.09	250	120
Faisalabad	Pb	0.21	3.13	1000	319
Peshawar	Pb	0.70	10.44	1000	96
Haroonabad	Pb	0.04	0.60	1000	1676

[a]Calcareous, alluvial soils.
[b]Based on wastewater irrigation application at 1.5m depth per year (15,000m^3 ha^{-1}).
[c]Considering cation exchange capacity (CEC) of the soils: 5-15 cmol$_c$ kg^{-1}.

ameliorate soils once they reach the loading limits of certain metals and metalloids. The amounts of metals removed by crops are small (<10 per cent of the added metal) compared with the amounts applied to the soils (Page and Chang, 1985).

EMERGING CONTAMINANTS OF CONCERN

With changes in lifestyle and increase in living standards, more and more contaminants are being added to wastewater, including endocrine disruptor compounds, hormones, residual pharmaceuticals and active residues of personal care products (PCPs), among others. Endocrine disruptors (sometimes also referred to as hormonally active agents) include the estradiol compounds commonly found in the contraceptive pill, phytoestrogens, pesticides and industrial chemicals such as phenols (Table 6.9). They are exogenous substances that can act like hormones in the human endocrine system and disrupt the functions of endogenous hormones. These substances tend to be present at very low concentrations even in treated wastewater and may have adverse physiological effects in animals and humans. At least 45 chemicals have been identified as potential endocrine disrupting contaminants, including industrial contaminants such as dioxins and polychlorinated biphenyls (PCBs), insecticides like dichlorodiphenyltrichloro-ethane (DDT) and carbaryl, and herbicides (2,4-D and atrazine).

In addition to containing endocrine disruptor compounds, wastewater may convey hormones. Irrigation with hormone-rich wastewater can increase the

Table 6.9 *Maximum tolerable concentrations of selected pesticides, emerging contaminants and other pollutants in wastewater-irrigated soils*

Pollutant	Soil concentration mg kg^{-1}	Pollutant	Soil concentration mg kg^{-1}
Aldrin	0.48	Methoxychlor	4.27
Benzene	0.14	PAHs (as benzo[a]pyrene)	16.0
Chlordane	3.00	PCBs	0.89
Chloroform	0.47	Pentacholorophenol	14.0
2,4-D	0.25	Pyrene	41.0
DDT	1.54	Styrene	0.68
Dicholorobenzene	15.0	2,4,5-T	3.82
Dieldrin	0.17	Tetrachloroethane	1.25
Dioxins	0.00012	Tetrachloroethylene	0.54
Heptachlor	0.18	Toluene	12.0
Hexacholorobenzene	1.40	Toxaphene	0.0013
Lindane	12.0	Trichloroethane	0.68

Source: Based on Human Health Protection (Chang et al., 2002; WHO, 2006a)

endogenous production of hormones (phytohormones) in legume crops such as alfalfa. Ingestion of the forage crop by sheep and cattle might cause infertility problems in the animals (Shore et al., 1995). For many substances, such as steroid oestrogens, biodegradation and sorption are the main fate processes. However, there remains a paucity of information on the persistence of many of these substances in soil (Young et al., 2004).

A related group of concern is residual pharmaceuticals (e.g. analgesics, caffeine, cholesterol-reducing drugs and antibiotics). Some tend to survive even advanced wastewater treatment. There are concerns that soils irrigated with wastewater containing such contaminants may not retain them, resulting in their percolation through the soil to the groundwater. Although many residual pharmaceuticals may not be toxic, they can have health implications through their effects on the immune and hormonal systems of animals and humans.

The levels of active residues of PCPs are also increasing in wastewater. Percolation of PCPs through wastewater-irrigated soils has implications for groundwater quality deterioration with possible subsequent effects on human health. There may also be some unspecified toxic effects in the form of antibiotic-resistant bacteria development by repeated exposure of the pathogens to antibiotic levels in wastewater and contaminated streams (Bouwer, 2005).

While the presence of these chemicals in the environment and the potential ecological consequences are generally alarming, the concentrations found in surface-water bodies and other environmental compartments so far are very low. Possible health effects have been related mainly to aquatic life (Young et al., 2004) but not positively in humans, although there are many indications of possible adverse effects (Bouwer, 2005; Colborn et al., 1993). There is, however, still little data concerning the occurrence and fate of organic micro-pollutants: during and after irrigation; in view of crop uptake; and possible human health impacts through the food-crop chain.

Many of the chemicals might face rapid microbial degradation or adsorption by the soil organic matter and are unlikely to enter the plant tissue through the root (Chang et al., 2002). But even if this might happen, the comparison of common concentration in raw wastewater with other sources of these chemicals so far points to very low risk for human health (Toze, 2006b). More studies are needed; especially in view of quantitative simulation models for risk assessment.

RISK ASSESSMENT

Chemicals can affect the health of soils, crops and humans. For some heavy metals the 'soil–plant barrier' protects the food chain from these elements, in other cases bioaccumulation occurs (see Chapter 11). Acceptable levels of chemical parameters therefore depend on their behaviour, the proposed reuse applications of the water (e.g. food vs. fodder vs. fuel production) and site-specific factors, such as the degree of dilution with water from other sources.

To develop numerical limits of pollutant loading rates in the land application of wastes in general, essentially the same informational elements are needed (Chang et al., 2002):

- Hazard identification – the toxic chemicals to be considered are identified.
- Dose-response evaluation and risk characterization – the maximum permissible exposure level in the exposed subjects is determined for each chemical, based on the dose-response characteristics associated with a predetermined acceptable risk level.
- Exposure analysis – realistic exposure scenarios depicting the routes of pollutant transport are formulated to identify the subjects of exposures.

Analysing wastewater quality as a risk indicator is appropriate where dose-response relationships between water quality, soil quality, plant growth and human health have been well established. This is, for example, the case for salinity indicators and most macro- and micronutrients as they are affecting soil and crop health, but remains an increasingly difficult challenge where human health is concerned.

In this case, dose-response relationships may be derived from data obtained in epidemiological investigations, extrapolations from animal studies, or toxicity assays on mammalian or bacterial cells. Epidemiological data can provide the most realistic cause–effect relationships, but are only available for a very limited number of chemicals. Another challenge, especially in developing countries, is the required investment in analytical laboratory capacity. The long latency period of disorders caused by many environmental toxicants, such as cancer, reduces the quality of

---

BOX 6.1 QUANTITATIVE CHEMICAL RISK ASSESSMENT

Quantitative chemical risk assessment (QCRA) is a tool increasingly used in risk-management decision-making, following the success of its microbiological equivalent (QMRA, see Chapters 3, 4, and 5). In QCRA, available data and information regarding toxicity is combined with estimates of exposure to calculate the likelihood and severity of human health effects. In some circumstances, limitations in evaluating chemical toxicity and exposure potential introduce significant uncertainties into such a risk assessment. Like in QMRA, probabilistic approaches, such as Monte Carlo techniques, can be used to quantify the uncertainty in the human health risk-assessment process (Washburn et al., 1998). Based on the assumption that food-chain transfer is the primary route of exposure to potentially hazardous pollutants in wastewater and sewage sludge, numerical limits defining the maximum permissible pollutant concentrations in soils were presented for a set of organic and inorganic pollutants by Chang et al. (2002), while Weber et al. (2006) showed a modelling example of how to predict environmental (no-effect) concentrations in the absence of comprehensive quantitative analytical data.

---

the data by hindering the determination of the effects (Weber et al., 2006). Risk-assessment models are required (see Box 6.1).

Once established, dose-response relationships will allow proposition of an acceptable daily intake (ADI) for each specific chemical. To derive the numerical limits for pollutant input in land application, the process quantitatively backtracks the pollutant transport through the food chain (and/or other exposure routes) to arrive at an acceptable pollutant concentration for the receiving soil to determine the 'predicted no-effect concentration'. In order to demonstrate an acceptable risk to health or the environment, its value should be larger than the analysed or 'predicted environmental concentration' (Weber et al., 2006).

Among nutrients and heavy metals, excess or deficiency in crops does not only depend on absolute individual concentrations but on the balance of the elements, on the kind of organic matter available which might bind them and on the soil conditions (like acidity and the redox status) which can determine their solubility and uptake by roots. In these cases, wastewater analysis can only give a first indication; soil analysis might be more appropriate. This also applies to organic contaminates which are in the soil and subject to a range of biotic and abiotic processes. An often neglected option for metals and metalloids is the analysis of the crops on the respective farms especially when transmission through the food chain is of interest. Plant analysis usually provides a much more accurate assessment of possible uptake than soil or water analysis. However, it also reflects uptake from all locally available sources of nutrients or contaminants in the soil, which might be irrigation water, chemical farm inputs or, particularly in urban farming, also traffic exhaust (Bakare et al., 2004). Such a situation would require a comparative analysis before conclusions about a particular source can be drawn.

In all cases, sampling and analysis will have to consider spatial and temporal variations in water quality and accumulation of contaminants in the soil or plants over time. This requires ideally long-term monitoring or a set-up which allows comparing sites with different exposures.

While the assessment of soil and water salinity can be carried out in the field with an electrode, the analysis of nutrients usually requires laboratory equipment. Depending on the concentration of the elements in the sample in general the equipment gets more complex and expensive moving from macronutrients to micronutrients or heavy metals. Although many research institutions and universities in developing countries will have laboratories to analyse most of the macro- and some micronutrients, external support is often required in view of heavy metals or organic contaminants. A low-cost alternative is to predict the risk based on environmental factors and application practices using, for example, the Pesticide Impact Rating Index (PIRI), a free software package developed by CSIRO in Australia (www.clw.csiro.au/research/biogeochemistry/organics/projects/piri.html).

When the concentrations of constituents such as heavy metals or organic contaminants are known in the plant tissue, or in food in general, which is eventually consumed by a particular consumer group, it is possible to calculate human exposure (intake). The exposure of the consumer is then compared to the 'acceptable daily intake' (ADI, see above), for example, where the intake of a component such as pesticides might be unavoidable, or to the 'tolerable daily intake' (TDI), such as for heavy metals. The exposure can be obtained using the basic equation: Exposure (mg/kg body weight/day) = Consumption (mg/kg body weight/day) × Residue (mg/kg). As TDIs are regarded as representing a tolerable intake for a lifetime, they are not so precise that they cannot be exceeded for short periods of time. Short-term exposure to levels exceeding the TDI is not a cause for concern, provided the individual's intake averaged over longer periods of time does not appreciably exceed the level set (WHO, 2006b).

Detailed information on sampling and analysis of common contaminants can be found in standard text books for soil, water and plant analysis, or the WHO website of the Water, Sanitation, Hygiene and Health Unit at www.who.int/water_sanitation_health/en.

Conclusions

While from the microbiological perspective wastewater is perceived more as a biophysical hazard, its chemical content presents a more complex situation with both positive and negative impacts on soils, crops and water bodies, which are important considerations not only for the farmer but also for managing wastewater treatment and discharge.

The concentrations of nutrients vary widely in wastewater. Although reliable availability for irrigation and nutrient-supplying capacity are considered to be major drivers for untreated wastewater use in agriculture, maintaining adequate levels of nutrients in wastewater is a challenging task because of the possible negative impacts of their excessive addition to soils. In terms of salt content, there are no economically viable means to remove the salts once they enter wastewater because the techniques are prohibitively expensive, and are only used to produce high-quality recycled water. However, wastewater containing an adequate proportion of divalent cations such as calcium can be used as an amendment for calcium-deficient soils such as sodic and saline-sodic soils.

Some metals and metalloids supplied through wastewater irrigation are essentially required for adequate plant growth, but are toxic at elevated concentrations. Most of the industries in developing countries discharge untreated effluent containing variable concentrations of metals and metalloids. Since there is often no separation of industrial and domestic wastewater, the wastewater channels can carry a blend of industrial and domestic wastewater. Depending on the level of industrialization and type of industries, the exact metals and metalloids discharged and their concentrations vary widely. In many developing countries, impacts might remain localized but the situation requires careful monitoring, especially in transitional economies.

However, the quality of chemical risk assessments varies considerably between different hazards. While the effects of excess nutrient or heavy metal levels on soil productivity or crop health have been studied for some time, there is only limited information on other factors such as the fate and impact of organic contaminants in irrigation water with regard to human health. There is a significant need for computer-based models similar to those developed for microbiological risk assessments (see Chapter 5).

Like the supply of nutrients through wastewater irrigation, the presence of organic matter in wastewater may have positive or negative implications depending on the nature of the organic materials added through wastewater irrigation. In terms of positive effects, organic matter added through wastewater improves soil structure, acts as a storehouse of essential nutrients for crop growth and enhances charge characteristics of irrigated soils. In addition, the organic carbon status of wastewater-irrigated soils increases irrespective of soil and agro-climatic conditions.

The search for win–win solutions would entail preserving the positive outcomes of wastewater irrigation while monitoring, assessing and, if required, minimizing possible negative effects (see Chapter 11). However, this often requires management interventions beyond the farm level. In other words, the agricultural and sanitation sector will have to work together.

REFERENCES

Asano, T., Burton, F. L., Leverenz, H., Tsuchihashi, R. and Tchobanoglous, G. (2007) *Water Reuse: Issues, Technologies, and Applications*, McGraw-Hill, New York

Ayers R. S. and Westcot D. W. (1985) *Water Quality for Agriculture,* Irrigation and Drainage, Paper 29, Rev 1, FAO, Rome

Baddesha, H. S., Chhabra, R. and Ghuman, B. S. (1997), *Journal of the Indian Society of Soil Science*, no 45, pp258–364

Baddesha, H. S., Rao, D. L. N., Abrol, I. P. and Chhabra, R. (1986) 'Irrigation and nutrient potential of raw sewage waters of Haryana', *Indian Journal of Agricultural Sciences*, no 56, pp584–91

Bahri, A. (2009) 'Managing the other side of the water cycle: Making wastewater an asset', *Technical Committee (TEC) Paper No 13*, Global Water Partnership, Stockholm

Bakare, S., Denloye, A. A. and Olaniyan, F. O. (2004) 'Cadmium, lead and mercury in fresh and boiled leafy vegetables grown in Lagos, Nigeria', *Environmental Technology*, vol 25, no 12, pp1367–70

Binns, J. A., Maconachie, R. A. and Tanko, A. I. (2003) 'Water, land and health in urban and peri-urban food production: The case of Kano, Nigeria', *Land Degradation and Development*, no 14, pp431–44

Bond, W. J. (1998) 'Effluent irrigation – An environmental challenge for soil science', *Australian Journal of Soil Research*, vol 36, pp543–55

Bouwer, H. (2005) 'Adverse effects of sewage irrigation on plants, crops, soils, and groundwater', in V. Lazarova and A. Bahri (eds) *Water Reuse for Irrigation: Agriculture, Landscapes, and Turf Grass*, CRC Press, Boca Raton, FL, pp235–63

Buechler, S. and Mekala, G. D. (2005) 'Local responses to water resource degradation in India: Groundwater farmer innovations and the reversal of knowledge flows', *Journal of Environment and Development*, no 14, pp410–38

Central Soil Salinity Research Institute (2004) 'Use of urban and industrial effluent in agriculture', *Annual Progress Reports (2000–2003)*, NATP-MM Project (CSSRI), Karnal, India

Chang A. C., Pan, G., Page, A. L. and Asano, T. (2002) *Developing Human Health-Related Chemical Guidelines for Reclaimed Wastewater and Sewage Sludge Applications in Agriculture*, report for World Health Organization, Geneva, www.who.int/water_sanitation_health/wastewater/gwwuchemicals.pdf

Colborn, T., Vom Saal, F. S. and Soto, A. M. (1993) 'Developmental effects of endocrine disrupting chemicals in wildlife and humans', *Environmental Health Perspectives*, vol 101, pp378–84, www.ehponline.org/members/1993/101-5/colborn-full.html

Ensink, J. H. J., van der Hoek, W., Matsuno, Y., Munir, S. and Aslam, M. R. (2002) 'Use of untreated wastewater in peri-urban agriculture in Pakistan: Risks and opportunities', *Research Report 64,* International Water Management Institute (IWMI), Colombo, p22

Grattan, S. R. and Grieve, C. M. (1999) 'Salinity–mineral nutrient relations in horticultural crops', *Scientia Horticulturae*, vol 78, pp127–57

Gupta, A. P., Narwal, R. P. and Antil, R. S. (1998) 'Sewer water composition and its effect on soil properties', *Bioresource Technology*, vol 65, pp171–3

Hamilton, A. J., Boland, A. M., Stevens, D., Kelly, J., Radcliffe, J., Ziehrl, A., Dillon, P. J. and Paulin, R. (2005) 'Position of the Australian horticultural industry with respect to the use of reclaimed water', *Agricultural Water Management*, vol 71, pp181–209

Hamilton, A. J., Stagnitti, F., Xiong, X., Kreidl, S. L., Benke, K. K. and Maher, P. (2007) 'Wastewater irrigation: The state of play', *Vadose Zone Journal*, no 6, pp823–40

Hussain, S. I. (2000) 'Irrigation of crops with sewage effluent: Implications and movement of lead and chromium as affected by soil texture, lime, gypsum and organic matter', PhD thesis, Department of Soil Science, University of Agriculture, Faisalabad, p190

IWMI (International Water Management Institute) (2003) 'Confronting the realities of wastewater use in agriculture', *Water Policy Briefing 9*, IWMI, Colombo, p6

Jayaraman, C., Perumal, R. and Ramultu, S. (1983) *In Proceedings of the National Seminar on Utilisation of Organic Wastes*, Tamil Nadu Agricultural University, Madurai, India; cited from Minhas and Samra (2004)

Jiménez, B. and Asano, T. (2008) 'Water reclamation and reuse around the world', in B. Jiménez and T. Asano (eds) *Water Reuse: An International Survey of Current Practice, Issues and Needs*, IWA Publishing, London, pp3–26

Kaul, S. N., Juwarkar, A. S., Kulkarni, V. S., Nandy, T., Szpyrkowicz, L. and Trivedy, R. K. (2002) *Utilisation of Wastewater in Agriculture and Aquaculture*, Scientific Publishers, Jodhpur, p675

Keraita, B. N. and Drechsel, P. (2004) 'Agricultural use of untreated urban wastewater in Ghana', in C. A. Scott, N. I. Faruqui and L. Raschid-Sally (eds) *Wastewater Use in Irrigated Agriculture*, CABI Publishing, Wallingford, UK, pp101–12

Keraita, B. N., Jiménez, B. and Drechsel, P. (2008) 'Extent and implications of agricultural reuse of untreated, partly treated and diluted wastewater in developing countries', *CAB Reviews: Perspectives in Agriculture, Veterinary Science, Nutrition and Natural Resources*, vol 3, no 58, pp1–15

Khan, M. J., Bhatti, A. U., Hussain, S. and Wasiullah (2007) 'Accumulation of heavy metals in soil receiving sewage effluent', *Soil and Environment*, vol 26, pp139–45

Lal, R. (2001) 'Potential of desertification control to sequester carbon and mitigate the greenhouse effect', *Climatic Change*, vol 51, pp35–72

Lal, R. (2004) 'Soil carbon sequestration impacts on global climate change and food security', *Science*, vol 304, pp1623–7

Lazarova, V. and Bahri, A. (2005) *Water Reuse for Irrigation: Agriculture, Landscapes, and Turf Grass*, CRC Press, Boca Raton, FL

Mapanda, F., Mangwayana, E. N., Nyamangara, J. and Giller, K. E. (2005) 'The effect of long-term irrigation using wastewater on heavy metal contents of soils under vegetables in Harare, Zimbabwe', *Agricultural Ecosystem and Environment*, vol 107, pp151–65

McCartney, M., Scott, C. A., Ensink, J. H. J., Jiang, B. B. and Biggs, T. W. (2008) 'Salinity implications of wastewater irrigation in the Musi River catchment, India', *Ceylon Journal of Science*, no 37, vol 1, pp49–59

Minhas, P. S. and Samra, J. S. (2003) 'Quality assessment of water resources in Indo-Gangetic basin part in India', *Central Soil Salinity Research Institute*, Karnal, India, p68

Minhas, P. S. and Samra, J. S. (2004) 'Wastewater use in peri-urban agriculture: impacts and opportunities', *Central Soil Salinity Research Institute*, Karnal, India, p75

Mitra, A. and Gupta, S. K. (1999) 'Effect of sewage water irrigation on essential plant nutrient and pollutant element status in a vegetable growing area around Calcutta', *Indian Journal of Society of Soil Science*, vol 47, pp99–105

Murtaza, G., Ghafoor, A. and Qadir, M. (2008) 'Accumulation and implications of cadmium, cobalt and manganese in soils and vegetables irrigated with city effluent', *Journal of the Science of Food and Agriculture*, vol 88, pp 100–107

Murtaza, G., Ghafoor, A., Qadir, M., Owens, G., Aziz, M. A., Zia, M. H. and Ullah, S. (2009) 'Disposal and use of sewage on agricultural lands in Pakistan: A review', *Pedosphere* (in press)

Page, A. L. and Chang, A. C. (1985) 'Fate of wastewater constituents in soil and groundwater: Trace elements', in G. S. Pettygrove and T. Asano (eds) *Irrigation with Reclaimed Municipal Wastewater – A Guide Manual*, Lewis Publishers, Chelsea, MI, pp13.1–13.16

Pescod, M. B. (ed) (1992) *Wastewater Treatment and Use in Agriculture*, Irrigation and Drainage Paper 47, FAO, Rome

Pettygrove, G. S. and Asano, T. (eds) (1985) *Irrigation with Reclaimed Municipal Wastewater – A Guide Manual*, Lewis Publishers, Chelsea, MI

Qadir, M., Ghafoor, A. and Murtaza, G. (2000) 'Cadmium concentration in vegetables grown on urban soils irrigated with untreated municipal sewage', *Environment, Development and Sustainability*, vol 2, pp11–19

Qadir, M. and Minhas, P. S. (2008) 'Wastewater use in agriculture: Saline and sodic waters', in S.W. Trimble (ed) *Encyclopedia of Water Science*, Taylor & Francis, New York, pp1307–10

Qadir, M. and Schubert, S. (2002) 'Degradation processes and nutrient constraints in sodic soils', *Land Degradation and Development*, vol 13, pp275–94

Qadir, M., Wichelns, D., Raschid-Sally, L., McCornick, P. G., Drechsel, P., Bahri, A. and Minhas, P. S. (2009) 'The challenges of wastewater irrigation in developing countries', *Agricultural Water Management* (in press)

Qadir, M., Wichelns, D., Raschid-Sally, L., Minhas, P. S., Drechsel, P., Bahri, A. and McCornick, P. (2007) 'Agricultural use of marginal-quality water – opportunities and challenges', in D. Molden (ed) *Water for Food, Water for Life: A Comprehensive Assessment of Water Management in Agriculture*, Earthscan, London, pp425–57

Raschid-Sally, L. and Jayakody, P. (2008) 'Drivers and characteristics of wastewater agriculture in developing countries: Results from a global assessment, Colombo, Sri Lanka', *IWMI Research Report 127*, International Water Management Institute, Colombo

Scott, C. A., Faruqui, N. I. and Raschid-Sally, L. (2004) *Wastewater Use in Irrigated Agriculture: Confronting the Livelihoods and Environmental Realities*, CABI Publishing, Wallingford, UK, p193

Scott, C. A., Zarazúa, J. A. and Levine, G. (2000) 'Urban-wastewater reuse for crop production in the water-short Guanajuato River Basin, Mexico', *IWMI Research Report 41*, International Water Management Institute (IWMI), Colombo

Sharma, R. K., Agrawal, M. and Marshall, F. (2007) 'Heavy metal contamination of soil and vegetables in suburban areas of Varanasi, India', *Ecotoxicology and Environmental Safety*, vol 66, pp258–66

Shore, L. S., Kapulnik, Y., Gurevich, M., Wininger, S., Badamy, H., Shemesh, M. (1995) 'Induction of phytoestrogen production in *Medicago sativa* leaves by irrigation with sewage water', *Environmental and Experimental Botany*, vol 35, pp363–9

Simmons, R. W., Ahmad, W., Noble, A. D., Blummel, M., Evans, A. and Weckenbrock, P. (2009) 'Effect of long-term un-treated domestic wastewater reuse on soil quality, wheat grain and straw yields and attributes of fodder quality', *Irrigation and Drainage Systems* in press

Toze, S. (2006a) 'Reuse of effluent water – benefits and risks', *Agricultural Water Management*, vol 80, pp147–59

Toze, S. (2006b) 'Water reuse and health risks – real vs. perceived', *Desalination*, no 187, pp41–51

United Nations Industrial Development Organization (UNIDO) (2000) *Industrial Policy and the Environment in Pakistan*, UNIDO, Vienna

United States Environmental Protection Agency (USEPA) (2004) *Guidelines for Water Reuse*, EPA/625/R-04/108, USEPA, Washington, DC

Washburn S., Arsnow, D. and Harris, R. (1998) 'Quantifying uncertainty in human health risk assessment using probabilistic techniques', in J. L. Rubio, C. A. Brebbia, J. L. Uso (eds) *Risk Analysis*, WIT Press, Southampton, UK, pp213–22

Weber, S., Khan, S. and Hollender, J. (2006) 'Human risk assessment of organic contaminants in reclaimed wastewater used for irrigation', *Desalination*, no 187, pp53–64

WHO (2006a) *Guidelines for the Safe Use of Wastewater, Excreta and Greywater, Volume 2: Wastewater Use in Agriculture*, World Health Organization, Geneva

WHO (2006b) *Guidelines for Drinking-Water Quality (electronic resource), incorporating first addendum, vol. 1, Recommendations*, 3rd ed., WHO, Geneva, www.who.int/water_sanitation_health/dwq/gdwq0506.pdf

Yadav, R. K., Goyal, B., Sharma, R. K., Dubey, S. K. and Minhas, P. S. (2002) 'Post-irrigation impact of domestic sewage effluent on composition of soils, crops and ground water – A case study', *Environment International*, vol 28, pp481–6

Young, W. F., Whitehouse, P., Johnson, I. and Sorokin, N. (2004) *Proposed Predicted-No-Effect-Concentrations (PNECs) for Natural and Synthetic Steroid Oestrogens in Surface Waters*, R&D Technical Report P2-T04/1, Environment Agency R&D Dissemination Centre, c/o WRc, Swindon, UK, http://publications.environment-agency.gov.uk/pdf/SP2-T04-TR1-e-p.pdf?lang=_e

7

Risk Analysis Integrating Livelihood and Economic Impacts of Wastewater Irrigation on Health

Marites M. Tiongco, Clare A. Narrod and Kelly Bidwell

ABSTRACT

This chapter provides a brief review of methods and approaches for evaluating the consequences of using wastewater to irrigate vegetables. The following five objectives are considered: (a) analysing poor producers' and consumers' knowledge, attitudes and perceptions of the risks associated with pathogen contamination/ exposure, and the economic consequences on health and livelihoods; (b) analysing the costs and benefits of non-treatment interventions at the farm level (e.g. drip irrigation and cessation of irrigation prior to harvest) and post-harvest level (e.g. washing and disinfection of vegetables after harvesting); (c) identifying cost-effective interventions for reducing the risk of waterborne disease associated with wastewater use for irrigation; (d) estimating producers' and consumers' willingness to pay for or adopt non-treatment interventions at multiple stages along the food chain; and (e) evaluating the long-term economic and livelihood impacts of adopting those non-treatment interventions that are identified as cost-effective and targeted at poor producers and consumers. The chapter concludes by synthesizing a methodological framework for the collection and analysis of data to assess the livelihood and economic impacts of illness caused by microbial pathogens from wastewater.

INTRODUCTION

It is estimated that up to 20 million hectares of agricultural land in developing countries are being irrigated with raw or diluted wastewater (see Chapter 1 and Jiménez and Asano, 2004; Scott et al., 2004). Ensink et al. (2004) stated that the use of wastewater for irrigating agricultural crops, including high-value crops such as fruits and vegetables is practised in many parts of the world because of the scarcity of clean water resources and because wastewater is seen by small-scale producers as a cheap means to improve soil fertility and add essential nutrients for their crops. Although wastewater has a high nutrient value, it also has a food-safety risk due to the possibility of the transmission of pathogens (including bacteria, viruses, and protozoa) on fruits and vegetables posing a potential human health hazard.

Direct consumption of food cultivated on land irrigated with wastewater and ingestion of soil resulting from improper hygiene that transfers soil from hands to mouth (not washing soiled hands before eating) are examples of exposure pathways to pathogenic micro-organisms from organic manure, fertilizers, pesticides and effluents causing infectious diseases including typhoid fever, rotavirus infection, cholera and hepatitis A (IWMI, 2006; Scott et al., 2004). In addition, farmers and irrigation workers can acquire helminth infections and parasitic diseases due to direct contact with untreated wastewater and contaminated soils, especially if exposed for a long duration (Ensink, 2006). Despite this knowledge, it is often difficult to get farmers, particularly poor small-scale producers, to alter behaviour by applying risk-reducing practices to wastewater irrigation, because food production using wastewater generates significant livelihood[1] opportunities (Buechler and Devi 2005a, 2005b; Hamilton et al., 2005; Toze, 2006). Therefore, effective risk reduction strategies must account for farmers' practices and attitudes towards the adoption of intervention to mitigate these risks.

The chapter evaluates methods to assess the cost-effectiveness of such interventions and suggests that overcoming this challenge must address four interrelated issues. First, small-scale producers using wastewater are often not well informed of the potential health risks of infection and disease both to themselves and to consumers of wastewater-irrigated produce. Second, small-scale producers primarily act on knowledge of the positive, short-term economic effects on livelihood security even though they may understand the negative, long-term health implications. Third, interventions to reduce the food-safety risk associated with using wastewater for irrigation in urban and peri-urban areas tend to be large-scale and not cost-effective for the poor to implement. In the case of consumers, their behavioural choices may be influenced by past behaviour and experiences, and their perception of relative risk. For example, if consumers have been eating raw vegetables for years and have not become ill, they may view themselves as not being at risk, or that the probability of contamination is very low, and so they could be reluctant to make long-term changes in their food preparation and consumption practices. Finally, decision-makers do not have sufficient information as to whether producers and consumers would be willing to pay for or adopt interventions to reduce health risks if cost-effective measures were available.

To better understand the complexity of these issues and find possible solutions to minimize risk of infection and illness from consuming and producing vegetables irrigated with wastewater, a risk analysis can be carried out. Risk analysis is an internationally recognized framework used for identifying and assessing disease and food-safety risks, for evaluating risk-management options and for assessing public-health and food-safety challenges (see Box 7.1). It involves a risk assessment in terms of both biological and economic impacts, an evaluation of risk-management choices and a risk-communication strategy so as to identify a portfolio of cost-effective control measures to reduce a specified risk. Although there have been a number of risk assessments on the use of wastewater on food crops (Asano et al., 1992; Fattal et al., 2004; van Ginneken and Oron, 2000; Hamilton et al., 2006; Petterson et al., 2001; Shuval et al., 1997; Tanaka et al., 1998), to the authors' knowledge there are no risk analyses that incorporate adoption of interventions into the framework, with the exception of the theoretical approach presented by Malcolm et al. (2004) and Chapters 13 and 16 of this book. Understanding awareness, knowledge and perceptions towards risk, as well as assessing people's willingness to pay for or adopt those cost-effective risk-reducing strategies are important determinants in making choices as to which measure to adopt. Further, although risk management has a monitoring and review component, it does not monitor and evaluate the long-term impact of adopting a mitigation strategy on livelihood outcomes. As there are many poor and small-scale producers involved in food production in developing countries who use wastewater, there is a need to understand the economic impact of food-safety hazards on their livelihood outcomes (income, health and nutrition and gender equality) and on stakeholders' willingness to adopt cost-effective risk-reducing strategies.

In this chapter, we propose the use of a modified risk analysis framework that takes into account people's willingness to pay for or adopt cost-effective ways to reduce health risks associated with wastewater use and to improve livelihoods. We explore how the risk analysis framework and the methodologies for evaluating the costs and benefits, and cost-effectiveness of risk-reducing options, can be integrated with methodologies for assessing perceptions, knowledge and attitudes about risk, and willingness to pay for or adopt control measures. An attempt is made to identify appropriate methodologies for evaluating the long-term impacts of adopting cost-effective non-treatment interventions targeted at producers and consumers, specifically how these affect productivity and livelihood outcomes.

Box 7.1 Risk analysis framework

Risk analysis is a useful tool for decision-making that 'maps' an action or event on to measurable endpoints. Risk analysis typically consists of three essential components that are integrated with each other: risk assessment, risk management and risk communication (see Figure 7.1). In the case of foodborne diseases, the risk assessment involves the evaluation of the likelihood of a foodborne hazard as well as the biological and economic consequences of that hazard. In other words, it helps to understand what can go wrong, how disease introduction or spread can happen, how likely microbiological risks arising from wastewater use for irrigation can be characterized and the consequences. Risk management involves evaluation of how best to mitigate the risk and to determine, using cost–benefit and cost-effective analyses, the cost to society of the action. Risk communication involves identifying ways to interact with the public as stakeholders and informing them of risk-assessment findings such as cost-effective risk-reduction measures and decision tools to aid decision-makers. Additionally, it supports decision-makers in making adequately informed decisions, evaluating policy alternatives and establishing food-safety control measures.

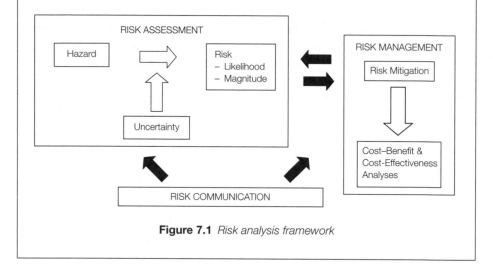

Figure 7.1 *Risk analysis framework*

Economic methods for evaluating impact of disease and interventions to reduce risk

The effects of wastewater use on health and its social and economic consequences for farmers, agricultural labourers and their household members, and consumers of wastewater-irrigated produce, have been studied in some areas but these studies lack the evaluation of economic consequences on livelihood outcomes such as income, wealth and food and nutrition security (Blumenthal et al., 2000; Ensink et al., 2003; Feenstra et al., 2000; van der Hoek et al., 2002; Shuval et al., 1986).

In the case of health risks, it is necessary to take a farm to fork perspective for microbial risks because pathogens can enter virtually anywhere along the food chain. Health impacts can arise through farmers' or others' contact with irrigation water, or through direct or indirect contact of non-contaminated vegetables with contaminated ones, and through unhygienic handling, i.e. soiled hands transmitting pathogens to vegetables. In health economics, disability-adjusted life years (DALYs, see chapters 2 and 3) are used to facilitate the comparison of the economic risks and cost-effectiveness of various forms of interventions. Currently this approach is the best measure available for quantifying health benefits in terms of: reduced diarrhoeal and gastrointestinal infections, and helminth and related intestinal nematode infections; improved irrigation water quality; and reduced cost of illness to consumers (costs of illness include medicines, hospitalization and doctor's consultation) and reduced productivity loss (e.g. forgone earnings). Thus, quantifying the economic impacts of wastewater-based microbial pathogen exposure on health is important in order to provide decision-makers with evidence-based information on the economic efficiency and technological feasibility of the risk reduction strategies at selected points along the food chain.

However, it is difficult to quantify the magnitude of the economic impact of foodborne disease on human health due to exposure to excreta-related pathogens and consumption of pathogen-contaminated crops irrigated with wastewater. Factors such as multiplication of microbial pathogens as the contaminated product moves along the food chain and the reaction of market actors and consumers have to be taken into consideration. For instance, consumers may lose confidence in the safety of the products they consume as a result of a waterborne disease outbreak, which further leads to market-share losses due to decline in demand for fruit and vegetables. Consumer responses usually depend on the existing information they have, their level of awareness and the changes in relative prices when making choices about the products they purchase or consume, particularly if there is a food- safety issue that would affect their well-being. Addressing the impact on consumer confidence in food safety could be a basis for estimating costs and benefits of reducing risk and preventing disease.

Approaches for assessing the costs and benefits of interventions

There are two widespread economic approaches to valuing changes to health and risk: cost–benefit analysis and cost-effectiveness analysis. Cost–benefit analysis (CBA) is used to understand the efficiency of the intervention relative to the baseline (no intervention) in an objective, quantitative way so as to determine where an intervention should be initiated, continued, or abandoned. The costs of an intervention and benefits of its impact are often evaluated in terms of the public's willingness to pay to acquire (benefits) or the willingness to pay to avoid them (costs); see next section on evaluating willingness to pay. Direct costs can

---

Box 7.2 Non-treatment interventions

The risk of using untreated wastewater for irrigation can be reduced through non-treatment options or multiple combinations of these options. These include farm-level wastewater management and harvest and post-harvest interventions.

At the farm level, farmers can reduce health risks (such as skin infections, muscular pains, intestinal nematode infections and sore feet) and crop contamination by adopting the following farming practices:

- drip irrigation: uses drip kits and containers for wastewater storage;
- improving methods of water distribution such as the use of flood and furrow irrigation or watering cans to fetch water (primarily to reduce collection of protozoan ova);
- avoiding soil splash when using watering cans (e.g. by lowering the height of application or using water hoses);
- ceasing irrigation before harvesting (one to several days before harvest) to allow natural pathogen die-off;
- avoiding stirring up sediment while fetching water with cans;
- reducing contact with irrigation water.

Not washing harvested crops in irrigation water can reduce pathogen contamination. At the post-harvest stage, which includes handling and transport, market display, storage and preparation in the kitchen, the following can be practised:

- Improving vegetable-washing before serving using vinegar (broad availability but the most expensive option) and disinfectants such as chlorine tablets (available at selected vendors) and potassium permanganate (available in about every third pharmacy in the cities sampled by Keraita, 2008);
- improving food safety and hygiene.

A combination of low-cost non-treatment options from farm to post-harvest comprises the 'multiple-barrier approach' (see Chapters 2 and 12) supported by the new WHO Guidelines where intervention measures are placed along the food chain to achieve aggregate effect in reducing health risks (WHO, 2006).

Source: Keraita (2008); Qadir et al. (2008)

---

be estimated using any or a combination of the following approaches: economic-engineering analysis; cost survey analysis; econometric estimations of costs; and simulation (Fearne et al., 2004; Havelaar et al., 2006; Valeeva et al., 2004).

In the economic-engineering analysis approach, the costs of an intervention are estimated for each individual procedure needed to implement it, and then the total cost is the summation of individual costs. These include the costs of implementing and monitoring risk-mitigation measures as shown in Table 7.1. In addition to these structural costs are incidental costs (productivity losses) and market-revenue losses that are related to detection of contamination or exposure. This approach also allows for efficiency analysis via estimation of cost functions based on available

Table 7.1 *Cost estimates of non-treatment interventions at the farm level[a]*

Interventions (see Keraita, 2008)	Fixed costs[b] (US$)	Operation, maintenance and labour costs (US$/yr)	Total cost estimates year 1 (US$)
Drip kits[c]			
Locally made	105	36	141
Imported	175	36	211
Current practice without intervention	10	15	25
Improved use of watering cans	10	20	30
Cessation before harvest[d]	Forgone benefit (yield loss)		
For 2 days	40	14	54
For 4 days	70	13	83
For 6 days	100	12	112
Pond use for improved sedimentation	17	25	42
Sand filtration (two rows of sand bags)	24	43	67

[a] Based on a typical farm of ca. 0.03ha (irrigated vegetable farming in urban areas in Ghana)
[b] Cost related to the preparation of the water sources (stream, dugout) not included
[c] Based on the requirement of 1 kit/0.004ha i.e. about 7 kits per farm, incl. water buckets
[d] Losses are estimated as 5% of total harvest per day. Selling price of lettuce estimated as 1 US$/m^2
Source: Hope and Keraita (2009)

technical and economic data. The main advantage of the engineering approach is its transparency as it is easy to understand how the numbers were estimated (Fearne et al., 2004).

Benefits can be derived from the value of reduction of economic costs based on the costs associated with implementing each intervention that would likely reduce the risk of illness from microbial pathogens or avoid crop-production losses, or in terms of savings due to reduced costs of illness or changes in the composition of demand (Smith et al., 2007; Bennett et al., 2004; Disney et al., 2003). Indirect benefits result from increases in productivity or costs offset, for example, reduced cost of illness and lives saved due to reduced mortality. An intervention would be considered Pareto optimal if it improves the situation for some people, but does not make anybody worse off. Thus, for governments, acceptable interventions (or policies) are typically those for which expected benefits are greater than or equal to expected costs.

Once the risks from microbial pathogens due to wastewater use have been estimated and described, and the costs and benefits of risk-reduction measures have been calculated, a cost-effectiveness analysis (CEA) can then be conducted to understand the trade-offs of the risk-reduction methods available. To do this, information is needed on the economic costs of chronic exposure (which also include infection, illness and death) to the disease, the investments and costs associated with the different risk-reduction options, the probability of effectiveness of the various risk-reduction measures and the probabilities of chronic exposure under different risk-reduction measures.

Simulation can be performed using different sets of scenarios: do nothing or no intervention (baseline); a single intervention; or a combination of interventions.

The difference between the baseline and a single intervention or combination is the gain in health (DALYs averted) or income due to the reduction in disease burden from the interventions. The costs of each intervention are then compared with the gains to identify the most cost-effective intervention (or a combination of interventions) at different levels of resource availability. The comparison of the different interventions against the most cost-effective shows areas of efficiency, while an intervention for higher resource levels shows what should be done if those resources are available.

To illustrate, four hypothetical options (A, B, C, D) to reduce risk are considered. As shown in Figure 7.2, the x-axis is the marginal cost of adding one of the new options compared to the baseline. The y-axis is the percentage reduction in risk over the baseline. Option D can be excluded as a choice since option B is superior to option D in the sense that B is both more effective and less costly. Choices of adoption strategy can be limited to non-dominated options A, B and C, which could result in maximum possible benefits for a given cost (Glauber and Narrod, 2001; Malcolm et al., 2004). Option C is the optimal risk-mitigation measure, where the marginal benefit of the risk-mitigation policy is equal to the marginal cost.

Results of the CEA are important inputs for risk-management decisions. They help weigh available options for reducing risk of illness due to wastewater use in terms of efficiency, technological feasibility and practicality at selected points along the food chain.

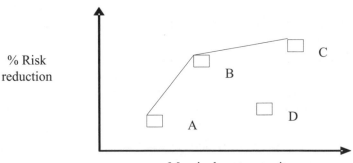

Figure 7.2 *Risk reduction/cost trade-off*

Evaluating willingness to pay for an intervention

The willingness to pay (WTP) for or adopt control strategies and willingness to test technologies or interventions such as those described above can be estimated using stated preference methods such as contingent valuation or conjoint analysis (Hammitt, 2000). Subsequently, the estimated WTP can be compared to the costs of these strategies and technologies to determine those that are the most economically efficient. In the contingent valuation method, consumers will be given a hypothetical scenario involving the choice between different risk levels of food contamination, from no contamination as the base scenario to a high level of contamination (for a thorough review of the application of this method, see Birol et al., 2006; Buzby et al., 1995, 1998; Latouche et al., 1998). Then consumers are presented with a price to see if they are willing to pay that amount for a certain safety level and, after responding positively, they are then presented with a higher price for even more safety and so on. If the consumer responds 'no' the first time, the second price is some amount and safety level lower than the first price.

In a conjoint analysis, consumers are asked to rank a number of attributes related to the vegetable including attributes on food safety and price. Unlike contingent valuation, the conjoint method does not ask directly whether a consumer would be willing to pay for a vegetable with particular attributes (Halbrendt et al., 1995). A limitation of these direct valuation methods is incomplete information of the respondents or information bias, since if contamination is not visible to the naked eye, they are not able to observe the level of risk, or even if they are able to see it, the consequences of contamination such as severity and health costs are difficult to judge (for more details of this problem on information bias and other biases, see Birol et al., 2006).

Finally, WTP can be modelled as a function of the severity and duration of illness, reduction in probability and respondent characteristics (Hammitt and Haninger, 2007).

Approach for assessing economic impacts on livelihoods

Various approaches – qualitative or quantitative analysis or a combination of both – can be used to assess the impact of microbial pathogen exposure from using wastewater for irrigation on livelihood outcomes including farm income, wealth (savings/insurance), food and nutrition security, and gender equality. Here, the best known Sustainable Livelihood Framework (SLF) documented by the UK Department for International Development (DFID) is used to enable understanding of the impact of wastewater-based microbial pathogen exposure on livelihood assets, transforming structures and processes, and livelihood strategies (DFID, 2000).[2] Impacts of pathogen exposure/contamination on all of these components will affect various livelihoods outcomes including farm income, wealth (savings/insurance), food and nutrition security, and gender equality.

Household livelihood outcomes in turn determine the level of future vulnerability of the households to various shocks and stresses, including excreta-related diseases such as diarrhoea and helminth infections, and outbreaks of hepatitis A and viral enteritis.

Qualitative methods such as focus group discussions and participatory rapid appraisal of the knowledge, attitudes and perceptions of health consequences of producing or consuming fruits and vegetables irrigated with wastewater would capture the dynamic changes in livelihood strategies. A participatory value-chain mapping can also be done to understand the basic relationships between value-chain actors and the structure of flows of products from raw material supply to the end consumer market, and to assess the value of losses due to microbial contamination (Hellin et al., 2005). This involves participatory observation, semi-structured interviews and focus group discussions to map the flow of produce irrigated with wastewater from farm to final consumer, in order to identify the key actors along the chain and understand the role of wastewater irrigation in their livelihoods (income, health and nutrition). Mapping the value chain can also help identify high- and low-risk areas along the chain, market failures and coordination mechanisms, incentives that may impede or facilitate the uptake of the multiple-barrier approach to prevent contamination and reduce health risks at all stages of the chain. It can also identify regulatory and market issues that may hinder or enhance functions of institutions and organizations providing services such as input supplies, market information, credit and quality standards that the different actors need to help them decide whether to adopt or apply control and preventive measures.

Quantitative methods such as regression analysis, covariate and propensity score-matching, and difference-in-difference estimators and empirical models for estimating differential treatment effects can be used to analyse the impact on livelihoods. This will involve structured household and quantitative value-chain surveys that will enable understanding of the full economic impacts of pathogen reduction measures on the poor's livelihood asset portfolio[3] and outcomes including income, health and nutrition. The quantity and quality of these assets and access to them are influenced by pathogen contamination, including trends (e.g. during the hungry season), shocks (e.g. diarrhoeal outbreak) and stresses (e.g. chronic diarrhoea). Households are viewed as being sustainable if they can cope with trends, shocks and seasonality without compromising their future ability to survive these.

Interventions to control or reduce risk of pathogen contamination/exposure can occur at various stages along the food chain, from production, during harvest and post-harvest. These may include wastewater treatment technologies and non-treatment options: water-quality improvements, human-exposure control, farm-level wastewater management, and harvest and post-harvest interventions (see Box 7.2 above and Qadir et al., 2008, for a detailed description of these risk-reduction interventions). Wastewater treatment technologies can achieve 1–6 log units of pathogen reduction and a tolerable disease burden of $<10^{-6}$ DALYs per person per year but this treatment is very expensive to implement in developing countries (Carr, 2001; WHO, 2006). There are non-treatment measures such as drip irrigation and washing of produce that protect farmers and consumers at low cost and can effectively minimize crop and human exposure by up to 6 log units of pathogen reduction (WHO, 2006).

Regression analysis could be used to examine impacts on livelihood outcomes with the measure of pathogen exposure as an explanatory variable controlling for various household-level factors that affect livelihood outcomes such as income from vegetable production and morbidity of adults and children. The measure of exposure can be grouped into high versus low exposure, and with and without disease or diarrhoeal outbreak.

Methods for evaluating the long-term economic impacts of interventions

The choice of method to evaluate the long term impact of cost-effective interventions on livelihoods and health is guided by the nature of the problem, the intervention chosen and its related goal and purpose, which in this case is reducing pathogen contamination/exposure resulting from wastewater irrigation. First, it is necessary to conduct a baseline survey to obtain good pre-intervention measures of both livelihood strategies and livelihood outcomes, because this will be crucial to obtaining good measures of intervention impacts when a package of cost-effective control measures is introduced. The baseline survey will collect information related to health, education, behaviours, preferences and water usage, and address questions on how illness/disease due to contact with untreated wastewater results in asset loss (either via price or via short-term loss of market to sell vegetable crops irrigated with wastewater). A baseline risk assessment is also needed to estimate exposures and prevalence of pathogen contamination.[4]

Surveys on knowledge, attitude, perception and practices (KAPP) towards wastewater use for irrigation and food preparation, as well as behavioural experiments (choice experiments or actual field experiments), could be employed to determine the farmers' and consumers' willingness to adopt cost-effective mitigation measures. Behavioural experiments are also useful in investigating what kind of institutions would be preferred by what type of households and how households' preferences for different institutional mechanisms (e.g. incentives, subsidies) are affected by their livelihood outcomes (e.g. income from vegetable production, total income, food and nutrition security, etc.).

Currently, assessment of the poor's knowledge and perceptions of the risk of foodborne diseases associated with crops irrigated with wastewater is limited (Faruqui et al., 2004). There is a need for a comprehensive evaluation of WTP for intervention technologies with consideration of the sustainability, cultural acceptability, economic feasibility, ethical acceptability and overall effectiveness of potential interventions. One step towards achieving this is to determine why there is inadequate understanding of the risk of foodborne disease associated with irrigating with wastewater and ways to mitigate that risk, followed by identifying effective ways to enhance understanding. A proven approach to doing this is value-chain analysis that focuses on the awareness, attitudes, perceptions, knowledge and practices of value-chain actors regarding wastewater use so as to understand how best to encourage farmers (and other actors along the value chain) to adopt risk-reduction measures. Such an analysis provides insight into the rationale behind value-chain actors' lack of understanding of the potential health risks associated with wastewater use for irrigation.

A structured questionnaire as well as participatory assessment can be used to collect KAPP information for wastewater irrigation. Questions can be ranked and scored according to cost-effectiveness in preventing infection due to wastewater use. These scores are the weighted measure of KAPP related to reduction of risk of infection. For example, five points can be awarded to the most important mitigation measure and one point for the least important. The percentage score is the sum of scores divided by the sum of available points (proportional piling). Results from this KAPP could help in understanding why the poor's management of wastewater use is inadequate. If the stakeholders were made aware of the health and income-loss risks, and which strategies were cost-effective to adopt, they might be more willing to implement such strategies.

Given the health risks associated with wastewater use and the importance of targeting effective and appropriate mitigation strategies, it is important not only to understand what farmers or consumers say they will do or say they prefer, but to truly observe what they actually do or actually choose. Randomized controlled trials allow us to observe the greatest impact of interventions on assets and livelihood outcomes (incomes, health and nutritional status), in real conditions, of different strategies and approaches to induce behaviour-change (Dupas et al., ongoing). This would involve counterfactual analysis to generate distributions of livelihood outcomes without interventions (control group), and to compare these to the actual distributions (treatment group) (DiNardo et al., 1996). The intervention's impact can be calculated from simple mean difference between the outcomes of the control and the treatment groups: Impact = Mean (Outcome of Eligible Random Treatment group) − Mean (Outcome of Eligible Random Control group). Data can also be further analysed to understand the differential impact on different subgroups within the sample.

Random assignment also assures the direction of causality, i.e. offering watering cans or drip kits to farmers causes a reduced disease burden on lettuce leaves. In a case where the intervention is only offered to better-educated farmers from the outset it is possible that this group is likely to be different from less-educated farmers in a variety of ways, such as differing hygiene practices and other behaviours which impact on health; thus, the impact of the intervention on this group will not be representative of the impact on all farmers. Additionally, if the control group is not identical to the treatment group, such as better-educated farmers receiving the programme compared to less-educated farmers serving as the control, the evaluation will not accurately show the programme's effects. These farmers are likely to have different behaviours and perhaps different health realities independent of the intervention, so the programme's affect on one group will be very different from the potential programme affect on the other, and the two groups will be experiencing different external events. The benefit of assigning the treatment or programme randomly is that we know there are no significant differences between the treatment and control groups. In choosing the treatment group, selection bias may be encountered. This problem of selection bias can be removed from impact estimates by 'instrumenting' adoption, that is, by finding exogenous variables that explain adoption but do not affect the outcomes. However, it is difficult to find such exogenous instruments and so instrumental variables may only identify part of the treatment effect.

With baseline data collected before the intervention, there should be one or more follow-up evaluation surveys (comparable questionnaires or interviews to the baseline) on the same groups after the interventions are put in place. The data collected would allow for the double difference method to measure the long-term economic impact (lower medical costs and lower productivity losses) and health impact (lowest pathogen levels and more than 50 per cent reduction in foodborne illness). As the first difference, it compares treatment (participants/adopters of intervention) and control (non-participants/non-adopters of interventions) groups. Subsequently, before and after intervention outcomes are compared as the second difference. The impact of the intervention is the mean difference between the 'before' and 'after' values of the outcome for each of the treatment and control groups.

CONCLUSIONS

Increasing use of wastewater for irrigating vegetable crops will continue as long as wastewater treatment remains limited while populations and demand for food increase, especially in the developing world. As verified in the other chapters of this volume, wastewater irrigation poses a health problem for the entire food chain, thus requiring a multidisciplinary approach for analysis. This chapter provided a discussion of various methods to evaluate the economic impacts of a disease, the costs and benefits of interventions and the willingness to adopt or pay for interventions. Second, the chapter aimed to provide a methodological framework to enable the collection and analysis of data to measure the economic impacts of illness/disease caused by microbial pathogens from wastewater on household assets; livelihood strategies to reduce the risk of illness/ waterborne disease; diversification patterns such as investment in non-treatment interventions or shifting to other livelihoods activities; and the various indicators of producer livelihoods, including income, nutrition and food security, and gender equality. The proposed framework addresses some of the challenges in evaluating cost-effective interventions and strategies for the poor to adopt so as to reduce the risk of illness/disease associated with wastewater use.

The lack of awareness and knowledge of poor producers and consumers of the potential impact of wastewater use for irrigation on health, as well as lack of information on appropriate food hygiene and sanitary practices, can all be addressed through KAPP analysis. In prioritizing interventions to improve health and livelihood outcomes, poor people's knowledge and perception of risk, as well as their willingness to pay for or adopt cost-effective ways to reduce health risks associated with wastewater use, must be taken into consideration. Promoting behaviour-change requires a longer period of time, incentives and frequent reinforcement, especially to those most vulnerable or at risk.

Randomized controlled trials can and should be used both to measure impact and to conduct product-innovation testing. Testing product or programme innovations, however, involves offering a programmatic innovation to a randomly selected pool of farmers, consumers, business owners, etc., while the control group has only access to the standard programme or services. Randomized controlled trials can be beneficial in developing and improving programmes and measuring the impact on usage, disease burden, operational efficiency and marketing.

To conclude, it would be ideal to use a combination of a before and after approach, and a with and without intervention approach, to capture the changes in the difference. The problem with this counterfactual analysis is finding a group 'without intervention' not too close to the 'with intervention' group, so as to avoid spillover effects or contamination. It is also possible that the 'without intervention' group, when the baseline data are collected, will have some intervention introduced between the time of the baseline and endline surveys. A mid-term survey is therefore suggested to allow an initial check on impact and to allow analysis of changes in impact over time. Data collection should be designed to include baseline, follow-up and endline surveys for the evaluation of interventions to reduce the risk of infection/contamination associated with wastewater use over the long term. In the final instance, interventions that are implemented should be proven to protect the livelihoods of the poor producers, traders and consumers so that adoption of these interventions will become sustainable in the long run.

NOTES

1   We take livelihoods as the set of activities, e.g. crop farming, livestock rearing and off-farm employment, on which (poor) households base their welfare or well-being (Chambers and Conway, 1992). A household's livelihood is sustainable when it can cope with and recover from external shocks (such as civil conflict or emergence of

new human, crop or livestock diseases) and stresses (e.g. recurrent adverse weather and seasonality), and can maintain or enhance its capabilities and assets, while not undermining the natural resource base (Chambers and Conway, 1992; Ellis, 2000; Scoones, 1998).

2   The three components of the framework are: (a) livelihood assets: changes in a household's asset portfolio including, for example, changes in irrigation facilities; changes in human capital in the form of information and education, as well as better health and nutrition; changes in infrastructure (e.g. good agricultural practices, hygienic handling practices, better storage facilities) to improve income, food security and health; (b) transforming structures and processes: changes in institutions, such as minimum standards for microbial pathogen reduction, implementation of hazard analysis and critical control points (HACCP) regulations at different stages of the value chain, capacity strengthening of laboratories and changes in markets (e.g. demand, prices, etc.). Attention will be given to the role of markets and institutions supporting markets access and reduced transaction costs to identify livelihood opportunities and constraints; (c) livelihood strategies: ex post strategies such as consuming rather than selling contaminated vegetables; ex ante mitigation strategies, such as adopting pathogen reduction measures in both production and consumption by, for instance, investing in drip or spray irrigation, washing and disinfecting of produce, etc.

3   Household assets consist of the stock of resources used to generate well-being (Jansen et al., 2005). Assets include human capital (e.g. number of household members, their gender and age, skills, knowledge (indigenous/local or formal through extension training), informal and formal education, good health, ability to work, household size and demographics); natural capital (e.g. climate, land (inherited or acquired), soil, water (treated or untreated), stream, borehole, soil (quality and fertility)); physical capital (numbers and types of livestock, production equipment and technologies, transportation); financial assets (cash, transfers, credit/debit, savings); location-specific factors such as access to infrastructure and public services; and social capital (social networks, social relations, membership in national or village-level producer associations, etc.).

4   When conducting the risk assessment, the exposure assessment will estimate the baseline prevalence of waterborne illness (e.g. acute gastroenteritis, diarrhoea, hepatitis A, amoebiasis, dysentery, etc.) associated with exposure to microbial pathogens (such as rotavirus, norovirus, *Legionella* spp., *Salmonella* spp., *E. coli*, *Giardia intestinalis*, helminths, and many more) in wastewater on a society.

REFERENCES

Asano, T., Leong, L. Y. C., Rigby, M. G. and Sakaji, R. H. (1992) 'Evaluation of the California wastewater reclamation criteria using enteric virus monitoring data', *Water Science and Technology*, vol 26, nos 7–8, pp1513–24

Bennett, R., Cooke, R. J. and Ijpelaar, J. (2004) 'Assessment economic impacts of TB and alternative control policies', SE3112, Final Project Report to the Department for Environment, Food and Rural Affairs, London

Birol, E., Karaousakis, K. and Koundouri, P. (2006) 'Using economic valuation techniques to inform water resources management: A survey and critical appraisal of available techniques and an application', *Science of the Total Environment*, vol 365, pp105–22

Blumenthal, U. J., Peasey, A., Ruiz-Palacios, G. and Mara, D. D. (2000) *Guidelines for Wastewater Reuse in Agriculture and Aquaculture: Recommended Revisions Based on New Research Evidence*, Task No 68, Part 1, WELL Study, London School of Hygiene and Tropical Medicine, London / Loughborough University, Loughborough

Buechler, S. and Devi, G. (2005a) 'Local responses to water resource degradation in India: Groundwater farmer innovations and the reversal of knowledge flows', *Journal of Environment and Development*, vol 14, no 4, pp410–38

Buechler, S. and Devi, G. (2005b) 'Household food security and wastewater-dependent livelihood activities along the Musi River in Andhra Pradesh, India', WHO, Geneva, www.who.int/water_sanitation_health/wastewater/gwwufoodsecurity.pdf

Buzby, J. C., Fox, J. A., Ready, R. C. and Crutchfield, S. R. (1998) 'Measuring consumer benefits of food safety risk reductions', *Journal of Agricultural and Applied Economics*, vol 30, pp69–82

Buzby, J. C., Ready, R. C. and Skees, J. R. (1995) 'Contingent valuation in food policy analysis: A case study of a pesticide-residue risk reduction', *Journal of Agricultural and Applied Economics*, vol 27, pp613–25

Carr, R. (2001) 'Excreta-related infections and the role of sanitation in the control of transmission', in L. Fewtrell and J. Bartram (eds) *Water Quality: Guidelines, Standards and Health; Assessment of Risk and Risk Management for Water-Related Infectious Disease*, International Water Association (IWA) on behalf on the World Health Organization, London, pp89–113

Chambers, R. and Conway, G. (1992) 'Sustainable rural livelihoods: Practical concepts for the twenty-first century', *IDS Discussion Paper No. 296*, Institute of Development Studies, Brighton, UK

Department of International Development (DFID) (2000) *Sustainable Livelihoods Guidance Sheets*, DFID, London, www.dfid.gov.uk

DiNardo, J., Fortin, N. M. and Lemieux, T. (1996) 'Labor market institutions and the distribution of wages, 1973–1992: A semiparametric approach', *Econometrica*, vol 64, pp1001–44

Disney, R., Emmerson, C. and Wakefield, M. (2003) 'Ill-health and retirement in Britain: A panel data-based analysis', Working Paper No. 03–02, Institute of Fiscal Studies, London

Dupas, P., Kremer, M. and Zwane, A. (ongoing) 'The demand for safe water among mothers of young children in Kenya', Innovations for Poverty Action, New Haven, CT, http://poverty-action.org/work/projects/0081

Ellis, F. (2000) *Rural Livelihoods and Diversity in Developing Countries*, Oxford University Press, Oxford

Ensink, J. H. J. (2006) 'Water quality and the risk of hookworm infection in Pakistani and Indian sewage farmers,' PhD thesis, London School of Hygiene and Tropical Medicine, University of London, London

Ensink, J. H. J., Mahmood, T., van der Hoek, W., Raschid-Sally, L. and Amerasinghe, F. P. (2004) 'A nationwide assessment of wastewater use in Pakistan: An obscure activity or a vitally important one?', *Water Policy*, vol 6, pp197–206

Ensink, J. H. J., van der Hoek, W., Matsuno, Y., Munir, S. and Aslam, M. R. (2003) 'The use of untreated wastewater in peri-urban agriculture in Pakistan: Risks and opportunities', *IWMI Research Report 64*, International Water Management Institute, Colombo

Faruqui, N. I., Scott, C. A. and Raschid-Sally, L. (2004) 'Confronting the realities of wastewater use in irrigated agriculture: Lessons learned and recommendations', in C. A. Scott, N. I. Faruqui and L. Raschid-Sally (eds) *Wastewater Use in Irrigated Agriculture: Confronting the Livelihood and Environmental Realities*, CABI Publishing, Wallingford, UK, pp173–85

Fattal, B., Lampert, Y. and Shuval, H. (2004) 'A fresh look at microbial guidelines for wastewater irrigation in agriculture: A risk assessment and cost-effectiveness approach', in C. A. Scott, N. I. Faruqui and L. Raschid-Sally (eds) *Wastewater Use in Irrigated Agriculture: Confronting the Livelihood and Environmental Realities*, CABI Publishing, Wallingford, UK, pp1–10

Fearne, A., Garcia, M., Bourlakis, M., Brennan, M., Caswell, J., Hooker, N. and Henson, S. (2004) 'Review of the economics of food safety and food standards', report prepared for Food Standards Agency, Imperial College, London

Feenstra, S., Hussain, R. and van der Hoek, W. (2000) 'Health risks of irrigation with untreated urban wastewater in the southern Punjab, Pakistan', *IWMI Pakistan Report*, no 107, International Water Management Institute, Lahore

Ginneken, M. van and Oron, G. (2000) 'Risk assessment of consuming agricultural products irrigated with reclaimed wastewater: An exposure model', *Water Resources Research*, vol 36, pp2691–9

Glauber, J. and Narrod, C. (2001) *A Rational Risk Policy for Regulating Plant Diseases and Pests*, AEI-Brookings Joint Center for Regulatory Studies, Washington, DC

Halbrendt, C., Pesek, J., Parsons, A. and Linder, R. (1995) 'Using conjoint analysis to assess consumers' acceptance of pST-supplemented pork', in J. A. Caswell (ed) *Valuing Food Safety and Nutrition*, Westview Press, Boulder, CO, pp129–53

Hamilton, A. J., Boland, A. M., Stevens, D., Kelly, J., Radcliffe, J., Ziehrl, A., Dillon, P. J. and Paulin, R. (2005) 'Position of the Australian horticultural industry with respect to the use of reclaimed water', *Agricultural Water Management*, vol 71, pp181–209

Hamilton, A. J., Stagnitti, F., Boland, A. M., Premier, R. and Hale, G. (2006) 'Quantitative microbial risk assessment models for consumption of raw vegetables irrigated with reclaimed water', *Applied and Environmental Microbiology*, vol 72, pp3284–90

Hammitt, J. K. (2000) 'Evaluating contingent valuation of environmental health risks: The proportionality test', *Association of Environmental and Resource Economists Newsletter*, vol 20, no 1, pp14–19

Hammitt, J. K. and Haninger, K. (2007) 'Willingness to pay for food safety: Sensitivity to duration and severity of illness', *American Journal of Agricultural Economics*, vol 89, no 5, pp1170–75

Havelaar, A. H., Bräunig, J., Christiansen, K., Cornu, M., Hald, T., Mangen, M.-J. J., Mølbak, K., Pielaat, A., Snary, E., Van Boven, M., Van Pelt, W., Velthuis, A. and Wahlström, H. (2006) *Towards an Integrated Approach in Supporting Microbiological Food Safety Decisions*, Report no 06-001 for the project on Network for the Prevention and Control of Zoonoses (project FOOD-CT-2004-506122) funded by the European Commission and co-supported by the Dutch Food and Consumer Safety Product Authority, Med-Vet-Net and RIVM, The Netherlands

Hellin, J., Griffith, A. and Albu, M. (2005) 'Mapping the Market: market-literacy for agricultural research and policy to tackle rural poverty in Africa', in F. R. Almond and S. D. Hainsworth (eds) *Beyond Agriculture – Making Markets Work for the Poor. Proceedings of an International Seminar, February 28–March 1, 2005*, Natural Resources International Limited and Practical Action, London

Hoek, W. van der, Ul Hassan, M., Ensink, J., Feenstra, S., Raschid-Sally, L., Munir, S., Aslam, R., Ali, N., Hussain, R. and Matsuno, Y. (2002) 'Urban wastewater: A valuable resource for agriculture – A case study from Haroonabad, Pakistan', *IWMI Research Report no 63*, International Water Management Institute, Colombo, p20

Hope, L. and Keraita, B. (2009) unpublished project data, IWMI Ghana, Accra

IWMI (2006) 'Recycling realities: Managing health risks to make wastewater an asset', *Water Policy Briefing no 17*, International Water Management Institute in partnership with the Global Water Partnership (GWP) Advisory Center at IWMI and the GWP Technical Committee, Colombo

Jansen, H. G. P., Siegel, P. B., Alwang, J. and Pichon, F. (2005) 'Geography, livelihoods and rural poverty in Honduras: An empirical analysis using an asset-based approach', Working Paper No 134, Ibero-America Institute for Economic Research (IAI), Göttingen

Jiménez, B. and Asano T. (2004) 'Acknowledge all approaches: The global outlook on reuse', *Water*, no 21, December 2004, pp32–7

Keraita, B. (2008) 'Low-cost measures for reducing health risks in wastewater-irrigated urban vegetable farming in Ghana', PhD dissertation, Faculty of Health Sciences, University of Copenhagen, Copenhagen

Latouche, K., Rainelli P. and Vermersch, D. (1998) 'Food safety issues and the BSE scare: Some lessons from the French case', *Food Policy*, no 23, pp347–56

Malcolm, S., Narrod, C., Roberts, T. and Ollinger, M. (2004) 'Evaluating the economic effectiveness of pathogen reduction technologies in cattle slaughter plants', *Agribusiness: An International Journal*, vol 20, no 1, pp109–24

Petterson, S. R., Ashbolt, N. and Sharma, A. (2001) 'Microbial risks from wastewater irrigation of salad crops: A screening-level risk assessment', *Water Environment Research*, vol 72, pp667–72

Qadir, M., Wichelns, D., Raschid-Sally, L., McCornick, P. G., Drechsel, P., Bhari, A. and Minhas, P. S. (2008) 'The challenges of wastewater irrigation in developing countries', *Agricultural Water Management*, in press, doi 10.1016/j.agwat.2008.11.004

Scoones, I. (1998) 'Sustainable rural livelihoods: A framework for analysis', IDS Working Paper no 72, University of Sussex, Institute of Development Studies, Brighton, UK

Scott, C. A., Faruqui, N. I. and Raschid-Sally, L. (2004) 'Wastewater use in irrigated agriculture: Management challenges in developing countries', in C. A. Scott, N. I. Faruqui and L. Raschid-Sally (eds) *Wastewater Use in Irrigated Agriculture: Confronting the Livelihood and Environmental Realities*, CABI Publishing, Wallingford, UK, pp1–10

Shuval, H. I., Adin, A., Fattal, B., Rawitz, E. and Yekutiel, P. (1986) *Wastewater Irrigation in Developing Countries – Health Effects and Technical Solutions*, World Bank Technical Paper no 51, UNDP Project Management Report, Washington, DC

Shuval, H. I., Lampert, Y. and Fattal, B. (1997) 'Development of a risk assessment approach for evaluating wastewater reuse standards for agriculture', *Water Science and Technology*, no 35, pp15–20

Smith, G. C., Bennett, R., Wilkinson, D. and Cooke, R. (2007) 'A cost–benefit analysis of culling badgers to control bovine tuberculosis', *Veterinary Journal*, vol 173, no 2, pp302–10

Tanaka, H., Asano, T., Schroeder, E. D. and Tchobanoglous, G. (1998) 'Estimating the safety of wastewater reclamation and reuse using enteric virus monitoring data', *Water Environment Research*, vol 70, no 1, pp39–51

Toze, S. (2006) 'Reuse of effluent water–benefits and risks', *Agricultural Water Management*, no 80, pp147–59

Valeeva, N. I., Meuwissen, M. P. M. and Huirne, R. B. M. (2004) 'Economics of food safety in chains: A review of general principles', *NJAS Wageningen Journal of Life Sciences*, vol 51, no 4, pp369–90

WHO (2006) *Guidelines for the Safe Use of Wastewater, Excreta and Greywater, Volume 2: Wastewater Use in Agriculture*, World Health Organization, Geneva

Part 3

Minimizing Health Risks

8

Wastewater Treatment for Pathogen Removal and Nutrient Conservation: Suitable Systems for Use in Developing Countries

*Blanca Jiménez, Duncan Mara, Richard Carr
and François Brissaud*[1]

ABSTRACT

This chapter summarizes the main characteristics of wastewater treatment processes, especially those suitable for use in developing countries, from the perspective of their potential to produce an effluent suitable for safe agricultural irrigation; it thus concentrates on pathogen removal and nutrient conservation. Wastewater treatment processes are divided into two principal categories: 'natural' systems which do not rely on the consumption of large amounts of electrical energy and which are therefore more suitable for use in developing countries; and conventional electromechanical systems which are wholly energy-dependent and which, if used in low income regions, require high levels of financial investment for their construction and skilled manpower for their successful operation and maintenance. The removal of viral, bacterial, protozoan and helminthic pathogens achieved by the most commonly used natural and conventional treatment processes are detailed, and recommendations are made for process selection.

INTRODUCTION

In order to treat municipal wastewater so that it can be safely used for agricultural purposes it is important to conserve nutrients while at the same time removing pathogens. This imposes constraints for process selection that are very different from those used for organic matter (i.e. biochemical oxygen demand, BOD) removal which is the principal concern of wastewater treatment prior to discharge to surface waters. To achieve effective pathogen removal requires a very careful selection of treatment processes since several pathogen groups – viral, bacterial, protozoan and helminthic – have to be removed to varying degrees and, in developing countries, at the lowest possible cost.

The information presented in this chapter, which is complementary to that in Chapter 9 (faecal sludge treatment), and Chapters 10 and 12 (both on post-treatment options), is a summary of the main characteristics of wastewater treatment processes, especially those suitable for use in developing countries, viewed from the perspective of their potential to produce an effluent suitable for agricultural irrigation, rather than to describe their design and operational principles (which can be found in the specialist literature and some of the references given herein).

WASTEWATER CHARACTERISTICS

Worldwide, municipal wastewaters have a broadly similar composition with regard to their content of organic matter and nutrients, but not their microbiological characteristics. Due to the difference in health conditions of people living in industrialized and developing countries, the pathogen content is notably different (Jiménez, 2003) and therefore the appropriate treatment options are also different. Table 8.1 shows the pathogen contents in wastewaters from different countries, from which it is apparent that, in order to attain values of ≤ 1 helminth egg per litre and $\leq 10^3$–10^4 faecal coliforms per 100ml in treated wastewater to be used for agricultural irrigation (as recommended in the 2006 WHO Guidelines – see Chapters 2 and 5), the removal efficiencies required are of the order of 95–99.99 per cent for helminth eggs[2] and 3–6 log units[3] for faecal coliforms.

Removal of helminth eggs, bacteria and viruses is commonly achieved by wastewater stabilization ponds and other 'natural' treatment processes. However, when more 'conventional' or energy-intensive processes (e.g. activated sludge) are used, disinfection methods such as chlorination, ozonation and UV radiation are generally required for pathogen inactivation. These disinfection methods remove bacteria and viruses, but not helminth eggs as these are very resistant and behave quite differently from bacteria and viruses during treatment. Protozoan (oo)cysts are only slightly less resistant than helminth eggs (details of the removal mechanisms of helminth eggs can be found in Jiménez, 2007, 2009). Thus, special care must be

Table 8.1 *Concentrations of micro-organisms in wastewater and wastewater sludge in different countries*

Micro-organism	Country/Region	Wastewater	Sludge
Helminth eggs (per litre)	Developing countries	70–3000	70–735
	Brazil	166–202	75
	Egypt	N/A	Mean: 67 Max: 735
	Ghana	0–15	76
	Jordan	300	N/A
	Mexico	6–98 (up to 330 in poor areas)	73–177
	Morocco	214–840	N/A
	Pakistan	142 (*Ascaris*) 558 (*Ascaris, Ancylostoma* and *Necator*)	N/A
	Ukraine	20–60	N/A
	France	9–10	5–7
	Germany	N/A	< 1
	Great Britain	N/A	< 6
	Irkutsk, Russia	19	N/A
	USA	1–8	2–13
Faecal coliforms (per 100ml)	Ghana	10^4–10^9	
	Mexico	10^7–10^9	
	USA	10^6–10^9	
Salmonella spp. (per 100ml)	Mexico	10^6–10^9	
	USA	10^3–10^6	
Protozoan cysts (per litre)	Mexico	978–1814 (*Entamoeba histolytica, Giardia lamblia* and *Balantidum coli*)	
	USA	28 (*Cryptosporidium*)	

Source: Jiménez (2005, 2007); Jiménez et al. (2004); N/A not available

taken when selecting a process that removes helminth eggs and protozoan (oo)cysts from wastewater to the required degree.

CLASSIFICATION OF TREATMENT STEPS

Conventionally there are four treatment steps to be considered: preliminary, primary, secondary and tertiary.

Preliminary treatment comprises screening and grit removal for the extraction of coarse suspended solids, such as fats, oils and greases, sand, gravel, rocks and any large floating materials (e.g. plastics, wood, etc.). Pathogen or nutrient concentration levels are not affected. In developed countries sophisticated proprietary equipment, often with remote operation and control, is employed. Developing countries commonly rely on low-cost equipment like manually raked bar screens and manually cleaned grit channels.

Primary treatment is commonly primary sedimentation, although septic tanks, Imhoff tanks, upflow anaerobic sludge-blanket (UASB) reactors, and anaerobic ponds, including high-rate anaerobic ponds (HRAP), also serve this purpose. In these processes, which have a hydraulic retention time of a few hours, almost all the settleable solids in the wastewater sediment sink to the base of the reactor, from where they are regularly removed (commonly continuously or at least once a day for primary sedimentation tanks, every few weeks for UASBs, and every one to three years for septic and Imhoff tanks and anaerobic ponds). The sludge so produced contains viable pathogens (notably helminth eggs) and requires further treatment before any application to agricultural land (other than by subsurface soil injection).

Secondary treatment systems follow primary treatment and are most frequently biological processes coupled with solid/liquid separation. Secondary aerobic treatment processes comprise a biological reactor followed by a secondary sedimentation tank to remove and concentrate the biomass produced from the organic compounds in the wastewater. Aerobic reactors use either suspended-growth processes (e.g. aerated lagoons, activated sludge, oxidation ditches) or fixed-film processes (trickling filters, rotating biological contactors). Although conventional secondary treatment systems are designed primarily for the removal of BOD, suspended solids and often nutrients (nitrogen and phosphorus), they can, with optimized performance, also reduce bacterial and viral pathogens by approximately 90 per cent, protozoan (oo)cysts by 0–1 log unit and helminth eggs by around 2 log units, depending on the concentration of suspended solids.

Tertiary treatment refers to treatment processes downstream of secondary treatment such as: additional solids removal by flocculation, coagulation and sedimentation; granular medium filtration; and/or disinfection. When tertiary treatment processes are used, the overall sequence of wastewater treatment processes is often described as 'advanced wastewater treatment'. Tertiary treatment, and in some cases even secondary (depending on the process selected), is typically unaffordable and often too complex to operate satisfactorily in many low-income countries.

Since these wastewater treatment processes can be applied at different treatment steps (primary, secondary, tertiary or even in between), each treatment process will be analysed in this chapter as a single unit and its role at different levels of treatment discussed.

DESCRIPTION OF TREATMENT PROCESSES

'Natural' wastewater treatment processes include waste stabilization ponds, wastewater storage and treatment reservoirs, septic tanks, Imhoff tanks, UASB reactors, high-rate anaerobic ponds and constructed wetlands, which use a low amount of energy for operation. Energy-intensive systems include aerated lagoons, activated sludge systems including oxidation ditches, biofilters and rotating biological contactors – all of these, except oxidation ditches and aerated lagoons, are preceded by primary sedimentation and all are followed by secondary sedimentation and, if required, by disinfection, commonly through chlorination or maturation ponds. Infiltration-percolation can be used for the further treatment of primary and secondary effluents, and soil-aquifer treatment for tertiary-treated effluents.

Waste stabilization ponds

Waste stabilization ponds (WSP) are shallow basins that use natural factors such as biodegradation, sunlight, temperature, sedimentation, predation and adsorption to treat wastewater (Mara, 2004). WSP systems usually consist of anaerobic, facultative and maturation ponds arranged in series. For optimal performance the ponds should be designed in such a way as to minimize hydraulic short-circuiting and care must be taken during operation to avoid irregular solids accumulation modifying the flow pattern. In tropical environments well-designed and properly operated WSP systems are very efficient at removing all kinds of pathogens without the addition of chemicals: they can reliably achieve a 2–4 log unit removal of viruses, a 3–6 log unit removal of bacterial pathogens, a 1–2 log unit removal of protozoan (oo)cysts and up to a 3 log unit (i.e. very close to 100 per cent) removal of helminth eggs – the precise values depend on the number of ponds in series and their retention times (Grimason et al., 1996; Mara, 2004; Mara and Silva, 1986; Oragui et al., 1987).

Protozoan (oo)cysts and helminth eggs are removed by sedimentation and thus remain in the pond sludge. Viruses are removed by adsorption onto solids, including algae; if these solids settle, the adsorbed viruses also remain in the pond sludge. Bacteria are removed or inactivated by several mechanisms including temperature, pH values >9.4 (induced by rapid algal photosynthesis), and a combination of high light intensity (>450nm wavelength) and high dissolved oxygen concentrations (Curtis et al., 1992).

To remove helminth eggs, a minimum total retention time in a WSP series of 5–20 days, depending on their number in the raw wastewater, is required (Mara, 2004). To control *Cryptosporidium* almost 38 days are needed (Grimason et al., 1996; Mara, 2004; Shuval et al., 1986). When a series of ponds are used, most of the helminth eggs are retained in the first pond. Helminth eggs remain viable for several years in the pond sludge: for example, from a survey of several WSP in Mexico, a content of 14 viable eggs per g TS was found in sludge stored for at least nine years (Nelson et al., 2004).

WSP are most effective in warm climates. In colder climates they can still be effective but they require a longer retention time and thus an even greater land area. In hot, arid and semi-arid climates substantial water loss occurs due to evaporation, causing not only a net loss of irrigation water but also an increase in the effluent salinity. Values up to 20–25 per cent of water loss have been reported (Duqqah,

2002; Jiménez, 2005; Jiménez, 2007). In the centre of Mexico, farmers have refused to use treated wastewater due to its high salinity and in Pakistan farmers have avoided the use of treated wastewater in favour of untreated wastewater for similar reasons (Clemett and Ensink, 2006).

WSP are most commonly the lowest-cost treatment option in tropical environments where inexpensive land is available (Arthur, 1983). They are relatively easy to operate and maintain, and do not require electricity. However, the growth of vegetation in or near the ponds must be controlled to prevent the creation of vector-breeding habitats.

Wastewater storage and treatment reservoirs

Wastewater storage and treatment reservoirs (WSTR), also called effluent-storage reservoirs, are used in several arid and semi-arid countries. They offer the advantage of storing and treating wastewater until it can be used during the irrigation season, so allowing the whole year's wastewater to be used in the irrigation season and therefore increasing agricultural production by increasing the area of land irrigated. Procedures for designing WSTR are detailed in Juanicó and Dor (1999) and Mara (2004). WSTR are generally used after primary treatment, typically after an anaerobic pond, although they can be used to store and treat secondary effluents (i.e. to upgrade an existing wastewater treatment plant).

WSTR remove 2 to 4 log units of viruses, 3 to 6 log units of bacterial pathogens and 1 to 2 log units of protozoan (oo)cysts. If treatment reservoirs are operated as batch systems with retention times over 20 days the complete removal of helminth eggs can be achieved (Jiménez, 2007; Juanicó and Milstein, 2004). WSTR have much lower evaporative losses compared to those from WSP: 14 per cent vs. 25 per cent (Mara et al., 1997).

In addition to large WSTR, small intermediate storage ponds can be utilized for pathogen removal prior to wastewater use in urban agriculture. Such reservoirs reduce helminth egg numbers by around 70 per cent, provided care is taken not to disturb the sediments when removing the WSTR contents for use (Drechsel et al., 2008). They are easy to operate and maintain, and if considered as part of the irrigation system, they result in a low investment cost. However, they may facilitate vector breeding if they are not well maintained and operated, and algal development may clog the irrigation distribution system (such as sprinklers and emitters).

Septic tanks, Imhoff tanks, UASBs and high-rate anaerobic ponds

These are all natural treatment systems roughly equivalent to primary treatment but with the potential to capture the anaerobically produced biogas which, as it comprises over 60 per cent methane, can be used for cooking and lighting at household level or, at larger treatment works, for electricity generation.

Septic tanks, which date from the late 19th century, are simple wastewater solid/liquid separation tanks often used at household level with on-site drainfields or soakaways to dispose of the settled effluent from the tank, although they can also be used at small wastewater treatment works with the settled effluent being treated further in WSP or a constructed wetland. Imhoff tanks, which were developed in Germany in 1906, are a modification of septic tanks for small treatment works: the tank has an improved design to facilitate better solid/liquid separation.

A more recent development, dating from the 1980s, is the UASB reactor. These are normally only used at wastewater treatment plants (either small or large – the largest in the world, in Belo Horizonte, Brazil, has a design population of 1 million). In a UASB the wastewater enters the reactor at its base and is treated during its passage through a sludge bed (the sludge 'blanket') formed by tight floccules of anaerobic bacteria. The hydraulic retention time is 6–12 hours (Mara, 2004). The treatment process is designed primarily for the removal of organic matter, but UASBs remove 86–98 per cent of helminth eggs, and effluent egg numbers are highly variable. In Brazil for example, UASB effluents contain three to ten eggs per litre, but with high numbers in the raw wastewater (up to 320 eggs per litre) effluent numbers can be as high as 45 per litre (Sperling et al., 2002, 2003, 2004). To remove helminth eggs from UASB effluents completely and reliably, it is recommended to treat the effluent further in WSP which also reduce faecal coliform levels to those recommended in the 2006 WHO Guidelines. Investigations of effluent nitrogen and phosphorus levels in UASB effluents do not indicate significant losses (Ali et al., 2007; van Lier et al., 2002); however, losses may occur due to increased pH in polishing ponds treating UASB effluents (Cavalcanti, 2003).

UASBs are often considered a low-cost technology; however, they are more expensive but not more efficient than conventional anaerobic ponds (Peña et al., 2000). A lower-cost but equally efficient alternative to UASBs is the high-rate anaerobic pond which combines the simplicity of conventional anaerobic ponds and the higher performance of UASBs, including the option of biogas recovery, at a much lower cost than the latter (Peña Varón, 2002).

Constructed wetlands

Constructed wetlands are beds of aquatic macrophytes which grow in soil, sand or gravel. There are three main types: surface-flow, subsurface horizontal-flow and vertical-flow systems. Although, in principle, any aquatic macrophyte can be grown in constructed wetlands, and high-value ornamental flowers and trees have been grown successfully in constructed wetlands, the majority are planted with reeds and/or rushes (e.g. *Juncus*, *Phragmites*) (Belmont et al., 2004).

Constructed wetlands are usually secondary or tertiary treatment units, in which case they are preceded by a septic tank, Imhoff tank, UASB, anaerobic pond or a conventional wastewater treatment plant. They are used to remove organic matter (BOD), solids and nutrients. Wetlands are generally promoted as a good option to control pathogens. However, although wetlands have been installed in several developing countries, in practice few data on the pathogen removals obtained are available due to the high cost and complexity of the analytical techniques involved. The available information mostly refers only to faecal coliforms. From the small amount of available data, pathogen removal is highly variable and depends on the climate, the type of wetland and the plants used. Pathogen removal is achieved via filtration, adsorption on to soil or plant roots and predation by micro-organisms (Jiménez, 2007). Wetlands can remove 90–98 per cent of faecal coliforms, 67–84 per cent of MS2 coliphages and 60–100 per cent of protozoa (Jiménez, 2003). Further details are given in Rivera et al. (1995) and IWA Specialist Group (2000).

Constructed wetlands can be sources of nuisance mosquitoes, some of which have public-health implications (e.g. *Culex quinquefasciatus*, the vector in many parts of the developing world of Bancroftian filariasis). Reports from the eastern USA, southern Sweden and Australia detail this phenomenon and present possible environmental management solutions (Russell, 1999; Schäfer et al., 2004). Clearly, locating constructed wetlands (especially surface-flow wetlands) at safe distances from human settlements is important.

Primary sedimentation

Primary treatment is achieved in tanks having a retention time of two to six hours. Removal occurs through sedimentation, therefore small pathogens such as bacteria and viruses are only removed if they are adsorbed on to or are trapped within a matrix of settleable solids. For helminth eggs, removal efficiencies of less than 30 per cent can be expected.

Coagulation-flocculation

Coagulation-flocculation has been sometimes used as the main treatment process to produce a treated wastewater suitable for agricultural use at a reasonable cost. This requires low coagulant doses combined with high-molecular-weight and high-density-charge flocculants to reduce sludge production (Jiménez, 2009). Two coagulation-flocculation technologies fulfil this requirement: chemically enhanced primary treatment (CEPT) and advanced primary treatment (APT). These differ in that CEPT uses a conventional settler and APT uses a high-rate lamellar settler. Hydraulic retention time is four to six hours for the former but only half to one hour for the latter. They are both efficient at removing helminth eggs while allowing part of the organic matter and nutrient (nitrogen and phosphorus) content to remain in the dissolved and colloidal fractions of the treated water. However, in both cases the effluent produced still needs a disinfection step to inactivate bacteria and viruses; this can be achieved with chlorine or UV light (Jiménez, 2007). Helminth eggs and some protozoa are removed along with the suspended solids following the same coagulation-flocculation removal principles. The low total suspended solids (TSS) content achieved during the process has the additional advantage of allowing the use of the treated effluent for sprinkler or drip irrigation.

Different coagulants can be used, with ferric and alum coagulants being the most common (Jiménez, 2003). Lime has been used at very high doses (more than 1000mg/litre) to coagulate but also to raise the pH to inactivate 4.5 log of faecal coliforms using a contact time of 9–12 hours. Unfortunately, sludge production is high and lime easily forms deposits creating clogging problems (Gambrill, 1990; Jiménez and Chávez, 2002; Jiménez and Chávez Mejia, 1997). The cost of the APT is only one-third of the cost of a conventional activated sludge system, including sludge treatment and disposal (within 20km) (Jiménez and Chávez, 2002). APT removes 1 log of faecal coliforms, 1 log *Salmonella* spp., 50–80 per cent of protozoa cysts (*Giardia, Entamoeba coli* and *E. histolytica*) and 90–99 per cent of helminth ova (Jiménez et al., 2001). From a content of up to 120 eggs/litre, APT may consistently produce an effluent with 0.5–3 eggs/litre (Chávez et al., 2004; Jiménez et al., 2001). With regard to nutrients, the total nitrogen removal is of the order 13 per cent with ferric chloride, 17 per cent with alum and 12 per cent with lime; the main fraction removed is organic nitrogen. Phosphorus removal was 20 per cent for ferric chloride, 15 per cent for alum and 54 per cent for lime.

Coagulation-flocculation can also be used as a tertiary treatment process. Chemicals (e.g. ferric chloride, ferrous chloride, aluminium sulphate, calcium oxide) are added to secondary effluents which cause very small particles to combine or aggregate; these larger aggregated particles then settle out of the liquid. Increasing particulate matter removal also increases viral and bacterial removals as they are often solids-associated – for example, viruses can be reduced by 2–3 log units under optimal conditions (Jiménez, 2003).

Secondary biological treatment

There are several options to treat wastewater biologically at a secondary level, all of them aerobic. These processes efficiently remove organic matter and, to a lesser extent, nutrients. They are high cost and complex to operate. The most widely used process is activated sludge, but other secondary treatments include aerated lagoons, oxidation ditches and trickling filters. There is an extensive specialized literature describing these processes and detailing their design (e.g. Metcalf and Eddy, Inc., 2003).

It is worth noting that Arthur (1983), in an economic comparison of WSP, aerated lagoons, oxidation ditches and trickling filters for the city of Sana'a, found that WSP were the least cost option up to land prices of US$50,000–150,000 (depending on the discount rate used), above which oxidation ditches were the cheapest treatment option, with aerated lagoons and trickling filters always being much more expensive. (The costing methodology used by Arthur was very rigorous and it still recommended for use today.)

Membrane bioreactors

Effluents from activated sludge aeration tanks may be further treated by passage through membranes. These membranes have a very small pore size (20–500nm), so they operate in the ultrafiltration and microfiltration ranges. They are thus able to achieve essentially complete reduction (i.e. >6 log units) of all pathogens, including viruses. However, membranes are very complex and expensive to operate, and membrane fouling is a particular concern, although costs and the complexity of operation are decreasing as the technology improves (Stephenson et al., 2000). Membrane bioreactors provide an extremely efficient, but correspondingly very expensive, combination of secondary and tertiary treatment. Often the effluent quality is far in excess of what is required (and thus may be considered to be a suboptimal use of scarce resources).

Filtration

Filtration is a useful treatment step to remove protozoan (oo)cysts and helminth eggs from effluents resulting from a primary or a secondary treatment step, whether this is physicochemical (Landa et al., 1997) or biological, such as activated sludge (Jiménez, 2007). During filtration, pathogens and other particulate matter are removed as they pass through sand or other porous granular media. Pollutants are retained by sieving, adsorption, straining, interception and sedimentation. There are several types of filtration including high-rate granular filtration (>2 m^3/m^2h), slow sand filtration, and single and multiple media filtration. Efficient slow sand filtration requires optimal maturation of the surface microbiological layer (the 'schmutzdecke'), cleaning and refilling without short-circuiting (WHO, 2004).

Rapid sand filtration removes approximately 1 log unit of faecal coliforms, pathogenic bacteria (*Salmonella* and *Pseudomonas aeruginosa*) and enteroviruses, 50–80 per cent of protozoan cysts (*Giardia*, *Entamoeba coli* and *E. histolytica*) and 90–99 per cent of helminth ova (Jiménez et al., 2001) from coagulated primary effluent (these efficiencies can be improved if coagulants are added at the filter entrance). The specific size of the sand medium is 0.8–1.2mm, the minimum filter depth is 1m, filtration rates are 7–10m^3/m^2h and the filtration cycles are 20–35 hours. Under these conditions, the effluent consistently contains <0.1 helminth egg per litre (Jiménez, 2007; Landa et al., 1997). In dual media filtration, used as a tertiary treatment and combined with a coagulation process, bacterial reduction can increase from approximately 1 log unit to 2–3 log units (WHO, 2004).

Conventional disinfection

The effectiveness of disinfection depends upon several factors, including the type of disinfectant, its contact time with the wastewater, temperature, pH, effluent quality and type of pathogen (WEF, 1996). Chlorine (free chlorine), ozone and ultraviolet radiation are the principal disinfectants used to treat wastewater, although chloramines may be used for advanced primary treatment effluents. Disinfection should be optimized for each type of disinfectant. In general, bacteria are highly susceptible to all three disinfectants; helminth eggs and protozoan (oo)cysts are most resistant to chlorine and ozone; and certain viruses (e.g. adenoviruses) are most resistant to UV disinfection. Chlorine inactivates 1–3 log units of viruses, 2 log units of bacteria, 0–1.5 log units of protozoan (oo)cysts, but almost no helminth eggs. Similar results are found with the other disinfectants, but ozonation is much more efficient at inactivating viruses and UV radiation results in better inactivation of protozoa.

Infiltration-percolation

Infiltration-percolation consists essentially of intermittently infiltrating wastewater through 1.5 to 2.0m deep unsaturated coarse sand beds. These systems treat primary or secondary effluents. As the mean hydraulic load of primary and secondary effluents cannot exceed, respectively, about 0.25 and 0.65m^3 per day per m^2 of sand-bed area, the use of infiltration-percolation systems is restricted to small works serving only a few thousand people, although they can be used to serve populations up to approximately 25,000 when treating secondary effluents. Larger plants would require too much filter surface and sand volume.

This low-energy consumption technology is proven to be an efficient means of reclaiming primary or secondary effluents prior to reuse. Full-scale plant monitoring has shown that E. coli numbers are reliably reduced to <1000 per 100ml (Salgot et al., 1996). Helminth eggs are completely removed, as are protozoa such as Giardia and Cryptosporidium (Alcalde et al., 2006).

Soil-aquifer treatment

Pumping tertiary-treated wastewater into a local aquifer (but not one used as a source of drinking water) is one way of storing the wastewater until it is required for irrigation. However, this is an expensive option and it has only been occasionally used – for example, the Dan Region scheme in Israel, which is a very large-scale soil-aquifer treatment (SAT) scheme (120–140Mm^3/yr) that has now been operational for more than 30 years (Icekson-Tal et al., 2003). SAT is particularly suitable for unrestricted irrigation as it provides storage as well as treatment to a level comparable to drinking-water quality. However, operation and maintenance are not simple: for example, particular attention has to be paid to optimizing the operation of the recovery wells to prevent high sand concentrations in the pipes and to minimize biofilm growth and iron and manganese deposits (Bixio et al., 2005).

COMPARISON OF TREATMENT METHODS

Table 8.2 summarizes the main characteristics of the wastewater treatment processes presented here, as well as some others not described in detail. The selection of a specific treatment process needs to be based on local climatic conditions and economic and human resource capabilities.

CONCLUSIONS

For agricultural irrigation in developing countries, it is important to select wastewater treatment processes that both reduce pathogen numbers and retain the nutrients. These are demands that are often difficult to reconcile and therefore a detailed analysis for each particular situation is required. As illustrated by WHO (2006), it is important to reduce pathogen levels before wastewaters are used for crop irrigation. For this to be achieved in practice, only locally viable treatment methods should be selected. Where, for example, institutional capacities to build and maintain treatment plants are limited, as is common in many developing countries, 'low-tech' natural systems should be used, commonly in conjunction with post-treatment health-protection control measures (see Chapter 5). In high-income countries, wastewater treatment coverage becomes more comprehensive and more advanced processes become financially and operationally feasible, so allowing society to rely on wastewater treatment more and more to prevent food contamination from wastewater irrigation.

In addition, knowledge of the types of pathogens and their expected numbers in local wastewaters is required in order to ensure that the selected process is capable of efficiently inactivating or removing them. It is also important to consider the amount and quality of sludge produced during wastewater treatment and how it will be disposed of or locally reused.

Table 8.2 *Characteristics of wastewater treatment processes with reference to their applicability to treatment prior to agricultural reuse in developing countries*

Process and operating conditions	Efficiency	Nutrient content	Advantages	Disadvantages
Natural treatment processes				
Waste stabilization ponds (5–20 days' retention time)	Organic matter: high Viruses, bacteria and protozoa: high Helminth eggs: 70–99% with high reliability	Low to medium	Low investment and operating costs. Simple to operate. Requires no electricity. Low sludge production. Appropriate for warm climates with medium to low evaporation rates. Permits the whole year's wastewater to be used in the irrigation season, so enabling a greater area to be irrigated and thus more crops produced. Does not require a conventional disinfection step	Water loss due to evaporation can be high, so leads to increased effluent salinity. High land demand. Algal content in the effluent may clog sprinklers if used. Can facilitate vector breeding if not properly maintained.
Wastewater storage and treatment reservoirs	Suspended solids: medium Organic matter: low Viruses, bacteria and protozoa: high Helminth eggs: 70–99% with high reliability	High	Very low investment and operating costs. Requires no electricity.	Sludge may contain viable pathogens and needs to be carefully managed
UASB reactors and HRAP (6–12 hours' retention time)	Organic matter: very high Helminth eggs: 60–96% with low reliability	Medium to high	Low cost. Low sludge production. Requires no electricity.	Effluent can cause odour problems. Effluent requires further (i.e. secondary) treatment. Sludge needs further treatment.

Table 8.2 *(Continued)*

Process and operating conditions	Efficiency	Nutrient content	Advantages	Disadvantages
Constructed wetlands (4 days' retention time in surface-flow wetlands)	Organic matter: high Pathogens: high for all, but with low reliability Helminth eggs: 60–100%	Low to medium	Low cost. Easy to operate. Requires no electricity. May improve the environment for other species (e.g. birds, rodents).	High land demand. Pathogen removal variable depending upon a variety of factors. Needs further treatment (e.g. filtration) to reliably remove helminth eggs. May facilitate mosquito breeding. Wildlife excreta may cause deterioration of effluent quality.

Primary sedimentation

Process and operating conditions	Efficiency	Nutrient content	Advantages	Disadvantages
Primary sedimentation (2–6 hours' retention time)	Organic matter: low Helminth eggs: 30% with low reliability	High	Low cost. Simple technology.	Low bacterial and viral removals. Effluent needs further treatment. Sludge needs further treatment.
CEPT (low coagulant doses; 3–4 hours' retention time) Advanced primary treatment (low coagulant doses when flocculants are used, high-rate settlers, 0.5–1 hour overall retention time)	Organic matter: medium Helminth eggs: high with high reliability	Medium	Low to medium cost compared to activated sludge (third of the cost). High efficiency and reliability. Low area requirement, notably for the APT.	Conventional disinfection is required to inactivate bacteria. Produces more sludge than primary sedimentation, stabilization ponds and wetlands. Sludge needs to be disinfected. Need to use chemicals.

Secondary treatment processes

Process and operating conditions	Efficiency	Nutrient content	Advantages	Disadvantages
Aerated lagoon plus settling pond	Organic matter: high	Low to medium	Technology widely available and well understood. No need for primary sedimentation. Less expensive and complex than other high-rate processes.	Requires electricity. Requires larger land area than other high-rate processes. Sludge needs disinfection. Needs a conventional disinfection step to inactivate viruses and bacteria.

Table 8.2 *(Continued)*

Process and operating conditions	Efficiency	Nutrient content	Advantages	Disadvantages
Oxidation ditches	Organic matter: high	Low to medium	Technology widely available and well understood. No need for primary sedimentation.	Requires electricity. Sludge needs disinfection Needs a conventional disinfection step to inactivate viruses and bacteria.
Trickling filters plus secondary settlers	Organic matter: high Helminth eggs: medium removal with medium reliability	Low to medium	Medium operating costs. High reliability. Technology widely available and well understood.	High investment costs. Needs trained staff. Sludge needs disinfection. Needs a conventional disinfection step to inactivate viruses and bacteria. Fly control required.
Activated sludge plus secondary sedimentation (4–8 hours' retention time in the reactor)	Organic matter: high Helminth eggs: 70–90% with low reliability	Low to medium	Removes organic matter with high reliability. Technology widely available and well understood. Easy to control.	High investment and operating costs. High energy demand. Needs trained staff. Sludge needs disinfection. Sludge bulking reduces helminth egg removal. Needs a conventional disinfection step to inactivate viruses and bacteria.
Membrane bioreactors	Organic matter, suspended solids and pathogens: high	Low	Removes all pathogens. Technology still under development.	High cost and complexity. Sludge needs disinfection. Membrane fouling. Needs trained staff.
Tertiary treatment processes				
Slow sand filtration	Organic matter: medium Pathogens: low to high	Medium to high	Technology well known.	More information is needed on pathogen removal. Requires large amount of space. Handling of filters during washing and sludge removal may create health concerns.

Table 8.2 *(Continued)*

Process and operating conditions	Efficiency	Nutrient content	Advantages	Disadvantages
Rapid sand filtration ($2m^3/m^2h$ with 0.8–1.2mm sand and 1m height) Cycle duration up to 35h, for a primary treatment	Helminth eggs: high (90–99%) (very high if coagulant is added)	High if used for primary effluent	High efficiency. High reliability. Improves pathogen removal. Well understood technology. Low additional cost.	Complementary process to biological or chemical wastewater treatment. Implies an additional cost.
Coagulation-flocculation as a tertiary treatment	Organic matter: high Nutrient: high	Low	Improves removal of viruses and other pathogens. Low additional cost.	High total cost (primary + secondary + tertiary treatment). Increases sludge production. Sludge needs to be disinfected.

Disinfection

Process and operating conditions	Efficiency	Nutrient content	Advantages	Disadvantages
Chlorination: doses and contact time depend on the characteristic of the effluent to be treated	Bacteria, viruses and some protozoa: high	–	Medium cost but it is the lowest cost for a conventional disinfection method. Well understood technology.	Needs to be applied to effluents with low organic matter and suspended solids contents. Creates disinfection by-products. Hazardous chemical.
Ozonation: doses and contact time depend on the characteristics of the effluent to be treated	Bacteria and some protozoa: high Viruses: very high	–	High efficiency of virus inactivation.	Needs to be applied to effluents with low organic matter and suspended solids contents. Higher cost and complexity than chlorination. Low efficiency of helminth inactivation at economical doses. Needs to be generated on site. Production of hazardous by-products.
UV radiation: doses and contact time depend on the characteristics of the effluent to be treated	Bacteria, viruses and protozoa: high	–	Similar or higher than cost of chlorination. Effective in inactivating bacteria, viruses	Needs to be applied to effluents with low organic matter and suspended solids content and high transmittance. Does not inactivate

Table 8.2 *(Continued)*

Process and operating conditions	Efficiency	Nutrient content	Advantages	Disadvantages
			and some protozoa. No toxic chemicals used or produced. Technology well known.	helminth eggs or all protozoa. Performance can be reduced by particulate matter and biofilm formation. Needs good maintenance of lamps.
Soil-aquifer treatment				
Infiltration-percolation: application of primary or secondary effluents to a sand bed for infiltration into local groundwater	Helminth eggs and protozoa: high (due to removal in sand bed) Bacteria and viruses: high (due to die-off in ground-water)	Low	No water losses due to evaporation. Simple operation.	Requires large land area. Needs good maintenance of sand bed.
Soil-aquifer treatment: pumping tertiary-treated waste-water into a local aquifer for storage until next irrigation season	High (due to die-off during long storage)	Low	No water losses due to evaporation.	Only to be used only for effluents with low organic matter and suspended solids contents. High cost and complexity. Pump maintenance often problematic.

Source: Alcalde et al. (2006), Asano and Levine (1998), Clancy et al. (1998), Jiménez (2003, 2005), Jiménez and Chávez (2002), Jiménez and Navarro (2009), Karimi et al. (1999), Landa et al. (1997), Lazarova et al. (2000), Mara (2004), Metcalf and Eddy, Inc. (1991, 2003), NRMMC and EPHCA (2005), Rivera et al. (1995), Rojas-Valencia et al. (2004), Rose et al. (1996), Schwartzbrod et al. (1989), Sobsey (1989), Sperling and Chernicharo (2005), Sperling et al. (2003), Strauss (1996), WHO (2004, 2006)

NOTES

1   The opinions expressed in this chapter are those of the authors and do not necessarily reflect the views or policies of the World Health Organization.

2   It is important to note that helminth egg removal efficiency provides more information when expressed as a percentage, rather than in log units (as in WHO, 2006), due to their much lower numbers in wastewater compared to those of bacteria and viruses and the need to achieve single-digit effluent qualities.

3   Log units are, strictly, log_{10} units, such that a 4 log unit reduction (for example) = 99.99 per cent removal.

REFERENCES

Alcalde, L., Folch, M., Tapias, J. C., Huertas, E., Torrens, A. and Salgot, M. (2006) 'Wastewater reclamation systems in small communities', *Water Science and Technology*, vol 55, no 7, pp149–54

Ali, M., Al-Sa'ed, R. and Mahmoud, N. (2007) 'Start-up phase assessment of a UASB-septic tank system for treating domestic septage', *Arabian Journal for Science and Engineering*, vol 32, no 1C, pp65–75

Arthur, J. P. (1983) *Notes on the Design and Operation of Waste Stabilization Ponds in Warm Climates of Developing Countries*, Technical Paper no 7, World Bank, Washington, DC

Asano, T. and Levine, A. D. (1998) 'Wastewater reclamation, recycling, and reuse: An introduction', in T. Asano (ed) *Wastewater Reclamation and Reuse*, Technomic Publishing Company, Lancaster, PA, pp1–56

Belmont, M. A., Cantellano, E., Thompson, S., Williamson, M., Sanchez, A. and Metcalfe, C. D. (2004) 'Treatment of domestic wastewater in a pilot scale natural treatment system in Mexico', *Ecological Engineering*, vol 23, pp299–311

Bixio, D., de Heyder, B., Cikurel, H., Muston, M., Miska, V. et al. (2005) 'Municipal wastewater reclamation: Where do we stand? An overview of treatment technology and management practice', *Water Science and Technology: Water Supply*, vol 5, no 1, pp77–85

Cavalcanti, P. F. F. (2003) 'Integrated application of UASB reactor and ponds for domestic sewage treatment in tropical regions', PhD thesis, Wageningen University, Wageningen, The Netherlands

Chávez, A., Jiménez, B. and Maya, C. (2004) 'Particle size distribution as a useful tool for microbial detection', *Water Science and Technology*, vol 50, no 2, pp179–86

Clancy, J. L., Hargy, T. M., Marshall, M. M. and Dyksen, J. E. (1998) 'UV light inactivation of *Cryptosporidium* oocysts', *Journal of the American Water Works Association*, vol 90, no 9, pp92–102

Clemett, A. E. V. and Ensink, J. H. J. (2006) 'Farmer driven wastewater treatment: A case study from Faisalabad, Pakistan', in *Proceedings of the 32nd WEDC International Conference, Colombo, Sri Lanka*, WEDC, Loughborough, pp99–104, available at http://wedc.lboro.ac.uk/conferences/pdfs/32/Clemett.pdf

Curtis, T. P., Mara, D. D. and Silva, S. A. (1992) 'Influence of pH, oxygen and humic substances on ability of sunlight to damage faecal coliforms in waste stabilization pond water', *Applied and Environmental Microbiology*, vol 58, no 4, pp1335–45

Drechsel, P., Keraita, B., Amoah, P., Abaidoo, R., Raschid-Sally, L. and Bahri, A. (2008) 'Reducing health risks from wastewater use in urban and peri-urban sub-Saharan Africa: Applying the 2006 WHO Guidelines', *Water Science and Technology*, vol 57, no 9, pp1461–6

Duqqah, M. (2002) 'Treated sewage water use in irrigated agriculture. Theoretical design of farming systems in Seil Al Zarqa and the Middle Jordan Valley in Jordan', PhD thesis, Wageningen University, Wageningen, The Netherlands

Gambrill, M. P. (1990) 'Physicochemical treatment of tropical wastewater', PhD thesis, University of Leeds, Leeds

Grimason, A., Smith, H., Thitai, W., Smith, P., Jackson, M. and Girwood, R. (1996) 'Occurrence and removal of *Cryptosporidium* oocysts and *Giardia* cysts in Kenyan waste stabilization ponds', *Water Science and Technology*, vol 36, no 7, pp97–104

Ickson-Tal, N., Avraham, O., Sack, J. and Cikurel, H. (2003) 'Water reuse in Israel – The Dan region project: evaluation of the water quality and reliability of plant's operation', *Water Science and Technology: Water Supply*, vol 3, no 4, pp231–7

IWA Specialist Group (2000) *Constructed Wetlands for Pollution Control. Processes, Performance, Design and Operation*, IWA Publishing, London, pp156

Jiménez, B. (2003) 'Health risks in aquifer recharge with recycled water', in R. Aertgeerts and A. Angelakis (eds) *Aquifer Recharge Using Reclaimed Water*, WHO Regional Office for Europe, Copenhagen, pp54–172

Jiménez, B. (2005) 'Treatment technology and standards for agricultural wastewater reuse: A case study in Mexico', *Irrigation and Drainage Journal*, vol 54, pp23–33

Jiménez, B. (2007) 'Helminth ova removal from wastewater for agriculture and aquaculture reuse', *Water Science and Technology*, vol 55, nos 1–2, pp485–93

Jiménez, B. (2009) 'Helminth ova control in wastewater and sludge for agricultural reuse', in W. O. K. Grabow (ed) *Encyclopaedia of Biological, Physiological and Health Sciences, Water and Health*, vol 2, UNESCO/EOLSS Publishers Co Ltd, Oxford, pp429–49

Jiménez, B., Barrios, J., Mendez J. and Diaz, J. (2004) 'Sustainable management of sludge in developing countries', *Water Science and Technology*, vol 49, no 10, pp251–8

Jiménez, B. and Chávez, A. (2002) 'Low-cost technology for reliable use of Mexico City's wastewater for agricultural irrigation', *Technology*, vol 9, nos 1–2, pp95–108

Jiménez, B. and Chávez Mejia, A. (1997) 'Treatment of Mexico City wastewater for irrigation purposes', *Environmental Technology*, vol 18, pp721–30

Jiménez, B., Maya, C. and Salgado, G. (2001) 'The elimination of helminth ova, faecal coliforms, *Salmonella* and protozoan cysts by various physicochemical processes in wastewater and sludge', *Water Science and Technology*, vol 43, no 12, pp179–82

Jiménez, B. and Navarro, I. (2009) 'Methodology to set regulations for safe reuse of wastewater and sludge for agriculture in developing countries based on a scientific approach and following the new WHO Guidelines', in A. Dividewi (ed) *Handbook of Research on IT Management and Clinical Data Administration in Healthcare*, ISI Global, New York, pp690–709

Juanicó, M. and Dor, I. (1999) *Hypertrophic Reservoirs for Wastewater Storage and Reuse: Ecology, Performance, and Engineering Design*, Springer Verlag, Heidelberg

Juanicó, M. and Milstein, A. (2004) 'Semi-intensive treatment plants for wastewater reuse in irrigation', *Water Science and Technology*, vol 50, no 2, pp55–60

Karimi, A. A., Vickers, J. C. and Harasick, R. F. (1999) 'Microfiltration goes to Hollywood: The Los Angeles experience', *Journal of the American Water Works Association*, vol 91, no 6, pp90–103

Landa, H., Capella, A. and Jiménez, B. (1997) 'Particle size distribution in an effluent from an advanced primary treatment and its removal during filtration', *Water Science and Technology*, vol 36, no 4, pp59–165

Lazarova, V., Savoye, P., MacGovern, L., Shields, P., Tchobanoglous, G., Sakaji, R. and Yates, M. (2000) 'Wastewater disinfection by UV: Evaluation of the MS2 phages as a biodosimeter for plant design', in *Proceedings of the Water Reuse Association Symposium*

2000, Napa, CA, 12–15 September, Water Reuse Association, Alexandria, VA (CD-ROM)

Lier, J. B. van, Zeeman, G. and Huibers, F. (2002) 'Anaerobic (pre-)treatment for the decentralized reclamation of domestic wastewater, stimulating agricultural reuse', in *Proceedings of the Latin American Workshop and Symposium 'Anaerobic Digestion 7', Mérida, Yucatán, 22–25 October*, www.cepis.ops-oms.org/bvsacd/unam7/anaerobic.pdf

Mara, D. (2004) *Domestic Wastewater Treatment in Developing Countries*, Earthscan, London

Mara, D. D., Pearson, H. W., Oragui, J. I., Cawley, L. R., de Oliveira, R. and Silva, S. A. (1997) 'Wastewater storage and treatment reservoirs in Northeast Brazil', *TPHE Research Monograph no 12*, School of Civil Engineering, University of Leeds, Leeds

Mara, D. D. and Silva, S. A. (1986) 'Removal of intestinal nematode eggs in tropical waste stabilization ponds', *Journal of Tropical Medicine and Hygiene*, vol 89, pp71–4

Metcalf and Eddy, Inc. (1991) *Wastewater Engineering: Treatment, Disposal and Reuse*, 3rd ed., McGraw-Hill, New York

Metcalf and Eddy, Inc. (2003) *Wastewater Engineering: Treatment, Disposal and Reuse*, 4th ed., McGraw-Hill, New York

Nelson, K., Jiménez-Cisneros, B., Tchobanoglous, G. and Darby, J. (2004) 'Sludge accumulation, characteristics, and pathogen inactivation in four primary waste stabilization ponds in central Mexico', *Water Research*, vol 38, no 1, pp111–27

NRMMC and EPHCA (2005) *National Guidelines for Water Recycling: Managing Health and Environmental Risks*, National Resource Management Ministerial Council and Environment Protection and Heritage Council of Australia, Canberra

Oragui, J. L., Curtis, T. P., Silva, S. A. and Mara, D. D. (1987) 'Removal of excreted bacteria and viruses in deep waste stabilization ponds in northeast Brazil', *Water Science and Technology*, vol 19, pp569–73

Peña, M. R., Rodrigues, J., Mara, D. D. and Spulveda, M. (2000) 'UASBs or anaerobic ponds in warm climates? A preliminary answer from Colombia', *Water Science and Technology*, vol 42, nos 10–11, pp59–65

Peña Varón, M. R. (2002) 'Advanced primary treatment of domestic wastewater in tropical countries: Development of high-rate anaerobic ponds', PhD thesis, University of Leeds, Leeds

Rivera, F., Warren, A., Ramirez, E., Decamp, O. and Bonilla, P. (1995) 'Removal of pathogens from wastewaters by the root zone method (RZM)', *Water Science and Technology*, vol 32, no 3, p211–18

Rojas-Valencia, M. N., Orta-de-Velásquez, M. T., Vaca-Mier, M. and Franco, V. (2004) 'Ozonation byproducts issued from the destruction of micro-organisms present in wastewaters treated for reuse', *Water Science and Technology*, vol 50, no 2, pp187–93

Rose, J. B., Dickson, L. J., Farrah, S. R. and Carnahan, R. P. (1996) 'Removal of pathogenic and indicator micro-organisms by a full-scale water reclamation facility', *Water Research*, vol 30, no 11, pp2785–97

Russell, R. C. (1999) 'Constructed wetlands and mosquitoes: Health hazards and management options – An Australian perspective', *Ecological Engineering*, vol 12, pp107–124

Salgot, M., Brissaud, F. and Campos, C. (1996) 'Disinfection of secondary effluents by infiltration-percolation', *Water Science and Technology*, vol 33, nos 10–11, pp271–6

Schäfer, L., Lundström, J. O., Pfeffer, M., Lundkvist, E. and Landin, J. (2004) 'Biological diversity versus risk for mosquito nuisance and disease transmission in constructed wetlands in southern Sweden', *Medical and Veterinary Entomology*, vol 18, no 3, pp256–61

Schwartzbrod, J., Stien, J. L., Bouhoum, K. and Baleux, B. (1989) 'Impact of wastewater treatment on helminth eggs', *Water Science and Technology*, vol 21, no 3, pp295–7

Shuval, H., Adin, A., Fattal, B., Rawutz, E. and Yekutiel, P. (1986) *Wastewater Irrigation in Developing Countries: Health Effects and Technical Solutions*, World Bank Technical Paper no 51, World Bank, Washington, DC

Sobsey, M. (1989) 'Inactivation of health-related micro-organisms in water by disinfection processes', *Water Science and Technology*, vol 21, no 3, pp179–95

Sperling, M. von, Bastos, R. K. X. and Kato, M. T. (2004) 'Removal of *E. coli* and helminth eggs in UASB-polishing pond systems', paper presented at the 6th International Water Association Specialist Conference on Waste Stabilization Ponds, Avignon, France, 27 September–1 October

Sperling, M. von and Chernicharo, C. A. L. (2005) *Biological Wastewater Treatment in Warm Climate Regions*, IWA Publishing, London

Sperling, M. von, Chernicharo, C., Soares, A. and Zerbini, A. M. (2002) 'Coliform and helminth egg removal in a combined UASB reactor–baffled pond system in Brazil: Performance evaluation and mathematical modelling', *Water Science and Technology*, vol 5, no 10, pp237–42

Sperling, M. von, Chernicharo, C., Soares, A. and Zerbini, A. M. (2003) 'Evaluation and modeling of helminth egg removal in baffled and unbaffled ponds treating effluent', *Water Science and Technology*, vol 48, no 2, pp113–20

Stephenson, T., Judd, S., Jefferson, B. and Brindley, K. (2000) *Membrane Bioreactors for Wastewater Treatment*, IWA Publishing, London

Strauss, M. (1996) *Health (Pathogen) Considerations Regarding the Use of Human Waste in Aquaculture*, EAWAG, Dübendorf, Switzerland, www.eawag.ch/organization/ abteilungen/sandec/publikationen/publications_wra/downloads_wra/human_waste_ use_health__pathogen__risks_in_aquaculture.pdf

WEF (1996) *Wastewater Disinfection, Manual of Practice No. FD-10*, Water Environment Federation, Alexandria, VA

WHO (2004) *Guidelines for Drinking Water Quality*, 3rd ed., World Health Organization, Geneva

WHO (2006) *Guidelines for the Safe Use of Wastewater, Excreta and Greywater, Volume 2: Wastewater Use in Agriculture*, World Health Organization, Geneva

9

Low-Cost Options for Pathogen Reduction and Nutrient Recovery from Faecal Sludge

Doulaye Koné, Olufunke O. Cofie and Kara Nelson

ABSTRACT

Recently, the application of excreta-based fertilizers has attracted attention due to the strongly increasing prices of chemically produced fertilizers. Faecal sludge from on-site sanitation systems is rich in nutrients and organic matter, constituents which contribute to replenishing the humus layer and soil nutrient reservoir and to improving soil structure and water-holding capacity. Hence, it represents an important resource for enhancing soil productivity on a sustainable basis. However, there is little in the scientific literature about the performance of treatment technology allowing recovery of nutrient resources from human waste. This paper reviews the state of knowledge of different processes that have been applied worldwide. Their pathogen removal efficiency as well as nutrient and biosolids recovery performances are assessed. The chapter outlines the gaps in research for further development.

INTRODUCTION

Contrary to wastewater management, the development of strategies and treatment options adapted to the conditions prevailing in developing countries to cope with faecal sludges (FS), the by-products of on-site sanitation installations, have long been neglected. In recent years though, an encouraging number of initiatives for improved FS management, including the devising of appropriate FS treatment schemes, have emerged, for instance in several West African countries (Senegal, Mali, Ivory Coast, Burkina Faso, Ghana) and in Southeast Asia (Nepal, Philippines, Thailand, Vietnam) as well as in Latin America. These initiatives help urban dwellers and authorities to overcome the challenges posed by what might be designated the 'urban shit drama' – the indiscriminate and uncontrolled disposal of faecal sludges into drains, canals and open spaces, thereby creating a 'faecal film' prevailing in urban areas and impairing public health, causing pollution, and creating nose- and eyesores.

The authors estimate that in the order of one-third of the world population (approximately 2.4 billion urban dwellers) rely on on-site sanitation installations, namely unsewered family and public latrines and toilets, aqua privies and septic tanks. This situation is likely to last for decades to come, since city-wide sewered sanitation is neither affordable nor feasible for the majority of urban areas in developing countries. Using the figure of 1 litre FS/cap/day as an average FS generation rate in urban areas (based on literature data and our own investigations), in a city of 1 million inhabitants, in the order of 1000m³/d of FS should be collected and disposed of daily. However, reported daily collection rates for cities much larger than this (e.g. Accra, Bangkok and Hanoi) rarely exceed 300–500m³/d. This indicates that huge quantities, if not the major fractions, of the FS generated are disposed of unrecorded or clandestinely within the urban settlement area.

When full, latrines are emptied mechanically by emptying trucks, or manually by labourers or family members (sometime the only option for the poorest households). While mechanically emptied sludge, from planned and accessible areas, can be transported and disposed of several kilometres from people's homes, the manually emptied sludge from inaccessible low-income areas is usually deposited within the family's compound, into nearby lanes, in nearby drains or on open land. These practices, often unrecorded, represent a significant risk to public health and have a high disease impact on emptying operators, their families, the households living in the immediate area and on vulnerable populations in latrine-based cities. To achieve effective and sustained health protection for these exposed urban populations, future latrine provision programmes must develop an approach that links on-site sanitation infrastructure to the transport system and safe reuse or disposal/treatment of the emptied faecal sludge (solids, liquid, or a mixture of both). This approach could be different for the planned and densely populated slum areas.

The low-cost FS treatment processes considered by the authors to be potentially suitable for developing countries comprise mainly non-mechanized options as listed below. These options are not sufficiently documented and updated in the existing literature.

Faecal sludge low-cost treatment options considered in this chapter

- settling/thickening tanks or ponds (non-mechanized, batch-operated);
- unplanted drying beds;
- constructed wetlands;
- combined composting ('co-composting') with organic solid waste;
- pond treatment of FS supernatants or percolates;
- land application in hot arid to semi-arid regions;
- anaerobic digestion with biogas utilization;
- lime stabilization.

These options, with the exception of anaerobic digestion and lime stabilization, have been experimented upon and investigated during ten years of collaborative field research with selected partners in Latin America, West Africa and Asia. Information on mechanized and energy-intensive sludge processing systems currently used in industrialized countries is described in International Solid Wastes and Public Cleansing Association Working Group on Sewage and Waterworks Sludge (1998).

CHALLENGES IN TREATING FAECAL SLUDGES

The choice of a FS treatment option depends primarily on the characteristics of the sludges generated in a particular town or city and on the treatment objectives (agricultural reuse, landfilling of biosolids, or discharge of treated liquids into receiving water bodies). Like for wastewater, FS characteristics vary widely within and between cities, based on the types of on-site sanitation installations in use (e. g. dilution factor) and whether manual or mechanical emptying practices are used. Sludges from septic tanks are biochemically more stable due to the long storage periods compared to sludges from installations which are emptied weekly (e.g. public toilet vaults). In cities like Bangkok, Hanoi and Buenos Aires, for instance, septic tanks are the predominant form of on-site sanitation installations. When septic tanks are emptied, both the solid and liquid portions are usually pumped out. Where soak pits are used for infiltrating the septic tank supernatants, they may have to be emptied, too, due to clogging. This contributes to diluting the FS collected in a particular settlement. In West Africa, an important fraction of the urban population relies on public toilets, which are usually highly frequented. In Kumasi (Ghana), a city of 1 million inhabitants, 40 per cent of the population rely on unsewered public toilets, which are emptied at weekly intervals. The sludges collected from these installations are biochemically unstable (high in BOD_5) and exhibit high ammonium (NH_4^+-N) concentrations, as urine is disposed of with the faeces.

The specific challenges in treating FS in developing countries, as opposed to treating wastewater, lie in the fact that pathogen concentrations are higher by a factor of 10 to 100 in FS than municipal wastewater and that appropriate, affordable and enforceable discharge and reuse standards or guidelines pertaining to FS treatment are lacking. Table 9.1 lists FS characteristics observed by the authors and their partners in selected cities in Africa and Asia. The fact that FS exhibit widely varying characteristics calls for a careful selection of appropriate treatment options, especially for primary treatment. This may encompass solids–liquid separation or biochemical stabilization if the FS is still fresh and has undergone only partial degradation during on-plot storage and prior to collection. Faecal and wastewater treatment plant (WWTP) sludges may, in principle, be treated by the same type of modest-cost treatment options.

WHY RECYCLE HUMAN EXCRETA?

Faecal sludges are rich in nutrients and organic matter – constituents which contribute to replenishing the humus layer and soil nutrient reservoir and to

Table 9.1 *Faecal Sludge (FS) characteristics in selected cities in developing countries*

Parameters	Accra (Ghana)	Accra (Ghana)	Yaoundé (Cameroon)	Bangkok (Thailand)	Alcorta (Argentina)
Type of FS	Public-toilet sludge[a]	Septage[b]	Septage	Septage mean (range)	Septage mean (range)
TS (mg/l)	52,500	12,000	37,000	15,350 (2200–67,200)	(6000–35,000) (SS)
TVS (% of TS)	68	59	65	73	50 (VSS)
COD (mg/l)	49,000	7800	31,000	15,700 (1200–76,000)	4200
BOD$_5$ (mg/l)	7,600	840	N/A	2300 (600–5,500)	(750–2600)
TN (mg/l)	N/A	N/A	1100	1100 (300–5,000)	190
NH$_4$-N (mg/l)	3300	330	600	415 (120–1,200)	150
Ascaris (Eggs number/gTS)	N/A	(13–94)	2813	(0–14)	(0.1–16)

TS: total solids; SS: suspended solids; TVS: total volatile solids; VSS: volatile suspended solids; COD: chemical oxygen demand; BOD$_5$: biochemical oxygen demand; TN: total nitrogen.
[a]Sludge collected from latrines shared by a high-density population or latrines with very high emptying frequency (weeks, months).
[b]Sludge collected from septic tanks after two to five years. Septage is well digested and less concentrated in solids and nitrogen than public-toilet sludge.
Source: Based on investigations conducted by SANDEC's field research partners

improving soil structure and water-holding capacity. Hence, they represent an important resource for enhancing soil productivity on a sustainable basis. Unfortunately, in most urban areas of developing countries, FS management remains largely unregulated and chaotic, hence it causes contamination of soils and water bodies and endangers human health.

Many municipal decision-makers are well aware, though, that developing and applying sound recycling strategies would greatly contribute to alleviating the management problems. However, little action has been taken to recycle FS on a sustainable basis. It has been estimated that, worldwide, the global fertilizer industry produces some 170 million tons of fertilizer nutrients annually (International Fertilizer Industry Association, 2009), while at the same time 50 million tons of fertilizer equivalents are dumped into water bodies via sewered sanitation systems (Werner, 2007). Recovery of organic matter and nutrients from human waste as biosolids is an economic necessity and an urgently needed environmental protection strategy. As a consequence, strategies and low-cost technological options for excreta treatment have to be developed which allow the cost-effective and affordable recycling of organic matter and nutrients especially to urban and peri-urban agriculture.

Drangert (1998) reported the fertilization equivalent of human excreta, which is, in theory at least, nearly sufficient for a person to grow his own food. However, the value of nutrients that can be recovered during recycling would be less than that contained in the raw excreta since it is impossible to recover all the value in whatever treatment option is adopted. The nutrient content in FS shows that it is a potential resource which should be utilized by farmers to replenish soil fertility for increased crop yield. It could be mixed with organic solid waste to generate very good fertilizer material. The organic waste fraction in solid waste remains the largest proportion that can be recovered. The high content of organic matter (50–90 per cent) provides an opportunity for exploitation through composting processes (Allison et al., 1998; Asomani-Boateng and Haight, 1999).

NUTRIENT RECOVERY AND BIOSOLIDS SANITIZING PROCESSES

The separating of the solids and liquids which make up FS is the process-of-choice in FS treatment, unless it is decided to co-treat FS in an existing or planned wastewater treatment plant or if the FS loads are small compared to the flow of wastewater. Solids–liquid separation may be achieved through sedimentation and thickening in ponds or tanks or filtration, and drying in sludge drying beds. Table 9.2 provides an overview of how selected treatment processes or process combinations are able to achieve reductions of certain contaminants or constituents. The separated solids will in most cases require further storage, dewatering, drying or composting, resulting in biosolids usable as a soil conditioner-cum-fertilizer. Upon separation, the liquid fraction can be used directly for agriculture or other

Table 9.2 *Overview of selected options and expected removal (recovery) efficiencies in faecal sludge solid–liquid separation treatment systems*

Solids–liquid separation options	Design criteria	Treatment goal / achievable removal		
		Solids–liquid separation	Organic pollutants in liquid fraction, after separation	Parasites (helminth eggs)
Settling/ thickening tank	SAR[a]: 0.13m³/ m³ of raw FS HRT: ≥ 4 h S: 0.006 m²/cap (Accra)	SS: 60–70% COD: 30–50%	To be processed for further improvement in ponds or constructed wetlands	Concentrated in the settled and floating solids
Settling/ anaerobic pond	300–600g BOD₅/m³/d HRT: ≥ 15 days SAR: 0.02m³/m³ (Rosario) and 0.13m³/m³ (Accra)	BOD₅ > 60–70%	Filtered BOD₅ > 50%	Concentrated in the settled and floating solids
Unplanted drying/ dewatering beds	100–200kgTS/ m²/year S: 0.05 m²/cap (Accra)	SS: 60–80% COD: 70–90% NH₄⁺-N: 40–60%	To be treated for further improvement in ponds or constructed wetlands	100% retained on top of the filtering media
Planted drying beds (humification beds)	≤ 250kgTS/m²/ year SAR: 20cm/year (Bangkok)	SS > 80% SAR: 20cm/year	To be treated for further improvement in ponds or constructed wetlands	100% retained on top of the filtering media
Co-composting with solids waste	Mixing ratio FS/ SW = 1/2–1/3	N/A	N/A	1–2 log units
Facultative stabilization ponds	350kg BOD₅/ ha/d	Not for this purpose	> 60% removal of total BOD₅	Removed by settlement

[a]Solids Accumulation Rate = the amount of solids that accumulate in a treatment system until the operation is stopped.
S: surface area required per capita, HRT: hydraulic retention time
Source: Kone and Strauss (2004)

purposes such as aquaculture. In areas where reuse is not an option, it will undergo a polishing treatment to satisfy criteria for discharge into surface waters and/or to avoid groundwater pollution, where effluents are allowed to infiltrate.

Biosolids recovery through faecal sludge solids–liquid separation

The choice of either sedimentation tanks or ponds, besides depending on the type of sludges to be treated, is also determined by the mode of operation envisaged and by the provisions which are made for handling the mass of solids to be periodically removed from these primary treatment units. Solids quantities produced in sedimentation/thickening tanks, which, in their low-cost version, will be non-mechanized and batch-operated in loading/consolidating cycles of weeks to a few months, will be much smaller than the mass of solids to be emptied and handled from primary ponds. These have typical operating cycles of 6–12 months, unless measures are introduced, by which settled solids are evacuated at higher frequencies without stopping pond operations.

Settling ponds

Suspended solids (SS) retention efficiencies of up to 96 per cent are achieved in two alternating, batch-operated septage sedimentation ponds in Alcorta, Argentina (Ingallinella et al., 2002). The concomitant solids accumulation rate amounts to $0.02m^3/m^3$ of raw FS. The quality of the septage pond effluent (COD = 650mg/litre, BOD_5 = 150mg/litre, NH_4^+-N = 104mg/litre) resembles that of urban wastewater, allowing the combined treatment of the two liquids in a waste stablization pond (WSP) system comprising a facultative and a maturation pond (Ingallinella et al., 2002). Septage deliveries to the pond in operation are suspended and the supernatant transferred to the parallel pond when the settled solids layer has reached 50cm. The accumulated sludge is left to dewater until a total solids (TS) concentration of >20–25 per cent is achieved, allowing it to be shovelled. This lasts up to six months under the temperate-subtropical climate prevailing in the particular area (400km west of Buenos Aires). Bulking material such as grain husks, sawdust or woodchips could be used under such conditions to shorten the in situ storage and dewatering time. This type of settling pond design is based on an assumed pond-emptying frequency and on the known or expected solids accumulation rate.

Settling/thickening tanks

Twin, batch-operated, non-mechanized sedimentation/thickening tanks were put into use by the Accra (Ghana) Waste Management Department in 1989 to treat septage and public-toilet sludges at mixing ratios of approximately 3:1. The tanks were intensively investigated by the Ghana Water Research Institute and SANDEC from 1994–1997 (Heinss et al., 1998). Four distinct zones were observed to develop while FS loading was in progress: a lower bottom thickening zone with TS up to 140g/litre (14 per cent), an upper bottom zone with 60gTS/litre, a settled water zone with 3–4gTS/litre and a scum layer containing up to 200gTS/litre. The settled solids accumulation rate was $0.16m^3/m^3$ of raw FS and SS retention ranged from 60–70 per cent. The average COD and SS contents in the tank effluents amounted to 3000mg/litre and 1000mg/litre, respectively.

Unplanted drying/dewatering beds

Unplanted drying beds can be used for dewatering and drying of septage, septage/public-toilet sludge mixtures (at volumetric ratios > 2:1) and of primary pond sludges with initial TS content varying from 1.5 to more than 7 per cent. Dewatering performance varies with the initial TS and TVS (total volatile solids) content and the applied loads. Pescod (1971), in conducting septage dewatering/drying experiments on yard-scale drying beds in Thailand, found that 5–15 days of dewatering were necessary to reach a TS content of 25 per cent with initial solids loading rates varying from 70 to $475kgTS/m^2/year$ and a loading depth of 20cm. In Ghana, a dewatered sludge with 40 per cent TS was obtained from a mixture of septage/public-toilet sludge in 12 days, with an initial solids loading rate of $200kgTS/m^2/year$ and a loading depth of < 20cm. With a solids loading rate of $130\ TS/m^2/year$, a sludge with 70 per cent TS was obtained in nine days and a reduction in the percolating liquid (compared to the raw sludge mixture) of 60 per cent BOD_5 and 70 per cent COD was achieved (Heinss et al., 1998).

Planted dewatering/drying beds (constructed wetlands)

Constructed wetlands have been successfully operated by the Asian Institute of Technology (AIT) from 1997–2004, for treating septage in Bangkok, containing 14,000–18,000mgTS/litre. An optimum loading rate of $250kgTS/m^2$ per year was established, based on seven years of field research with three pilot constructed wetland beds (Koottatep et al., 2005). The beds were planted with *Typha angustifolia* (narrow-leaved cattail). Each bed had a surface of $25m^2$ and was fed with $8m^3$ of septage once a week. Impounding of the percolate proved necessary to secure sufficient humidity for the cattails, which developed wilting symptoms during dry seasons. Overall, 70–80 per cent TS, 96–99 per cent SS and 95–98 per cent total COD (TCOD) removals were achieved in the liquid fraction of the septage. TCOD removal was improved by impounding and so was nitrogen removal through denitrification. Ponding periods of six days were found to be optimal. The constructed wetlands were able to accumulate 70cm of sludge after four years of operation while maintaining their full permeability. The TS content of the dewatered sludge varied from 20–25 per cent in the uppermost layer (< 20cm) to 25–30 per cent in the deeper layers. Under steady loading conditions, the percolate quality was constant. TCOD in the percolate amounted to 250–500mg/litre, TS to 1500–4000mg/litre and SS to 100–300mg/litre. Experiments with biochemically unstable and highly concentrated sludges like those from public toilets in West African cities have not been conducted to date.

Nitrogen recovery

Settling tanks and ponds

Nitrogen lost in settling tanks (Table 9.2) is negligible due to the absence of nitrification under the fully anaerobic conditions prevalent. In pond schemes, nitrogen is stored in the organic form by newly forming biomass that later settles and accumulates in the sediments. Additional losses may occur by ammonia (NH_3) volatilization if overall hydraulic retention times are sufficiently long (weeks to months) and pH rises above 8, enabling the formation of NH_3 in the pH-dependant NH_4/NH_3 equilibrium (Heinss et al., 1998).

Unplanted drying beds

Organic nitrogen is filtered with the suspended solids retained on the bed surface (90–97 per cent). NH_3-N is lost by volatilization depending on local climatic conditions (wind, temperature, rain). Experiments from Ghana, conducted with different types of sludges, resulted in nitrogen recovery of 35–70 per cent (Cofie et al., 2006).

Planted dewatering/drying beds (constructed wetlands)

Nitrogen recovery of 55–60 per cent in planted dewatering beds treating septage is estimated to be due mainly to the accumulation of organic nitrogen in the dewatered sludge layers. Losses of nitrogen are due to NH_3 volatilization and nitrification/denitrification processes, and account for 15–35 per cent (Panuvatvanich et al., 2009). Percolate concentrations of 100–200mg/litre of organic and ammonia nitrogen and 50–150mg/litre of NH_4^+-N were observed at AIT's pilot scheme with initial concentrations of 1000 and 350mg/litre N, respectively (Koottatep et al., 2005).

Co-composting

The dynamics of nitrogen during co-composting of FS and organic solid waste have been documented (Cofie et al., 2006, 2009). Researchers found that the highest concentrations of ammonia-nitrogen recovered from co-composting of FS with organic solid waste occurred during the early stages of composting, when the organic matter degradation is most intense and NH_4-N is produced through the mineralization of organic nitrogen. NH_4-N concentration decreased continually during the thermophilic phase up to day 40 and then remained fairly stable afterwards until the end of maturation. It was observed that after 50 days of composting no further significant degradation of NH_4-N could be observed as the compost is maturing with a final value of 0.01 per cent of ammonium nitrogen.

For nitrate (NO_3-N), little nitrification can be observed under the thermophilic conditions. After the thermophilic phase, when the inner temperature is around 45°C, nitrification begins and a drastic decrease in ammonium concentration occurs. This started to occur after 30 days of composting. The nitrate value of 0.04 per cent at this point rose steadily and reached its maximum value of about 0.12 per cent after 60–70 days of composting.

Both organic nitrogen and total nitrogen (TN) have similar behaviour during co-composting of dewatered FS with organic solids waste. During the thermophilic phase, the nitrogen concentration remained fairly constant. During maturation the nitrogen levels rose higher than during the thermophilic phase. The final organic nitrogen value was about 1.05 per cent TS and the TN value was about 1.16 per cent TS.

Faecal sludge liquid fraction

Although high losses of nitrogen can occur in some of the above treatment processes, the effluent (or percolate) still contains high concentrations of nitrogen which can be used for irrigation. Where the possibility of recycling into agriculture exists, the salt content is often a limiting factor. Electrical conductivities (EC) observed in the supernatants of the Accra sedimentation tanks ranged from 8–10mS/cm but salt tolerance limits of even the most tolerable plants are 3mS/cm. Percolates from the AIT's planted dewatering units exhibited EC values of 2–5mS/cm. However, the long-term impact on soil salinity may be negligible as the high conductivity in the percolates or supernatants is mainly due to the high concentration of NH_4^+.

In Ghana, pond systems have been developed to polish effluent from the settling/thickening tank pre-treatment units. Algal growth was inhibited due to the excessive ammonia content caused by the highly concentrated public-toilet sludges. These exhibit NH_4^+-N + NH_3-N levels of > 3000mg/litre leading to NH_3-N levels in the FS liquids which are beyond the toxicity limits of algae (40–50mg NH_3-N/litre). In Kumasi, where septage and public-toilet sludges are collected and disposed in ponds at a volumetric ratio of 1:1, NH_3 volatilizing from the FS pond scheme causes eye irritation during periods of high temperature and during periods of insufficient winds. Ammonium concentrations in the public-toilet sludges, coupled with high ambient temperatures of >28°C, favour the release of obnoxious amounts of NH_3-N (Strauss et al., 1997).

Pathogen inactivation (biosolids sanitization)

The fate of pathogens during FS solid–liquid separation processes depends on their size and degree of particle association. Due to their large size, helminth eggs are concentrated with the solids, whereas bacteria and viruses may be found both in the liquid and attached to particles in the solids. Under most conditions, helminth eggs are expected to be the most resistant pathogens in FS. Although die-off of helminth eggs in the sludge layer of ponds has been documented (Nelson et al., 2004; Sanguinetti et al., 2005), some eggs can survive for many years. Low-cost treatment options such as planted drying beds, unplanted drying beds or co-composting can achieve high inactivation efficiency of helminths eggs when treating faecal sludge (Table 9.3).

Percolates from planted and unplanted drying beds are free of helminth eggs as they are filtered with the solids by the sand layer. In Cameroon, Kengne et al.

(2009) showed that the planted drying beds can reduce helminth egg concentration from 78.9 eggs/gTS to 4.0 eggs/gTS after a six-month loading period follow by six additional months' resting. No *Ancylostoma duodenale*, *Strongyloides stercoralis*, *Enterobius vermicularis* and *Taenia* sp. eggs were present after a four-month resting period for the sludge. During the six-month resting period, the biosolids dry-matter content increased from 51 to 77 per cent. However, the biosolids were not entirely sanitized after this storage period as regards compliance with the WHO Guidelines of less than one egg/gTS for safe agricultural practice (WHO, 2006). Hence prior to direct application on fields, further storage for at least one month protected from rain or other additional treatment may be necessary. Similar results were also obtained by Sanguinetti et al. (2005), who found a significant reduction of *Ascaris* egg viability with decreasing humidity (below 40 per cent) in unplanted drying beds in Argentina. From the authors' experience, a minimum six-month storage time is required to sanitize faecal sludge in planted dewatering beds under tropical conditions; the rate of sanitizing depends on the degree of drying.

Co-composting has been tested successfully as a means to sanitize faecal sludge due to the high temperatures produced during aerobic composting. In dewatered FS co-composted with municipal solid waste, greater than a 1 log unit removal of helminth eggs was achieved after two months (Koné et al., 2007). During the first month, the temperature at the centre of the compost pile was higher than 60°C, and near the edge it was initially above 45°C. These temperatures may increase the permeability of the *Ascaris* eggs' shell (Barrett, 1976), allowing transport of harmful compounds, as well as increasing the desiccation rate of the eggs (Capizzi-Banas et al., 2004; Feachem et al., 1983; Gaspard and Schwartzbrod, 2003). The decrease in moisture content in the eggs may reduce the helminth larvae's mobility and movement, thus contributing to their decay (Sanguinetti et al., 2005; Stromberg, 1997; Wharton, 1979).

Table 9.3 *Pathogen inactivation efficiency of selected low-cost faecal treatment options*

Treatment option or process	Helminth egg log reduction	Duration (months)	References
Settling ponds	3	4	Fernandez et al. (2004)
Planted dewateringdrying beds (constructed wetlands)	1.5	12	Koottatep et al. (2005)
Unplanted drying/dewatering beds (for pre-treatment)	0.5	0.3–0.6	Heinss et al. (1998)
Composting (windrow, thermophilic)	1.5–2.0	3	Koné et al. (2007)
pH elevation > 9	3	6	Chien et al. (2001)
Anaerobic (mesophilic)	0.5	0.5–1.0	Feachem et al. (1983); Gantzer et al. (2001)

Source: Adapted from WHO (2006)

Thus, the combination of unplanted drying beds and co-composting of subsequently dewatered sludge can produce hygienic biosolids safe for agricultural reuse. Additional options for treatment include maintaining high pH (Capizzi-Banas et al., 2004; Gaspard and Schwartzbrod, 2003), particularly in the presence of ammonia (Pecson et al., 2007; Pecson and Nelson, 2005). High pH can be achieved by addition of lime or ash; if quicklime (CaO) is used, heat is also generated. Because of the high NH_4^+-N content of FS (Table 9.3), rapid inactivation of *Ascaris* eggs by the neutral form of NH_4^+-N can occur. However, this process will also lead to rapid loss of NH_4^+-N due to volatilization, which is undesirable for nitrogen recovery. Also, this process has not yet been tested in the field for FS treatment.

Based on epidemiological and the quantitative microbial risk assessment (QMRA), Navarro et al. (2009) showed that higher helminth egg concentrations in biosolids did not significantly increase consumers' and farmers' health-risk exposure. Indeed, the current WHO Guidelines (WHO, 2006) were not developed using epidemiological evidence on this aspect. As a consequence, the indicative guideline value of 1 helminth egg/gTS in biosolids appears to be more stringent than necessary and unaffordable to achieve in most cases in developing countries.

Biosolids heavy metal content

Biosolids generated from constructed wetlands can be recycled in agriculture without reservation as regards heavy metal content, as tests in Bangkok exhibited relatively low trace element concentrations (mg/kgTS) of 63 Pb; 14 Ni; 26 Cr;

Table 9.4 *Trace elements in biosolids recovered from constructed wetlands*

Parameters	Trace elements concentration (mg/kgTS)				
	Biosolids (Kengne et al., 2009)	Co-compost MSW/FS: 3:1 (Cofie et al., 2008)	Co-compost MSW/FS: 2:1 (Cofie et al., 2008)	Limit values in EC eco label compost (Hogg et al., 2002)	Limit values in Spain sewage sludge (Hogg et al., 2002)
Fe	9579 ± 14	–	–	–	–
Pb	63 ± 32	24 ± 13	34 ± 41	100	750
Ni	14 ± 3	12 ± 2	9 ± 2	50	300
Cr	26 ± 4	90 ± 32	62 ± 20	100	1000
Cd	2.4 ± 0.8	0.4 ± 0.1	0.0 ± 0.2	1	20
Cu	575 ± 283	–	–	100	1000
Zn	703 ± 436	–	–	50	2500
Mn	186 ± 25	–	–	–	–
Se	32 ± 16	–	–	–	–
Si	2779 ± 551	–	–	–	–

24 Cd; 575 Cu; 703 Zn; 186 Mn and 32 Se (Table 9.4). These values are below the limits acceptable for sewage sludge application or disposal in most European countries (Hogg et al., 2002). Concentrations of Pb, Ni and Cr are even below the limiting values of the European Communities eco label composts. These results showed that FS emptied mechanically in Bangkok is not highly contaminated by heavy metals. However, this may be a concern in areas where industrial sludges are mixed with FS for disposal.

In addition to this, co-composting of FS with organic solid-waste-generated compost with an acceptable content of heavy metals was found to be less than even the strict Swiss standard for compost (ASCP, 2001), except for Mercury (Hg), which in principle may still be acceptable following other European standards as summarized by Brinton (2001). Hence co-composting does not pose any environmental problems regarding heavy metal accumulation on agricultural land. It was observed that the Ni and Cr concentrations in the 3:1 (solid waste: FS) mixing ratio are significantly higher than in the 2:1 mixture. This observation implies that heavy metals are introduced to compost by the organic solid waste rather than FS. Therefore, the use of FS as a nitrogen source does not introduce high levels of heavy metals into the finished compost.

CONCLUSIONS

Human excreta collected as FS from on-site sanitation systems in developing countries can be converted into safe biosolids or pathogen-free liquid for reuse in agriculture. Although pathogen concentrations, particularly helminth eggs, are high in FS, filtration systems such as drying beds (planted and unplanted) concentrate them into the solids fraction, hence delivering a liquid phase free of helminths.

Comparing planted and unplanted drying beds, the concentration of pathogens in the sludge accumulated from the planted drying beds is reduced because of the reduction in moisture content. Other factors such as lack of nutrients also play an important role in pathogen decay. However, sludge accumulated by unplanted drying beds may still contain helminth eggs if the drying time is not long enough. Hence, these sludges need to be further treated, i.e. by co-composting before safe reuse in agriculture.

Thermophylic co-composting with organic solid waste produces safe biosolids as helminth eggs are inactivated mainly during the heating phase. Because of its high nitrogen content, dewatered faecal sludge constitutes a good complementary substrate to organic solid waste, which is rich in carbon.

The biosolids produced from these processes are rich in nutrients and safe, from the perspective of heavy metal concentrations, when compared to existing guidelines for biosolids reuse in agriculture. Considering the current food crisis, the potential for reusing by-products of FS processing systems will provide a tangible mitigation strategy to enhance agricultural soil productivity and farmers' incomes, as this product is available at competitive prices compared to industrial fertilizer.

Gaps in research

The world sanitation community has recently defined sustainable sanitation as systems which take into consideration all aspects of sustainability. They should protect and promote human health by providing a clean environment and breaking the cycle of disease. In order to be sustainable a sanitation system has to be not only economically viable, socially acceptable, and technically and institutionally appropriate, it should also protect the environment and the natural resources. Hence, when improving an existing sanitation system and/or designing a new one, it is suggested that the following sustainability criteria be considered: health aspects, environment and natural resources; technology and operation; financial and economic issues; and socio-cultural and institutional aspects (Sustainable Sanitation Alliance, SuSanA, 2008). This opens interesting prospects for FS-based products as organic fertilizer in agricultural applications in developing countries. Indeed, a range of pollutants can occur in FS, including pharmaceutical compounds, natural and artificial hormones, and pathogens. In view of the fact that the application of pharmaceuticals in developing and transition countries is increasing, the application of untreated FS on a large scale could lead to unforeseeable environmental risks (Lienert et al., 2007). Therefore, in addition to sanitizing FS, the removal of micropollutants and their derivatives is considered to be a key factor contributing to sustainability if FS is to be applied for reuse in agriculture (Shannon et al., 2008; UNEP, 2002).

When developing new treatment options in developing countries, the availability of sufficient and reliable energy often dictates the choice of the technology or sanitation systems. Energy consumption during the operation of a particular sanitation system is also a key aspect concerning its environmental and economic sustainability (van Timmeren and Sidler, 2007). It is estimated that 75 per cent of sub-Saharan Africans (550 million people) and some 50 per cent of South Asians (700 million people) do not have access to electricity. Given the problems for energy-generation faced by these economies, low-energy processing systems need to be developed for sustainable operation and regular production of FS-based fertilizer, especially in farming areas.

Linking urban sanitation infrastructure and service provision to city development can draw sufficient financial resources for building infrastructure and securing operation and maintenance costs, as city planners might see the direct economic benefits of recycling. It is also an opportunity to close the nutrient loop in urban excreta and wastewater management. Such a linkage can be established with agriculture, which contributes an important share to urban food supply.

In the years to come, more than 2.6 billion people without access to improved sanitation will have to be serviced (WHO and UNICEF, 2006). The majority will likely use on-site sanitation, the predominant option in developing countries. Considering this, it can be assumed that for decades to come growing quantities of FS, dehydrated faeces and urine will have to be dealt with.

Thus, the goals and requirements of human waste or FS collection and treatment systems can be summarized as follows:

- recovery of nutrients and biosolids;
- removal of micropollutants;
- increase the concentration of nutrients;
- sanitizing of faecal sludge for reuse;
- economical, energy efficient and market-driven implementation.

REFERENCES

Allison, M., Harris, P. J. C., Hofny-Collins, A. H. and Stephens, W. (1998) *A Review of the Use of Urban Waste in Peri-urban Interface Production Systems*, Henry Doubleday Research Association, Coventry, UK

Asomani-Boateng, R. and Haight, M. (1999) 'Reusing organic solid waste in urban farming in African cities: A challenge for urban planners', *Third World Planning Review*, vol 21, no 4, pp411–28

Association of Swiss Compost Plants (ASCP) Guidelines (2001) *Quality Criteria for Composts and Digestates from Biodegradable Waste Management*, Association of Swiss Compost Plants in collaboration with Swiss Biogas Forum, Münchenbuchsee, Switzerland

Barrett, J. (1976) 'Studies on induction of permeability in *Ascaris lumbricoides* eggs', *Parasitology*, vol 73, pp109–121

Brinton, W. F. (2001) 'An international look at compost standards', *Biocycle*, vol 42, no 4, pp74–6

Capizzi-Banas, S., Deloge, M., Remy, M. and Schwartzbrod, J. (2004) 'Liming as an advanced treatment for sludge sanitization: Helminth eggs elimination – *Ascaris* eggs as model', *Water Research*, no 38, pp3251–8

Chien, B. T., Nga, N. H., Stenström, T.-A. and Winblad, U. (2001) 'Biological study on retention time of microorganisms in faecal materials in urine-diverting eco-san latrines in Vietnam', 1st International Conference on Ecological Sanitation, Nanning, People's Republic of China, internet dialogue on ecological sanitation, www.ias.unu. edu/proceedings/icibs/ecosan/bui.html

Cofie, O., Abraham, E. M., Olaleye, A. O. and Larbi, T. (2008) 'Recycling human excreta for urban and peri-urban agriculture in Ghana', in L. Parrot, A. Njoya, L. Temple, F. Assogba-Komlan, R. Kahane, M. Ba Diao and M. Havard (eds) *Agricultures et Développement Urbain en Afrique Subsaharienne. Environnement et Enjeux Sanitaires*, L'Harmattan, Paris, pp191–200

Cofie, O. O., Agbottah, S., Strauss, M., Esseku, H., Montangero, A., Awuah, E. and Koné, D. (2006) 'Solid–liquid separation of faecal sludge using drying beds in Ghana: Implications for nutrient recycling in urban agriculture', *Water Research*, vol 40, no 1, pp75–82

Cofie, O., Koné, D., Rothenberger, S., Moser, D. and Zubruegg, C. (2009) 'Co-composting of faecal sludge and organic solid waste for agriculture: Process dynamics', *Water Research*, no 43, pp4665–4675

Drangert, J. O. (1998) 'Fighting the urine blindness to provide more sanitation options', *Water South Africa*, vol 24, no 2, pp157–64

Feachem, R. G., Bradley, D. J., Garelick, H. and Mara, D. D. (1983) *Sanitation and Disease: Health Aspects of Excreta and Wastewater Management,* John Wiley & Sons, Chichester

Fernandez, R. G., Ingallinella, A. M., Sanguinetti, G. S., Ballan, G. E., Bortolotti, V., Montangero, A. and Strauss, M. (2004) 'Septage treatment in waste stabilization ponds', in *Proceedings, 9th International IWA Specialist Group Conference on Wetlands Systems for Water Pollution Control and to the 6th International IWA Specialist Group Conference on Waste Stabilization Ponds*, Avignon, France, 27 September–1 October, www.sandec.ch/FaecalSludge/Documents/Settage%treatment%20WSP.pdf

Gantzer, C., Gaspard, P., Galvez, L., Huyard, A., Dumouthier, N. and Schwartzbrod, J. (2001) 'Monitoring of bacterial and parasitological contamination during various treatment of sludge', *Water Research*, vol 35, no 16, pp3763–70

Gaspard, P. G. and Schwartzbrod, J. (2003) 'Parasite contamination (helminth eggs) in sludge treatment plants: Definition of a sampling strategy', *International Journal of Hygiene and Environmental Health*, vol 206, no 2, pp117–22

Heinss, U., Larmie, S. A. and Strauss, M. (1998) *Solid Separation and Pond Systems for the Treatment of Faecal Sludges in the Tropics: Lessons Learnt and Recommendations for Preliminary Design*, SANDEC Report no 05/98, EAWAG/SANDEC, Dübendorf, Switzerland

Hogg, D., Barth, J., Favoino, E., Centemero, M., Caimi, V., Amlinger, F., Devliegher, W., Brinton, W. and Antler, S. (2002) *Comparison of Compost Standards within the EU, North America and Australasia*, Waste and Resources Action Programme, Banbury, UK, pp1–97

Ingallinella, A. M., Sanguinetti, G., Koottatep, T., Montangero, A. and Strauss, M. (2002) 'The challenge of faecal sludge management in urban areas – Strategies, regulations and treatment options', *Water Science and Technology*, vol 46, pp285–94

International Fertilizer Industry Association (IFA) (2009) www.fertilizer.org/ifa/Home-Page/ABOUT-IFA

International Solid Wastes and Public Cleansing Association Working Group on Sewage and Waterworks Sludge (1998) *Sludge Treatment and Disposal Management Approaches and Experiences*, EEA, Copenhagen

Kengne, I. M., Akoa, A. and Koné, D., (2009) 'Recovery of biosolids from constructed wetlands used for faecal sludge dewatering in tropical regions', *Environmental Science and Technology*, vol 43, pp6816–21

Koné, D., Cofie, O., Zurbrugg, C., Gallizzi, K., Moser, D., Drescher, S. and Strauss, M. (2007) 'Helminth eggs inactivation efficiency by faecal sludge dewatering and co-composting in tropical climates', *Water Research,* vol 41, no 19, pp4397–402

Koné, D. and Strauss, M. (2004) 'Low-cost options for treating faecal sludges (FS) in developing countries – Challenges and performance', paper presented to the 9th International IWA Specialist Group Conference on Wetlands Systems for Water Pollution Control and to the 6th International IWA Specialist Group Conference on Waste Stabilisation Ponds, Avignon, France, 27 September–1 Octocber 2004.

www.eawag.ch/organisation/abteilungen/sandec/publikationen/publications_ewm/downloads_ewm/FS_treatment_Avignon.pdf

Koottatep, T., Surinkul, N., Polprasert, C., Kamal, A. S. M., Koné, D., Montangero, A., Heinss, U. and Strauss, M. (2005) 'Treatment of septage in constructed wetlands in tropical climate: Lessons learnt from seven years of operation', *Water Science and Technology*, vol 51, no 9, pp119–26

Lienert, J., Gudel, K. and Escher, B. I. (2007) 'Screening method for ecotoxicological hazard assessment of 42 pharmaceuticals considering human metabolism and excretory routes', *Environmental Science and Technology*, vol 41, no 12, pp 4471–8

Navarro, I., Jiménez, B., Cifuentes, E. and Lucario, S. (2009) 'Application of helminth ova infection dose curve to estimate the risks associated with biosolid application on soil', *Journal of Water and Health*, vol 7, no 1, pp31–44

Nelson, K. L., Cisneros, B. J., Tchobanoglous, G. and Darby, J. L. (2004) 'Sludge accumulation, characteristics, and pathogen inactivation in four primary waste stabilization ponds in central Mexico', *Water Research*, vol 38, no 1, pp111–27

Panuvatvanich, A., Koottatep, T., Koné, D. et al. (2009) 'Influence of sand layer depth and percolate impounding regime on nitrogen transformation in vertical-flow constructed wetlands treating faecal sludge', *Water Research*, vol 43, no 10, pp2623–30

Pecson, B. M., Barrios, J. A., Jiménez, B. E. and Nelson, K. L (2007) 'The effects of temperature, pH, and ammonia concentration on the inactivation of *Ascaris* eggs in sewage sludge', *Water Research*, vol 41, no 13, pp2893–902

Pecson, B. M. and Nelson, K. L. (2005) 'Inactivation of *Ascaris suum* eggs by ammonia', *Environmental Science and Technology*, vol 39, no 20, pp7909–14

Pescod, M. B. (1971) 'Sludge handling and disposal in tropical developing countries', *Journal of Water Pollution Control Federation*, vol 43, no 4, pp555–70

Sanguinetti, G. S., Tortul, C., Garcia, M. C., Ferrer, V., Montangero, A. and Strauss, M. (2005) 'Investigating helminth eggs and *Salmonella* sp. in stabilization ponds treating septage', *Water Science and Technology*, vol 51, no 12, pp239–47

Shannon, M. A., Bohn, P. W., Elimelech, M., Georgiadis, J. G., Marinas, B. J. and Mayes, A. M. (2008) 'Science and technology for water purification in the coming decade', *Nature*, vol 452, no 7185, pp301–10

Strauss, M., Larmie, S. A. and Heinss, U. (1997) 'Treatment of sludges from on-site sanitation – Low-cost options', *Water Science and Technology*, vol 35, no 6, pp129–36

Stromberg, B. E. (1997) 'Environmental factors influencing transmission', *Veterinary Parasitology*, vol 72, nos 3–4, pp247–56

SuSanA (2008) *Towards More Sustainable Sanitation*, Sustainable Sanitation Alliance, Eschborn, Germany, www.susana.org

Timmeren, A. van and Sidler, D. (2007) 'The sustainable implant: Decentralized sanitation and energy reuse (Desaer) in the built environment', *Construction Innovation*, vol 7, no 1, pp 22–37

UNEP (2002), *Environmentally Sound Technologies for Wastewater and Stormwater Management. An International Source Book*, Technical Publication Series 15, IWA Publishing, London, 613pp

Werner, C. (2007) 'Ecological sanitation: Introduction and health aspects of the reuse of wastewater and excreta', presentation, 11 November 2007, Towards Sustainable Global Health, Bonn, www.gtz.de/de/dokumente/en-water-health-ecosan.pdf

Wharton, D. A. (1979) '*Ascaris* sp.: Water loss during desiccation of embryonating eggs', *Experimental Parasitology*, vol 48, no 3, pp398–406

WHO (2006) *Guidelines for the Safe Use of Wastewater, Excreta and Greywater*, vol 4, World Health Organization, Geneva, 182pp

WHO and UNICEF (2006) *Joint Monitoring Programme for Water Supply and Sanitation – Meeting the MDG Drinking Water and Sanitation Target: The Urban and Rural Challenge of the Decade*, World Health Organization, Geneva, 47pp

10

Farm-Based Measures for Reducing Microbiological Health Risks for Consumers from Informal Wastewater-Irrigated Agriculture

Bernard Keraita, Flemming Konradsen and Pay Drechsel

ABSTRACT

This chapter presents farm-based measures that have been developed and tested in the informal irrigation sector to reduce microbiological health risks for consumers from wastewater irrigation of vegetables commonly eaten uncooked. The measures target poor smallholder farmers or farmer associations in developing countries as part of a multiple-barrier approach for health-risk reduction along the farm to fork pathway. Measures discussed include treatment of irrigation water using ponds, filters and wetland systems; water application techniques; irrigation scheduling; and crop selection. In addition, the chapter highlights some practical strategies to implement these measures, based largely on field experiences in Ghana. Although most measures discussed do not fully eliminate possible health risks, they can significantly complement other pathogen barriers. Which measures fit, either alone or in combination, will depend on local site characteristics and practices. Further studies are required to develop new measures or adapt them to other irrigation practices and systems in developing countries.

INTRODUCTION

Wastewater-irrigated agriculture is increasingly becoming a common phenomenon, and more so with increasing global water scarcity. Wastewater irrigation creates both opportunities and problems. The opportunities of wastewater irrigation are that it provides convenient disposal of waste products and adds valuable plant nutrients and organic matter to soils and crops (van der Hoek et al., 2002). Wastewater also provides reliable irrigation water and supports urban food supply, especially with perishable crops, making it a source of livelihood for many farmers and produce traders. On the other hand, wastewater irrigation, especially with untreated wastewater, facilitates transmission of diseases from excreta-related pathogens and vectors, skin irritants and toxic chemicals like heavy metals and pesticides. Of most concern in developing countries are excreta-related pathogens and skin irritants (Blumenthal et al., 2000; van der Hoek et al., 2005). These risks affect the sustainability of wastewater irrigation and need to be addressed. This chapter focuses on risk reduction measures for excreta-related pathogens, i.e. microbiological health risks for consumers of increasingly popular salad greens.

For many years, wastewater treatment was seen as the panacea for reducing health risks in wastewater-irrigated agriculture. The WHO, in its 2006 Guidelines for safe use of wastewater in agriculture, reviewed more than 20 studies on removal of various pathogens by different treatment processes (WHO, 2006). The studies show that biological processes, as they take place in pond systems, are especially effective in pathogen removal. Indeed, in many developed and middle-income countries, such as the USA, Tunisia, Spain, France, Israel and Jordan, wastewater is effectively treated before application to agricultural fields (Jiménez and Asano, 2008). In these countries, wastewater irrigation is formal, well regulated and controlled by well-established agencies (McCornick et al., 2004).

However, this is not the situation in most developing countries, which lack resources for effective wastewater treatment facilities; hence, large volumes of wastewater generated, especially in urban areas, remain untreated. Estimates show median levels of treated wastewater to be about 35 per cent in Asia, 14 per cent in Latin America and not even 1 per cent in sub-Saharan Africa (WHO, 2000). This treatment is often minimal or partial (primary level) and the effluent quality is poor. Therefore, in these countries, partially treated wastewater from the few existing treatment systems and large amounts of untreated wastewater are discharged into urban drainage systems and natural waterways, which farmers end up using on their farms. A recent survey suggests that wastewater without any significant treatment is used for irrigation purposes in and around four out of five cities in the developing world (Raschid-Sally and Jayakody, 2008). Hence, while source treatment of wastewater is important, implementing supplementary, or in the worst case alternative, on-farm measures appears, for the time being, to be a realistic approach to reduce health risks posed by wastewater irrigation.

In the following sections some simple measures are described that have been tested on leafy vegetables such as lettuce and spring onions, which are commonly eaten raw as salad or part of urban fast food. Measures include the use of alternative sites for agricultural production, alternative water sources, different types of pond systems, low-cost filtration, improved ways of water fetching and application, and the choice of alternative crops. Examples refer in most cases to detailed studies in Ghana, supported by field studies in Burkina Faso, Senegal, Togo and India.

ON-FARM WATER TREATMENT MEASURES

The WHO (2006) describes measures for risk reduction outside conventional wastewater treatment facilities which might be called 'post-treatment' or 'non-treatment' options (see Chapter 2). The term 'non-treatment' suits measures such as drip irrigation but not those measures which transfer conventional treatment processes to the farm. Pond-based systems are an example as ponds alone or in combination can be of very different sizes (down to 2–4m³), fitting even small farms.

Pond-based systems

Pond systems are widely used as simple biological wastewater treatment systems in many low-income countries as they are cheaper than most conventional systems. In ponds, helminth eggs and protozoa cysts are mainly removed by sedimentation (Sperling et al., 2004), while pathogenic bacteria and viruses are removed by a combination of various factors that create an unfavourable environment for their survival (Curtis et al., 1992). However, in drier climates evaporation can cause the salinity of the pond water to increase, which makes it less suitable for cultivation (Clemett and Ensink, 2006). In addition, pond systems can be important breeding sites for mosquitoes, which are vectors for a number of diseases.

Waste storage and treatment reservoirs (WSTR)

WSTR have traditionally been used as storage reservoirs for pre-treated wastewater from waste stabilization ponds (WSP) intended for irrigation use (Mara, 2004). During storage, further pathogen removal is achieved (Athyde-Junior et al., 2000; Cifuentes et al., 2000). Guidelines for designing WSTRs are detailed in Juanicó and Dor (1999) and Mara (2004). The use of a three batch-fed pond system (fill-rest-use) has shown best results for pathogen removal (Mara et al., 1996). Sometimes called the 'Chinese three-tank' system, at any one time, one tank is being filled by the farmer, one is settling and the settled water from the third is being used for irrigation. It requires a one-day period of quiescent settling to remove almost all helminth eggs and achieve a 1–2 log reduction of other pathogens. In general, when WSTR are properly designed, operated and maintained, they can achieve a 2–4-log unit removal of viruses, a 3–6 log unit removal for bacteria pathogens and 100 per cent removal for helminth eggs (Juanicó and Milstein, 2004; WHO, 2006).

Simple on-farm sedimentation ponds

In Ghana, as in many other countries in West Africa, shallow dugout ponds, which are usually about 1m deep and have a surface area between 2 and 6m^2, are widely used at urban irrigated vegetable farming sites. In most cases, they are used as storage reservoirs that surface run-off and wastewater effluents are channelled into (Figure 10.1). Other variations include the use of mobile drums or concrete structures. Ponds are common in areas where irrigation water sources are far away. Farmers fill them manually or by pumping water from streams or tube wells. The key advantage of the ponds is the reduced walking distance, especially where watering cans are used. Depending on the size of the reservoir and irrigation frequency, refilling is done after one or several days. While the water is stored, sedimentation takes place and studies in Ghana showed that these ponds are very effective in removing helminths (reduced to less than one egg per litre) when sedimentation is allowed for two to three days. Removal of faecal coliforms in the same period was about 2 log units. In contrast to the reduction of worm eggs, the die-off of coliforms was only significant during the dry season.

Digging a pond requires up to two man-days. With an additional plank to stand on (see below) the cost might be around US$20. The installation costs would be higher where concrete ponds are used as is common in other parts of West Africa (Figure 10.2). There are different measures possible that can enhance sedimentation in these ponds like using natural flocculants and means to optimize pathogen die-off. These measures could help further to lessen the pathogen load in these mini-ponds.

Filtration techniques

There is a wide range of filtration systems that can be used for treating irrigation water (Morel and Diener, 2006). For on-farm installation, sand-filters with slow application rates (slow sand-filters) are a possible option. However, sand should be of correct configuration i.e. effective size (ES) of 0.15–0.40mm and uniformity coefficient (UC) of 1.5–3.6 (Metcalf and Eddy, Inc., 1995). Sand-filters remove pathogenic micro-organisms from polluted water by first retaining them in the filtration media before they are eliminated (Stevic et al., 2004). Retention is achieved mainly through straining, in which larger micro-organisms (protozoans and helminths) are physically blocked as they move through the well-packed filter media, and adsorption, in which smaller ones like bacteria get attached to the

Figure 10.1 *One of several dugout ponds farmers are using on informal urban vegetable farms in Kumasi, Ghana*

filtration media. Elimination of pathogenic micro-organisms is achieved mainly by exposing them to unfavourable environmental conditions such as high temperature and also through predation by other organisms like protozoans. Similarly to man-made sand-filters, soils can act as natural bio-filters, especially if smaller textures (silt, clay) are dominant.

The typical pathogen removal range reported by the WHO based on a review of several studies for slow sand-filters is 0–3 log units and 1–3 log units for bacteria and helminths respectively (WHO, 2006). Studies in Ghana using 0.5–1m deep columns filled with uniform sand of mean ES of 0.17mm and UC 3.6 achieved over 98 per cent of bacteria removal, equivalent to an average of 2 log units per 100ml, and 71–96 per cent of helminths were removed (Keraita et al., 2008b). This removal was significant but not adequate as irrigation water had very high initial levels of indicator organisms. For an urban vegetable farm of 0.1ha, a column sand-filter with a surface area of 0.4m^2 placed on a simple stand and with

Figure 10.2 *Concrete reservoir used by smallholders in Lomé, Togo. Ponds are interconnected through tubes and filled with a pump from a tube well; at other locations, also from streams*

a water-storage tank costed about US$100. This amount was less than 5 per cent of the average net revenue made by farmers if the system could be used for five years or more. The greatest limitation of sand-filters is clogging which farmers can address e.g. via a textile pre-filter to remove debris.

Farmers in West Africa also use other forms of infiltration systems. In Ouagadogou, Burkina Faso, wells are sunk next to wastewater canals, creating a hydraulic gradient which enables canal water to infiltrate the soil layer towards the well. In doing that, filtration takes place, leading to a reduction in micro-organisms and turbidity. Wastewater can also be allowed to pass through sand-filter trenches, sand embankments, column sand-filters and simple sandbags as farmers channel irrigation water to collection storage ponds. These types of filter will mostly affect protozoa and helminths. In Togo, Ghana and Senegal, farmers use different forms of sieves, but mostly folded mosquito nets on the watering-can intake hole to prevent particles like algae, waste and organic debris from entering the watering cans (Figure 10.3). In doing that, some pathogens adsorbed to organic matter are removed. Studies on this kind of simple filter system showed about 1 log unit removal for bacteria and 12–62 per cent for helminths when a normal nylon cloth material was used (Keraita et al., 2008b). Filtration materials can also be attached to irrigation equipment such as pumps. In all cases it is recommended to fine-tune the mesh size to find the best balance between easy water fetching and maximal debris filtration. As farmers are already used to these types of coarse filter systems

Figure 10.3 *Watering cans with mosquito mesh to avoid debris (Dakar, Senegal)*

to eliminate visible obstacles, an opportunity exists for adaptive field studies with high adoption potential.

Use of irrigation infrastructure

Irrigation infrastructure such as water reservoirs and weirs in irrigation canals can facilitate pathogen removal. Though not designed for this purpose, water-storage reservoirs can enhance sedimentation of helminths and bacterial die-off, especially in drier climates. Weirs, which are used for regulating irrigation water, act as traps for helminth eggs. A study done along the Musi river in Hyderabad, India, showed that irrigation infrastructure (mainly weirs, see Figure 10.4) can significantly improve water quality (Ensink et al., 2006). In the study, no helminth eggs were found 40km downstream from where 133 eggs/litre were reported at a point on the Musi river closest to the city. Corresponding *E. coli* levels showed a reduction by 5 log units from 7 log units per 100ml of water. Similar systems can be observed at micro-level where farmers block wastewater streams to create in-stream ponds (with overflow) for water fetching. In some instances, whole cascades of such barriers can be found (IWMI, 2008).

IMPROVED WATER FETCHING AND APPLICATION MEASURES

Fetching of irrigation water

In tests in Ghana, careful collection of irrigation water with a watering can, that did not disturb the sediment at the collection point in the stream or dugout, reduced

Figure 10.4 *Weir in the Musi river, downstream of Hyderabad, Andhra Pradesh, India*

helminth egg counts in irrigation water by 70 per cent. Most eggs settled on the first day of sedimentation. After three days without disturbance of the pond the average number of eggs in the pond water was less than one egg per litre (Keraita et al., 2008a). However, farmers in Ghana have to irrigate continuously due to high temperatures and use the dugouts regularly in the morning and afternoon on most sunny days without rain, thereby disturbing the water continuously. This could be avoided with a set of ('Chinese three-tank') dugouts as described above. Another option is the use of a wooden log across the pond to avoid entering the water (Figure 10.5). Water can also be fetched with a watering can connected to a rope, removing the need to step into the pond or stream (Figure 10.6). Deeper pond designs prevent the watering can from touching the sediment layer during water fetching (Drechsel et al., 2008). Investment costs are limited to labour (especially if a Chinese three-tank system is used) and the required behaviour-change during water fetching.

Water from irrigation channels along the Musi River in India is pumped onto fields. The foot valve apparatus at the inlet pipe is usually heavy, which helps to keep the pipe in place under water. In many instances the pipe touches the sludge layer in the canal and sediments are sucked in, increasing the risk of metal and helminth egg contamination. U-shaped pump ends (Figure 10.7) could reduce this threat (Luque Ruiz, 2009).

Figure 10.5 *Farmer standing on a wooden log while fetching water from a small dugout pond (Kumasi, Ghana)*

Figure 10.6 *Farmer fetching water with a can on a rope from a wastewater stream (Ouagadougou, Burkina Faso)*

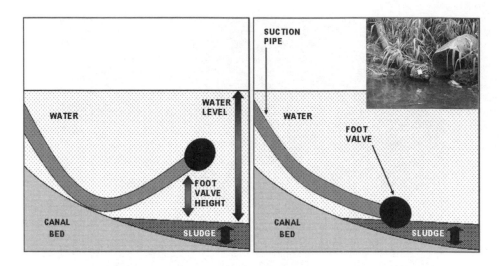

Figure 10.7 *Lifting pumps inflow valves out of the sediment of irrigation channels near Hyderabad, India*

Irrigation methods

With regard to reducing crop contamination, good irrigation methods should minimize contact between the edible parts of the plant and contaminated irrigation water. Overhead irrigation methods such as sprinkler irrigation and watering cans have the highest potential to transfer pathogens to leafy vegetables as water is applied on edible parts and due to the wider movement of pathogens through aerosols (Pescod, 1992). Flood and furrow irrigation methods apply water on the surface and are less likely to contaminate high growing crops; but for low-lying crops and root crops contamination is still high. Localized techniques, such as drip irrigation, have minimal pathogen transfer to crop surfaces because water is directly applied to the roots (Pescod, 1992).

Several studies have been conducted on the effects of sprinkler, drip (both surface and subsurface) and furrow irrigation on crop contamination (Armon et al., 2002; Bastos and Mara, 1995; El Hamouri et al., 1996; Oron et al., 2001; Solomon et al., 2002). The studies show that drip irrigation results in comparatively lower contamination on crops than furrow and sprinkler irrigation. However, drip kits, as promoted in developed countries, are very expensive and prone to clogging as polluted water usually has high turbidity levels (Capra and Scicolone, 2007; Martijn and Redwood, 2005). Nevertheless, low-cost drip irrigation techniques like bucket drip kits (Figure 10.8) (sacks can also be used) have shown a high potential for use and adoption in low-income countries (Kay, 2001). Similar to more sophisticated kits, the low-cost types promoted, for example, by International Development Enterprises (IDE) in India can be tailored to local vegetable-bed

Figure 10.8 *Simple drip irrigation kit made in India and tested in Ghana for lettuce. Adjustments are needed to increase the planting density*

sizes. Studies done in Ghana using bucket drip kits showed higher reduction in contamination (up to 6 log units) especially during the dry season (Keraita et al., 2007b) as compared to the often cited 2–4 log units (WHO, 2006).

There are hardly any documented studies on traditional or modified traditional irrigation methods involving watering cans, buckets, subsurface clay pods or calabashes in relation to crop contamination. Studies in Ghana showed a great potential in reducing vegetable contamination by modifying the handling of watering cans to reduce splashing of contaminated soils on to the crops. Using a watering can with an outflow rose (a cap with holes in) and watering from a height <0.5m (Figure 10.9) reduced thermotolerant coliforms by 2.5 log units and helminths by 2.3 eggs per 100g of lettuce compared with using a watering can with no end cap, from a height >1m (Keraita et al., 2007a). The required changes are of very low cost, but further studies are needed to verify the effectiveness on different types of soil and crop cover.

Scheduling of water application

Timing of irrigation, including frequency, is not only important for pathogen reduction but also for reducing salinity. One of the most widely documented field water-management measures to reduce pathogens is cessation of irrigation, in which irrigation is stopped a few days before crops are harvested. This results in

Figure 10.9 *Holding the watering can at low height and using an outflow rose reduces splashing of already contaminated soil on the crop (Kumasi, Ghana)*

exposure to conditions that are unfavourable to pathogen growth including heat, desiccation and sunlight (Shuval et al., 1986). Studies have provided some ranges of potential survival times for pathogens on crops, soils and water in temperate and tropical climates (see Table 12.2, Chapter 12), along with identifying how environmental conditions influence pathogen survival (Feachem et al., 1983; Shuval et al., 1986; Yates et al., 1987). In short, pathogen inactivation on crops is more rapid in hot, sunny weather than in cool, cloudy or rainy conditions.

WHO (2006) gives a pathogen die-off range of between 0.5 and 2 log units per day between final irrigation to consumption, while Fattal et al. (2004) use 3 log units in their risk-assessment models. In another study, it was revealed that when trickling filter effluent with 10^6 thermotolerant coliforms per 100ml was used to spray-irrigate lettuces, initial concentrations of indicator bacteria exceeded 10^5 thermotolerant coliforms per 100g fresh weight. Once irrigation ceased, no *Salmonella* could be detected after five days, and the levels of thermotolerant coliforms after 7–12 days were comparable to those detected on lettuces irrigated with freshwater (Vaz da Costa-Vargas et al., 1996). In Ghana, studies from field trials showed an average daily reduction of 0.65 log units of thermotolerant coliforms on lettuce (Keraita et al., 2007a). However, they also showed that cessation in hot climates has correspondingly high yield losses (1.4 tons/ha of fresh weight) that may make it harder for farmers to adopt the method. Indeed, in Accra or Kumasi, farmers irrigate lettuce preferably twice a day, while in the cooler Addis Ababa lettuce is irrigated thrice a week, which offers greater possibility for die-off.

Enforcement of irrigation cessation in hot climates has raised reservations that some crops, especially leafy vegetables and salad crops, will lose their freshness and thereby their market value (Vaz da Costa-Vargas et al., 1996). It has been suggested that irrigation cessation should be used for fodder crops that do not have to be harvested at the peak of their freshness (Blumenthal et al., 2000). As much as 99 per cent elimination of detectable viruses has been reported after two days' exposure to sunlight, supporting regulations of a suitable time interval between irrigation and crop-handling or grazing time (Feigin et al., 1991). Enforcement can be difficult especially where vegetable farming is an informal activity and not regulated, as is the case in many low-income countries. In addition, in countries like Ghana, where farmers do not market the vegetables they produce but wait for vegetable traders to visit their fields and select the crops they like, special arrangements will have to be made with the traders for successful timing of the measure (Keraita et al., 2007a).

Crop selection

Some crops are more prone to contamination from pathogens than others. For example, crops with their edible parts more exposed to contaminated soils and irrigation water like low-growing leafy vegetables or root crops (e.g. carrots) will be more prone to pathogen contamination. The WHO, in its Guidelines for safe use of wastewater in agriculture, advises crop restrictions, especially for crops eaten raw (WHO, 2006). However, a shift in the type of crops planted is only feasible if the market value of the alternative crops is similar. Crop restrictions can be hard to implement if necessary conditions such as law enforcement, market pressure and demand for cleaner vegetables are not in place. So while there have been successful crop-restriction schemes in India, Mexico, Peru and Chile (Blumenthal et al., 2000; Buechler and Devi, 2003), this has not been possible in other countries where wastewater irrigation is informal, such as in sub-Saharan Africa.

Alternative farmland and/or safer irrigation water

Wastewater use could be reduced if authorities have the possibility to provide farmers with safer irrigation water or an alternative location where water is not polluted. In Accra, Ghana, for example, groundwater was found at a convenient depth for treadle pumps, but the water was saline due to salt intrusion from the sea. In other cities, the groundwater level was in many sites too deep (more than 15m) to make borehole drilling an economic option for farmers. However, Ghana's Ministry of Food and Agriculture extended their national initiative to support small-scale irrigation and started borehole drilling on several urban farming sites. This risk-mitigation strategy was apparently successful in Benin where the city authorities of Cotonou and Seme-Kpodji and various national ministries agreed to allocate about 400ha of alternative farmland to urban farmers. The new site has shallow non-saline groundwater, which can easily be lifted by treadle pump for all-season irrigation. About 1000 farmers declared their interest to move to this peri-urban site despite its distance from the urban markets (Drechsel et al., 2006).

ENHANCING ADOPTION OF RISK-REDUCTION MEASURES

Many initiatives to address wastewater irrigation-related health risks in low-income countries remain at the risk-assessment level or pilot stage. To have the desired impact, recommended measures have to be integrated into routine farming practice. In this section, practical experience of some approaches is shared, drawing on several interlinked 'wastewater projects' conducted in Ghana between 2004 and 2009. The projects were supported by the Knowledge Sharing in Research project of the Consultative Group on International Agricultural Research (CGIAR). More details and lessons can be found in Chapters 16 and 17.

Innovative knowledge sharing

The project in Ghana encouraged and facilitated knowledge exchanges among farmers as well as between farmers and scientists. Research findings were synthesized according to the expressed wishes of the extension service to make them as user-friendly as possible. The materials illustrated safer irrigation practices and were translated into different regional languages. They included training media (radio and video) for extension offices and farmers as well as illustrated flip-charts/posters. In addition, the project prepared modules for farmer field schools, to actually demonstrate best practices. The module preparation was supported by the Food and Agriculture Organization (FAO) and involved farmers' representatives, extension officers from the Ministry of Food and Agriculture and communication experts. To enhance communication along the farm to fork pathway, all key stakeholders took part in so-called 'road shows', allowing them to follow the crops from the farm to the kitchen to observe and discuss sources of risks and options for risk reduction, and to understand the necessity of a multiple-barrier approach.

Involving authorities

Equally important is to involve local authorities and relevant government ministries from the initial stages. In Ghana, the project involved local authorities, the Ministry of Food and Agriculture, the private sector interested in food safety and other relevant agencies such as food-safety regulators. Some of them were involved as research partners, others coordinated training events which incorporated project results, and others were kept updated through policy briefs and participation in project meetings. The latter applies in particular to those agencies setting policies and regulations for wastewater reuse, and aids the institutionalization of safe practices. They also have a mandate to offer extension services to farmers. Dissemination of safe practices developed during the project will be done by the extension officials from the Ministry of Food and Agriculture. The target is to incorporate safer irrigation practices in the ministries' extension and training curricula.

Linking with other projects

Waste reuse projects should also be linked to other relevant projects or government projects with common goals. These could include government poverty-reduction programmes for the urban poor, initiatives for urban food security, nutritional programmes that emphasize consumption of green vegetables, health programmes and ongoing policy revisions. In Ghana, the project results influenced the Irrigation Policy launched in 2008 and the currently ongoing agricultural byelaw revision in the capital city, Accra. As wastewater use is just one of the routes by which excreta-related diseases are transmitted in poor communities, improved irrigation practices might not have much effect on the occurrence of intestinal infections when sanitation or hygiene remains unimproved. In such situations, linking vegetable-washing with a handwashing campaign might be very cost-effective.

Incentives

To enhance adoption of safer practices in waste reuse, farmers will need some form of incentive. This applies to most forms of behaviour-change, but in particular to situations where recommended practices involve increased inputs, such as personal labour. Studies have shown that people are more likely to adopt innovations if they get direct benefits for themselves rather than for the general population (Frewer et al., 1998). On this basis, incentives are even more important as the main beneficiaries are not the farmers but the consumers of their produce (exotic vegetables produced are for sale, not for farm household consumption). The most obvious incentive for farmers to adopt safe practices would be higher economic returns for safer vegetables. If a related market demand exists, producer groups could be encouraged to sell their products outside the existing marketing channels to avoid mixing-up safe and unsafe produce. This could be done by linking farmers directly to large unit consumers like hotels and designated selling-points of safe produce in markets and supermarkets or hotels. Other incentives could be institutional support from government institutions like the provision of extension services for training farmers, loans, awards and land-tenure security. Certification standards and labelling could be steps in the medium term. The media should be partners in these efforts to promote good practices and recognize progressive farmers. More details are presented in Chapter 16.

CONCLUSIONS

Farm-based measures can contribute to the reduction of health risks deriving for consumers from irrigated agriculture. These measures should play a complementary role to wastewater treatment and other post-harvest measures to comprehensively reduce risks associated with wastewater irrigation. Unfortunately, farm-based measures have not yet received the needed attention in research, perhaps due to the traditional focus on conventional wastewater treatment as the best solution for health protection. Although many principles of wastewater treatment could also be applied on farm, field-testing of these measures is scarce and their potential to reduce health risks is relatively unknown or not yet fully proven. There is an urgent need for scientists to work with farmers to adapt the technologies and improve their efficiency in pathogen removal.

Assessments to provide evidence for health-risk reduction are also needed. These are particularly important and urgent in high-risk areas like urban vegetable farming in developing countries where farmers often have no other choice than using untreated wastewater for irrigation. A key challenge for the adoption of farm-based measures is that they require behaviour-change without obvious and direct benefit. This requires incentive systems which can range from supporting market demand to social marketing. It also requires that farmers are equipped with knowledge on health risks and can rely on institutional support, like from the extension service.

The options of farm-based measures for health-risk reduction presented here are biased to experiences gained in West Africa. There, watering cans are extensively used in urban vegetable production while in other regions, such as Eastern Africa, topography favours gravity-flow and furrow or flood irrigation systems. Which measures fit (alone or in combination) a particular situation, will depend on local site characteristics and practices. Further studies are required to address other smallholder irrigation systems and crops to develop new measures or adapt the ones presented here.

REFERENCES

Armon, R., Gold, D., Brodsky, M. and Oron, G. (2002) 'Surface and subsurface irrigation with effluents of different qualities and presence of *Cryptosporidium* oocysts in soil and on crops', *Water Science and Technology,* vol 46, no 3, pp115–22

Athyde-Junior, G. B., Mara, D. D., Pearson, H. W. and Silva, S. A. (2000) 'Faecal coliform die-off in wastewater storage and treatment reservoirs', *Water Science and Technology,* vol 42, no 10, pp139–47

Bastos, R. K. X. and Mara, D. D. (1995) 'The bacterial quality of salad crops drip and furrow irrigated with waste stabilization pond effluent: An evaluation of WHO Guidelines', *Water Science and Technology,* vol 12, pp425–30

Blumenthal, U. J., Peasey, A., Ruiz-Palacios, G. and Mara, D. D. (2000) *Guidelines for Wastewater Reuse in Agriculture and Aquaculture: Recommended Revisions Based on New Research Evidence,* Task No 68, Part 1, WELL Study, London School of Hygiene and Tropical Medicine, London / Loughborough University, Loughborough

Buechler, S. and Devi, G. (2003) 'Household food security and wastewater dependent livelihood activities in Andhra Pradesh, India', unpublished background document prepared for the WHO Guidelines (2006)

Capra, A. and Scicolone, B. (2007) 'Recycling of poor quality urban wastewater by drip irrigation systems', *Journal of Cleaner Production,* vol 15, pp1529–34

Cifuentes, E., Blumenthal, U., Ruiz-Palacios, G., Bennett, S. and Quigley, M. (2000) 'Health risk in agricultural villages practicing wastewater irrigation in Central Mexico: Perspectives for protection', in I. Chorus, U. Ringelband, G. Schlag and O. Schmoll (eds) *Water Sanitation and Health,* IWA Publishing, London, pp249–56

Clemett, A. E. V., and Ensink, J. H. J. (2006) 'Farmer driven wastewater treatment: A case study from Faisalabad, Pakistan', *Conference Proceedings from the 32nd WEDC International Conference on Sustainable Development of Water Resources, Water Supply and Environmental Sanitation,* WEDC, Colombo

Curtis, T. P., Mara, D. D. and Silva, S. A. (1992) 'Influence of pH, oxygen and humic substances on ability of sunlight to damage faecal coliforms in waste stabilization ponds', *Applied Environmental Microbiology,* vol 58, pp1335–43

Drechsel, P., Graefe, S., Sonou, M. and Cofie, O. (2006) *Informal Irrigation in Urban West Africa: An Overview,* Research Report no 102, IWMI, Colombo, www.iwmi.cgiar. org/Publications/IWMI_Reports/PDF/pub102/RR102.pdf

Drechsel, P., Keraita, B., Amoah, P., Abaidoo, R., Raschid-Sally, L. and Bahri, A. (2008) 'Reducing health risks from wastewater use in urban and peri-urban sub-Saharan Africa: Applying the 2006 WHO Guidelines', *Water Science and Technology,* vol 57, no 9, pp1461–6

El Hamouri, B., Handouf, A., Mekrane, M., Touzani, M., Khana, A., Khallayoune, K. and Benchokroun, T. (1996) 'Use of wastewater for crop production under arid and saline conditions: Yield and hygienic quality of crop and soil contaminations', *Water Science and Technology,* vol 33, nos 10–11, pp327–34

Ensink, J. H. J., Brooker, S., Cairncross, S. and Scott, C. A. (2006) 'Wastewater use in India: The impact of irrigation weirs on water quality and farmer health', *Conference Proceedings from the 32nd WEDC International Conference on Sustainable Development of Water Resources, Water Supply and Environmental Sanitation,* WEDC, Colombo

Fattal, B., Lampert, Y. and Shuval, H. (2004) 'A fresh look at microbial guidelines for wastewater irrigation in agriculture: A risk-assessment and cost-effectiveness approach', in C. A. Scott, N. I. Faruqui and L. Raschid-Sally (eds) *Wastewater Use in Irrigated Agriculture: Confronting the Livelihood and Environmental Realities*, CABI Publishing, Wallingford, UK pp59–68

Feachem, D. G., Bradley, D. J., Garelick, H. and Mara, D. D. (1983) *Sanitation and Disease: Health Aspects of Excreta and Wastewater Management*, John Wiley and Sons, Bath

Feigin, A., Ravina, I. and Shalhevet, J. (1991) *Irrigation with Treated Sewage Effluent: Management for Environmental Protection*, Springer Verlag, Heidelberg

Frewer, L. J., Howard, C. and Shepherd, R. (1998) 'Understanding public attitudes to technology', *Journal of Risk Research*, vol 1, no 3, pp221–35

Hoek, W. van der, Tuan Anh, V., Dac Cam, P., Vicheth, C. and Dalsgaard, A. (2005) 'Skin diseases among people using urban wastewater in Phnom Penh', *Urban Agriculture Magazine*, vol 14, pp30–31

Hoek, W. van der, Ul Hassan, M., Ensink, J. H. J., Feenstra, S., Raschid-Sally, L., Munir, S. and Aslam, M. R. (2002) *Urban Wastewater: A Valuable Resource for Agriculture*, International Water Management Institute Research Report 63, IWMI, Colombo

IWMI (2008) 'Health risk reduction in a wastewater irrigation system in urban Accra, Ghana', www.youtube.com/watch?v=f_EnUGa_GdM

Jiménez, B. and Asano, T. (2008) *Water Reuse: An International Survey, Contracts, Issues and Needs around the World*, IWA Publishing, London, p648

Juanicó, M. and Dor, I. (1999) *Hypertrophic Reservoirs for Wastewater Storage and Reuse: Ecology, Performance, and Engineering Design*, Springer Verlag, Heidelberg

Juanicó, M. and Milstein, A. (2004) 'Semi-intensive treatment plants for wastewater reuse in irrigation', *Water Science and Technology*, vol 50, no 2, pp55–60

Kay, M. (2001) *Smallholder Irrigation Technology: Prospects for Sub Saharan Africa*, IPRTRID, FAO, Rome

Keraita, B., Drechsel, P. and Konradsen, F. (2008a) 'Using on-farm sedimentation ponds to reduce health risks in wastewater irrigated urban vegetable farming in Ghana', *Water Science and Technology*, vol 57, no 4, pp519–25

Keraita, B., Drechsel, P. and Konradsen, F. (2008b) 'Potential of simple filters to improve microbial quality of irrigation water used in urban vegetable farming in Ghana', *Journal of Environmental Science and Health, Part A*, vol 43, pp749–55

Keraita, B., Konradsen, F., Drechsel, P. and Abaidoo, R. C. (2007a) 'Reducing microbial contamination on lettuce by cessation of irrigation before harvesting', *Tropical Medicine and International Health*, vol 12, no 2, pp8–14

Keraita, B., Konradsen, F., Drechsel, P. and Abaidoo, R. C. (2007b) 'Effect of low-cost irrigation methods on microbial contamination of lettuce', *Tropical Medicine and International Health*, vol 12, no 2, pp15–22

Luque Ruiz, F. J. (2009) 'Investigation of methods to reduce cadmium and helminth eggs in irrigated wastewater', MSc thesis (Water Science, Policy and Management), Oxford University, Oxford

Mara, D. D. (2004) *Domestic Wastewater Treatment in Developing Countries*, Earthscan, London

Mara, D. D., Pearson, H. W., Oragui, J. I., Crawley, L. R., de Oliveira, R. and Silva, S. A. (1996) *Wastewater Storage and Treatment Reservoirs in Northeast Brazil*, TPHE Research Monograph no 12, University of Leeds, Department of Civil Engineering, Leeds

Martijn, E. and Redwood, M. (2005) 'Wastewater irrigation in developing countries – Limitations for farmers to adopt appropriate practices', *Irrigation and Drainage*, vol 54, pp63–S70

McCornick, P. G., Hijazi, A. and Sheikh, B. (2004) 'From wastewater reuse to water reclamation: Progression of water reuse standards in Jordan', in C. A. Scott, N. I. Faruqui and L. Raschid-Sally (eds) *Wastewater Use in Irrigated Agriculture: Confronting the Livelihood and Environmental Realities*, CABI Publishing, Wallingford, UK, pp113–25

Metcalf and Eddy, Inc. (1995) *Wastewater Engineering: Treatment, Disposal and Reuse*, McGraw-Hill, New York, p1819

Morel, A. and Deiner, S. (2006) *Greywater Management in Low and Medium Income Countries; A Review of Different Treatment Systems for Households or Neighborhoods*, EAWAG, Dübendorf, Switzerland

Oron, G., Armon, R., Mandelbaum, R., Manor, Y., Campos, C., Gillerman, L., Salgot, M., Gerba, C., Klein, I. and Enriquez, C. (2001) 'Secondary wastewater disposal for crop irrigation with minimal risks', *Water Science and Technology*, vol 43, no 10, pp139–46

Pescod, M. B. (ed) (1992) *Wastewater Treatment and Use in Agriculture*, Irrigation and Drainage Paper 47, FAO, Rome

Raschid-Sally, L. and Jayakody, P. (2008) 'Drivers and characteristics of wastewater agriculture in developing countries: Results from a global assessment, Colombo, Sri Lanka', *IWMI Research Report 127*, International Water Management Institute, Colombo

Shuval, H. I., Adin, A., Fattal, B., Rawitz, E., Yekutiel, P. (1986) *Wastewater Irrigation in Developing Countries: Health Effects and Technical Solutions*, World Bank Technical Paper no 51, World Bank, Washington, DC

Solomon, E. B., Potenski, C. J. and Matthews, K. R. (2002) 'Effect of irrigation method on transmission to and persistence of *Escherichia coli* O157:H7 on lettuce', *Journal of Food Protection*, vol 65, no 4, pp673–6

Sperling, M. von, Bastos, R. K. X. and Kato, M. T. (2004) 'Removal of *E. coli* and helminth eggs in UASB–polishing pond systems', *Water Science and Technology*, vol 51, no 12, pp91–7

Stevik, T. K., Aa, K., Auslan, G. and Hanssen, J. F. (2004) 'Retention and removal of pathogenic bacteria in wastewater percolating through porous media', *Water Research*, vol 38, pp1355–67

Vaz da Costa-Vargas, S., Bastos, R. K. X. and Mara, D. D. (1996) *Bacteriological Aspects of Wastewater Irrigation*, Dept. of Civil Engineering, Tropical Public Health Engineering, University of Leeds, Leeds

WHO (2000) *Global Water Supply and Sanitation Assessment 2000 Report*, World Health Organization (WHO) / United Nations Children's Fund (UNICEF), Geneva and New York

WHO (2006) *Guidelines for the Safe Use of Wastewater, Excreta and Greywater, Volume 2: Wastewater Use in Agriculture*, World Health Organization, Geneva

Yates, M. V., Yates, S. R., Wagner, J. and Gerba, C. P. (1987) 'Modeling virus survival and transport in the subsurface', *Journal of Contaminant Hydrology*, vol 1, pp329–45

11

Farm-Based Measures for Reducing Human and Environmental Health Risks from Chemical Constituents in Wastewater

Robert Simmons, Manzoor Qadir and Pay Drechsel

ABSTRACT

There is a significant imbalance between the number of publications describing potential and actual environmental and health impacts from chemically contaminated wastewater, and reports outlining concrete options to minimize the related risks where conventional wastewater treatment is not available. This gap applies more to inorganic and organic contaminants than excess salts or nutrients. This chapter outlines some of the options available that could be considered in and around the farm, looking at heavy metals, salts, excess nutrients and organic contaminants. The emphasis is placed on low-cost options applicable in developing countries. While such measures can reduce negative impacts to a certain extent, it remains crucial to ensure that hazardous chemicals are replaced in production processes; industrial wastewater is treated at source and/or separated from other wastewater streams used for irrigation purposes; and fertilizer application rates and related possible subsidies adjusted to avoid over-fertilization.

INTRODUCTION

Where irrigation with untreated, partly treated or diluted wastewater cannot be avoided or is otherwise common, negative impacts on irrigated crops, soils and groundwater that can affect human and environmental health are likely (Ayers and Westcot, 1985; Murtaza et al., 2009; Pescod, 1992; Pettygrove and Asano, 1985; WHO, 2006b). Several chapters in this book focus on pathogenic threats, related risk assessments and risk mitigation. This chapter has its focus on non-pathogenic contaminants. As outlined in Chapter 6, aside from organic chemicals, debris and solutes, non-pathogenic components of polluted irrigation water can comprise a range of elements that can be essential plant nutrients, undesirable salts or metals and metalloids in toxic concentrations, depending on their concentration and solubility.

The high concentrations of chemical constituents that need to be addressed in wastewater-irrigated environments can be roughly divided into:

- metals and metalloids, such as cadmium (Cd), chromium (Cr), cobalt (Co), molybdenum (Mo), nickel (Ni), zinc (Zn), lead (Pb), arsenic (As), selenium (Se), mercury (Hg), copper (Cu) and manganese (Mn), among others;
- nutrients such as nitrogen (N), phosphorous (P), potassium (K), calcium (C) and magnesium (Mg), which in high concentrations might suppress other nutrients and/or affect plant growth and aquatic life;
- salts and specific ionic species such as sodium (Na), boron (B) and chloride (Cl);
- persistent organic pollutants (POPs), such as pesticides as well as so-called emerging contaminants, like residual pharmaceuticals, endocrine disruptor compounds and active residues of personal care products.

To avoid potential negative impacts, conventional wastewater-treatment options, which can control the release of most of these contaminants into the environment, remain the key to protecting water quality for beneficial uses including agriculture.

In theory, it could be expected that, with increasing economic development and industrialization, treatment standards, regulations and capacities grow concomitantly, allowing a society at each development stage to deal with its own waste. However, there are many development pathways, and growth in each sector of the economy does not always run in parallel. The so-called emerging economies or markets are a good example of this process. China, India, Pakistan and Mexico are some of the largest countries in this group, but they are also those most often cited for large-scale industrial water pollution and irrigation with highly polluted water (Jiménez and Asano, 2008). Many other low-income countries show, at a smaller scale, similar challenges of emerging industrial sectors or mining activities while institutional, technical and/or regulatory capacities for wastewater treatment are not yet in place. The result is a situation in which not only microbiological contaminants, but also industrial effluent, pose a threat to farmers and consumers of wastewater-irrigated food. The related possible environmental and health impacts are described in a range of papers (Abaidoo et al., 2009; Hamilton et al., 2007; Stevens and McLaughlin, 2006) but they are usually brief in answering what could be done where appropriate conventional treatment facilities are missing. This chapter tries to address the gap by outlining some options for non-pathogenic contaminants including salts.

METALS AND METALLOIDS

All of the potentially toxic metals are naturally present in the environment in trace amounts and are ingested with food, water and air. Human bodies have the ability to deal with these background levels. The World Health Organization (WHO) has established guidelines on allowable consumption of various toxins (WHO, 2006a) and guidance values in irrigation water (WHO, 2006b). Several of these metals and metalloids are of particular concern due to their adverse effects on agricultural productivity as well as environmental and human health. In a review of wastewater use in the Australian horticultural production industry, Hamilton et al. (2005) classified potentially phytotoxic metals in wastewater into four groups based on their retention in soil, translocation in plants, phytotoxicity and potential risk to the food chain (Table 11.1). They categorized Cd, Co, Se and Mo as posing the greatest risk to human and animal health because they may accumulate in crops without damaging them. Indeed, the visible symptoms of toxicity vary from plant to plant, even if they contain elevated concentrations of toxic metals and metalloids (Clemens, 2001). The recent the guidelines of the WHO also consider Cd to be of particular concern because of both high levels of toxicity and bioaccumulation in crops (WHO, 2006b).

Metals such as Cd, Hg and Pb do not have any essential function but they are detrimental, even in small quantities, to plants, animals and humans, and accumulate because of their long biological half-life (Goethberg et al., 2002). Other metals and metalloids, such as Mn, Zn, B and Cu are essential micronutrients in small concentrations, but harmful to crops in higher concentrations. Some, such as Cu and Zn, become toxic to plants before they reach high enough concentrations to be toxic to humans, thus plants function here as a barrier mitigating potential health risks (Hamilton et al., 2005; Johnson, 2006).

Although wastewater treatment is the best choice in managing wastewater in agriculture, the costs involved in engineering-based technologies for wastewater treatment are prohibitively high for most developing countries. Even where wastewater treatment plants are externally funded, they usually only treat a small fraction of the wastewater produced and, depending on their type, can face significant maintenance problems. However, some farm-based measures and low-

Table 11.1 *Metal bio-availability grouping*

Group	Metal	Soil adsorption	Phytotoxicity	Food chain risk
1	Ag, Cr, Sn, Ti, Y and Zr	Low solubility and strong retention in soil	Low	Little risk because they are not taken up to any extent by plants
2	As, Hg and Pb	Strongly sorbed by soil colloids	Plant roots may adsorb them but not translocate to shoots; generally not phytotoxic except at very high concentrations	Pose minimal risks to the human food chain
3	B, Cu, Mn, Mo, Ni and Zn	Less strongly sorbed by soil than Groups 1 & 2	Readily taken up by plants and phytotoxic at concentrations that pose little risk to human health	Conceptually the 'soil–plant barrier' protects the food chain from these elements
4	Cd, Co, Mo and Se	Least of all metals	Pose human and/or animal health risks at plant tissue concentrations that are not generally phytotoxic	Bioaccumulation through the soil–plant–animal food chain

Source: From Hamilton et al. (2005)

cost treatment options can reduce the risk to the environment and human health (WHO, 2006b).

The key steps to follow are:

- identifying which geographical areas have elevated risk based on consideration of potential metal sources;
- quality-assured testing of soil and plant samples to verify the level of risk;
- identifying alternative varieties of the same desired crop that take up the least metal or convert the toxin to less toxic forms when grown in high-risk areas;
- developing irrigation, fertilization and residue management strategies that help to minimize metal uptake by plants;
- recommending cultivation of other crops with lower health risk (crop restrictions) if the measures mentioned above fail to safeguard humans;
- zoning affected areas for non-agricultural land use or land rehabilitation.

Most knowledge refers to the last option and industrially contaminated sites in developed countries where the affected land has a high value and costs of remediation are met by the state or by the polluter. In these cases, in situ and ex situ engineering options are applied (Table 11.2).

However, within the economic constraints of developing countries and in terms of farm-based strategies aimed at addressing wastewater-induced contamination of metal/metalloids, viable risk-reduction options can be categorized as:

Table 11.2 *In situ and ex situ engineering options adopted for remediated metal/metalloid contaminated soils*

Element	Method/Treatment/Amendment	References
Cd, Zn, As, Ti, Pb, Cu, Cr	Removal and replacement of contaminated soil	Iimura (1981)
	Containment: caps, vertical barriers, etc.	USEPA (1997)
	Solidification/stabilization: cement-based, polymer-microencapsulation, vitrification	Dutré et al. (1998); USEPA (1997)
	Separation/concentration: soil-washing, soil-flushing	USEPA (1997)
	Electrokinetics	Virkutyte et al. (2002)
Cd, Mn, Ti, Cr	Microwave immobilization	Abramovitch et al. (2003)
Cd, Cu, Pb, Zn	Suphidization pre-treatment and Denver floatation	Vanthuyne and Maes (2002)

- Soil-based treatment with non-toxic amendments to form insoluble complexes of metals and metalloids, rendering their availability at low concentrations in the root zone.
- Plant-based strategies for soils and waters contaminated with metals and metalloids through the cultivation of specific plant species capable of accumulating target ionic species in their shoots, thereby removing them from the soil or water. These mechanisms include phytoremediation (including hyper-accumulation and phytomining), chelate-enhanced phytoextraction and the use of transgenic crops.

Soil-based treatment

Hamilton et al. (2007) describe increasing total heavy metal concentrations in soils irrigated with sewage for up to a century. The authors also found that potentially bio-available forms of the metals have increased. However, the authors also report that plant tissue showed relatively low concentrations as the metals were strongly absorbed in the soil. Steering the processes that limit the solubility and plant availability of heavy metals and metalloids in soils is possible, e.g. through the use of soil amendments including gypsum, lime ($CaCO_3$), phosphate materials, hydrous Fe and Mn oxides, clay minerals and organic matter (Table 11.3).

These amendments have been shown to immobilize metals and metalloids through:

- formation of insoluble metal phosphate minerals;
- sorption of contaminants on Fe and Mn oxide surface-exchange sites, co-precipitation – formation of contaminant Fe and Mn compounds;
- sorption of contaminants on exchange sites of organic materials including manures, composts and sludges;

Table 11.3 *Soil amendments utilized for the in situ immobilization of metals and metalloids*

Element	Method/Treatment/Amendment	References
Pb	Hydroxyapatite (HA)	Chlopecka and Adriano (1997); Zhu et al. (2004)
Cd	Alkaline biosolids, lime-stabilized biosolids	Basta et al. (2001); Wong et al. (2004)
Cd/Zn	Sepiolite	Alvarez-Ayuso and García-Sánchez (2003)
Ti, Zn, Cd, Mn, Pb, Hg and Co	Zeolite (natural and synthetic)	Chlopecka and Adriano (1997); García-Sánchez et al. (1999); Haidouti (1997); Malliou et al. (1994); Oste et al. (2002)
Pb	Phosphoric acid (H_3PO_4) and calcium dihydrogen phosphate ($Ca(H_2PO_4)_2$)	Brown et al. (2004); Chen et al. (2003); Melamed et al. (2003)
Cd and Pb	Iron oxide waste by-product	Chlopecka and Adriano (1997)
Cd, Pb and Zn	Di-ammonium phosphate (DAP)	McGowen et al. (2001)
Pb	Phosphate rock	Basta et al. (2001); Hettiarachchi et al. (2001)
Pb, Cd, Zn	Triple super phosphate (TSP)	Hettiarachchi et al. (2001); Hettiarachchi and Pierzynski (2002)
Cd, Pb and Zn	Phosphate clay	Singh et al. (2001)
Pb	Mn oxide	Hettiarachchi and Pierzynski (2002)
Cd	Liming	McLaughlin and Singh (1999)
Cr (Cr(VI) reduction to Cr(III))	Organic amendments	Bolan et al. (2003)
Ni	Limestone	Kukier and Chaney (2001)
As	Simultaneous addition of lime and $FeSO_4$	Warren et al. (2003); Warren and Alloway (2003)
As	Goethite	Garcia-Sànchez et al. (1999)
As	Water treatment sludges and red mud	Lombi et al. (2004)

- sorption of contaminants on mineral surface-exchange sites or incorporation into the mineral structure of zeolites, natural aluminosilicates and aluminosilicate by-products.

The aforementioned amendments form insoluble complexes of metals and metalloids, reducing their availability at low concentrations in the root zone and reducing their assimilation by plants (Hussain, 2000; Zhu and Alva, 1993).

Although soil-based management via addition of amendments to immobilize metals/metalloids offers great opportunity to minimize element bio-availability, practical limitations must be considered. These include the management of sites co-contaminated with several elements; cost and availability of amendments; cost of long-term monitoring programmes; and suitability to particular soil and climatic conditions. Care should also be taken in the post-management phase, particularly if the site is exposed to acidic water (low pH) which may transform insoluble complexes into soluble forms.

Plant-based treatments

Soils contaminated with metals and metalloids can be improved through the use of certain plant species. This approach is broadly known as phytoremediation (Chaney et al., 2007; Cunningham et al., 1995; Salt et al., 1996). As an important category of phytoremediation, phytoextraction involves the use of pollutant-scavenging plants to absorb and concentrate metals and metalloids from the soil into above-ground biomass, which may be harvested to remove the elements from the field (Table 11.4). Plants able to accumulate high concentrations of metals are known as hyperaccumulators (Box 11.1).

BOX 11.1 HYPERACCUMULATORS

Three internationally recognized hyperaccumulator definitions are used to describe the efficiency of phytoextraction for a given metal or metalloid, namely:

- Translocation Factor;
- Extraction Coefficient;
- Bioaccumulation Factor.

The Translocation Factor or shoot/root quotient is defined as the ratio of a given heavy metal in plant shoots as compared with that in the plant root. A Translocation Factor >1.0 indicates preferential partitioning of metals to the shoot (Baker and Whiting, 2002; Branquinho et al., 2007; González and González-Chávez, 2006). The Extraction Coefficient has been described as the heavy metal concentration in the shoot divided by the (total) heavy metal concentration in soil and can be used to evaluate the ability of a plant to accumulate a heavy metal (Branquinho et al., 2007; Chen et al., 2004). Finally, the Bioaccumulation Factor is defined as the ratio of metal concentration in plant shoots to the extractable concentration of metal in the soil and is used for the quantitative expression of accumulation (Branquinho et al., 2007; Derem et al., 2006).

The concentrations of metals accumulated in hyperaccumulator plants may be 100 times greater than those occurring in non-accumulator plants growing on the same substrates (Chaney et al., 2007). Currently, there are more than 400 plant species categorized as hyperaccumulators of metals and metalloids (Cobbett, 2003).

Table 11.4 *Selected case studies on phytoremediation*

Element	Plant Species	Reference
As	*Pteris vittata* L. and *Pityrogramma calomelanos*	Francesconi et al. (2002); Tu and Ma (2002); Wongkongkatep et al. (2003); Zhang et al. (2002)
Cd/Zn	*Thlaspi caerulescens*	Brown et al. (1994, 1995a, 1995b); Lombi et al. (2001); Schwartz et al. (2003)
Ni	*Alyssum murale, Phyllanthus serpentinus, Berkheya coddii*	Abou-Shanab et al. (2003); Chaney et al. (2007); Kersten et al. (1979); Robinson et al. (1999)
Se	*Astragalus racemosus*	Parker et al. (1991)
Mn	*Alyxia rubricaulis, Phytolacca acinosa* Roxb.	Brooks et al. (1981); Xue et al. (2004)
Ti	*Biscutella laevigata, Iberis intermedia*	Anderson et al. (1999)
Cu	*Aelanthus biformifolius, Haumaniastrum katangense*	Brooks (1977); Brooks et al. (1978)
Co	*Haumaniastrum robertii*	Brooks et al. (1978)

Because the costs of growing a phytoremediation crop are minimal as compared to those of soil removal and replacement, the use of plants to remediate hazardous soils is seen as having great promise (Chaney et al., 2007). This is particularly pertinent for elements that may provide economic phytomining potential (Ni, Co, Ti and Au). Following harvest of the metal-enriched plants, their weight and volume can be reduced by burning the dried biomass which results in a high-grade 'metal ore'.

Chelate-enhanced phytoextraction utilizing ethylenediaminetetraacetic acid (EDTA) and high biomass producing plant species such as *Brassica juncea* (L.) Czern (Indian mustard) has also been investigated (Kumar et al., 1995). However, an observed drawback was the equally enhanced leaching of Pb down the soil profile (Greman et al., 2003; Madrid et al., 2003; Römkens et al., 2001; Wu et al., 2004).

In addition to phytoextraction, phytoremediation can also be achieved through reduction in the bio-availability of metals in the soil (phytostabilization), volatilization of pollutants such as Hg and Se from the foliage (phytovolatilization) and removal of contaminants by plant roots from flowing water (rhizofiltration) (Pilon-Smits, 2005). Rhizofiltration is particularly effective in applications where low metal concentrations and large volumes of water are involved (Salt et al., 1996).

However, phytoremediation has certain limitations which need to be addressed in general and on a site- and contaminant-specific basis. These include:

- Phytoextraction of metals and metalloids may take years/decades which limits its practical applicability.
- It is restricted to sites where the concentration of the contaminants (or co-contaminants) are not toxic to the plants proposed for phytoremediation.
- A specific phytoremediation 'prescription' cannot be applied to every site with a certain chemical contaminant because different site-specific conditions may not be suitable for the target plant.
- In situ phytoremediation is often restricted to sites conducive to growth of the selected plant with the contaminant located within the root zone.
- It is limited by bio-availability of pollutants, only a fraction of which may be bio-available but regulatory clean-up standards require that all the pollutant is removed. In this scenario phytoremediation may not be applicable.

Crop choice and crop restriction

As described above, crops vary in their absorption behaviour and thus risk potential for humans. In addition, some crops are consumed in larger quantities than others and some are only used as fodder plants and might not enter the human food chain. Thus, crop selection can contribute to decreasing human health risks. For example, in the case of irrigation with untreated wastewater, leafy vegetables accumulate certain metals such as Cd in greater amounts than non-leafy species (Qadir et al., 2000). Bellows (1999) gives as a rule of thumb a heavy metal absorption ratio of 1:10 for fruits and seeds versus leaves and roots. This favours cereals, legumes like beans and peas, tomatoes or fruits over vegetables such as lettuce, cauliflower, carrots or spinach. However, consideration must be given to the quantities of e. g. rice or leafy vegetables actually consumed, and hence contribution to dietary intake of the metal or metalloid, before farmers are challenged to change their cropping pattern. There is a strong relationship between the long term consumption of Cd-contaminated rice and human Cd disease (Kobayashi et al., 2002; Nordberg, 2003).

A shift in crop choice is only feasible and sustainable if there is a market and comparative market value for the alternative crop, unless subsidies are provided. Changed cropping practices might also require additional training and different tools, or even long-term tenure security if, for example, tree crops are recommended. Crop restrictions can therefore be hard to implement if necessary conditions are not in place. There are, however, examples of successful or partly successful implementation of crop restriction in wastewater use schemes in several countries such as India, Mexico, Peru, Chile, Jordan and Syria (Blumenthal et al., 2000; Qadir et al., 2007b). However, the probability of success appears much lower in sub-Saharan Africa and other countries where wastewater irrigation is not confined to (regulated) irrigation schemes but takes place along polluted streams and thus remains informal.

Zoning

Where there are no further options to maintain the farm, the affected areas might have to be mapped and taken out of production. Simmons et al. (2009) developed a General Linear Regression Model to predict the spatial distribution of soil Cd in a Cd/Zn co-contaminated cascading irrigated rice-based system in Thailand. Preliminary validation indicated that the model can predict soil Cd based on minimal soil sampling and the field's proximity to primary outlets from in-field irrigation channels and subsequent inter-field irrigation flows. Previous research (Simmons et al., 2005) and subsequent health studies confirming Cd-induced renal dysfunction in the exposed population (Swaddiwudhipong et al., 2007; Teeyakasem et al., 2007) also demonstrated the validity of assessing health risks through monitoring Cd intake via dietary exposed pathways in comparison to the Joint FAO/WHO Expert Committee on Food Additives (JECFA) Provisional Tolerable Weekly Intake values established for Cd. While Cd is of high risk, as stated above, soil sampling alone might not be a sufficient indicator of the actual health risk. This is reiterated in the example of arsenic (Box 11.2). However, zoning and taking contaminated areas out of food production should be accompanied by adequate compensation for farmers /landowners or alternative income-generating livelihood opportunities, associated with training and assured markets or subsidies.

BOX 11.2 THE CASE OF ARSENIC

Sources of arsenic contamination in rice fields include geologic soil materials that are naturally high in arsenic; irrigation with contaminated groundwater; residual arsenical pesticides; or application of poultry manure from chickens treated with arsenical antiparasite food additives. In Bangladesh, which has widespread geologic arsenic contamination, the many documented cases of arsenic poisoning have been caused by consumption of contaminated drinking water, not food, although arsenic is of more concern in rice than in other grain crops because flooded soil conditions make arsenate, which mimics the plant nutrient phosphate, more available to plants. However, far more arsenic accumulates in leaves than in grain and, according to Johnson (2006), experiments have so far failed to measure arsenic concentrations above published safe limits in rice grain, even in very contaminated soil. This situation may have changed. Williams et al. (2006) predicted that a daily consumption of rice in Bangladesh with a common total arsenic level of 0.08μg As g^{-1} is similar to a drinking-water intake with the allowed arsenic concentration of 10μg per litre. Meharg et al. (2008) reported that inorganic arsenic is in particular elevated in the bran layer of unpolished (brown) rice and less in white rice. According to FAO, planting rice in raised beds around 15cm above the ground and not in conventional flooded fields counteracted yield losses and resulted in lower arsenic levels in crops and in the soil, as a pilot field study in Bangladesh revealed (Duxbury et al., 2007).

NUTRIENTS IN EXCESS

Wastewater usually contains valuable plant nutrients, such as N, P and K. Depending on whether raw or diluted wastewater is used, the concentrations of the nutrients can vary significantly and might reach levels that can replace fertilizers or are in excess of crop needs and, if biased to certain nutrients, might affect others. Although availability of these nutrients is considered to be a driving force for wastewater irrigation in some developing countries, managing appropriate levels of nutrients in wastewater is a challenging task. Related studies usually encounter a variety of challenges which reduce the management options for farmers.

In general, nutrients in irrigation water are immediately available to the crop, as long as they remain dissolved in the water and soil solution, but may be rendered less available by several soil processes. Some processes result in permanent loss (leaching, volatilization and erosion) and others in nutrient accumulation in the soil (microbiological immobilization, adsorption and precipitation). Hence the proportions of nutrients taken up by plants are different from the proportions of nutrients applied via wastewater (or fertilizers). Because soils and wastewater seldom contain nutrients in optimum ratios, guidelines are needed to optimize wastewater irrigation. A related concept has been presented by Janssen et al. (2005). It requires, however, information on nutrient levels in water, soils and plants, which may not be readily available to resource-poor wastewater farmers or relevant government departments unless obtained through site-specific field trials.

To avoid excessive or unbalanced additions of particular nutrients to wastewater-irrigated soils and crops, farmers can select crops which are less sensitive to high nutrient levels or which can take advantage of high amounts of P and N. Higher N-levels are thus more welcome in farms specializing in leafy vegetables than grains. In addition, fodder grass is well suited to wastewater-irrigation and acts as a scavenger for N and P applied via wastewater. Reduction efficiencies of 84 per cent for N and 54 per cent for P have been reported from wastewater irrigated pastures in Zimbabwe (Nhapi et al., 2002). However, land- and soil-based options depend not only on the type of crop but also local soil and site conditions. Medium- to fine-textured soils, for example, may hold more nutrients than sandy soils, thereby releasing lower quantities in the water percolating through the soil and adding to the groundwater. Groundwater-quality monitoring is required where groundwater is shallow and used for drinking purposes.

Where farmers do not have the option to grow crops which benefit from high N or P levels, the irrigation water might first pass through other systems to transform part of its nutrient load into biomass. This could be an on-farm pond covered with duckweed or a wetland system, like the traditional tank cascades found in Sri Lanka (Awuah et al., 2004; Mahatantila et al., 2008; Nhapi, 2004). In all of these cases, however, it is necessary to remove the net biomass growth in order to prevent eventual decay of the biomass and re-release of the nutrients (Strom, 2006).

Observations from larger urban settings in developed countries show that effluent treatment by land application for cropping and forestry is often less economical than other treatment techniques. This might be due to the increasing economic land value near cities, but in particular the need in temperate climates to cater for the cold season when soils might be sealed by ice, with plants not growing or in dormant state (Jayawardane et al., 2001). In addition, where soils have restricted internal drainage capacity, soil degradation can occur through waterlogging and salinization (Jayawardane et al., 2001; Su et al., 2005). Hence most land-disposal processes are dependent on freely draining soils and the existence of some diversion structure to store effluent during periods of low absorption capacity or plant water demand.

To overcome the constraints associated with conventional land disposal of wastewater in Australia, the Filtration and Irrigated Cropping for Land Treatment and Effluent Reuse (FILTER) technique was developed for the treatment and reuse of secondary sewage effluent (Gardner et al., 2001; Jayawardane, 1995). The FILTER technique combines the use of nutrient-rich wastewater for intensive cropping with biological and physio-chemical filtration through the soil to a subsurface drainage system. It was initially tested on eight 1-ha experimental plots and subsequently trialled on four (4-ha) commercial-scale plots. FILTER plots were constructed by deep ripping to around 1m depth and installing the subsurface drainage system at this depth. The sewage effluent was applied as flood irrigation at the top end of the FILTER plots. Besides nutrient removal, other beneficial effects were reduced suspended solids, oil and grease, and an increased N/P ratio in the drainage water (Blackwell and Arakel, 2004). An obvious disadvantage is the cost factor and equipment required for the set-up of the system, even at smaller scale. However, there might be options for low-cost adaptations.

In cases where there are excess nutrient levels such as N or salts (see below), wastewater can be diluted with freshwater, where possible, to decrease the nutrient concentration and increase the benefits through a higher volume of irrigation water. This option might have a strong seasonal dimension and is only possible where wastewater streams are separated from other surface-water bodies. Where freshwater is not available, the quantity of wastewater applied per unit area can be decreased. The same applies to wastewater with high levels of organic matter. In this case, wastewater should not be applied continuously to allow soil to biodegrade organic matter.

SALTS AND SPECIFIC IONIC SPECIES

Wastewater contains more soluble salts than freshwater because salts are added to it from different sources (Qadir et al., 2007b). There are no economically viable means to remove the salts once they enter wastewater because the techniques, such as cation exchange resins or reverse-osmosis membranes, are prohibitively expensive and are only used to produce high-quality recycled water (Toze, 2006a).

For remediation purposes, wastewater can be divided into: saline wastewater containing excess levels of soluble salts; sodic wastewater characterized by excess levels of sodium (Na^+); and saline-sodic wastewater having both salts and Na^+ in excess concentrations.

The last category is most prevalent. Salinity in wastewater is characterized by its electrical conductivity (EC) expressed in terms of deci-Siemens per metre (dS m^{-1}). Sodicity is assessed by sodium adsorption ratio (SAR), which is expressed as the relative amounts of Na^+ to that of divalent cations, calcium (Ca^{2+}) and magnesium (Mg^{2+}).

For long-term irrigation with saline and/or sodic wastewater, there is a need for site-specific preventive measures and management strategies, which may include:

- appropriate selection of crop or crop variety capable of producing profitable yield with saline wastewater;
- selection of irrigation methods to reduce crop exposure;
- application of wastewater in excess of crop water requirement (evapotranspiration) to leach excess salts from the root zone;
- wastewater irrigation in conjunction with freshwater, if available, through cyclic applications and/or blending;
- in the case of salt-sensitive crops, via careful seedbed preparation and planting techniques;
- in the case of highly sodic wastewater, through the application of Ca^{2+} (e.g. via gypsum or alternative calcium-rich wastewater) to mitigate Na^+ effects on soils and crops.

Crop selection and diversification

Research efforts have led to the identification of a number of field crops, forage grasses and shrubs, biofuel crops, fruit trees and agroforestry systems which can suit a variety of salt-affected environments and local or regional markets (Maas and Grattan, 1999; Qadir et al., 2008). Salt tolerance depends on several soil, crop and climatic factors and is generally divided into four classes: sensitive; moderately sensitive; moderately tolerant; and tolerant. Relative salt tolerance threshold values for a range of crops as a function of average root-zone salinity are given in Table 11.5. Absolute tolerances will, however, vary depending on climate, soil conditions and cultural practices.

The genetic diversity among these crops provides a range of cropping options, especially as salinity tolerance often varies between different varieties of the same crop. For some crops particular salt-tolerant varieties have been created. Local extension officers and crop-research institutes will be able to provide advice on their in- and output markets.

Table 11.5 *Yield potentials of some grain, forage, vegetable and fibre crops as a function of average root-zone salinity*

Common name	Botanical name	Yield potential (%) at specified salinity (dS m^{-1})		
		50%	80%	100%
Durum wheat	*Triticum durum* Desf.	19	11	6
Barley	*Hordeum vulgare* L.	18	12	8
Cotton	*Gossypium hirsutum* L.	17	12	8
Rye	*Secale cereale* L.	16	13	11
Sugar beet	*Beta vulgaris* L.	16	10	7
Wheat	*Triticum aestivum* L.	13	9	6
Purslane	*Portulaca oleracea* L.	11	8	6
Sorghum	*Sorghum bicolor* (L.) Moench	10	8	7
Alfalfa	*Medicago sativa* L.	9	5	2
Spinach	*Spinacia oleracea* L.	9	5	2
Broccoli	*Brassica oleracea* L.	8	5	3
Egg plant	*Solanum melongena* L.	8	4	1
Rice	*Oryza sativa* L.	7	5	3
Potato	*Solanum tuberosum* L.	7	4	2
Maize	*Zea mays* L.	6	3	2
Carrot	*Daucus carota* L.	6	3	1

Source: Based on the salt-tolerance data of different crops and percentage decrease in yield per unit increase in root-zone salinity in terms of dS m^{-1} as reported by Maas and Grattan (1999)

Crop-diversification systems based on salt-tolerant plant species are likely to be the key to future agricultural and economic growth in regions where saline wastewater is used for irrigation. Such systems, linked to secure markets, should support farmers in finding the most suitable and sustainable crop-diversifying systems to mitigate any perceived production risks, while ideally also enhancing the productivity per unit of saline wastewater and protecting the environment. In all cases, farmers are encouraged to test the actual performance of suggested varieties on their fields.

Irrigation method

There are different ways to irrigate crops, such as surface or flood irrigation, manual irrigation with watering cans, furrow irrigation, sprinkler irrigation and micro-irrigation such as drip or trickle irrigation. Some are more suitable for saline water or other types of low-quality water than others. The clogging of drip irrigation systems is an example. Another one is sprinkler irrigation which may cause injury to crops from the sodium and chloride salts absorbed directly through wetted leaf surfaces, especially where climatic conditions favour evaporation (Ayers and Westcot, 1985). Several factors affect salt accumulation in leaves: leaf age, shape,

Table 11.6 *Parameters for evaluation of commonly used irrigation methods in relation to risk reduction*

Evaluation parameter	Irrigation method			
	Furrow irrigation	Border irrigation	Sprinkler irrigation	Drip irrigation
Foliar wetting and consequent leaf damage resulting in poor yield	No foliar injury as the crop is planted on the ridge	Some bottom leaves may be affected but the damage is not so serious as to reduce yield	Severe leaf damage can occur resulting in significant yield loss	No foliar injury occurs under this method of irrigation
Root zone salt accumulation with repeated applications	Salts tend to accumulate in the ridge which could harm the crop	Salts move vertically downwards and are not likely to accumulate in the root zone	Salt movement is downwards and root zone is not likely to accumulate salts	Salt movement is radial along the direction of water movement. A salt wedge is formed between drip points
Ability to maintain high soil water potential	Plants may be subject to stress between irrigations	Plants may be subject to water stress between irrigations	Not possible to maintain high soil water potential throughout the growing season	Possible to maintain high soil water potential throughout the growing season and minimize the effect of salinity
Suitability to handle brackish wastewater without significant yield loss	Fair to medium. With good management and drainage acceptable yields are possible	Fair to medium. Good irrigation and drainage practices can produce acceptable yields	Poor to fair. Most crops suffer from leaf damage and yield is low	Excellent to good. Almost all crops can be grown with very little reduction in yield

Source: Adapted from Pescod (1992)

angle, and position on plant; type and concentration of salt; ambient temperature; air velocity; irrigation frequency; and length of time the leaf remains wet (Maas and Grattan, 1999). Since the problem is related more to the frequency than the duration of sprinkler irrigation, infrequent and heavy irrigations should be preferred over frequent and light irrigations (Qadir and Minhas, 2008). Several parameters for the evaluation of commonly used irrigation methods in relation to risk reduction are given in Table 11.6.

Irrigation, drainage, and root-zone salinity management

While using saline water or wastewater, the volume of irrigation water applied should be in excess of crop water requirement (evapotranspiration) and predictable rainfall should be taken into consideration as it leaches excess salts from the root zone. Salinity control by effective leaching of the root zone therefore becomes an important option for farmers who do not have limited water allocations. In order to calculate leaching requirement, farmers will need assistance to analyse the electrical conductivity of their soils and irrigation water so that the following equation can be used.

$$LR = EC_w / [5(EC_e) - (EC_w)] \qquad\qquad 11.1$$

LR refers to leaching requirement (additional water fraction of the irrigation water) needed to control salts in the root zone within the salt tolerance level of a specific crop with the routine surface irrigation method, i.e. the fraction of infiltrated water that must pass through the root zone to keep soil salinity within a specific level. EC_w is electrical conductivity of applied irrigation water expressed in terms of dS m^{-1}. EC_e refers to the average soil salinity (determined from the extract of saturated soil paste; also expressed as dS m^{-1}) in the root zone that can be tolerated by the crop under consideration. The values given in Table 11.5 for different crops can be used. These values also provide information on yield loss by these crops as the salinity of the growth medium increases.

The LR is needed to calculate the total water requirement (AW) of the crop. This can be estimated from Equation 11.2 (Ayers and Westcot, 1985).

$$AW = ET / (1 - LR) \qquad\qquad 11.2$$

AW refers to the depth of applied water per unit area on a yearly or seasonal basis (mm yr^{-1}); ET is the annual or seasonal crop water consumption expressed as evapotranspiration (mm yr^{-1}); and LR is the leaching requirement expressed as a fraction (see above). Both AW and ET can also be expressed in terms of m^3 of water (1mm = 10m^3 ha^{-1}).

The leaching required to maintain salt balance in the root zone may be achieved either by applying sufficient water at each irrigation to meet the LR or by applying, less frequently, a leaching irrigation sufficient to remove the salts accumulated from previous irrigations. The leaching frequency depends on the salinity status in water or soil, salt tolerance of the crop and climatic conditions (Qadir and Minhas, 2008). The amount of rainfall should be taken into consideration while estimating the leaching requirement and selecting the leaching method. Although leaching is essential to prevent root-zone salinity, leaching under saline wastewater irrigation may result in the movement of nitrates, metals, metalloids and salts to the groundwater. Therefore, monitoring of groundwater levels and quality is an essential indicator of environmental performance (Lazarova and Bahri, 2005).

Adequate soil drainage is considered to be an essential prerequisite to achieving leaching requirement vis-à-vis salinity control in the root zone. Natural internal drainage alone may be adequate if there is sufficient storage capacity in the soil profile or a permeable subsurface layer occurs that drains to a suitable outlet. An artificial system must be provided if such natural drainage is not present. Otherwise the resultant root-zone salinity control will not be sustainable. Besides, adequate soil drainage, land-levelling and adequate depth of groundwater are also basic components to maintain salinity in the root zone at a specific level. The suitable depth of groundwater depends on climate, groundwater quality and crop(s) to be grown.

Conjunctive use with freshwater

Saline wastewater can be used for irrigation in conjunction with freshwater, if available, through cyclic and blending approaches. Several studies have evaluated different aspects of these approaches on a field scale (Oster, 1994; Qadir and Oster, 2004; Rhoades, 1989; Sharma and Rao, 1998; Shennan et al., 1995). These approaches allow a good degree of flexibility to fit into different situations. Guidelines pertaining to water quality for irrigation in terms of salinity- and sodicity-related parameters were mentioned in Chapters 2 and 6 in this volume.

The cyclic strategy involves the use of saline wastewater and non-saline irrigation water in crop rotations that include both moderately salt-sensitive and salt-tolerant crops. Typically, the non-saline water is also used before planting and during initial growth stages of the salt-tolerant crop while saline water is usually used after seedling establishment (Oster, 1994; Rhoades, 1989). The cyclic strategy requires a crop-rotation plan that can make best use of the available good-quality water and saline wastewater, and takes into account the different salt sensitivities among the crops grown in the region, including the changes in salt sensitivities of crops at different stages of growth. The advantages of the cyclic strategy include:

- Steady-state salinity conditions in the soil profile are never reached because the quality of irrigation water changes over time.
- Soil salinity is kept lower over time, especially in the topsoil during seedling establishment.
- A broad range of crops, including those with high economic-value and moderate salt sensitivity, can be grown in rotation with salt-tolerant crops.
- Conventional irrigation systems can be used.

Studies addressing the cyclic use of drainage waters (Oster, 1994; Rhoades, 1989; Shennan et al., 1995) have shown that this strategy is sustainable for cotton, wheat, safflower (*Carthamus tinctorius* L.), sugar beet, tomato (*Lycopersicon esculentum* Mill.), cantaloupe (*Cucumis melo* L.) and pistachio (*Pistacia vera* L.), provided that the problems of crusting or poor aeration are dealt with through optimum management. Sharma and Rao (1998) provided further evidence from a study area where waters with various levels of salinity (EC = 6, 9, 12, 18.8 dS m^{-1}) were used successfully for seven years to irrigate different crops like wheat, pearl millet (*Pennisetum glaucum* (L.) R. Br.) and sorghum with acceptable yield reductions but without any serious degradation of a coarse-textured soil. The soil salinity levels were managed satisfactorily by monsoon rains and in part pre-sowing irrigation of 70mm with low-salinity canal water. However, the extent of salt leaching was heavily dependent on the total amount of monsoon rainfall and subsurface drainage.

Blending consists of mixing good- and poor-quality water supplies before or during irrigation. Saline wastewater can be pumped directly into the nearest irrigation canal or water channel. The quantity of saline wastewater pumped into the canal can be regulated so that target salinities in the blended water can be achieved (Oster, 1994; Rhoades, 1989). Water qualities are altered, according to the availability of different irrigation water qualities and quantities, between or within an irrigation event. Blending saline waters with good-quality irrigation waters has been a common practice in several countries such as India, Pakistan and the USA (Minhas, 1996; Qadir and Oster, 2004).

Seedbed preparation and planting techniques

Since most crops are salt-sensitive at germination stage, it is important to avoid the use of saline wastewater at this critical time. Under field conditions, it is possible, by modifications of planting practices, to minimize salt-accumulation around the seed and to improve the standing of crops that are sensitive to salts during germination. These modifications can include sowing near the bottom of the furrows on both sides of the ridges, raising seedlings with freshwater and their transplanting, using mulches to carry over soil moisture for longer period and increasing the seed or seedling rate per unit area (plant density) to compensate for possible decrease in germination and growth (Minhas, 1996; Tanji and Kielen, 2002).

Soil and water treatment

Irrigation with sodic wastewater needs provision of a source of Ca^{2+} to mitigate Na^+ effects on soils and crops. Gypsum ($CaSO_4 \cdot 2H_2O$) is the most commonly used source of Ca^{2+}; its requirement for sodic water depends on the Na^+ concentration and can be estimated through simple analytical tests. Gypsum can be added to the soil, applied with irrigation water by using gypsum beds or placing gypsum stones in water channels. In the case of calcareous soils containing precipitated or native calcite ($CaCO_3$), none or a much lower rate of gypsum application may work well. Plant residues and other organic matter left in or added to the field can also improve the chemical and physical conditions of soils irrigated with sodic wastewater. In addition, biological treatment of salt-prone wastewater by standard activated sludge culture can be triggered by the inclusion of salt-tolerant organisms to improve treatment efficiency.

Where available, high-electrolyte waters containing an adequate proportion of divalent cations such as Ca^{2+} can be used for sodic and saline-sodic soil amelioration. These waters can improve soil hydraulic properties without the need to apply a calcium-supplying amendment (Qadir et al., 2007a; Quirk, 2001). However, the ratio of divalent cations, particularly Ca^{2+}, to total cations (TC) in the applied water should be at least 0.3. Synthesis of the data on total cationic and Ca^{2+} concentrations in several wastewater samples suggests that wastewaters have a wide range of calcium to TC ratio ($C_{Ca}:C_{TC}$), i.e. from as low as 0.03 to as high as 0.80 (Table 11.7). These contrasting observations reveal that the use of wastewater to irrigate sodic soils should be carefully planned as the $C_{Ca}:C_{TC}$ should be over the threshold value of 0.3. Several studies have demonstrated that adequate amounts of Ca^{2+} supplied through irrigation water or applied to the soil in the form of some amendment improve soil structure and counterbalance the negative effects of high concentrations of Na^+ when sodic soils are brought under cultivation (Oster et al., 1999; Qadir et al., 2001).

The applicability of the high-electrolyte water is effective under certain conditions:

- The sodic soil under amelioration and management has smectite- and montmorillonite-type clay minerals with low hydraulic conductivity.
- The soil physical condition has deteriorated and hydraulic conductivity is so low that the time required for amelioration or the amount of amendment required is excessive.
- The irrigation water to be used following amelioration is so low in electrolyte concentration that water transmission would decrease adversely.

Table 11.7 *Concentrations of total cations (mmol$_c$ per litre) and calcium (mmol$_c$ per litre), and ratio of calcium to total cations in wastewater samples*

Total cations $(C_{TC})^a$	Calcium (C_{Ca})	$C_{Ca} : C_{TC}$	Reference
7.0	1.6	0.23	Kaul et al. (2002)
10.0	2.7	0.27	Kaul et al. (2002)
17.0	3.7	0.22	Mitra and Gupta (1999)
19.0	5.0	0.26	Mitra and Gupta (1999)
8.0	2.5	0.31	Arora et al. (1985)
9.0	2.8	0.31	Baddesha et al. (1986)
9.0	7.2	0.80	CSSRI (2004)
21.0	11.0	0.52	CSSRI (2004)
44.0	1.5	0.03	Ensink et al. (2002)

$^aC_{TC} \approx EC$ (dS m^{-1}) x 10.

ORGANIC CONTAMINANTS

Exposure of consumers, farmers and crops in developing countries to organic contaminants is probably much higher through direct pesticide application than via contaminated irrigation water. The challenge of any related risk (and its mitigation) starts with its assessment, which is costly if based on actual analysis (see Chapter 6). A possible alternative for pesticides is to predict the risk based on easier to measure environmental factors and application practices, using, for example, the free Pesticide Impact Rating Index (PIRI) software, mentioned in Chapter 6, which was developed in Australia but also been applied elsewhere, like Sri Lanka. More difficult and costly would be the analysis of organic contaminants of emerging concern, like residual pharmaceuticals or endocrine disruptor compounds. This limits the current knowledge on their actual risk in wastewater irrigation, which has so far been ranked as relatively low compared, for example, to pathogenic hazards (Chang et al., 2002; Toze, 2006b; WHO, 2006b).

To address organic contaminants preventive measures are therefore more suitable than any soil or water treatment. Key activities include the use of alternative pesticides or integrated pest management. In order to avoid pesticides entering streams used for irrigation or other purposes, buffer zones, run-off reduction and the use of wetlands for remediation could be considered. Containment of contaminated water in dams or wetlands may provide time for pesticides to be removed by sediments or through degradation. Farming practices that reduce run-off, such as the provision of vegetation cover or vegetated bufferstrips (Box 11.3), can significantly reduce the probability of environmental impacts (Finlayson and Silburn, 1996; Kennedy, 1999; USDA, 2000). In spiking trials, the FILTER system has also been shown to reduce pesticide loads by more than 98 per cent (Biswas et al., 2000).

The key removal mechanisms for most organic substances are adsorption and biodegradation in soils and sediments (WHO, 2006b). Removal efficiencies are greater in soils rich in silt, clay and organic matter. Black carbon, in particular, can play a significant role in fixing highly toxic polycyclic aromatic hydrocarbons, polychlorinated biphenyls, dioxins, polybrominated diphenylethers and pesticides (Koelmans et al., 2006).

Chemical stability and slow natural attenuation of certain POPs, such as polychlorinated biphenyls (PCBs) and 1,1,1-trichloro-2,2-bis(4-chlorophenyl) ethane (DDT), make remediation of these compounds a particularly intractable environmental challenge. The approach usually taken is to isolate affected sites and either remove the contaminated soil or rely on phytoremediation as described above.

Box 11.3 Buffer-strips

There is a dearth of empirical evidence on the performance of various options for mitigating diffuse pollution from agriculture. Especially, riparian buffers have received significant attention over the past 20 years. Ranges for positive buffer efficacy were found to be 30–100 per cent for soil sediment, 30–95 per cent for total phosphorus, 10–100 per cent for total nitrogen, 30–100 per cent for pesticides and 53–100 per cent for faecal indicator organisms. Since many of the experiments underpinning these data were conducted under 'ideal' operating conditions, it is likely that buffer performance in nature will be lower. Overall, the evidence base suggests that buffers provide at least useful short-term benefits, while longer-term impacts remain questionable owing to risks of pollution swapping (Collins et al., 2009).

CONCLUSIONS

There is a variety of management options for smallholder farmers in developing countries to address the challenges and risks of exposure to heavy metals or excessive salts and nutrients through irrigation water. These measures include soil- and water-based interventions as well as changes in crops and crop varieties. Currently available techniques that have been successfully applied to remediate metal or metalloid contaminated soils include in situ and ex situ engineering options, irrigation management options, in situ soil-based immobilization, phytoremediation, chelate-enhanced phytoextraction, etc. In certain cases, farmers and authorities might have no other choice than to cultivate better adapted and non-edible crops, or to zone the areas for non-agricultural land use. In view of possible organic contaminants, appropriate pest and pesticide management will remain more important than soil and water treatment. All methods have however also their drawbacks in effectiveness, duration and economics (Iskandar and Adriano, 1997; Zaurov et al., 1999). Due to the additional risk of bioaccumulation it is in many cases not possible to provide details on the general effectiveness of measures in terms of health-risk reduction, which will largely depend on a variety of site conditions, as well as spatial and temporal factors. While our knowledge is much advanced in view of challenges related to excess nutrients and salts, large gaps remain for heavy metals and, in particular, organic contaminants. A key constraint to risk assessments and mitigation is the missing capacity to analyse and monitor these constituents, especially in developing countries. It remains, therefore, crucial to support pollution preventing policies and measures, including the reduction of possible fertilizer subsidies where they have led to over-fertilization. In the case of metals, metalloids, nutrients and emerging contaminants, pre-treatment and/or segregation of industrial wastewater from the domestic and municipal wastewater stream (eventually used for irrigation) should have highest priority

(Patwardhan, 2008). Also, the sources of salts in wastewater can be reduced by using technologies in the industrial sector that reduce salt consumption vis-à-vis discharge into the sewage system. In addition, many hazardous chemicals can be replaced in production processes and restrictions can be imposed on the use of certain products for domestic use that are major sources of, for example, salts in wastewater (Lazarova and Bahri, 2005).

REFERENCES

Abaidoo, R. C., Keraita, B., Drechsel, P., Dissanayake, P. and Maxwell, A. X. (2009) 'Soil and crop contamination through wastewater irrigation and options for risk reduction in developing countries', in P. Dion (ed) *Soil Biology and Agriculture in the Tropics*, Springer Verlag, Heidelberg (in press)

Abou-Shanab, R. A., Angle, J. S., Delorme, T. A., Chaney, R. L., Van Berkum, P., Moawad, H., Ghanem, K. and Ghozlan, H. A. (2003) 'Phizobacterial effects on nickel extraction from soil and uptake by *Alyssum murale*', *New Phytologist*, vol 158, pp219–24

Abramovitch, R. A., ChangQing, L., Hicks, E. and Sinard, J. (2003) 'In situ remediation of soils contaminated with toxic metal ions using microwave energy', *Chemosphere*, vol 53, pp1077–85

Alvarez-Ayuso, E. and García-Sánchez, A. (2003) 'Sepiolite as a feasible soil additive for the immobilization of cadmium and zinc', *Science of the Total Environment*, vol 305, nos 1–3, pp1–12

Anderson, C. W. N., Brooks, R. R., Chiarucci, A., LaCoste, C. J., Leblanc, M., Robinson, B. H., Simcock, R. and Stewart, R. B. (1999) 'Phytomining for nickel, thallium and gold', *Journal of Geochemical Exploration*, vol 67, pp407–15

Arora, B. R., Azad, A. S., Singh, B. and Shekon, G. S. (1985) 'Pollution potential of municipal wastewater of Ludhina, Punjab', *Indian Journal of Ecology*, vol 12, pp1–7

Awuah, E., Oppong-Peprah, M., Lubberding, H. J. and Gijzen., H. J. (2004) 'Comparative performance studies of water lettuce, duckweed, and algal-based stabilization ponds using low-strength sewage', *Journal of Toxicology and Environmental Health*, vol 67, pp1727–39

Ayers R. S. and Westcot, D. W. (1985) *Water Quality for Agriculture,* Irrigation and Drainage, Paper 29, Rev 1, FAO, Rome

Baddesha, H. S., Rao, D. L. N., Abrol, I. P. and Chhabra, R. (1986) *Indian Journal of Agricultural Sciences*, vol 56, pp584–91

Baker, A. J. M. and Whiting, S. N. (2002) 'In search of the holy grail – A further step in understanding metal hyperaccumulation', *New Phytologist*, vol 155, pp1–7

Basta, N. T., Gradwohl, R., Snethen, K. L. and Schroder, J. L. (2001) 'Chemical immobilization of lead, zinc and cadmium in smelter-contaminated soils using biosolids and rock phosphate', *Journal of Environmental Quality*, vol 30, no 4, pp1222–30

Bellows, A. C. (1999) 'Urban food, health, and the environment: The case of Upper Silesia, Poland', in M. Koc, R. MacRae, L. J. A. Mougeot and J. Welsh (eds) *For Hunger-Proof Cities: Sustainable Urban Food Systems*, International Development Research Centre, Ottawa, pp131–5

Biswas, T. K., Naismith, A. N. and Jayawardane, N. S. (2000) 'Performance of a land FILTER technique for pesticide removal from contaminated water', in J. A. Adams and A. K. Metherell (eds) *Soil 2000: New Horizons for a New Century*, Lincoln University, Christchurch Canterbury, New Zealand, pp23–4

Blackwell, J. and Arakel, A. (2004) 'Can integration of sequential biological concentration and the SAL-PROCTM processes result in sustainable management of irrigation drainage?', Desalination Conference, October 2004, El Paso, TX, www.geo-processors. com/files/Geo_InternationalSalinityForum05.pdf

Blumenthal, U. J., Peasey, A., Ruiz-Palacios, G. and Mara, D. D. (2000) *Guidelines for Wastewater Reuse in Agriculture and Aquaculture: Recommended Revisions Based on New Research Evidence*, Task No 68, Part 1, WELL Study, London School of Hygiene and Tropical Medicine, London / Loughborough University, Loughborough

Bolan, N. S., Adriano, D. C., Natesan, R. and Koo, B.-J. (2003) 'Effects of organic amendments on the reduction and phytoavailability of chromate in mineral soil', *Journal of Environmental Quality*, vol 32, pp120–28

Branquinho, C., Serrano, H. C., Pinto, M. J. and Martins-Loução, M. A. (2007) 'Revisiting the plant hyperaccumulation criteria to rare plants and earth abundant elements', *Environmental Pollution*, vol 146, pp437–43

Brooks, R. R. (1977) 'Copper and cobalt uptake by *Haumaniastrum* species', *Plant Soil*, no 48, pp541–4

Brooks, R. R., Morrison, R. S., Reeves, R. D. and Malaisse, F. (1978) 'Copper and cobalt in African species of *Aeolanthus* Mart', *Plant Soil*, no 50, pp503–7

Brooks, R. R., Trow, J. M., Veillon, J.-M. and Jaffre, T. (1981) 'Studies on manganese-accumulating Alyxia from New Caledonia', *Taxon*, vol 30, pp420–23

Brown, S. L., Angle, J. S., Chaney, R. L. and Baker, A. J. M. (1995a) 'Zinc and cadmium uptake by *Thlaspi caerulescens* and *Silene cucubalis* grown on sludge-amended soils in relation to total soil metals and soil pH', *Environmental Science and Technology*, vol 29, pp1581–5

Brown, S. L., Chaney, R. L., Angle, J. S. and Baker, A. J. M. (1994) 'Zinc and cadmium uptake by *Thlaspi caerulescens* and *Silene cucubalis* in relation to soil metals and soil pH', *Journal of Environmental Quality*, vol 23, pp1151–7

Brown, S. L., Chaney, R. L., Angle, J. S. and Baker, A. J. M. (1995b) 'Zn and Cd uptake of *Thlaspi caerulescens* grown in nutrient solution', *Soil Science Society of America Journal*, vol 59, pp125–133

Brown, S. L., Chaney, R., Hallfrisch, J., Ryan, J. A. and Berti, W. R. (2004) 'In situ soil treatments to reduce the phyto- and bio-availability of lead, zinc and cadmium', *Journal of Environmental Quality*, vol 33, pp522–31

Central Soil Salinity Research Institute (2004) 'Use of urban and industrial effluent in agriculture', *Annual Progress Reports (2000–2003)*, NATP-MM Project (CSSRI), Karnal, India

Chaney, R. L., Angle, J. S., Broadhurst, C. L., Peters, C. A., Tappero, R. V. and Sparks, D. L. (2007) 'Improved understanding of hyperaccumulation yields commercial phytoextraction and phytomining technologies', *Journal of Environmental Quality*, vol 36, pp1429–43

Chang, A. C., Pan, G., Page, A. L. and Asano, T. (2002) 'Developing human health-related chemical guidelines for reclaimed water and sewage sludge applications in agriculture', report for WHO, www.who.int/water_sanitation_health/wastewater/gwwuchemicals. pdf

Chen, M., Ma, L. Q., Singh, S. P., Cao, R. X. and Melamed, R. (2003) 'Field demonstration of in situ immobilization of soil Pb using P amendments', *Advances in Environmental Research*, vol 8, pp 93–102

Chen, Y., Shen, Z., Li, X. (2004) 'The use of vetiver grass (*Vetiveria zizanioides*) in the phytoremediation of soils contaminated with heavy metals', *Applied Geochemistry*, vol 19, pp1553–65

Chlopecka, A. and Adriano, D. C. (1997) 'Influence of zeolite, apatite and Fe-oxide on Cd and Pb uptake by crops', *Science of the Total Environment*, vol 207, nos 2–3, pp195–206

Clemens, S. (2001) 'Molecular mechanisms of plant metal tolerance and homeostasis', *Planta*, vol 212, pp475–86

Cobbett, C. (2003) 'Heavy metals and plants – Model system and hyperaccumulators', *New Phytologist*, vol 159, pp289–93

Collins, A. L. Hughes, G., Zhang, Y. and Whitehead, J. (2009), 'Mitigating diffuse water pollution from agriculture: Riparian buffer strip performance with width', *CAB Reviews: Perspectives in Agriculture, Veterinary Science, Nutrition and Natural Resources*, vol 4, no 39, p15

Cunningham, S. D., Berti, W. R. and Huang, J. W. (1995) 'Phytoremediation of contaminated soils', *Trends in Biotechnology*, vol 13, pp393–7

Derem, A., Denayer, F. O., Petit, D. and Haluwyn, C. V. (2006) 'Seasonal variations of cadmium and zinc in *Arrhenatherum elatius*, a perennial grass species from highly contaminated soils', *Environmental Pollution*, vol 140, pp62–70

Dutré, V., Kestens, C., Scaep, J. and Vandecasteele, C. (1998) 'Study of the remediation of a site contaminated with arsenic', *Science of the Total Environment*, vol 220, nos 2–3, pp185–94

Duxbury, J. M., Panaullah, G. and Koo-Oshima, S. (2007) *Remediation of Arsenic for Agriculture, Sustainability, Food Security and Health in Bangladesh*, FAO Water Working Paper, FAO, Rome

Ensink, J. H. J., van der Hoek, W., Matsuno, Y., Munir, S. and Aslam, M. R. (2002) *Use of Untreated Wastewater in Peri-urban Agriculture in Pakistan: Risks and Opportunities*, Research Report 64, International Water Management Institute (IWMI), Colombo, p22

Finlayson, B. and Silburn, M. (1996) 'Soil, nutrient and pesticide movements from different land use practices, and subsequent transport by rivers and streams', in H. M. Hunter, A. G. Eyles and G. E. Rayment (eds) *Downstream Effects of Land Use*, Department of Natural Resources, Queensland, pp9–14

Francesconi, K., Visoothiviseth, P., Sridokchan, W. and Goessler, W. (2002) 'Arsenic species in an arsenic hyperaccumulating fern *Pityrogramma calomelanos*: A potential phytoremediator of arsenic-contaminated soils', *Science of the Total Environment*, vol 284, nos 1–3, pp27–35

García-Sánchez, A., Alastuey, A. and Querol, X. (1999) 'Heavy metal adsorption by different minerals: Application to the remediation of polluted soils', *Science of the Total Environment*, vol 242, nos 1–3, pp179–88

Gardner, E. A., Morton, D., Sands, J., Mathews, P., Cook, F. J. and Jayawardane, N. S. (2001) 'The FILTER system for tertiary treatment of sewage effluent by land application – its performance in a subtropical environment', *Water Science and Technology*, vol 10, pp335–42

Goethberg, A., Greger, M. and Bengtsson, B. E. (2002) 'Accumulation of heavy metals in water spinach (*Ipomea aquatica*) cultivated in the Bangkok region, Thailand', *Environmental Toxicology and Chemistry*, vol 21, no 9, pp1934–9

González, R. C. and González-Chávez, M. C. A. (2006) 'Metal accumulation in wild plants surrounding mining wastes', *Environmental Pollution*, vol 144, pp84–92

Greman, H., Vodnik, D., Velinkonja-Bolta, S. and Lestan, D. (2003) 'Ethylenediamine-dissuccinate as a new chelate for environmentally safe enhanced lead phytoextraction', *Journal of Environmental Quality*, vol 32, pp500–506

Haidouti, C. (1997) 'Inactivation of mercury in contaminated soils using natural zeolites', *Science of the Total Environment*, vol 208, nos 1–2, pp105–9

Hamilton, A. J., Boland, A.-M., Stevens, D., Kelly, J., Radcliffe, J., Ziehrl, A., Dillon, P. J. and Paulin, R. (2005) 'Position of the Australian horticultural industry with respect to the use of reclaimed water', *Agricutural Water Management*, vol 71, pp181–209

Hamilton, A. J., Stagnitti, F., Xiong, X., Kreidl, S. L, Benke, K. K. and Maher, P. (2007) 'Wastewater irrigation: The state of play', *Vadose Zone Journal*, vol 6, no 4, pp823–40

Hettiarachchi, G. M. and Pierzynski, G. M. (2002) 'In situ stabilization of soil Pb using phosphorous and manganese oxide', *Journal of Environmental Quality*, vol 31, pp564–72

Hettiarachchi, G. M., Pierzynski, G. M. and Ransom, M. D. (2001) 'In situ stabilization of soil lead using phosphorous', *Journal of Environmental Quality*, vol 30, pp1214–21

Hussain, S. I. (2000) 'Irrigation of crops with sewage effluent: Implications and movement of lead and chromium as affected by soil texture, lime, gypsum and organic matter', PhD thesis, Department of Soil Science, University of Agriculture, Faisalabad, p190

Iimura, K. (1981) 'Chemical forms and behavior of heavy metals in soils', in K. Kitagishi and I. Yamane (eds) *Heavy Metal Pollution in Soils of Japan*, Japan Science Society Press, Tokyo, pp27–35

Iskandar, I. K. and Adriano, D. C. (eds) (1997) *Remediation of Soils Contaminated with Metals*, Advances in Environmental Science, Science Reviews, Northwood, UK

Janssen, B. H., Boesveld, H. and Rodriguez, M. J. (2005) 'Some theoretical considerations on evaluating wastewater as a source of N, P and K for crops', *Irrigation and Drainage*, vol 54, no S1, ppS35–S47

Jayawardane, N. S. (1995) *Wastewater Treatment and Reuse through Irrigation, with Special Reference to the Murray Basin and Adjacent Coastal Areas*, Division of Water Resources – Divisional Report, no 95/1, CSIRO, Collingwood, Australia

Jayawardane, N. S., Biswas, T. K., Blackwell, J. and Cook, F. J. (2001) 'Management of salinity and sodicity in a land FILTER system, for treating saline wastewater on a saline-sodic soil', *Australian Journal of Soil Research*, vol 39, pp1247–58

Jiménez, B. and Asano, T. (2008) 'Water reclamation and reuse around the world', in B. Jiménez and T. Asano (eds) *Water Reuse: An International Survey of Current Practice, Issues and Needs*, IWA Publishing, London

Johnson, S. (2006) 'Are we at risk from metal contamination in rice?', *Rice Today*, July–September 2006, p36

Kaul, S. N., Juwarkar, A. S., Kulkarni, V. S., Nandy, T., Szpyrkowicz, L. and Trivedy, R. K. (2002) *Utilization of Wastewater in Agriculture and Aquaculture*, Science Publishers, Jodhpur, p675

Kennedy, I. R. (1999) 'Environmental fate and transport of cotton pesticides', in S. A. Hahndorf and P. A. Jones (eds) *Proceedings 1998 Riverine Environment Forum*, Murray-Darling Basin Commission, Canberra, pp51–60

Kersten, W. J., Brooks, R. R., Reeves, R. D. and Jaffre, T. (1979) 'Nickel uptake by New Caledonian species of *Phyllanthus*', *Taxon*, vol 28, pp529–34

Kobayashi, E., Okudo, Y., Suwazono, Y., Kido, T., Nishijo, M., Nakagawa, H. and Nogawa, K. (2002) 'Association between total cadmium intake calculated from the cadmium concentration in household rice and mortality among inhabitants of the cadmium-polluted Jinzu River basin of Japan', *Toxicology Letters*, no 129, pp85–91

Koelmans, A. A., Jonker, M. T. O., Cornelissen, G., Bucheli, T. D., VanNoort, P. C. M. and Gustafsson, O. (2006) 'Black carbon: The reverse of its dark side', *Chemosphere*, vol 63, pp365–77

Kukier, U. and Chaney, R. L., (2001) 'Amelioration of nickel phytotoxicity in muck and mineral soils', *Journal of Environmental Quality*, vol 30, pp1949–60

Kumar, P. B. A. N., Dushenkov, V., Motto, H. and Raskin, I. (1995) 'Phytoextraction: The use of plants to remove heavy metals from soils', *Environmental Science and Technology*, vol 29, pp1232–8

Lazarova, V. and Bahri, A. (2005) *Water Reuse for Irrigation: Agriculture, Landscapes, and Turf Grass*, CRC Press, Boca Raton, FL

Lombi, E., Hamon, R. E., Wieshammer, G., McLaughlin, M. J. and McGrath, S. P. (2004) 'Assessment of the use of industrial byproducts to remediate a copper and arsenic contaminated soil', *Journal of Environmental Quality*, vol 33, pp902–10

Lombi, E., Zhao, J. J., Dunham, S. J. and McGrath, S. P. (2001) 'Phytoremediation on heavy metal contaminated soils. Natural hyperaccumulation versus chemically enhanced phytoextraction', *Journal of Environmental Quality*, vol 30, pp1919–26

Maas, E. V. and Grattan, S. R., (1999) 'Crop yields as affected by salinity', in R.W. Skaggs and J. van Schilfgaarde (eds) *Agricultural Drainage*, ASA-CSSA-SSSA, Madison, WI, pp55–108

Madrid, F., Liphadzi, M. S. and Kirkham, M. B. (2003) 'Heavy metal displacement in chelate-irrigated soil during phytoremediation', *Journal of Hydrology*, vol 272, pp107–19

Mahatantila, K., Chandrajith, R., Jayasena, H. A. H. and Ranawana, K. B. (2008) 'Spatial and temporal changes of hydrogeochemistry in ancient tank cascade systems in Sri Lanka: Evidence for a constructed wetland', *Water and Environment Journal*, vol 22, pp17–24

Malliou, E., Loizidou, M. and Spyrellis, N. (1994) 'Uptake of lead and cadmium on clinoptilolite', *Science of the Total Environment*, vol 149, no 3, pp139–44

McGowen, S. L., Basta, N. T. and Brown, G. O. (2001) 'Use of diammonium phosphate to reduce heavy metal solubility and transport in smelter-contaminated soil', *Journal of Environmental Quality*, vol 30, pp493–500

McLaughlin, M. J. and Singh, B. R. (1999) *Cadmium in Soils and Plants*, Kluwer Academic Publishers, Dordrecht, The Netherlands, p271

Meharg, A. A., Lombi, E., Williams, P. N., Scheckel, K. G., Feldmann, J., Raab, A., Zhu, Z. and Islam, I. (2008) 'Speciation and localization of arsenic in white and brown rice grains', *Environmental Science and Technology*, vol 42, no 4, pp1051–57

Melamed, R., Cao, X., Chen, M. and Ma, L. Q. (2003) 'Field assessment of lead immobilization in a contaminated soil after phosphate application', *Science of the Total Environment*, vol 305, nos 1–3, pp117–27

Minhas P. S. (1996) 'Saline water management for irrigation in India', *Agricultural Water Management*, vol 30, pp1–24

Mitra, A. and Gupta, S. K. (1999) 'Effect of Sewage water irrigation on essential plant nutrient and pollutant element status in a vegetable growing area around Calcutta', *Indian Journal of Society of Soil Science*, no 47, pp99–105

Murtaza, G., Ghafoor, A., Qadir, M., Owens, G., Aziz, M. A., Zia, M. H. and Ullah, S. (2009) 'Disposal and use of sewage on agricultural lands in Pakistan: A review', *Pedosphere* (in press)

Nhapi, I. (2004) 'Potential for the use of duckweed-based pond systems in Zimbabwe', *Water SA*, vol 30, no 1, p115

Nhapi., I., Mawere, M., Veenstra, S. and Gijzen, H. (2002) 'Effluent polishing via pasture irrigation in Harare, Zimbabwe', *Water Science and Technology*, vol 46, no 9, pp287–95

Nordberg, G. (2003) 'Cadmium and human health: A perspective based on recent studie in China', *Journal of Trace Elements and Experimental Medicine*, vol 16, no 4, pp307–319

Oste, L. A., Lexmond, T. M. and van Reimsdijk, W. H., (2002) 'Metal immobilization in soils using synthetic zeolites', *Journal of Environmental Quality*, vol 31, pp813–21

Oster, J. D. (1994) 'Irrigation with poor quality water', *Agricultural Water Management*, vol 25, pp271–97

Oster, J. D., Shainberg, I. and Abrol, I. P. (1999) 'Reclamation of salt affected soils', in R.W. Skaggs and J. van Schilfgaarde (eds) *Agricultural Drainage*, ASA-CSSA-SSSA, Madison, WI, pp659–91

Parker, D. R., Page, A. L. and Thomason, D. N. (1991) 'Salinity and boron tolerances of candidate plants for the removal of selenium from soils', *Journal of Environmental Quality*, vol 20, pp157–64

Patwardhan, A. D. (2008) *Industrial Waste Water Treatment*, Prentice Hall of India, New Delhi, p292

Pescod, M. B. (ed) (1992) *Wastewater Treatment and Use in Agriculture*, Irrigation and Drainage Paper no 47, FAO, Rome

Pettygrove, G. S. and Asano, T. (eds) (1985) *Irrigation with Reclaimed Municipal Wastewater – A Guide Manual*, Lewis Publishers, Chelsea, MI

Pilon-Smits, E. (2005) 'Phytoremediation', *Annual Review of Plant Biology*, vol 56, pp15–39

Qadir, M., Ghafoor, A. and Murtaza, G. (2000) 'Cadmium concentration in vegetables grown on urban soils irrigated with untreated municipal sewage', *Environment, Development and Sustainability*, vol 2, pp11–19

Qadir, M. and Minhas, P. S. (2008) 'Wastewater use in agriculture: Saline and sodic waters', in S.W. Trimble (ed) *Encyclopedia of Water Science*, Taylor & Francis, New York, pp1307–10

Qadir, M. and Oster, J. D. (2004) 'Crop and irrigation management strategies for saline-sodic soils and waters aimed at environmentally sustainable agriculture', *Science of the Total Environment*, vol 323, pp1–19

Qadir, M., Schubert, S., Ghafoor, A. and Murtaza, G. (2001) 'Amelioration strategies for sodic soils: A review', *Land Degradation and Development*, vol 12, pp357–86

Qadir, M., Sharma, B. R., Bruggeman, A., Choukr-Allah, R. and Karajeh, F. (2007a) 'Non-conventional water resources and opportunities for water augmentation to achieve food security in water scarce countries', *Agricultural Water Management*, vol 87, pp2–22

Qadir, M., Tubeileh, A., Akhtar, J., Labri, A., Minhas, P. S. and Khan, M. A. (2008) 'Productivity enhancement of salt-affected environments through crop diversification', *Land Degradation and Development*, vol 19, pp429–53

Qadir, M., Wichelns, D., Raschid-Sally, L., Minhas, P. S., Drechsel, P., Bahri, A. and McCornick, P. (2007b) 'Agricultural use of marginal-quality water – Opportunities and challenges', in D. Molden (ed) *Water for Food, Water for Life: A Comprehensive Assessment of Water Management in Agriculture*, Earthscan, London, pp425–57

Quirk, J. P. (2001) 'The significance of the threshold and turbidity concentrations in relation to sodicity and microstructure', *Australian Journal of Soil Research*, vol 39, pp1185–217

Rhoades, J. D. (1989) 'Intercepting, isolating and reusing drainage waters for irrigation to conserve water and protect water quality', *Agricultural Water Management*, vol 16, pp37–52

Robinson, B. H., Brooks, R. R. and Clothier, B. E. (1999) 'Soil amendments affecting nickel and cobalt uptake by *Berkheya coddii*: Potential use for phytomining and phytoremediation', *Annals of Botany*, vol 84, pp689–94

Römkens, P., Bouwman, L., Japenga, J. and Draaisma, C. (2001) 'Potentials and drawbacks of chelate-enhanced phytoremediation of soils', *Environmental Pollution*, vol 116, pp109–21

Salt, D. E., Blaylock, M., Kumar, P. B. A. N., Dushenkov, S., Ensley, B. D., Chet, I. and Raskin, I. (1996) 'Phytoremediation: A novel strategy for the removal of toxic metals from the environment using plants', *Biotechnology*, vol 13, pp468–74

Schwartz, C., Echevarria, G. and Morel, J. L. (2003) 'Phytoextraction of cadmium with *Thlaspi caerulescens*', *Plant and Soil*, vol 249, pp27–35

Sharma, D. P. and Rao, K. V. G. K. (1998) 'Strategy for long term use of saline drainage water for irrigation in semi-arid regions', *Soil Tillage Research*, vol 48, pp287–95

Shennan, C., Grattan, S. R., May, D. M., Hillhouse, C. J., Schactman, D. P., Wander, M., Roberts, B., Burau, R. G., McNeish, C. and Zelinski, L. (1995) 'Feasibility of cyclic reuse of saline drainage in a tomato–cotton rotation', *Journal of Environmental Quality*, vol 24, pp476–86

Simmons, R. W., Noble, A. D., Pongsakul, P., Sukreeyapongse, O. and Chinabut, N. (2009) 'Cadmium-hazard mapping using a general linear regression model (Irr-Cad) for rapid risk assessment', *Environmental Geochemistry and Health*, vol 31, pp71–9

Simmons R.W., Pongsakul, P., Saiyasitpanich, D. and Klinphoklap, S. (2005) 'Elevated levels of cadmium and zinc in paddy soils and elevated levels of cadmium in rice grain downstream of a zinc mineralized area in Thailand: Implications for public health', *Environmental Geochemistry and Health*, vol 27, pp501–11

Singh, S. P., Ma, L. Q. and Harris, W. G. (2001) 'Heavy metal interactions with phosphatic clay', *Journal of Environmental Quality*, vol 30, pp1961–8

Stevens, D. and McLaughlin, M. J. (2006) 'Managing risks to soil and plant health from key metals and metalloids in irrigation waters', in D. Stevens (ed) *Growing Crops with Reclaimed Wastewater*, CSIRO Publishing, Collingwood, Australia, pp139–46

Strom, P. F. (2006) 'Introduction to phosphorus removal. Invited presentation for Wastewater Treatment Operator's Workshop', 91st Annual Meeting, NJWEA, Atlantic City, NJ

Su, N., Bethune, M., Mann, L. and Heuperman, A. (2005) 'Simulating water and salt movement in tile-drained fields irrigated with saline water under a Serial Biological Concentration management scenario', *Agricultural Water Management*, vol 78, pp165–80

Swaddiwudhipong, W., Limpatanachote, P., Mahasakpan, P., Krintratun, S. and Padungtod, C. (2007) 'Cadmium-exposed population in Mae Sot District, Tak Province: 1. Prevalence of high urinary cadmium levels in the adults', *Journal of the Medical Association of Thailand*, vol 90, pp143–8

Tanji, K. and Kielen, N. C. (2002) *Agricultural Drainage Water Management in Arid and Semi-arid Areas*, Irrigation and Drainage Paper 61, FAO, Rome

Teeyakasem, W., Nishijo, M., Honda, R., Satarug, S., Swaddiwudhipong, W. and Ruangyuttikarn, W. (2007) 'Monitoring of cadmium toxicity in a Thai population with high-level environmental exposure', *Toxicology Letters*, vol 169, pp185–95

Toze, S. (2006a) 'Reuse of effluent water – Benefits and risks', *Agricultural Water Management*, vol 80, pp147–59

Toze, S. (2006b) 'Water reuse and health risks – Real vs. perceived', *Desalination*, vol 187, pp41–51

Tu, C. and Ma, L. Q. (2002) 'Effects of arsenic concentration and forms on arsenic uptake by the hyperaccumulator', *Journal of Environmental Quality*, vol 31, pp641–7

USDA (2000) *Conservation Buffers to Reduce Pesticide Losses*, United States Department of Agriculture, Natural Resources Conservation Service, Washington, DC

USEPA (1997) *Technology Alternatives for the Remediation of Soils Contaminated with As, Cd, Cr, Hg and Pb*, EPA/540/S-97/500, Office of Emergency and Remedial Response, Washington, DC

Vanthuyne, M. and Maes, A. (2002) 'The removal of heavy metals from contaminated soil by a combination of sulfidisation and floatation', *Science of the Total Environment*, vol 290, nos 1–3, pp69–80

Virkutyte, J., Sillanpaa, M. and Latostenmaa, P. (2002) 'Elektrokinetic soil remediation – Critical review', *Science of the Total Environment*, vol 289, pp97–121

Warren, G. P. and Alloway, B. J. (2003) 'Reduction of arsenic uptake by lettuce with ferrous sulphate applied to contaminated soil', *Journal of Environmental Quality*, vol 32, pp767–72

Warren, G. P., Alloway, B. J., Lepp, N. W., Singh, B., Bochereau, F. J. M. and Penny, C. (2003) 'Field trials to assess the uptake of arsenic by vegetables from contaminated soils and soil remediation with iron oxides', *Science of the Total Environment*, vol 311, nos 1–3, pp19–33

WHO (2006a) *Guidelines for Drinking-Water Quality, Incorporating First Addendum: Volume 1, Recommendations*, 3rd ed., WHO, Geneva, www.who.int/water_sanitation_health/dwq/gdwq0506.pdf

WHO (2006b) *Guidelines for the Safe Use of Wastewater, Excreta and Greywater, Volume 2: Wastewater Use in Agriculture*, World Health Organization, Geneva

Williams, P. N., Islam, M. R. , Adomako, E. E., Raab, A., Hossain, S. A., Zhu, Y. G., Feldmann, J. and Meharg, A. A. (2006) 'Increase in rice grain arsenic for regions of Bangladesh irrigating paddies with elevated arsenic in groundwaters', *Environmental Science and Technology*, vol 40, no 16, pp4903–8

Wong, J. W. C., Wong, W. W. Y., Wei, Z. and Jadadeesan, H. (2004) 'Alkaline biosolids and EDTA for phytoremediation of an acidic loamy soil spiked with cadmium', *Science of the Total Environment*, vol 324, nos 1–3, pp235–46

Wongkongkatep, J., Fukushi, K., Parkpian, P., DeLaune, R. D. and Jugsujinda, A. (2003) 'Arsenic uptake by native fern species in Thailand: Effect of chelating agents on hyperaccumulation of arsenic by *Pityrogramma calomelanos*', *Journal of Environmental Science and Health*, vol 38, no 12, pp2773–84

Wu, L. H., Luo, Y. M., Xing, X. R. and Christie, P. (2004) 'EDTA-enhanced phytoremediation of heavy metal-contaminated soil with Indian mustard and associated potential leaching risk', *Agriculture, Ecosystems and Environment*, vol 102, pp307–18

Xue, S. G., Chen, Y. X., Reeves, R. D., Baker, A. J. M., Lin, Q. and Fernando, D. R. (2004) 'Manganese uptake and accumulation by the hyperaccumulator plant *Phytolacca acinosa* Roxb (Phytolaccaceae)', *Environmental Pollution*, vol 131, pp393–9

Zaurov, D. E., Perdomo, P. and Raskin, I., (1999) 'Optimizing soil fertility and pH to maximize cadmium removal by Indian mustard from contaminated soils', *Journal of Plant Nutrition*, vol 22, pp977–86

Zhang, W., Cai, Y., Tu, C. and Ma, L. Q. (2002) 'Arsenic speciation and distribution in an arsenic hyperaccumulating plant', *Science of the Total Environment*, vol 300, nos 1–3, pp167–77

Zhu, B. and Alva, A. K. (1993) 'Trace metal and cation transport in a sandy soil with various amendments', *Soil Science Society of America Journal*, vol 57, no 3, pp723–7

Zhu, Y. G., Chen, S. B. and Yang, J. C. (2004) 'Effects of soil amendments on lead uptake by two vegetable crops from a lead-contaminated soil from Anhui, China', *Environment International*, vol 30, no 3, pp351–6

12

Applying the Multiple-Barrier Approach for Microbial Risk Reduction in the Post-Harvest Sector of Wastewater-Irrigated Vegetables

Sanja Ilic, Pay Drechsel, Philip Amoah and Jeffrey T. LeJeune

ABSTRACT

Post-harvest interventions are an important component of a multiple-barrier approach for health-risk reduction of wastewater-irrigated crops as recommended by the 2006 edition of the WHO Guidelines for safe wastewater irrigation. This approach draws on principles of other risk-management approaches, in particular the hazard analysis and critical control point (HACCP) concept. Post-harvest measures are of particular importance as they can address possible on-farm pre-contamination, and also contamination that may occur after the crops leave the farm. Key factors influencing microbial contamination along the farm to fork pathway are basic hygiene and temperature management. Both factors are, however, hardly under control in most developing countries where microbial contamination and proliferation are supported by low education, limited risk awareness, rudimentary technical infrastructure and unenforced regulations. In the face of these challenges, the most successful strategies to enhance food safety will involve interventions at multiple control points along the production chain, with emphasis on local safety targets and innovative educational programmes fitting local knowledge, culture and risk perceptions. The WHO (2006) recommended health-based targets for risk reduction in wastewater irrigation provide the required flexibility for risk mitigation in line with the concept of food-safety objectives (FSO).

INTRODUCTION

Microbial infections of foodborne origin are a major public-health problem internationally and a significant cause of death in developing countries (WHO, 1996, 2006). Underlying problems of food safety differ considerably between developing countries and the more developed part of the world (Nicolas et al., 2007). Food safety in developing countries is influenced by a number of factors. In the context of wastewater irrigation, the main concern is the increasing environmental pollution in urban areas, which does not support the changing behaviour of urban consumers towards more international diets, in particular fruits and salads that are eaten raw. There is a high risk of contamination (not only affecting fruits and vegetables) at all stages of production, processing and distribution which is very difficult to control through regulations given the common constraints in supporting infrastructure (cool chain) and institutional capacities.

Approaches to address this challenge have been discussed over many years in different divisions of the WHO and FAO dealing with food quality and health. The WHO Guidelines (2006) for safe wastewater irrigation present only one of several concepts. However, although different terminologies are used, there is considerable agreement on the best way forward.

The best known initiative is the *Codex Alimentarius* which calls upon countries to work towards international food safety and quality standards. Related recommendations, also for vegetables eaten raw, are outlined in international codes of best practices (CAC, 2003a, 2003b). Acknowledging the complexity of the current food-safety situation within and across many countries, the WHO and FAO advocate targeted interventions using microbiological risk analysis as the basis for building food-safety control programmes. Partly through the activities of *Codex Alimentarius* and expert consultations, both organizations have developed a series of guidelines and reports that detail the various steps in risk analysis and management (FAO/WHO, 2008; Gorris, 2005).

Quantitative microbial risk assessment can help in identifying critical control points (Seidu et al., 2008). However, in many countries the results are predictable given the general substandard situation. The critical control point concept is similar to the multiple-barrier approach recommended by different national and international agencies for drinking-water safety and also by WHO (2006) in view of wastewater-related food-safety issues. The approach recognizes that while each individual barrier may be not be able to completely remove or prevent contamination, and therefore protect public health, implemented together, the barriers work to provide greater assurance that the water or food will be safe at the point of consumption.

Where a quantitative risk assessment is not available, it is still possible to set local food-safety objectives (FSO) (Box 12.1) which relate operational food-safety management to public-health goals (FAO/WHO, 2002). Health-based FSO relate to the time/point of consumption, which gives flexibility to the individual contribution of different control points to the overall risk reduction target. This flexibility also acknowledges that food chains can be very different, but nevertheless should comply with a common health-based target (Gorris, 2005). In the context of health-based targets, the ultimate goal is to have a measurable impact on specific health outcomes, such as diarrhoeal diseases. Whereas metrics and threshold targets for 'upstream' parameters (irrigation water quality, for example) may vary from

BOX 12.1 TERMS AND DEFINITIONS FOR THE KEY CONCEPTS IN RISK-BASED FOOD CONTROL

APPROPRIATE LEVEL OF PROTECTION (ALOP)

Level of protection deemed appropriate by the country establishing a sanitary or phytosanitary measure to protect human, animal or plant life or health within its territory (WTO, 1995).

Food-Safety Objective (FSO)

The maximum frequency and/or concentration of a hazard in a food at the time of consumption that provides or contributes to the appropriate level of protection (ALOP) (CAC, 2004).

Health-based targets

Health-based targets are set by national authorities as a defined level of health protection for a given exposure. This can be based on a measure of disease or the absence of a specific disease related to that exposure (WHO 2004, 2006).

Control measures (CM)

Any action and activity that can be used to prevent or eliminate a food-safety hazard or to reduce it to an acceptable level (it can be microbiological specifications, guidelines on pathogen control, hygiene codes, microbiological criteria, specific information, e.g. labelling, training, education, and others (ICMSF, 2002).

Multiple-barrier approach

Protection against contaminants occurs at each step along the water to food pathway, beginning at the wastewater source, continuing at the treatment facility and extending through the farm and market chain to the kitchen where the food is prepared and eventually served (WHO, 2006; modified).

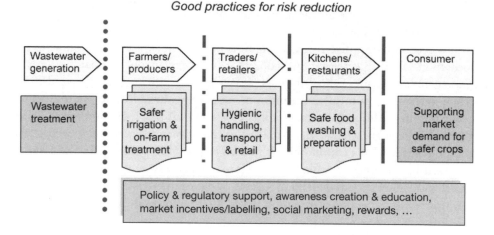

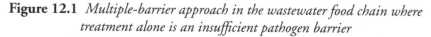

Figure 12.1 *Multiple-barrier approach in the wastewater food chain where treatment alone is an insufficient pathogen barrier*

Source: Based on the HACCP concept, IWMI (unpublished)

system to system, and are often unattainable, the FSO approach is viewed as a success as long as the end result of improved health is achieved through one or more control points (barriers) before the food gets served.

The 2006 edition of the WHO Guidelines for safe wastewater irrigation (WHO, 2006) mirrors this philosophy and recommends a 'multiple-barrier' approach for health-risk reduction, especially where conventional wastewater treatment is not effective (Figure 12.1). Health-based targets are expressed in averted DALYs (see Chapter 2). The Guidelines draw on the hazard analysis and critical control point (HACCP) system and its prerequisites: good agricultural practices (GAP), good manufacturing practices (GMP) and good hygiene practices (GHP) which are recognized by the *Codex Alimentarius* Commission as a cost-effective way to enhance food safety at all stages of the food supply chain (WHO, 1996).

Although microbiologically polluted irrigation water is a major contributor to on-farm contamination of vegetable crops, it is only one of many risk factors in the farm to fork continuum. There are other pathogen sources and non-pathogenic threats. Looking only at pathogens, they can contaminate the edible tissues of plants at any stage from production to consumption via soilborne, seedborne, airborne or waterborne routes. Considering the differences in existing food-production chains, with an enormous variety in structures, logistics and stakeholders, and that they will undoubtedly change rapidly, scale-up and diversify continuously, food-safety management at any scale (regional, national, local, factory) is a challenge (Gorris, 2005). This shows the crucial need for multiple precautions at various pathogen barriers or critical control points. In Chapter 10, the authors introduced farm-based measures, while this chapter focuses on barriers in the post-harvest sector. These address two important objectives: minimizing any existing contamination during primary production (i.e. on farm); and avoiding any additional contamination that may occur through cross-contamination and suboptimal hygiene practices during harvesting, transport, processing, marketing/handling and food preparation.

BIOPHYSICAL FACTORS AFFECTING RISK REDUCTION

Contaminants originating from wastewater may attach to the plant surface, may be taken up by roots or may be internalized into the plant tissue elsewhere. From a food-safety standpoint, the latter route is debatably less significant given the low concentrations of pathogens which can enter the tissue of healthy plants compared to what can be deposited on the surface. Although it has been shown that some human pathogens, such as *Salmonella* spp., can survive and grow within certain vegetables, their replication is generally limited under these conditions (Jablasone et al., 2004; Serani et al., 2008; Shi et al., 2007; Solomon et al., 2002; Tsai and Ingham, 1997; Zhuang et al. 1995). It is more likely for pathogens to enter plants that are wounded or damaged (Aruscavage et al., 2008; Fatemi et al., 2006).[1] The greater risk factor, in terms of quantitative pathogen exposure, is the contamination of the crop surface, especially where the surface is large, like on leafy vegetables.

Understanding the ecology of bacterial pathogens on plant surfaces can lead to the development of intervention strategies to prevent, reduce or remove contamination. Virtually any fruit or vegetable can serve as a vehicle for any pathogen, providing that the pathogen survives in high enough numbers on the product until such time as it is consumed. Common factors influencing pathogen survival include initial dose of contamination, time and environmental conditions (Table 12.1). Table 12.2 shows the die-off rate of different pathogen groups on the crop surface.

Environmental conditions play a key role in the survival of micro-organisms on plant surfaces which are subject to extreme fluctuations in temperature and moisture (Bunster et al., 1989) and related bacterial numbers and diversity (Ailes et al., 2008; Ilic et al., 2008). This offers opportunities for interventions. Natural die-off of bacteria has been described as an important method to minimize safety risks by increasing the interval between the last irrigation (and contamination) and harvest to several days (Aruscavage et al., 2006; Keraita et al., 2007). Unfortunately, the same does not apply to the interval between harvest and consumption: once harvested, (leafy) vegetables begin to decay rapidly and cannot be kept on the shelf to facilitate natural die-off.

It can get even worse. As crops are transported from the farm to the table, contamination, recontamination and cross-contamination issues are gaining in importance. Consequently, instead of naturally decreasing contamination levels

Table 12.1 *Factors affecting pathogen survival in the environment*

Factor	Comment
Humidity/precipitation	Humid environments favour pathogen survival.
	Dry environments facilitate pathogen die-off.
	Rainfall can result in splashing of contaminated soil on crops.
Temperature	Most important factor in pathogen die-off.
	The impact of temperature varies for different pathogens. High temperatures lead to rapid die-off, normal temperatures lead to prolonged survival.
	Freezing temperatures can also cause pathogen die-off.
Acidity/alkalinity (pH)	Some viruses survive longer in more acid, i. e. lower pH soils, while alkaline soils are associated with more rapid die-off of viruses.
	Neutral to slightly alkaline soils favour bacterial survival.
Sunlight (UV radiation)	Direct sunlight leads to rapid pathogen inactivation through desiccation and exposure to UV radiation.
Foliage/plant type	Certain vegetables have sticky surfaces (e.g. zucchini) or can absorb pathogens from the environment (e.g. lettuce, sprouts) leading to prolonged pathogen survival.
	Root crops are more prone to contamination and facilitate pathogen survival.
Competition with native flora and fauna	Antagonistic effects from bacteria or algae may enhance die-off.
	Bacteria may be preyed upon by protozoa.

Source: Strauss (1985); modified

Table 12.2 *Survival times of selected excreted pathogens in soil and on crop surfaces at 20–30°C*

Pathogens	Survival time	
	In Soil	On crops
Viruses:		
Enteroviruses[a]	<100 but usually <20 days	<60 but usually <15 days
Bacteria:		
Faecal coliform	<70 but usually <20 days	<30 but usually <15 days
Salmonella spp.	<70 but usually <20 days	<30 but usually <15 days
Vibrio cholera	<20 but usually <10 days	<5 but usually <2 days
Protozoa:		
Entamoeba histolytica cysts	<20 but usually <10 days	<10 but usually < 2 days
Helminths:		
Ascaris lumbricoides eggs	Many months	<60 but usually <30 days
Hookworm larvae	<90 but usually <30 days	<30 but usually <10 days
Taenia saginata eggs	Many months	<60 but usually <30 days
Trichuris trichiura eggs	Many months	<60 but usually <30 days

[a]Includes polio-, echo- and coxsackie-viruses.
Source: Feachem et al. (1983)

after harvest, several studies have shown an increase in microbial load as vegetables move from the farm to the consumer (Ailes et al., 2008; Ensink et al., 2007; Ilic et al., 2008). Only when the temperature can be controlled and kept low can longer intervals allow for bacterial die-off; but where temperature cannot be controlled, extended time between harvest and consumption may support an increase in bacterial population numbers rather than a decrease (Box 12.2).

Box 12.2 Methodological challenges

There are many challenges in the detection and removal of pathogenic threats which demand some notes of caution when it comes to recommendations for risk reduction. A few are mentioned here:

- Test conditions: studies that have examined the survival of foodborne pathogens on plants have been mostly conducted under experimental conditions (Aruscavage et al., 2008; Jablasone et al., 2005; Stine et al., 2005). Serious limitations to the extrapolation of these experiments to real-life situations include the large initial inoculums often used and the unnatural (i.e. greenhouse/laboratory) conditions in which the plants are grown.
- Indicator quality: a general challenge is the use of indicator micro-organisms. The detection of specific pathogens such as *Shigella* spp., *E. coli* O157:H7 or *Salmonella* spp. (see Box 12.1) is both expensive and time-consuming. Therefore, many researchers, especially in developing countries, measure thermotolerant coliform contamination frequency and magnitude as a surrogate of pathogen survival and vegetable safety (Ailes et al., 2008). However, the use of coliforms as indicators of pathogen contamination is debatable as many coliforms are naturally present in the environment and on plant surfaces and therefore their presence might not indicate recent pathogen contamination. Moreover, this group of organisms may not exhibit the same survival or attachment behaviour as the pathogens. This is particularly important when considering or assessing their removal (Ilic et al., 2008).
- Tracing contamination: studies trying to trace the source of contamination often tend to compare independent sample sets taken, for example, at the farm gate and in markets (e.g. Armar-Klemesu et al., 1998). However, where markets receive their produce from different farms, it will require significant efforts and sample numbers to confirm the origin of any analysed difference in coliform counts. Amoah et al. (2007a) tried to bypass this problem by following vegetables from various farms – using wastewater or tap water for irrigation – to the final retail points. In this way, it was possible to identify the crucial points at which most contamination occurred in the farm to fork chain of activities.

OPTIONS FOR RISK REDUCTION ALONG
THE CONTAMINATION PATHWAY

Harvest

Different paths of contamination are possible during the harvest of leafy green vegetables (Franz and van Bruggen, 2008; Hope et al., 2008; McEvoy et al., 2009). While in more developed countries most concerns are addressed through standardized protocols and mechanized field operations, in developing countries basic hygiene is often violated due to the high dependency on manual labour combined with the lack of clean water or other resources and/or education.

Harvest is a key step along the contamination pathway as it involves the injury of plant tissues. As discussed above, cut surfaces are ideal sites for pathogen attachment and may also serve as an entryway of pathogens into the deeper tissues of the plant where they cannot be disinfected or washed away (Aruscavage et al., 2008). The cleaning and sanitization of equipment used during harvest is an important requirement (McEvoy et al., 2009), but of limited applicability in smallholder farms in developing countries where water for cleaning might not be available and tools are permanently in contact with hands, crops and soil. However, as mentioned above, plant injury and internalization of pathogens at harvest are only noteworthy where surface contamination is not a larger risk factor.

During harvesting and immediately after, fresh vegetables are also exposed to potential cross-contamination from the soil surface, other agricultural inputs (e.g. fresh manure) and handlers. It is important to implement basic sanitary practices to prevent contamination at this level. Using baskets or plastic sheets to avoid contact between utensils and produce and the ground or other potentially unsafe sources of contaminants can greatly contribute to the reduction of the risks of contamination during harvest.

In both northern and southern vegetable production systems, emphasis is often placed on performing parts of the processing while the crop is still on the farm. For example, in-field coring and packaging of lettuce heads in the USA has become a common industry practice (McEvoy et al., 2009). Likewise, in West Africa, it is common practice for vegetable sellers to buy their crops on the farm. This allows them to choose the best-looking ones. Still on the farm, they remove soil particles from freshly harvested vegetables (e.g. carrots, salad greens and cucumbers) by washing them in the streams or ponds usually used for irrigation, as reported, for example, in Niger, Benin, Burkina Faso and Senegal (Klutse et al., 2005). These water sources are often highly contaminated, which undermines growers' efforts to avoid contamination and poses a significant risk to the consumer as well as all stakeholders involved in subsequent crop handling (Hope et al., 2008). Raising awareness about microbial hazards among traders is required, as is the provision of acceptable alternative water sources in which to wash vegetables.

Transport and storage

The main risk factor for increased microbial loads on fresh vegetables during transportation and storage is elevated temperatures over extended periods of time. In many developing countries, there is, however, still a general lack of cool transport and storage. This explains why some crops, especially the most perishable such as lettuce, are often grown in the city close to the point of sale. This urban vicinity, on the other hand usually results in irrigation with contaminated surface water (Drechsel et al., 2008).

The lack of cool storage requires fast transport from farm to retail and exact prediction of quantities to be sold to avoid leftovers. In some countries, intermediate traders are gaining ground to supply to large outlets such as supermarkets. A common bottleneck in this situation is the heat exposure of vegetables already packed in closed plastic bags during transport and intermediate storage, i.e. before the supermarket is reached.

The rate and extent of microbial growth in fresh produce depend mainly on the initial microbial load and time/temperature exposures. In general, lower storage temperatures ensure a longer post-harvest life for fresh fruits and vegetables (Nunes, 2008). Storing produce in the shade is one of the few methods available to keep produce cooler where refrigeration in not feasible.

Another risk factor typical for developing countries is the lack of dedicated transport vehicles. Usually, market traders or farmers hire taxis or mini-vans which are used at other times for the transport of commuters, small livestock or other goods, which increases the general risk of cross-contamination.

In northeastern India, farmers often transport their produce from the field to the market by bullock/buffalo cart, as it is the cheapest available transport. While on-farm packaging practices are almost non-existent, some farmers use straw for crops such as tomatoes as a cushioning material to reduce mechanical damage. Traders further pack the tomatoes in smaller paper cartons with no ventilation and send them to distant markets, with a large proportion of the products damaged and decayed by the time they reach the consumer, which increases food-safety risks (Directorate of Research (Agri) Assam Agricultural University, 2005).

Processing and marketing

Handling, processing and packaging of leafy green vegetables is carried out differently in diverse environments throughout the world. International standards as supported by the *Codex Alimentarius* remain in many developing countries only a long-term target as local conditions, education, regulations and infrastructure (cooling, transport means, etc.) including monitoring cannot yet match what is possible in more developed countries.

The first processing step of fresh vegetables in local African and Asian market chains is often the removal of soil particles and dust to improve their general appearance and market value. In Ghana, for example, the simple removal of ('bad-looking') outer vegetable leaves in markets reduced the coliform counts by 0.5 log unit (lettuce) to 1 unit (cabbage) (M. Akple, pers. communication). Cutting the cabbage into smaller units, on the other hand, increased the surface area and coliform counts, which shows that every manipulation of fresh vegetables down the processing chain may be a source of contamination if prevention measures, such as cleanliness of processing equipment and the surroundings, including hygiene, health and adequate training of the involved staff, are lacking.

As in all stages of production and processing, workers may be the key sources of produce-contamination with pathogens, primarily viruses (norovirus, hepatitis A) and bacteria (*Shigella, Salmonella*, etc.). The two main and most basic steps for risk reduction would be to provide sufficient handwashing facilities and to avoid having ill individuals harvest or handle produce. However, both recommendations face significant challenges in developing countries. On the one hand, labour associations covering the health protection of formal and informal restaurant, vendor and catering staff are usually non-existent. On the other hand, the urbanization rate has outpaced development of sanitary infrastructure. For example, a market survey in Ghana's capital, Accra, found that only 31 per cent of the urban markets have a drainage system, 26 per cent have toilet facilities and 34 per cent are connected to pipe-borne water (Nyanteng, 1998). These data are very similar to those reported from a global survey on street-vended food (WHO, 1996).

Final point of sale

Where the lack of local infrastructure constrains the provision of acceptable hygienic conditions, as described in the previous section, relocation of markets or food stalls is often discussed, especially those that are informal. However, the WHO (1996) noted correctly that street-food vendors are, in many countries, part of the social and cultural fabric of their communities and, therefore, an effort should be made to keep them as close to their current business sites as possible, even though some sanitary facilities may not be available. The reasons are at least twofold:

1   The provision of new sites away from traditional locations often results in business disadvantages, thus there is low adoption and/or an informal reappearance of the stands near the former location.
2   Although better sanitary conditions might reduce the number of risk factors, they may not automatically impact on raw material contamination, cross-contamination, personnel hygiene behaviour, poor food preparation practices or hot and cold holding capacity.

Consequently, relocation should not be seen as a panacea for resolving the problems of low food safety. Indeed, risk mitigation has to start on farm (see Chapter 10) and continue during harvest.

The last point of sale can be a street-market, a supermarket or a restaurant offering, for example, a fresh salad. Although the standards of these entities vary greatly in developing countries, general food-safety considerations are similar and again are much dependent on the ability to keep the produce under low temperatures and well protected from contamination. Especially in hot climates, it is often impossible to conserve unsold leafy vegetables for the next day because of product quality deterioration. Even during the day, water is often used for refreshing or rehydrating (crisping) fruits and vegetables on display. Changing this water once during the day can already decrease the average faecal coliform counts on lettuce by up to 1 log unit, as a comparative analysis has indicated (Drechsel et al., 2000). However, in many developing countries where it is not easy to change water, vegetables are refreshed and washed over the day with the same water, which can lead to severe cross-contamination (Amoah et al., 2007a).

In theory, the use of chlorine tablets could help, but if solutions used for decontamination are not regularly changed, such processing water may itself become a source of contamination. Therefore, clear instructions on dosages and frequencies of water replenishment and disinfectants should be provided and followed. More important is the need to address the motivation for washing or refreshing vegetables in retail. The most obvious motivation is to display 'fresh' produce, which reflects customers' preferences and criteria for purchase; this does not automatically translate into 'safe' products but could be a starting point for awareness campaigns. Such campaigns should be based on local perception studies. In Kumasi, Ghana, public-health students worked as interns over several weeks in eating places of various types (street kiosks, canteens, restaurants), observing behaviour and trying to understand limitation and opportunities to increase food safety (Rheinländer et al., 2008). According to their findings, consumers avoided food-safety risk by assessing the neatness and trustworthiness of vendors. Vendors were also found to emphasize these attributes while ignoring basic food-safety practices.

Consumption at home and in restaurants

Diets vary and the consumption of raw salads is not common in every country or region. However, fresh leafy greens are increasingly eaten in urban centres, e.g. in sub-Saharan Africa, as a modern complement to rice-based fast food. In Ghana, for example, more than 90 per cent of the lettuce produced enters the street-food sector; in Accra alone, at least 200,000 residents of various socio-economic classes consume lettuce or cabbage every day. Most of this produce is grown in urban and peri-urban agricultural plots irrigated with polluted water (Amoah et al., 2005, 2007a; Obuobie et al., 2006).

While markets, transport and retail can be influenced (and, in some countries, also regulated) by governmental guidelines and control measures, consumer behaviour can hardly be controlled through formal regulations (Fischer et al., 2007). On the other hand, if risk awareness is provided, consumers should have a high incentive to practise safe food-handling behaviours because of the direct and immediate impacts on their own health. The challenge is to understand if this awareness is actually influencing behaviour and on what kind of information it is based. Surveys of 210 restaurants and 950 households in seven countries across West Africa showed, for example, that vegetable-washing is common in 56–90 per cent of the urban households and 80–100 per cent of the restaurants (Amoah et al., 2007b; Klutse et al., 2005).

The reasons for washing varied between cities and countries, broadly depending on educational and economic standards, the availability of certain disinfectants and local traditions. In some households, vegetables were washed primarily to remove dirt, sand, dust and, more seldom, chemical farming residues. In other households and restaurants it was performed explicitly to reduce the risk of pathogens and diarrhoeal diseases (Amoah et al., 2007b; Klutse et al., 2005). The most common disinfectants used in the restaurants throughout Francophone West Africa were bleach (Eau de Javel®) (55 per cent of cases) and potassium (K) permanganate (31 per cent), followed by salt, lemon or soap. In Anglophone Ghana, the use of bleach was unknown and the general awareness level related to pathogen contamination appeared to be much lower (Amoah et al., 2007b). Amongst the lower classes in the selected Francophone cities, there was a clear tendency for only water or water with salt, soap or lemon juice to be used, while in middle and upper class households and restaurants the use of bleach or permanganate appeared to be prevalent (Figure 12.2).

In Ghana, various salt and vinegar solutions are dominantly used besides cleaning in water only. Salt is preferred to vinegar for cost reasons, but both appeared highly ineffective in the low concentrations or contact times commonly used (Amoah et al., 2007b). Also Rosas et al. (1984) stressed that common washing practices very often do not reduce the coliform counts to safe levels. There can be large differences depending on contact time and sanitizer (Table 12.3). The observed differences in the knowledge of appropriate sanitizers between Francophone and Anglophone countries in West Africa call for an engagement of the private sector in food-safety campaigns.

Washing can also remove helminth eggs especially with good agitation and rubbing of the leaves. When washing in a bowl was compared to washing under running water (independent of sanitizing solution used) the latter was more effective in egg reduction. Washing in a bowl reduced the helminth egg population by half and sometimes more, while running water reduced the contamination level from the usual eight to nine eggs to one egg per 100g lettuce wet weight (Amoah et al., 2007b).

When it comes to internalized pathogens or pesticides on vegetable surfaces even thorough washing has its limitations (Box 12.3).

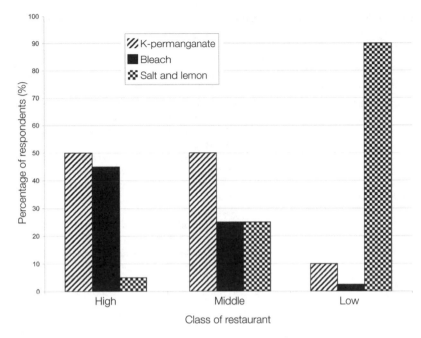

Figure 12.2 *Types of disinfectants used according to the category of restaurants in Cotonou, Benin*

Source: Amoah et al. (2007b)

Box 12.3 Limitations in view of internalized pathogens and pesticides

Surface treatments with sanitizers may substantially reduce surface contamination but are significantly less effective in reducing microbial populations that have been internalized in produce (Pao and Davis, 1999). Zhuang and Beuchat (1996) demonstrated that a 15 per cent solution of trisodium phosphate completely inactivated *Salmonella* on the surface of tomatoes while only resulting in a 2 log reduction of internal populations. Moreover, some pathogens, including bacteria and some viruses, adhere to fruits and vegetables in such a fashion that they cannot be easily removed or killed with conventional washing and disinfection procedures. The exact mechanisms are not yet fully understood.

In addition to microbial contamination, washing vegetables can effectively also reduce levels of pesticide contamination. Special care is, however, required for hydrophobic pesticides which cannot easily be removed with water, unless soap is used. For some fruits and vegetables, such as tomatoes, it is best to remove the skin when boiling cannot eliminate the threat. Cooking vegetables can be contra-effective when the melting point of the pesticide is over 100°C, like in the case of Lindane analysed on tomatoes in Ghana. In this case, the tomato skin cracks when boiled and the pesticide can enter the fruit body (Obuobie et al., 2006). Amoah et al. (2006) compared the general threat of microbial and pesticide contamination of green vegetables in Ghana's urban markets.

Table 12.3 *Effect of selected disinfection methods on faecal coliform levels on lettuce in West Africa*

Method	Log unit reductions[a]	Comments
Dipping in a bowl of water	1.0–1.4	• Increased contact time from a few seconds to 2 minutes improves the efficacy from 1–1.4 logs. • Not very efficient compared to washing with other sanitizers. • Not very effective for helminth eggs if washing has to be done in the same bowl of water. • Warming the water did not result in different counts.
Running tap water	0.3–2.2	• Effective compared with washing in a bowl, also for helminth egg removal. • Increased efficacy only with increased contact time from a few seconds to 2 minutes. • Limited application potential due to absence of tap water in poor households.
Dipping in a bowl with a salt solution	0.5–2.1	• Salt solution is a better sanitizer compared to dipping in water if the contact time is long enough (1–2 mins). • Efficacy improves with increasing temperature and increasing concentration, but high concentrations have a deteriorating effect on the appearance of some crops like lettuce.
Dipping in a bowl with a vinegar solution	0.2–4.7	• Very effective at high concentration (>20ml/l) but this could have possible negative effects on taste and palatability of the washed vegetables. • To achieve best efficacy and keep the sensory quality of product the contact time should be increased to 5–10 mins. • Efficacy is improved even at low concentration if carried out with a temperature over 30°C.
Dipping in a bowl with potassium permanganate solution	0.6–3.0	• Most effective at higher concentrations (200ppm), a temperature of 30°C or higher and a contact time of 5–10 mins. • Higher concentration colours washed vegetables purple which requires more water for rinsing or may raise questions of a negative health impact.
Dipping in a bowl with a solution containing a washing detergent (OMO™)	1.6–2.6	• Significant reductions could be achieved with 5–10 mins' contact time. • Residual perfumes and soap taste might affect consumer's sensory perception. • As OMO contains surfactants which could affect health, thorough rinsing is required
Dipping in a bowl of water with added household bleach	2.2–3.0	• Tested dosages (commercial bleach) resulted in 165–248μS/cm salinity (= concentration indicator). • Effective with 5–10 mins' contact time, and widely used in Francophone West Africa. • May pose a health risk if dosage is not well explained.
Dipping in a bowl of water containing chlorine tablets	2.3–2.7	• Effective at 100ppm but tablets not commonly available in some West African countries. • Effect of higher concentrations on efficacy not tested.

Source: Amoah et al. (2007b); modified; [a] ranges are due to different concentrations or contact times of disinfectant (see next column)

Education of stakeholders in post-harvest risk reduction

Education in food safety is critical for implementation of risk reduction and mitigation measures during post-harvest production of fresh produce in both developed and developing countries. In general, stakeholders at every level need to be included in food-safety education, including policy-makers. In the developing world there is a special need to improve both processors' and consumers' understanding of food safety. Educational campaigns should target the following three groups:

- Processors: in regions where cost is the main barrier to implementing safe practices, education efforts should aim to inform the stakeholders about available low-cost alternatives that can be successfully implemented locally. Educational programmes should also include cost–benefit comparisons and take into account cultural preferences and patterns of behaviour. Aside from conventional training workshops, there are also other educational approaches which try, for example, to show the invisible risk moving along the pathogen pathway (Box 12.4).
- Policy-makers: at the national and international level, the *Codex Alimentarius*, supported by the FAO and WHO, probably has the best potential and network to foster awareness and influence decision-making. Care has to be taken to support countries with appropriate steps towards achieving the international standards.
- Consumers: the educational activities may target the general consumer audience on various levels of society, such as schoolchildren, women, households, etc. As the main considerations differ from country to country, it is crucial to understand the barriers in each region and possible opportunities in order to implement a successful food-safety educational campaign. As the West African example showed, sometimes certain easy-to-buy disinfectants might simply not be known.

However, the step from increased awareness to actual behaviour-change is not an easy one and might require certain triggers and incentives as described in Chapter 16.

CONCLUSIONS

Due to poverty-related poor sanitary conditions in most developing countries, it is difficult to maintain appropriate hygienic standards in support of food safety. The enforcement of unrealistic standards, on the other hand, would neither be effective nor address the core of the problem, which is often the lack of understanding of hazards and safe practices (Nicolas et al., 2007). Therefore, regulations based on

---

BOX 12.4 ROAD SHOWS

Supported by the Knowledge Sharing in Research (KSinR) project of the Consultative Group on International Agricultural Research (CGIAR), alternative methods of awareness creation and education on wastewater irrigation and food safety were tried in Ghana. Instead of conventional training events, farmers, food caterers, market women, retailers and representatives from authorities met in their city for an urban road trip along the contamination pathway.

The participants were taken in a bus to one of their typical urban vegetable production sites with wastewater irrigation. From there the group toured wholesale and retail markets until they reached typical street-food restaurants serving the same vegetables that they had followed from the farm. At each of the stops, farmers, vendors or kitchen staff demonstrated common and locally fitting improved practices for health-risk reduction. Participants were encouraged to ask questions and discussed possible incentives for behaviour-change at each stop along the value chain.

The road trip was supported by the visualization of the invisible threat of microbiological hazards through the use of agar plates inoculated either with wastewater (showing growing bacterial colonies) or piped water (no bacterial colonies). The main learning objectives were for:

- participants to be aware of the presence of invisible risks moving from farm to table;
- participants to understand the concept of a multiple-barrier approach with joint responsibility for effective health-risk reduction;
- authorities to appreciate and support efforts of main stakeholders to contribute to solutions.

Source: Amoah et al. (2009)

---

international standards have very limited local application potential, although they are useful long-term goals. In addition, the application of the common HACCP concept is challenged by the multitude of existing sanitary hazards likely to affect the condition of the food along the farm to fork pathway as well as the many individual entities concerned, who often lack the collective organization, education, risk awareness and resources to undertake HACCP studies. While, for example, priority-setting via QMRA (see Chapter 2) would be desirable, the common lack of resources limits its application. What is required under these circumstances is an integrated but flexible approach, keeping in mind what is realistically possible, and the awareness and motivation level of all the concerned parties.

Agreeing on local FSO and striving for continuous improvement in the levels over time are key elements of an adapted concept. This mirrors the WHO (2006) recommended health-based targets for risk reduction in wastewater irrigation, which are, like the FSO, related to the time of consumption, i.e. the end of a food chain.

Critical control points remain important to avoid and/or reduce contamination. The studies in West Africa by Amoah et al. (2007b) found, for example, that it is very common practice to wash vegetables before consumption as raw salad. Although the reasons did not always reveal any understanding of pathogens and possible disease transmission, the fact that people adopted a washing behaviour can be considered a significant milestone on which a local food-safety campaign could build. While such post-harvest operations might not fully remove foodborne pathogens from leafy vegetables and herbs, they remain key steps complementing other options for risk reduction (FAO/WHO, 2008).

Given the basic need for food-safety education, a key pillar of any intervention will be awareness creation and training.

NOTE

1   The situation is different for chemicals, especially heavy metals. Also some crops, like cucumbers or carrots, are able to absorb smaller organic chemicals, like chlorobenzenes and polycyclic aromatic hydrocarbons (Collins et al., 2006).

REFERENCES

Ailes, E., Leon, J., Jaykus, L., Johnston, L., Clayton, H., Blanding, S., Kleinbaum, D., Backer, L. and Moe, C. (2008) 'Microbial concentrations on fresh produce are affected by postharvest processing, importation, and season', *Journal of Food Protection*, vol 71, pp2389–97

Amoah, P., Drechsel, P., Abaidoo, R. C. and Henseler, M. (2007a) 'Irrigated urban vegetable production in Ghana: Microbiological contamination in farms and markets and associated consumer risk groups', *Journal of Water and Health*, vol 5, no 3, pp455–66

Amoah, P., Drechsel., P., Abaidoo, R. C. and Klutse, A. (2007b) 'Effectiveness of common and improved sanitary washing methods in West Africa for the reduction of *coli* bacteria and helminth eggs on vegetables', *Tropical Medicine and International Health*, vol 12, supplement 2, pp40–50

Amoah, P., Drechsel, P., Abaidoo, R. C. and Ntow, W. J. (2006) 'Pesticide and pathogen contamination of vegetables in Ghana's urban markets', *Archives of Environmental Contamination and Toxicology*, vol 50, no 1, pp1–6

Amoah, P., Schuetz, T., Kranjac-Berisavjevic, G., Manning-Thomas, N. and Drechsel, P. (2009) 'From world cafés to road shows: Using a mix of knowledge sharing approaches to improve wastewater use in urban agriculture', *Knowledge Management for Development Journal*, December 2009 (in press)

Armar-Klemesu, M., Akpedonu, P., Egbi, G. and Maxwell, D. (1998) 'Food contamination in urban agriculture: Vegetable production using wastewater', in M. Armar-Klemesu and D. Maxwell (eds) *Urban Agriculture in Greater Accra Metropolitan Area*, Final

Report to IDRC, Centre file: 003149, Noguchi Memorial Institute for Medical Research, University of Ghana, Accra

Aruscavage, D., Lee, K., Miller, S. and LeJeune, J. T. (2006) 'Interactions affecting the proliferation and control of human pathogens on edible plants', *Journal of Food Science*, vol 71, ppR89–R99

Aruscavage, D., Miller, S. A., Ivey, M. L., Lee, K. and LeJeune, J. T. (2008) 'Survival and dissemination of *Escherichia coli* O157:H7 on physically and biologically damaged lettuce plants', *Journal of Food Protection*, vol 71, pp2384–8

Bunster, L., Fokkema, N. J. and Schippers, B. (1989) 'Effect of surface-active *Pseudomonas* spp. on leaf wettability', *Applied Environmental Microbiology*, vol 55, no 6, pp1340–45

CAC (*Codex Alimentarius* Commission) (2003a) 'Code of hygienic practice for fresh fruits and vegetables', Doc. CAC/RCP 53–2003

CAC (*Codex Alimentarius* Commission) (2003b) 'Recommended international code of practice. General principles of food hygiene', Doc. CAC/RCP 1–1969, Rev. 4–2003

CAC (*Codex Alimentarius* Commission) (2004) 'Report of the Twentieth Session of the Codex Committee on General Principles, Paris, France, 3–7 May 2004', ALINORM 04/27/33A, Appendix II, pp37–8, ftp://ftp.fao.org/codex/alinorm04/al0433ae.pdf

Collins, C., Martin, I. and Fryer, M. (2006) 'Evaluation of models for predicting plant uptake of chemicals from soil', Science Report SC050021/SR, UK Environment Agency, Bristol, UK, www.environment-agency.gov.uk/static/documents/Research/sc050021_2029764.pdf

Directorate of Research (Agri) Assam Agricultural University (2005) *Post Harvest Practices and Loss Assessment of Some Commercial Horticultural Crops of Assam*, Directorate of Research (Agri) Assam Agricultural University, Jorhat, India

Drechsel, P., Abaidoo, R. C., Amoah, P. and Cofie, O. O. (2000) 'Increasing use of poultry manure in and around Kumasi, Ghana: Is farmers' race consumers' fate?', *Urban Agricultural Magazine*, vol 2, pp25–7

Drechsel, P., Keraita, B., Amoah, P., Abaidoo, R., Raschid-Sally, L. and Bahri, A. (2008) 'Reducing health risks from wastewater use in urban and peri-urban sub-Saharan Africa: Applying the 2006 WHO Guidelines', *Water Science and Technology*, vol 57, no 9, pp1461–6

Ensink, J. H. J., Mahmood, T. and Dalsagaard, A. (2007) 'Wastewater irrigated vegetables: Market handling verses irrigation water quality', *Tropical Medicine and International Health*, vol 12, pp2–7

FAO/WHO (Food and Agriculture Organization of the United Nations / World Health Organization) (2002) 'Principles and guidelines for incorporating microbiological risk assessment in the development of food safety standards, guidelines and related texts', Report of a Joint FAO/WHO Consultation, Kiel, Germany, 18–22 March 2002, ftp://ftp.fao.org/docrep/fao/006/y4302e/y4302e00.pdf

FAO/WHO (Food and Agriculture Organization of the United Nations / World Health Organization) (2008) 'Microbiological hazards in fresh leafy vegetables and herbs: Meeting Report', *Microbiological Risk Assessment Series*, no 14. FAO, Rome, p151

Fatemi, P., LaBorde, L. F., Patton, J., Sapers, G. M., Annous, B. and Knabel, S. J. (2006) 'Influence of punctures, cuts, and surface morphologies of golden delicious apples on penetration and growth of *Escherichia coli* O157:H7', *Journal of Food Protection*, vol 69, pp267–75

Feachem, D. G., Bradley, D. J., Garelick, H. and Mara, D. D. (1983) *Sanitation and Disease: Health Aspects of Excreta and Wastewater Management*, John Wiley & Sons, Bath

Fischer, A. R. H., De Jong, A. E. I., Van Asselt, E. D. et al. (2007) 'Food safety in the domestic environment: An interdisciplinary investigation of microbial hazards during food preparation', *Risk Analysis*, vol 27, no 4, pp1065–82

Franz, E. and van Bruggen, A. H. C. (2008) 'Ecology of *E. coli* O157:H7 and *Salmonella* enterica in the primary vegetable production chain', *Critical Reviews in Microbiology*, vol 34, nos 3–4, pp143–61

Gorris, L. G. M. (2005) 'Food Safety Objective: An integral part of food chain management', *Food Control*, vol 16, pp801–9, www.esb.ucp.pt/twt/seg_alim/artigosCientificos/ LeonGorris/Gorris_FSO_Food_Control_upd.PDF

Hope, L., Keraita, B. and Akple, M. S. K. (2008) 'Use of irrigation water to wash vegetables grown on urban farms in Kumasi, Ghana', *Urban Agriculture Magazine*, vol 20, pp29–30

ICMSF (International Commission on Microbiological Specifications for Foods) (2002) *Microorganisms in Foods. Book 7, Microbiological Testing in Food Safety Management*, Kluwer Academic/Plenum, New York, NY

Ilic, S., Odomeru, J. and LeJeune, J. T. (2008) 'Coliforms and prevalence of *Escherichia coli* and foodborne pathogens on minimally processed spinach in two packing plants', *Journal of Food Protection*, vol 71, pp2398–403

Jablasone, J., Brovko, L. Y. and Griffiths, M. W. (2004) 'A research note: The potential for transfer of *Salmonella* from irrigation water to tomatoes', *Journal of the Science of Food and Agriculture*, vol 84, no 3, pp287–9

Jablasone, J., Warriner, K. and Griffiths, M. (2005) 'Interactions of *Escherichia coli* O157:H7, *Salmonella typhimurium* and *Listeria monocytogenes* plants cultivated in a gnotobiotic system', *International Journal of Food Microbiology*, vol 99, pp7–18

Keraita, B., Konradsen, F., Drechsel, P. and Abaidoo, R. C. (2007) 'Reducing microbial contamination on lettuce by cessation of irrigation before harvesting', *Tropical Medicine and International Health*, vol 12, supplement 2, pp8–14

Klutse, A., Tandja, C. T. and Sow, J. A. (2005) 'Circuit and practices in washing gardening products from production to consumption: An investigation report in West Africa', CREPA-IWMI, unpublished project report for CPWF, no 38

McEvoy, J. L., Luo, Y., Conway, W. et al. (2009) 'Potential of *Escherichia coli* O157:H7 to grow on field-cored lettuce as impacted by postharvest storage time and temperature', *International Journal of Food Microbiology*, vol 128, no 3, pp506–9

Nicolas, B., Razack, B. A., Yollande, I., Aly, S., Tidiane, O. C. A., Philippe, N. A., Da Silva, C. and Sababénédjo, T. A. (2007) 'Street-vended foods improvement: Contamination mechanisms and application of Food Safety Objective Strategy: Critical review', *Pakistan Journal of Nutrition*, vol 6, no 1, pp1–10, www.pjbs.org/pjnonline/fin533. pdf

Nunes, M. C. N. (2008) 'Impact of environmental conditions on fruit and vegetable quality', *Stewart Postharvest Review*, vol 4, no 4, pp1–14

Nyanteng, V. K. (1998) 'Draft summary report on food markets and marketing in the Accra metropolis', in *Food Supply and Distribution to Accra and its Metropolis. Workshop – Proceedings, Accra, Ghana, 13th–16th April 1998*, AMA-FAO

Obuobie, E., Keraita, B., Danso, G., Amoah, P., Cofie, O. O., Raschid-Sally, L. and Drechsel, P. (2006) *Irrigated Urban Vegetable Production in Ghana: Characteristics, Benefits and Risks*, IWMI-RUAF-IDRC-CPWF, Accra, p150, www.cityfarmer.org/GhanaIrrigateVegis.html

Pao, S. and Davis, C. L. (1999) 'Enhancing microbiological safety of fresh orange juice by fruit immersion in hot water and chemical sanitizers', *Journal of Food Protection*, vol 62, no 7, pp756–60

Rheinländer, T., Olsen, M. Bakang, J. A., Takyi, H., Konradsen, F. and Samuelsen, H. (2008) 'Keeping up appearances: Perceptions of street food safety in urban Kumasi, Ghana', *Journal of Urban Health*, vol 85, no 6, pp952–64

Rosas, I., Baez, A. and Coutino, M. (1984) 'Bacteriological quality of crops irrigated with wastewater in Xochimilco plots, Mexico City, Mexico', *Applied Environmental Microbiology*, vol 47, pp1074–9

Seidu, R., Heistad, A., Amoah, P., Drechsel, P., Jenssen, P. D. and Stenström, T.-A. (2008) 'Quantification of the health risk associated with wastewater reuse in Accra, Ghana: A contribution toward local guidelines', *Journal of Water and Health*, vol 6, no 4, pp461–71

Serani, S., Nasinyama, G. W., Nabulo, G., Lubowa, A. and Makoha, M. (2008) 'Biological hazards associated with vegetables grown on untreated sewage-watered soils in Kampala', in D. C. Cole, D. Lee-Smith and G. W. Nasinyama (eds) *Healthy City Harvests: Generating Evidence to Guide Policy on Urban Agriculture*, CIP/Urban Harvest and Makerere University Press, Lima, Peru, pp151–69

Shi, X., Namvar, A., Kostrzynska, M., Hora, R. and Warriner, K. (2007) 'Persistence and growth of different *Salmonella* serovars on pre- and postharvest tomatoes', *Journal of Food Protection*, vol 70, pp2725–31

Solomon, E. B, Yaron, S. and Matthews, K. R. (2002) 'Transmission of *Escherichia coli* 0157:H7 from contaminated manure and irrigation water to lettuce plant tissue and its subsequent internalization', *Applied and Environmental Microbiology*, vol 68, pp397–400

Stine, S. W., Song, I., Choi, C. Y. and Gerba, C. P. (2005) 'Effect of relative humidity on preharvest survival of bacterial and viral pathogens on the surface of cantaloupe, lettuce, and bell peppers', *Journal of Food Protection*, vol 68, no 7, pp1352–8

Strauss, M. (1985) 'Health aspect of nightsoil and sludge use in agriculture and aquaculture: Part II: Survival of excreted pathogens in excreta and faecal sludges', *IRCWD News*, vol 23, pp4–9

Tsai, Y. and Ingham, S. C. (1997) 'Survival of *Escherichia coli* O157:H7 and *Salmonella* spp. in acidic condiments', *Journal of Food Protection*, vol 60, no 7, pp751–5

WHO (1996) *Essential Safety Requirements for Street-Vended Food*, revised edition, Food Safety Unit, Division of Food and Nutrition, World Health Organization, Geneva, www.who.int/foodsafety/publications/fs_management/en/streetvend.pdf

WHO (2004) *Guidelines for Drinking-Water Quality*, 3rd edition, World Health Organization, Geneva

WHO (2006) *Guidelines for the Safe Use of Wastewater, Excreta and Greywater, Volume 2: Wastewater Use in Agriculture*, World Health Organization, Geneva

WTO (World Trade Organization) (1995) *The WTO Agreement on the Application of Sanitary and Phytosanitary Measures (SPS Agreement)*, World Trade Organization, Paris, www.wto.org/english/tratop_e/sps_e/spsagr_e.htm

Zhuang, R. Y. and Beuchat, L. R. (1996) 'Effectiveness of trisodium phosphate for killing *Salmonella montevideo* on tomatoes', *Letters in Applied Microbiology*, vol 22, pp97–100

Zhuang, R. Y., Beuchat, L. R. and Angulo, F. J. (1995) 'Fate of *Salmonella montevideo* on and in raw tomatoes as affected by temperature and treatment with chlorine', *Journal of Applied Environmental Microbiology*, vol 61, no 6, pp2127–31

13

Cost-Effectiveness Analysis of Interventions for Diarrhoeal Disease Reduction among Consumers of Wastewater-Irrigated Lettuce in Ghana

Razak Seidu and Pay Drechsel

ABSTRACT

Interventions proposed and implemented for the mitigation of diarrhoeal diseases associated with wastewater reuse in agriculture have received little, if any, comparative assessment of their cost-effectiveness. This chapter assesses the costs, outcomes and cost-effectiveness of the so-called 'treatment' and 'non- or post-treatment' interventions as well as a combination of these for wastewater irrigation in urban Ghana using an approach that integrates quantitative microbial risk assessment (QMRA), disability-adjusted life years (DALYs) and cost-effectiveness analysis (CEA). The cost-effectiveness ratios (CERs) for the treatment and non-treatment interventions assessed ranged from US$31/DALY to US$812/DALY averted. Risk-reduction measures targeting farming practices and the basic rehabilitation of local wastewater treatment plants were the most attractive interventions with a CER well below the threshold of US$150/DALY, sometimes considered as the upper limit for a health intervention to be cost-effective in developing countries. All combinations associated with the basic rehabilitation of the treatment plants, with either on-farm or post-harvest interventions or both, resulted in CERs within the range of US$40/DALY to US$57/DALY. However, the CERs for the construction of a new wastewater treatment plant either as an independent intervention or in combination with on-farm and post-harvest interventions were unattractive in view of health-risk reduction for wastewater irrigation. Although attractive, the CERs of non-treatment options are largely dependent on compliance (adoption) by farmers and food vendors. In this regard, the CER increased by almost fivefold when the adoption rate was only 25 per cent by farmers and food vendors; but was attractive as long as adoption rates did not fall below 70 per cent. On the other hand, the success of the treatment option depends on the functionality of the treatment plants which is not without challenges in a country like Ghana. Thus, this chapter stresses the need for a balanced risk-management approach through a combination of treatment and non-treatment interventions to hedge against failures that may affect CERs at any end. While this chapter provides a contribution to the debate on interventions for health-risk mitigation in wastewater irrigation, more case studies would be useful to verify the data presented here.

INTRODUCTION

Irrigation with raw, diluted and treated wastewater for vegetable production is increasingly becoming a central component of the urban food matrix in many countries due to depleting freshwater resources, increased demand for fresh vegetables and the need to reuse water based on a deeper understanding of sustainability issues. The benefits of the practice are many and encapsulate social, economic and environmental returns that dovetail neatly into food security, freshwater conservation and sustainable wastewater management. At the same time, wastewater irrigation can serve as a conduit for severe and sometimes fatal health consequences with a cost to society greater than its benefits if not undertaken in a safe manner. Many of the infectious pathogenic organisms of viral, bacterial, protozoan and parasitic origins implicated in gastroenteric diseases are present in wastewater and may be transmitted via the consumption of wastewater-irrigated vegetables. A review of several wastewater-irrigation studies worldwide showed clear evidence of direct correlations between the consumption of wastewater-irrigated vegetables and the occurrence of gastroenteric diseases including diarrhoea (Blumenthal and Peasey, 2002).

To reduce the health risk associated with wastewater irrigation while optimizing its benefits, a multi-pronged approach that progressively reduces microbial health hazards has been proposed by the most recent World Health Organization (WHO) Guidelines for wastewater irrigation (WHO, 2006). This approach to health-risk management appreciates the diverse and disparate socio-cultural, technical and institutional dynamics of wastewater irrigation and thus postulates a wide range of flexible and locally specific health-risk barriers. This is of particular importance where the main conventional risk barrier, i.e. wastewater treatment, does not sufficiently work, as in most developing countries. Here, so-called 'post-treatment' or 'non-treatment' options gain significance (see Chapter 2). These comprise measures for risk reduction along the farm to fork pathway, such as drip-kit irrigation or vegetable-washing.

Several of these health-risk barriers have been explored in different geographical areas in terms of their efficacy in view of risk reduction and, in some cases, their feasibility of implementation, acceptability and potential sustainability. One of these cases is Ghana. In urban Ghana, where wastewater irrigation is common and poses a significant health risk (Seidu et al., 2008), non-treatment interventions at the farm and post-harvest points have been explored in different cities, on farms, in markets and in street-food restaurants (see references in Drechsel et al., 2008). These studies, together with others elsewhere (WHO, 2006), have shown that a significant risk reduction is also possible where public health cannot yet rely on conventional wastewater treatment, especially if different options are combined. However, decisions as to which intervention to implement have largely accounted for only the efficacy of the interventions in terms of reduced bacterial counts or helminth eggs, without rigorous analysis of the health gains and cost-effectiveness.

An approach that has been used to address this gap is cost-effectiveness analysis (CEA). The approach provides a framework for the assessment of interventions in terms of their costs per standardized health benefit measured in DALYs averted (WHO, 2003). This approach, although widely used to assess water and sanitation interventions, is yet to be applied to wastewater irrigation to rigorously assess the different interventions proposed in the 2006 WHO Guidelines. This chapter presents the first attempt at applying a holistic CEA framework that integrates the health gains in terms of diarrhoeal disease reduction and cost of treatment and non-treatment interventions associated with wastewater irrigation in urban Ghana.

DESCRIPTION OF INTERVENTIONS

Both intervention types, treatment and non-treatment, were considered in comparison with the common (baseline) practices of wastewater irrigation, independently and in combination. For the non-treatment option a variety of improved practices were tested at different critical control points, i.e. on the farm, in markets and in kitchens of the street-food sector, in terms of their ability to reduce faecal coliforms and helminth eggs on vegetables mostly eaten raw (Drechsel et al., 2008). Chapters 10 and 12 in this book provide more details on this. For the promotion of these practices the International Water Management Institute (IWMI) and national partners suggested a 36-month campaign.

The campaign targeted farmers using wastewater for irrigation and street-food kitchens selling wastewater-irrigated salads as part of common urban fast-food dishes. For the CEA, the on-farm and off-farm components of the campaign were assessed separately and in combination. The campaign was largely based on social marketing, incentives and education (see also Chapter 16), and included improved irrigation practices such as cessation of irrigation, drip irrigation and improved overhead irrigation at the farm level, as well as more effective vegetable-washing practices at the post-harvest level.

A set of possible interventions was compiled at the farm and fast-food restaurant level, taking into account different possibilities and constraints at different locations. As some practices will have a higher applicability and adoption potential at one site than another their average risk reduction was used in the analysis presented here. Thus, in the assessment, the specific improved practices were categorized into two groups, on farm and post-harvest respectively, with no further distinctions between the different interventions. Aside from those 'non-treatment' options, the IWMI project carried out an inventory of all 70 (largely dysfunctional) wastewater treatment plants (WWTP) in Ghana to analyse, among things, their costs of rehabilitation. Nine smaller wastewater treatment plants with minor technical problems were selected for rehabilitation across five major cities in Ghana where wastewater irrigation is practised, each meeting the following criteria:

- The treatment plant had farmland available for irrigation purposes.
- Wastewater irrigation is undertaken in the town/city where the treatment plant is located.
- The readiness and willingness of local regulatory authorities and managers of the plant to use wastewater for irrigation.
- The cumulative area would be large enough to absorb the large majority of farmers currently using untreated wastewater.

In addition to the rehabilitation option, the ongoing construction of a smaller new wastewater treatment plant in Legon, Accra[1] (with a theoretically possible large-scale irrigation component) was assessed, using official cost estimates. Finally, all possible combinations of treatment and non-treatment options were assessed.

METHODS

An integrated approach combining QMRA, DALYs and CEA was applied to estimate quantitatively the health effects and cost-effectiveness of the interventions. For this, the QMRA framework presented by Haas et al. (1999) was followed while DALY estimations were based on Murray (1994). The cost-effectiveness of the interventions was constructed following the WHO guide to cost-effectiveness analysis (WHO, 2003). A detailed description of the methodology is presented as follows.

Health-risk assessment

Hazard identification

All diarrhoea-causing pathogenic organisms of viral, bacterial, protozoan and parasitic origins are present in wastewater and can be transmitted via the consumption of wastewater-irrigated vegetables. In Ghana, studies on the microbial hazards in wastewater have so far been limited to faecal coliforms and helminths (Amoah et al., 2007; Obuobie et al., 2006). However, epidemiological investigations of diarrhoea prevalence have consistently detected a wide range of pathogenic organisms including rotavirus (Reither et al., 2007), (non-typhi) *Salmonella* and *Cryptosporidium* (Adjei et al., 2004) suggesting that these organisms can potentially be found in the wastewater used for vegetable irrigation. Therefore, for this assessment, we chose rotavirus, *Cryptosporidium* and *Salmonella* respectively as representative organisms for the viral, protozoan and bacterial infections and diarrhoea cases.

Rotavirus has been used as a representative organism in health-risk assessments associated with wastewater irrigation in Ghana (Seidu et al., 2008) and elsewhere (Hamilton et al., 2006; Mara et al., 2007; Shuval et al., 1997). (Non-typhi) *Salmonella* has been found in street-salad vegetables potentially irrigated with wastewater (Mensah et al., 2002). It is also a major cause of foodborne diseases worldwide and has been used as a representative organism for bacterial infections in a risk-assessment study (Gerba et al., 2008). *Cryptosporidium* has also been used as a representative organism in quantitative microbial risk studies (Mara et al., 2007) and is widely associated with diarrhoeal diseases worldwide.

As indicated above, none of these organisms has been directly investigated and detected in wastewater in Ghana. Therefore, their concentrations in irrigation wastewater were determined by extrapolation using ratios (pathogenic bacteria/virus/protozoan to indicator bacteria) ranging from a conservative $1:10^5$ to the least conservative $1:10^6$ and $1:10^4$ to $1:10^5$ were used to predict the concentration of rotavirus and *Salmonella* in wastewater respectively (Gerba et al., 2008). For *Cryptosporidium*, a range of $1:10^6$ to $1:10^7$ (Mara et al., 2007) was used. For the wastewater treatment options, the faecal coliform concentrations reported for domestic wastewater in Ghana (Awuah et al., 1996) were used. For the non-treatment interventions (farm and post-harvest improved practices), the reported concentration of faecal coliforms in stormwater drains in Ghana (Keraita and Drechsel, 2004; Obuobie et al., 2006) and on crops (Amoah et al., 2007) were used. To account for uncertainty, the reported faecal coliform concentrations in the wastewater were assumed to follow a lognormal probability distribution (Table 13.1).

Exposure assessment, dose-response and risk of infection

Exposure to the pathogenic organisms for each of the interventions was modelled for wastewater-irrigated lettuce by accounting for the reductions in faecal coliforms

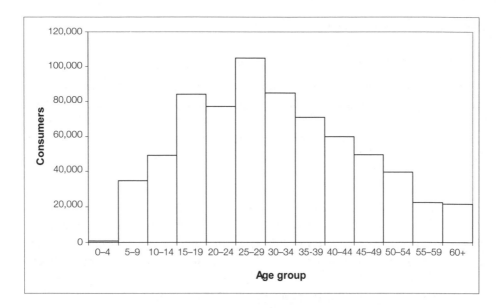

Figure 13.1 *Projected distribution of wastewater-irrigated lettuce consumer population in urban Ghana*

attributable to each of the interventions using the probability distributions in Table 13.1. The exposed consumer population was estimated from surveys of restaurants and food vendors serving wastewater-irrigated lettuce salad by following the distribution-consumption path described by Amoah et al. (2007) and was approximately 700,000 per day in Ghana's five largest cities where urban fast food is common (IWMI, 2009). From this survey and an earlier study (Obuobie et al., 2006), it was found that consumers in the streets of Accra and Kumasi, on average, ate about 13g of lettuce salad three times per week, resulting in an annual consumption of 1.87kg per person (IWMI, 2009). Since response to various pathogenic organisms is age-dependent, this was accounted for by stratifying consumers of lettuce at restaurants and fast-food vendors. Figure 13.1 shows a standardized age-cohort distribution of the exposed consumer population.

The dose of organisms D_i ingested by consuming irrigated lettuce was determined as:

$$D_i = Q_i . V_i . V_c . 10^{-n} \qquad \qquad 13.1$$

Q_i is the mass of lettuce consumed per meal (g); V_i is the volume of irrigation water left on lettuce after harvest (ml g^{-1}); V_c is the concentration of pathogens per volume of wastewater (number of pathogens g^{-1}); and n log unit reduction in pathogens associated with the interventions. V_i was assumed to be between 10.8ml

Table 13.1 *Efficacy of treatment and non-treatment interventions*

Concentration of faecal coliforms in irrigation water source	Interventions	Log_{10} reduction	References	Probability distribution used for reduction in faecal coliforms
Treatment options: Domestic wastewater Lognormal (10^8, 10^8)[a]	Wastewater treatment plant	3–6	WHO (2006)	Triangular (3, 4, 6)
		2–3	Hodgson (2000); Awuah et al. (1996)	
Non-treatment options: Stormwater drain wastewater Lognormal (10^6, 10^8)[b]	On farm: Cessation of irrigation	0.65–0.66 per day	Drechsel et al. (2008)	Uniform (2, 3)[c]
	On farm: Overhead irrigation at <0.5m	2–2.5	Drechsel et al. (2008)	
	On farm: Drip irrigation	3–4	Drechsel et al. (2008)	
	Post-harvest: Washing of vegetables with only clean water (cold water for 2 min)	1–1.4	Drechsel et al. (2008)	Uniform (1, 2)
	Post-harvest: Washing of lettuce with clean water and disinfectant	2.1–2.2	Drechsel et al. (2008)	

[a]Awuah et al. (1996).
[b]Obuobie et al. (2006) and Keraita and Drechsel et al. (2004).
[c]A maximum of 3 log unit reduction instead of 4 log was taken to account for problems of clogging associated with the use of drip kits by farmers in Ghana.

and 15ml (Mara et al., 2007; Seidu et al., 2008), a range based on the 10.8ml reported by Shuval et al. (1997).

For the dose-response relationships, the beta-Poisson dose-response model (which assumes the pathogen-host survival probability to vary according to a beta distribution) was used for rotavirus and *Salmonella* (non-typhi), as it best describes the dose-response relationships for both organisms (Haas et al., 1999) in human feeding trials involving rotavirus (Ward et al., 1986) and *Salmonella* of several strains (McCullough and Eisele, 1951a; 1951b; 1951c). For *Cryptosporidium* the single hit exponential dose-response model (which assumes constancy of the pathogen-host survival probability) best describes its dose-response relationship obtained from human feeding trials (DuPont et al., 1995; Haas et al., 1999). In the case of a single exposure, the beta-Poisson and exponential dose-response models are respectively expressed as:

$$P_{i\ (d)} = 1 - \left[1 + \left(\frac{D_i}{N_{50}}\right)\left(2^{\frac{1}{\alpha}} - 1\right)\right]^{-\alpha}$$

13.2

$$P_{i\ (d)} = 1 - e^{-(rD_i)}$$

13.3

$P_{i(d)}$ is the probability of becoming infected by ingesting D_i number of organisms, N_{50} is the median infection dose representing the number of organisms that will infect 50 per cent of the exposed population; and α and r are the dimensionless infectivity constants. For rotavirus, N_{50} and α are 6.17 and 0.253 respectively; for *Salmonella*, N_{50} is 23,600 and α is 0.3126; and for *Cryptosporidium* r is 0.0042 (Haas et al., 1999). We estimated the annual risk of infection for the organisms by accounting for the dose and frequency of consumption presented above using the formula:

$$P_A = 1 - (1 - P_{i(d)})^{156}$$

13.4

P_A is the annual risk of infection and $P_{i\ (d)}$ is as described above. All the models were constructed in Microsoft Excel and calculated with Monte Carlo simulation at 10,000 iterations using the @ Risk 4.5 (Palisade Corporation) software add-on to Excel.

Diarrhoea morbidity, mortality and Disability-Adjusted Life Years

Epidemiological data on the transition from infection with the selected pathogenic organisms to disease (mild or severe) or death are lacking for Ghana. Therefore, studies undertaken in other regions were relied on. For rotavirus, it was assumed that after infection 10–15 per cent are asymptomatic, while 85–90 per cent develop diarrhoea of which in Ghana 12 per cent of the cases are severe, with the rest suffering mild diarrhoea leading to full recovery. From the severe diarrhoea cases it was assumed that 5 per cent die (Havelaar and Melse, 2003).

Rotavirus diarrhoea-related disease is common among children. However, some studies have also reported the incidence of diarrhoea among adults infected with rotavirus. A rotavirus outbreak study among college students has reported that of the 83 cases of rotavirus infection, 93 per cent had diarrhoea with a full recovery (Fletcher et al., 2000). In another study of children with rotavirus in 28 families, 18 of 54 adult family members exposed to rotavirus developed evidence of infection, and all but four had diarrhoea (Grimwood et al., 1988).

Based on this, it was assumed that the severe diarrhoea cases and deaths can occur mainly in the consumer age groups of 1–14 years (i.e. over and above the widely reported key age group of 0–5 years who, from our survey, are not frequent consumers of street food served with wastewater-irrigated lettuce) and those over 60 years. The choice of this wide range, including those in the over 60 age group, was to account for potential outbreak incidence. It was further assumed that the other age groups (15–60 years) will develop mild diarrhoea with full recovery.

For *Cryptosporidium* infection, it is known that in developed countries, 71 per cent of infected immunocompetent persons develop gastroenteritis, while population-based outbreak studies and volunteer experiments report relapses of diarrhoea in 40–70 per cent of patients (Havelaar and Melse, 2003). The only well-documented *Cryptosporidium*-related mortality is the waterborne disease outbreak in Milwaukee where four deaths were reported out of 400,000 diarrhoea cases (Mackenzie et al., 1994). For the purposes of this study, it was assumed that 70 per cent of those infected with *Cryptosporidium* following consumption of lettuce will develop diarrhoea with a mortality rate of 0.1 per cent, to reflect the potentially high mortality rates in developing countries (Havelaar and Melse, 2003).

For *Salmonella*, studies based on the FoodNet database (Kennedy et al., 2004; Voetsch et al., 2004) were used. From these studies, it was estimated that 50.3 per cent and 49.7 per cent of consumers infected with *Salmonella* non-typhoid will develop bloody and non-bloody diarrhoea respectively. From the bloody diarrhoea cases, it was assumed that 20 per cent will be hospitalized as severe cases for an average of three days with a 0.6 per cent fatality rate (Kennedy et al., 2004; Voetsch et al., 2004).

To ascertain the efficacy of the interventions in comparison with the status quo, the burden of morbidity and mortality of the diarrhoeal disease cases resulting from the infections under each of the interventions was estimated using the DALY approach. DALY combines years of life lost by premature mortality with years lived with a disability, standardized using severity or disability weights (Murray, 1994). The approach was first introduced in the *World Development Report* (World Bank 1993) and was revised in 1996 for the *Global Burden of Disease* studies (Murray and Lopez, 1996). For each of the pathogenic organisms, the DALYs/year were calculated using the equation:

$$DALYs = YLLs + YLDs \qquad 13.5$$

YLL is the number of years of life lost due to mortality and YLD is the number of years lived with a disability, weighed with a factor between 0 and 1 for the severity of the disability or disease.

YLLs and YLDs were derived using the equations:

$$YLLs[r, K, \beta] = \frac{KCe^{ra}}{(r+\beta)^2} \{e^{-(r+\beta)(L+a)}[-(r+\beta)(L+a)-1]-e^{-(r+\beta)a}[-(r+\beta)a-1]\}$$
$$+ \frac{1-K}{r}(1-e^{-rl}) \qquad 13.6$$

$$YLDs[r, K, \beta] = D \{ \frac{KCe^{ra}}{(r + \beta)^2} \{ e^{-(r+\beta)(L+a)}[-(r + \beta)(L + a) - 1] - e^{-(r+\beta)a}[-(r + \beta)a - 1] \}$$

$$+ \frac{1-K}{r} (1 - e^{-rl}) \} \qquad\qquad 13.7$$

K = age weighting modulation factor; C = constant; r = discount rate; a = age of death; β = parameter from the age weighting function; L = standard expectation of life at age a.

For rotavirus the severity indexes of mild diarrhoea and severe diarrhoea were taken as 0.1 and 0.23. For *Cryptosporidium* and *Salmonella*, 0.067 was used as the severity index for watery diarrhoea cases. Bloody *Salmonella*-related diarrhoea was accounted for with a severity index of 0.39 (Havelaar and Melse, 2003). All mild and severe diarrhoea cases lasted seven days while the very severe cases with blood lasted 5.6 days based on bloody diarrhoea associated with *E. coli* O157 (Havelaar and Melse, 2003). Deaths resulting from all the diarrhoea cases irrespective of the organism involved had a severity index of 1. A standard life expectancy of 60 years (GSS, 2002) across all the age groups with a standard age-weighting modulation factor ranging from 0 to 1 was used, and the parameters β and C were set at 0.04 and 0.1658 respectively (Murray, 1996). The DALY model for the interventions was constructed and simulated in Excel and discounted at 3 per cent annually (WHO, 2003).

Costing interventions

The ingredient approach, which totals all the inputs as the products of their respective quantities and values, was used to estimate the cost of the interventions. For the suggested three-year campaign (IWMI, 2009) targeting farmers and fast-food vendors/restaurants, all relevant stakeholders including the Ghana Social Marketing Foundation, Ministry of Food and Agriculture (MOFA) and the Food and Drugs Board (FDB) were interviewed to get a feasible cost-assessment for the campaign.

For the nine treatment plants selected for rehabilitation, a facility assessment survey was carried out by local sanitation consultants to elicit information on the inputs/materials required for a basic (low-cost) upgrading towards effective operation (IWMI, 2009). In the case of the new wastewater treatment plant all costs were obtained from the appraisal reports of the African Development Bank-funded Accra Sewerage Improvement Project (ASIP) (IWMI, 2009). All cost streams obtained for the different interventions were separated as capital or recurrent. All cost items for the various interventions including their components are summarized in 2008 US dollars (Tables 13.2–13.3). Capital costs were annualized and recurrent costs discounted over three years for the non-treatment campaign and ten years for the treatment interventions. For comparability across regions, capital and recurrent costs for the interventions were annualized and

Table 13.2 *Summary of costs for non-treatment options (national campaign)*

Intervention	Component	Cost (US$) (36 months)	Total Cost (US$)
Campaign reaching all vegetable *farmers* in five major cities	Programme Management & Administration	300,000	1,100,000
	Training and Materials	440,000	
	Enforcement/Follow-Up	260,000	
	Marketing Study	100,000	
Campaign reaching all vegetable *street-food vendors/restaurants* in five major cities	Programme Management & Administration	310,000	1,820,000
	Training/Social Marketing	1,050,000	
	Enforcement/Follow-Up	240,000	
	Marketing Study	220,000	
Total			2,920,000

Source: IWMI (2009)

Table 13.3 *Summary of costs of two 'treatment' options*

	Selected Plants	Cost (US$)
1) WWTP Rehabilitation Restricted rehabilitation of core functions of selected plants with agricultural lands	Roman Ridge, Accra	5,500
	PRESEC, Accra	48,500
	KNUST, Kumasi	50,000
	Asafo, Kumasi	7,000
	Pantang, Accra	20,000
	Kamina Barracks, Tamale	20,000
	UCEW, Winneba	25,000
	Ankaful WWTP	25,000
	Volta Star WWTP, Juapong	17,000
	Total	**218,000**
	Total annual O&M incl. staff labour for all 9 plants	+333,000
2) Construction New construction of a small treatment plant with sewer rehabilitation and extension (part of the already funded and ongoing ASIP project)	University of Ghana, Accra: Sewer (re)connection	16,500,000
	Ponds and pumping station	6,700,000
	Total	**23,200,000**

Source: IWMI (2009)

discounted at 3 per cent as the base case and at rates of 0 per cent and 6 per cent for sensitivity analysis (WHO, 2003). To account for uncertainty around the cost estimates, the triangular probability distribution was fitted to all the capital and recurrent costs by taking the minimum and maximum likely values at +/– 20 per cent, respectively.

Cost-effectiveness

Cost-effectiveness of the interventions was modelled with the TreeAge ProHealth Suit Software (www.treeage.com) (Robberstad et al., 2007). The average cost-effectiveness ratios (CER) were calculated in US$ per DALY (i.e. the cost incurred for each DALY averted by the intervention) as well as the incremental cost-effectiveness ratios (ICER) (i.e. the additional cost needed for each additional unit of DALY averted resulting from investment in the intervention rather than its comparator) after accounting for the DALYs averted for each of the interventions in relation to the status quo (no intervention scenario). An expansion path analysis, based on the ICER, was also made to highlight dominated interventions (i.e. interventions that are both costly and less effective than their comparators) and for the ranking of the interventions. All costs and DALYs averted were discounted at 3 per cent as baseline with further sensitivity analysis at 0 per cent and 6 per cent, as suggested by the WHO. The cost-effectiveness ratios were compared with a cut-off value of US$150/DALY averted, which was used for many years as a rough economic evaluation criterion by which a health intervention in a developing country is considered cost-effective (World Bank, 1993). All interventions with cost-effectiveness ratios of < US$150/DALY were considered cost-effective while those > US$150/DALY were classified as unattractive.[2]

Sensitivity and uncertainty analysis

A one-way sensitivity analysis was also made to ascertain the effects of variations in the discount and campaign adoption rates as well as costs on the CER and ICER. The CER and ICER were calculated for each of the interventions by varying the discount rate for costs and benefits (DALYs) from 0 per cent to 6 per cent. As the calculations were based on a successful campaign with 100 per cent adoption, the sensitivity analysis was used to address lower adoption rates. Adoption rates of 25 per cent and 75 per cent representing pessimistic and optimistic scenarios respectively were assessed for the on-farm and post-harvest interventions. For the costs, as stated above, triangular distributions were applied for both the capital and recurrent costs with minimum and maximum values at 20 per cent below and above the most likely value, calculated from the ingredient approach (Robberstad et al., 2007). From the triangular distributions, 10,000 Monte Carlo simulations were made and CERs calculated. From these iterations mean CERs with 95 per cent confidence intervals were derived for each of the interventions.

RESULTS

Infection risks, diarrhoea cases and DALYs

The annual infection risk associated with the consumption of lettuce salad irrigated under the current wastewater-irrigation and post-harvest practices across the country showed a high viral infection risk. The median viral infection risk was of a magnitude of 10^{-1} per person per year (pppy) while those of bacterial and protozoan were 10^{-5} pppy indicating that the risks of bacterial and protozoan infection given the current wastewater irrigation practices met the WHO tolerable infection risk of 10^{-4} pppy. These infection risks resulted in 477,258 self-limiting (mild) diarrhoea cases, representing 0.68 episodes per consumer per year. This falls outside the range of diarrhoea incidence of 0.8–1.3 pppy for all ages in developing countries, but approximates the global average diarrhoea incidence of 0.7 pppy (Mathers et al., 2002). Of the 0.68 diarrhoea episodes, about 14 per cent and 0.1 per cent were severe and fatal respectively and translated into 12,016 DALYs annually, representing 0.017 DALYs pppy. This figure represents nearly 10 per cent of the WHO-reported DALYs occurring in urban Ghana due to various types of water- and sanitation-related diarrhoea (Prüss-Ustün et al., 2008).

Effectiveness of interventions

The assessment shows that 41–92 per cent of the total DALYs (related to the consumption of wastewater-irrigated salads) can be averted through the different on-farm and post-harvest interventions (Figure 13.2). A campaign targeting improved farm practices could avert up to 92 per cent of the DALYs while up to 74 per cent could be averted through interventions in the street-food sector. Also, the rehabilitation of the nine selected WWTPs with farmland nearby and well distributed over the country could allow a high DALY reduction of 82 per cent if farmers would agree to move to those sites. Building a new WWTP (independently of its level of sophistication and cost) would certainly be very effective in its treatment but could not accommodate all farmers (even in Accra, with the greatest amount of irrigated urban farming) and supply all required vegetables. Thus, it would only avert in the best case 44 per cent of the annual DALYs. Combined non-treatment options (on farm, off farm) or non-treatment options and the rehabilitation of the nine WWTPs would in all cases increase the health benefit by averting 94 per cent of the DALYs, which is not much more than the farm interventions alone if they are broadly adopted.

Cost-effectiveness of interventions

As presented in Table 13.4, the CERs ranged from US$31/DALY to US$812/DALY on average. Based on the rough CER benchmark of US$150/DALY, the

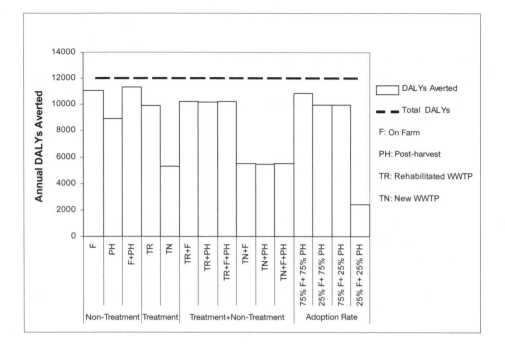

Figure 13.2 *DALYs averted by interventions*

most cost-effective interventions are those targeting health-risk reduction at the farm level (CER of US$31/DALY). Also, the low-cost rehabilitation of a larger number of existing but underperforming WWTPs well distributed over urban Ghana can be very cost-effective. These two options demand that farmers either adopt safer irrigation practices or move to sites with safer (treated) water. Also combining both options to offer farmers more choices is still very cost-effective (US$40/DALY) and so is the multiple-barrier approach combining low-cost rehabilitations, on-farm interventions and post-harvest (street-food) interventions. This is important as it offers more options and security for risk reduction while only marginally increasing the costs per DALY averted.

Only the construction of new WWTPs could not be considered as cost-effective in view of health-risk reduction related to wastewater-irrigated salads. The reason is not only the low coverage but the high costs, even of simple pond systems, if sewer connections are planned. Thus, increasing the number of new plants to cover all land needed for satisfying the current demand for salad greens would even decrease the CER despite averting all DALYs. This also applies to any non-treatment intervention combined with construction of a new WWTP.

The high cost-competitiveness of the WWTP rehabilitation is due to the limited investments needed to get the selected systems working again; the costs

Table 13.4 *Cost-effectiveness ratios of interventions*

Interventions	CER (US$/DALY)	
	Mean	CI (5–95%)
Non-Treatment Options Campaign		
100% adoption rate (AR) on farm	31	27–35
100% AR post-harvest	67	58–76
100% AR on farm + post-harvest	83	72–95
25% AR on farm + 75% AR post-harvest	95	82–108
75% AR on farm + 25% AR post-harvest	94	81–107
25% AR on farm + 25% AR post-harvest (pessimistic scenario case)	394	340–447
75% AR on-farm + 75% AR post-harvest (optimistic scenario case)	87	75–98
Treatment Options		
Rehabilitation of selected urban WWTPs	31	27–35
Construction of one new WWTP with household connections	786	678–893
Combined Options		
Rehabilitation + on farm	40	34–45
Rehabilitation + post-harvest	48	41–54
Rehabilitation + on farm + post-harvest	57	50–65
Construction + on farm	771	666–877
Construction + post-harvest	798	689–907
Construction + on farm + post-harvest	812	702–924

are even lower than the funds required for a national campaign on non-treatment options. However, as mentioned before, this option assumes no further costs on sewer to household connections and that the farmers move to those sites with treated wastewater. Where this would increase their transport costs, incentives will be needed to ensure that farmers do not maintain their current high-risk plots. Even though the CERs provide significant information regarding the efficacy of interventions, they cannot be used to rank the interventions without considering resource constraints. Therefore, an expansion path, based on the incremental cost-effectiveness of the interventions, was undertaken by first ranking all the interventions in terms of their effectiveness. Figure 13.3 shows the expansion path for the interventions given that there is no resource constraint. The associated incremental cost-effectiveness analysis shows that the most cost-effective path for the implementation of possible interventions is from the rehabilitation of the WWTPs to on-farm interventions to a combination of on-farm and post-harvest interventions. All other interventions were completely dominated, i.e. resulted in negative incremental effects against a comparator.

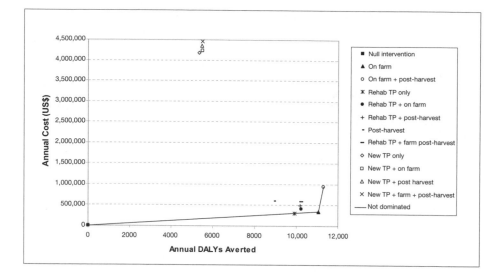

Figure 13.3 *Expansion path showing dominated interventions*

Sensitivity and uncertainty analysis

Discounting the cost and health benefits at 0 per cent and 6 per cent significantly affected the average CER, but this did not affect the ranking of the interventions in terms of incremental cost-effectiveness ratios (results not shown). Also, there was a remarkable effect of the campaign adoption at the farm and post-harvest sectors on the overall effectiveness and, hence, the cost-effectiveness of the interventions (Figure 13.2 and Table 13.4).

Generally, the relationship describing this phenomenon was exponential. Given the pessimistic scenario where only 25 per cent of farmers and food vendors adopted the improved practices of the campaign, only 20 per cent of the DALYs lost were averted, resulting in a CER of US$394/DALY, which is more than twice the benchmark CER and thus making the campaign unattractive. The optimistic scenario representing 75 per cent adoption of improved practices across the farm and post-harvest sectors averted about 90 per cent of the DALYs, leading to a CER of US$87/DALY. This shows that significant health gains can still be made cost-effectively at marginal non-compliance rates of up to 25 per cent for the optimistic scenario in this study across the farm and post-harvest sectors. Further calculations based on the exponential relation show that a maximum non-compliance (non-adoption) rate of about 30 per cent across the farm and post-harvest sectors could still make the campaign attractive in view of the US$150 benchmark.

DISCUSSION

The assessment has shown that the consumption of wastewater-irrigated lettuce is likely to significantly contribute to cases of diarrhoea and DALYs with a disproportionate impact on children. The results were compared with the EU-funded SWITCH project which used QMRA to assess the disease burden associated with contaminated piped drinking water, flooding, playing in open storm water drains, swimming at urban beaches and occupational contact with faecal matter in Accra (Lunani et al., 2009). It was found that for the same urban area and population the consumption of wastewater-irrigated vegetables appears to be the second highest in risk after children exposed to an open stormwater drain (IWMI, 2009).

Mensah et al. (2002) found a wide range of pathogenic organisms including *Staphylococcus aureus* in street-food salad in Accra and concluded that the lettuce and cabbage used in the preparation of the salad were potentially irrigated with wastewater and/or fertilized with poorly composted manure. In the same study, poor hygiene practices by street-food vendors serving salad were also implicated in the microbial contamination of the salad served. This study, together with others (Amoah et al., 2007; Obuobie et al., 2006; Seidu et al., 2008), stressed the importance of on-farm and post-harvest practices as control points for the reduction of the health hazards associated with wastewater irrigation.

As the results indicate, health-reduction measures at these points have the potential to avert a high number of DALYs and are cost-effective as well. Nevertheless, the sensitivity analysis showed the importance of strategies that support the adoption of non-treatment options as non-compliance of more than 30 per cent rendered the campaign increasingly unattractive in terms of costs and health gains.

Thus, strategies that ensure a consistent increase in the adoption of improved practices are vital. In this regard, constraints including the additional labour requirements (e.g. farm ponds) or investment needs (e.g. drip kits) of some of the improved practices, or risk of lower yields due to cessation of irrigation or furrow irrigation (see Chapter 12) have to be taken into account in the design of incentive systems and effective campaign programmes. A framework combining incentive systems, education, social marketing and regulations to achieve a high adoption rate as well as practical examples from participatory on-farm research are discussed in Chapters 16 and 17.

It should be stressed that the assessment here generally reflected an endemic situation, accounting for variations in the pathogenic organisms in the stormwater-drain irrigation water with probability distribution functions. These distributions did not account for an epidemic or outbreak situation. In an outbreak or epidemic situation, where the concentration of pathogenic organisms in the irrigation water is significantly elevated, even an adoption of 70–75 per cent may not reduce the total DALYs significantly as an elevated incidence of diarrhoea and DALYs could occur in a cluster of consumer population not affected by the intervention.

Given the sensitivity of the CERs of the non-treatment interventions to farmers' and vendors' adoption rates, it would not make sense to select a single critical control point. It is thus proposed that both treatment (rehabilitation of wastewater treatment plants for wastewater treatment) and non-treatment interventions (on-farm improved irrigation practices and post-harvest washing practices by fast-food vendors) be combined to increase the probability of DALY reduction while only marginally decreasing the CER. In this regard, a combination involving the basic rehabilitation of the nine Ghanaian wastewater treatment plants together with both or either of the non-treatment options will not only reflect best the 'multi-barrier' approach promoted by the WHO (2006) but also provide some safety against potential failures in the suggested campaigns.

It is, for example, uncertain whether the probability of behaviour-change will be higher among farmers than vendors or vice versa. To increase the probability of success, it is thus recommended to address both groups.

In the CEA of interventions to reduce health risks related to wastewater-irrigated vegetables, those involving the construction of a new wastewater treatment plant were less attractive. Despite the small size of the plant, a major cost factor in the Accra case was the rehabilitation and construction of household connections which dominated the actual pond construction by a factor of three to one.

However, WWTPs might be cost-effective in terms of other reduced health risks (e.g. if underground sewers replace open drains), household support and/ or environmental protection, which are not considered here. There is also no question about the effectiveness of WWTPs for pathogen and diarrhoeal disease reduction (Barreto et al., 2007; Kolahi et al., 2009; WHO, 2006). It is therefore recommended to be, on the one hand, location- and case-specific, but on the other, to carry out a more encompassing cost-effectiveness assessment that includes all locally relevant diarrhoeal-related risk factors that may be impacted by the construction of a WWTP and other benefits of WWTPs.

The estimated CERs for the interventions presented here are comparable with those of other water, sanitation and hygiene interventions worldwide, which range from US$3.35–$20/DALY for hygiene behaviour-change to up to US$6,396/ DALY for improved urban water supply and sanitation systems (Table 13.5). The comparison shows that the non-treatment options as well as low-cost rehabilitation of existing treatment plants can be as cost-effective as the promotion of hand-washing or water chlorination. Also, the estimated CER for the non-treatment (on-farm and post-harvest practices) and basic rehabilitation of treatment plants for vegetable irrigation compares favourably with an estimated cost-effectiveness ratio of US$516/DALY for the reduction of diarrhoea associated with the coverage of stormwater drains in Accra (IWMI, 2009). However, due to the fact that these CERs have been arrived at via different methodologies, such comparisons should be used with caution. On the other hand, we may be relatively confident that

Table 13.5 *CER of interventions for diarrhoeal disease reduction*

Intervention	CER (US$/DALY)	
	Mean	Range
Hygiene behaviour-change campaign	–	3–20
Chlorination at household level	–	46–266
Solar disinfection	54	40–74
Ceramic filtration	125	83–59
Basic sanitation (pit latrine) construction and promotion	≤ 270	–
Basic sanitation (promotion only)	11	–
Water supply via hand pumps/stand posts	94	–
Water supply via house connection	223	–
Oral rehydration therapy	1062	132–2570
Rotavirus immunization	2478	1402–8357
Cholera immunization	2945	1658–8274
Improved rural water supply and sanitation	1974	–
Improved urban water supply and sanitation	6396	–
A campaign leading to 75% adoption of safer irrigation and vegetable-washing practices[a]	87	75–98

Source: Cairncross and Valdmanis (2006); Clasen and Haller (2008); Hutton and Haller (2004); Keusch et al. (2006); Lvovsky (2001); [a]this study

an intervention with a CER of US$45/DALY is better than another one with US$450/DALY (Clasen and Haller, 2008).

The assessment applied QMRA to estimate health risks from extrapolated microbial hazards. The extrapolation of the empirically analysed thermotolerant coliform bacteria to the different pathogenic organisms remains, however, only an estimate based on the best available transfer functions; this may result in an underestimation or overestimation of the health risks with the accompanied DALYs and hence the CERs. The study of Donkor et al. (2008), for example, shows that in view of *E. coli* O157:H7, our assessment might be on the safe side. Such uncertainty surrounding the estimates has been accounted for by providing the 95 per cent confidence interval (CI) around the mean CER, to provide policy-makers with an opportunity to better assess intervention options on a continuum. However, a more rigorous study based on epidemiological investigations of the interventions and their associated impact on diarrhoea is needed to further validate the QMRA results and CERs arrived at in this assessment.

CONCLUSIONS

The health risk associated with wastewater irrigation in terms of diarrhoea cases and the associated DALYs can be significant. This study has demonstrated that by implementing on-farm and post-harvest interventions, both independently and in combination, the DALYs could be significantly reduced in a very cost-effective way. Although these interventions are attractive, their implementation and subsequent cost-effectiveness relies significantly on the adoption rates by farmers and vendors in the fast-food sectors. It is thus suggested that these interventions be well promoted, taking advantage of tangible or intangible incentives and combined with the rehabilitation of wastewater treatment plants where this is possible at low cost, to ensure, by an only marginally decreased CER, the best allocation of scarce resources. The study also suggests that the construction of new wastewater treatment ponds and related sewer systems is much less cost-effective in terms of public-health-risk reduction from the (limited) perspective of wastewater irrigation. Further studies looking at other 'non-treatment options', as well as the larger impact of treatment plants, are recommended.

NOTES

1   Based on a set of anaerobic, facultative and maturation ponds with a planned intake of 6424m³/day.
2   In more recent literature, other criteria are used, for example based on the GDP of a country. The Commission on Macroeconomics and Health classifies interventions that have a cost-effectiveness ratio of less than three times GDP per head as cost-effective (CMH, 2001).

REFERENCES

Adjei, A. A., Armah, H., Rodrigues, O., Renner, L., Borketey, P., Ayeh-Kumi, P., Adiku, T., Sifah, E. and Lartey, M. (2004) '*Cryptosporidium* spp.: A frequent cause of diarrhoea among children at the Korle-Bu Teaching Hospital, Accra, Ghana', *Japanese Journal of Infectious Diseases*, vol 57, pp216–19

Amoah, P., Drechsel, P., Henseler, M. and Abaidoo, R.C. (2007) 'Irrigated urban vegetable production in Ghana: Microbial contamination in farms and markets and associated consumer risk groups', *Journal of Water and Health*, vol 5, no 3, pp455–66

Awuah, E., Nkrumah, E. and Monney, J. G. (1996) 'The performance of the Asokwa Waste Stabilization Pond and the Condition of other Sewage Treatment Plants in Ghana', *University of Science and Technology Journal of Science Technology (Ghana)*, vol 16, nos 1–2, pp121–6

Barreto, M. L., Genser, B., Strina, A., Teixeira, M. G., Assis, A. M. O., Rego, R. F., Teles, C. A., Prado, M. S., Matos, S. M. A., Santos, D. N., dos Santos, L. A. and Cairncross, S. (2007) 'Effect of city-wide sanitation programme on reduction in rate of childhood diarrhoea in northeast Brazil: Assessment by two cohort studies', *Lancet*, vol 370, pp1622–8

Blumenthal, U. J. and Peasey, A. (2002) 'Critical review of epidemiological evidence of the health effects of wastewater and excreta use in agriculture', unpublished document

prepared for World Health Organization, Geneva, www.who.int/water_sanitation_
health/wastewater/whocriticalrev.pdf

Cairncross, S. and Valdmanis, V. (2006) 'Water supply, sanitation and hygiene promotion',
in D. Jamison et al. (eds) *Disease Control Priorities in Developing Countries*, Oxford
University Press and World Bank, Washington, DC, 2nd edition, pp771–92, www.
dcp2.org

Clasen, T. F. and Haller, L. (2008) *Water Quality Interventions to Prevent Diarrhoea: Cost
and Cost-Effectiveness*, World Health Organization, Geneva, www.who.int/water_
sanitation_health/economic/prevent_diarrhoea/en/index.html

CMH (Commission on Macroeconomics and Health) (2001) *Macroeconomics and Health:
Investing in Health for Economic Development*, Center for International Development at
Harvard University, Boston, MA

Donkor, E. S., Lanyo, R., Akyeh, M. L., Kayang, B. B., and Quaye, J. (2008) 'Monitoring
enterohaemorrhagic *Escherichia coli* O157:H7 in the vegetable food chain in Ghana',
Research Journal of Microbiology, vol 3, no 6, pp423–8

Drechsel, P., Keraita, B., Amoah, P., Abaidoo, R. C., Raschid-Sally, L. and Bahri, A.
(2008) 'Reducing health risk from wastewater use in urban and peri-urban sub-Saharan
Africa: Applying the 2006 WHO Guidelines', *Water Science and Technology*, vol 57, no
9, pp1461–6

DuPont, H. L., Chapel, C. L., Sterling, C. R., Okhuysen, P. C., Rose, J. B. and Jakubowski,
W. (1995) 'The infectivity of *Cryptosporidium parvum* in healthy volunteers', *New
England Journal of Medicine*, vol 332, no 13, pp855–9

Fletcher, M., Levy, M. E. and Griffin, D. D. (2000) 'Foodborne outbreak of Group A
rotavirus gastroenteritis among college students: District of Columbia, March–April
2000', *MMWR Morbidity and Mortality Weekly Report*, vol 49, pp1131–3

Gerba, C. P., Castro-Del Campo, N., Brooks, J. P. and Pepper, I. L. (2008) 'Exposure and
risk assessment of *Salmonella* in recycled residuals', *Water Science and Technology*, vol
57, no 7, pp1061–5

Grimwood, K., Lund, J. C., Coulson, B. S., Hudson, I. L., Bishop, R. F. and Barnes,
G. L. (1988) 'Comparison of serum and mucosal antibody responses following severe
acute rotavirus gastroenteritis in young children', *Journal of Clinical Microbiology*, vol
26, pp732–8

GSS (Ghana Statistical Service) (2002) *Population and Housing Census: Special Report on
20 Largest Cities*, Ghana Statistical Service, Accra

Haas, C. N., Rose, J. B. and Gerba, C. P. (1999) *Quantitative Microbial Risk Assessment*,
John Wiley & Sons, New York

Hamilton, A. J., Stagnitti, F., Premier, R., Boland, A. M. and Hale, G. (2006) 'Quantitative
microbial risk assessment models for consumption of raw vegetables irrigated with
reclaimed water', *Applied and Environmental Microbiology*, vol 76, pp3284–90

Havelaar, A. H. and Melse, J. M. (2003) *Quantifying Public Health Risk in the WHO
Guidelines for Drinking-Water Quality: A Burden of Disease Approach*, RIVM Report
no 734301022/2003, Rijksinstituut voor Volksgezondheid en Milieu, Bilthoven, The
Netherlands

Hodgson, I. O. A. (2000) 'Treatment of domestic sewage at Akuse (Ghana)', *Water SA*,
vol 26, no 3, pp413–16

Hutton, G. and Haller, L. (2004) *Evaluation of the Costs and Benefits of Water and Sanitation Improvements at the Global Level*, WHO/SDE/WSH/04.04, World Health Organization, Geneva, www.who.int/water_sanitation_health

IWMI (2009) 'Wastewater irrigation and public health: From research to impact – A road map for Ghana', report for Google.org prepared by IWMI, Accra, Ghana

Kennedy, M., Villar, R., Vugia, D. J., Rabatsky-Ehr, R., Farley, M. M., Pass, M., Smith, K., Smith, P., Cieslak, P. R., Imhoff, B. and Griffin, P. M. (2004) 'Hospitalizations and deaths due to *Salmonella* infections, FoodNet, 1996–1999', *Clinical Infectious Disease*, vol 38, no 3, pp142–8

Keraita, B. and Drechsel, P. (2004) 'Agricultural use of untreated wastewater in Ghana', in C. A. Scott, N. I. Faruqui and L. Raschid-Sally (eds) *Wastewater Use in Irrigated Agriculture: Confronting the Livelihood and Environmental Realities*, CABI Publishing, Wallingford, UK

Keusch, G. T., Fontaine, O., Bhargava, A., Boschi-Pinto, C., Bhutta, Z. A., Gotuzzo, E., Rivera, J. A., Chow, J., Shahid-Salles, S. A. and Laxminarayan, R. (2006) 'Diarrhoeal diseases', in D. T. Jamison et al. (eds) *Disease Control Priorities in Developing Countries*, 2nd edition, Oxford University Press, New York

Kolahi, A. A., Rastegarpour, A. and Sohrabi, M. R. (2009) 'The impact of an urban sewerage system on childhood diarrhoea in Tehran, Iran: A concurrent control field trial', *Transactions of the Royal Society of Tropical Medicine and Hygiene*, vol 103, no 5, pp 500–505

Lunani, I., Labite, H., van der Steen, P., Vairavamoorthy, K., Drechsel, P. and Lens, P. (2009) 'Quantitative Microbial Risk Analysis to evaluate health effects of interventions in the urban water system of Accra, Ghana', *Water Research* (submitted)

Lvovsky, K. (2001) 'Health and environment', *Environment Strategy Papers Series no. 1*, World Bank, Washington, DC

Mackenzie, W. R., Hoxie, N. J., Proctor, M. E., Gradus, M. S., Blair, K. A., Peterson, D. E., Kazmierczak, J. J., Addis, D. G., Fox, K. R., Rose, J. B. and David, J. P. (1994) 'A massive outbreak in Milwaukee of *Cryptosporidium* infection transmitted through the public water supply', *New England Journal of Medicine*, vol 331, no 3, pp161–7

Mara, D. D., Sleigh, P. A., Blumenthal, U. J. and Carr, R. M. (2007) 'Health risks in wastewater irrigation: Comparing estimates from quantitative microbial risk analyses and epidemiological studies', *Journal of Water and Health*, vol 5, no 1, pp39–50

Mathers, C. D., Stein, C., Ma Fat, D., Rao, C., Inoue, M., Tomijima, N., Bernard, C., Lopez, A. D. and Murray, C. J. L. (2002) *Global Burden of Disease 2000: Version 2 Methods and Results*, World Health Organization, Geneva

McCullough, N. B. and Eisele, C.W. (1951a) 'Experimental human salmonellosis. I. Pathogenicity of strains of *Salmonella meleagridis* and *Salmonella anatum* obtained from spray dried whole egg', *Journal of Infectious Diseases*, vol 88, no 3, pp278–89

McCullough, N. B. and Eisele, C. W. (1951b) 'Experimental human salmonellosis. III. Pathogenicity of strains of *Salmonella newport*, *Salmonella derby*, and *Salmonella bareilly* obtained from spray dried whole egg', *Journal of Infectious Diseases*, vol 89, no 3, pp209–13

McCullough, N. B. and Eisele, C. W. (1951c) 'Experimental human salmonellosis. IV. Pathogenicity of strains of *Salmonella pullorum* obtained from spray dried whole egg', *Journal of Infectious Diseases*, vol 89, no 3, pp259–65

Mensah, P., Yeboah-Manu, D., Owusu-Darko, K. and Ablordey, A. (2002) 'Street foods in Accra, Ghana: How safe are they?', *Bulletin of the World Health Organization*, vol 80, no 7, pp546–57

Murray, C. J. (1994) 'Quantifying the burden of disease: The technical basis for disability-adjusted life years', *Bulletin of the World Health Organization*, vol 72, no 3, pp429–45

Murray, C. J. L. (1996) 'Rethinking DALYs', in C. J. L. Murray and A. D. Lopez (eds) *The Global Burden of Disease. A Comprehensive Assessment of Mortality and Disability for Diseases, Injuries and Risk Factors in 1990 and Projected to 2020*, Harvard University Press, Cambridge, MA, pp1–97

Murray, C. J. L. and Lopez, A. D. (1996) *The Global Burden of Disease, Volume 1; A Comprehensive Assessment of Mortality and Disability from Diseases, Injuries, and Risk Factors in 1990 and Projected to 2020*, Harvard University Press, Cambridge, MA

Obuobie, E., Keraita, B., Danso, G., Amoah, P., Cofie, O. O., Raschid-Sally, L. and Drechsel, P. (2006) *Irrigated Urban Vegetable Production in Ghana: Characteristics, Benefits and Risks*, IWMI-RUAF-CPWF, Accra, Ghana, www.ruaf.org/node/1046

Prüss-Ustün, A., Bos, R., Gore, F. and Bartram, J. (2008) *Safer Water, Better Health: Costs, Benefits and Sustainability of Interventions to Protect and Promote Health*, World Health Organization, Geneva

Reither, K., Ignatius, R., Weitze, T., Seidu-Korkor, A., Anyidoho, L., Saad, E., Djie-Maletz, A., Ziniel, P., Amoo-Sakyi, F., Danikuu, F., Danour, S., Otchwemah, R. N., Schreier, E., Bienzle, U., Stark, K. and Mockenhaupt, F. P. (2007) 'Acute childhood diarrhoea in northern Ghana: Epidemiological, clinical and microbiological characteristics', *BMC Infectious Diseases*, vol 7, no 104, www.biomedcentral.com/1471-2334/7/104

Robberstad, B., Hemed, Y. and Norheim, O. F. (2007) 'Cost-effectiveness of medical interventions to prevent cardiovascular disease in a sub-Saharan African country – The case of Tanzania', *Cost-Effectiveness and Resource Allocation*, vol 5, no 3, www.resource-allocation.com/content/pdf/1478-7547-5-3.pdf

Seidu, R., Heistad, A., Amoah, P., Drechsel, P., Jenssen, P. D. and Stenström, T.-A. (2008) 'Quantification of the health risks associated with wastewater reuse in Accra, Ghana: A contribution toward local guidelines', *Journal of Water and Health*, vol 6, no 4, pp461–71

Shuval, H., Lampert, Y. and Fattal, B. (1997) 'Development of a risk assessment approach for evaluating wastewater reuse standards for agriculture', *Water Science and Technology*, vol 35, nos 11–12, pp15–20

Voetsch, A. C., Van Gilder, T. J., Angulo, F. J., Farley, M. M., Shallow, S. and Marcus, R. (2004) 'FoodNet estimate of the burden of illness caused by nontyphoidal *Salmonella* infections in the United States', *Clinical Infectious Diseases*, vol 38, pp127–34

Ward, R. L., Bernstein, D. I., Young, E. C., Sherwood, J. R., Knowlton, D. R. and Schiff, G. M. (1986) 'Human rotavirus studies in volunteers: Determination of infectious dose and serological response to infection', *Journal of Infectious Diseases*, vol 154, no 5, pp871–80

WHO (2003) *Making Choices in Health: WHO Guide to Cost-Effectiveness Analysis*, World Health Organization, Geneva

WHO (2006) *Guidelines for the Safe Use of Wastewater, Excreta and Greywater, Volume 2: Wastewater Use in Agriculture*, World Health Organization, Geneva

World Bank (1993) *World Development Report 1993: Investing in Health*, Oxford University Press, New York

Part 4

Wastewater Governance and Adoption of Risk-Reduction Options

14

Challenging Conventional Approaches to Managing Wastewater Use in Agriculture

Frans Huibers, Mark Redwood and Liqa Raschid-Sally

ABSTRACT

In developing countries urban wastewater management often fails to cope with increasing wastewater generation. Financial, technical and institutional limitations force authorities to discharge substantial amounts of untreated or partially treated wastewater into surface waters. Consequently, uncontrolled use of polluted water is increasingly common in the downstream peri-urban areas. Although wastewater use bears a significant risk on human health, such use is also productive and an asset for many. Agricultural use of wastewater is a strong manifestation of the urban–rural connection and transfers a waterborne risk from the wastewater disposal system to the food chain, requiring a paradigm shift in the approaches applied to risk minimization. Conventional models for urban wastewater treatment and management are based on top-down, technically driven approaches that do not, or do not sufficiently, consider the links between the social, economic and health aspects. This situation is understandable from historical and technological points of view, but does not provide innovative solutions to current problems in developing-country cities. A different approach is required, one that rethinks conventional wastewater system design and management. By adopting a systems approach to analysing both the water and food chains, one discovers the interactions of different stakeholders that treat and use (or abuse) water, the impacts on overall productivity and the risks. Governance systems to manage wastewater use in agriculture must incorporate decentralization to accommodate thinking at the bottom layer, encourage stakeholder engagement and provide coordination and policy cohesion for managing risks jointly from both the water and food chains.

INTRODUCTION

In developing countries, population growth, urbanization and economic development result in ever increasing wastewater flows exceeding present capacities of management, treatment and proper handling. Many cities, in developing countries, are growing at unprecedented rates (4–8 per cent annually), outpacing the ability of city managers to cope (Davis, 2006); despite billions invested in improved wastewater management, Ujang and Henze (2006) argue that 95 per cent of wastewater generated enters the environment with no proper treatment.

Worldwide, pollution of surface water close to cities, with impacts extending to downstream agricultural areas, is evident (Raschid-Sally and Jayakody, 2008; Scott et al., 2004). This has resulted in more than 10 per cent of the world's population consuming food that is irrigated with wastewater of varying quality (WHO, 2006). Agricultural use of urban wastewater and polluted water more generally represents a challenge not only because poor water quality has environmental consequences, but also because it is linked directly to the food chain. This situation is likely to persist into the future (see Chapter 1) and will undoubtedly expand to new areas experiencing urban growth. For better health protection, it is imperative to simultaneously address health risks associated with both water pollution and food contamination. In fact, this is our interpretation of how best to apply, in the contexts of developing countries, the 2006 World Health Organization (WHO) Guidelines for the safe use of wastewater in agriculture.

Research compiled by the UN has concluded that the conventional model of collection, treatment and discharge of wastewater often fails due to high costs and low capacity to pay, problems associated with governance and overemphasis on technologically driven processes (UN-Habitat, 2006; Chapter 15 in this volume). Such technology-driven, centralized or decentralized systems aim at quality levels acceptable to protect the natural environment. This implies that developed-country standards are often applied in developing countries whether or not there exists the capacity, both financial and institutional, to manage systems to meet these standards. While the new WHO Guidelines for the safe use of wastewater in agriculture provide the opportunity to tailor standards to local requirements, existing institutional arrangements in developing countries have problems accommodating them. Furthermore, few wastewater-management systems consider agricultural effluent use from the perspective of water and nutrient resource recovery, an essential point when addressing environmental and economic feasibility. Our paper presents and discusses an alternative paradigm to respond to this problem.

We hypothesize that conventional models of wastewater management do not work as they insufficiently take into account the downstream users of wastewater and do not appropriately value the social, economic and health implications of wastewater flows. For this reason, decentralized water services such as closed-loop, source separation and other ecological sanitation techniques may have a better chance of success, because they rely on principles of integration, prevention and resource recovery, rather than treatment and disposal.

It is indicative to note that the Australian Senate has taken a stand that in replacing ageing urban infrastructure, more serious consideration must be given to decentralized forms of service provision particularly linked to water recycling (Stenekes et al., 2006).

Using a water-chain approach (Figure 14.1) based on systems management principles helps to define which upstream and downstream issues are at stake and how they are linked, enabling identification of the way in which responsibilities are distributed to various stakeholders. The purpose of conceptualizing water and wastewater using a systems approach is to allow the succession of events to be addressed, from where water is accessed (the source) through the various uses (and reuses), to where it is disposed of, which is usually the environment. Thus, we contend that such an analytical approach can improve management through allowing users to optimize the ways that the resource should be managed (see below). Such a management strategy seeks not only to improve water quality through sustainable waste treatment, but also responds to user requirements for water and nutrients.

Following a water-chain approach also shows how pollution can affect the food that humans consume. Understanding the parallel food chain along the various contamination pathways that exist from the farm through the various transportation and marketing chains to the consumer would help to facilitate the simultaneous improvement of water quality and food quality (see Chapter 12). Risk reduction through applying the multiple-barrier approach advocated by the WHO implies that interventions could be made partly along the water chain and partly along the food chain in order to achieve cumulative risk reduction. Thus, risk management would apply a combination of safer irrigation and agricultural practices and post-harvest food-safety measures, which require different institutional arrangements to those currently existing in most countries. Safe and acceptable wastewater use would require stakeholder engagement – this has been clearly shown even in developed countries, where stakeholder participation has been known to make or break a project (Keremane and McKay, 2007; Nancarrow et al., 2008; Stenekes et al., 2006; Tsagarakis and Georgantzís, 2003).

Accounting for all of the above, it is argued here that for developing countries a new paradigm for wastewater governance, that accommodates agricultural use, should be based on four fundamental precepts (discussed in subsequent sections of this chapter):

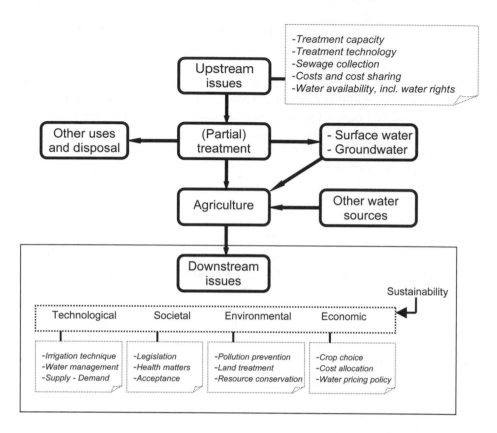

Figure 14.1 *The water chain: conceptual framework showing upstream-downstream links*

Source: Modified from Huibers and Raschid-Sally (2005)

- the use of the (reverse) water-chain approach to design wastewater systems;
- decentralization of wastewater management services and systems;
- policy coherence and coordination for linking sectors, attributes and costs;
- stakeholder involvement going beyond acceptance to involvement in decisions.

To effect this paradigm change, new institutional arrangements, including better coordination and collaboration, will be needed. This requires analysing existing institutions (both formal and informal) for wastewater management and food safety. Since much of the wastewater use takes place within urban and peri-urban areas, a review of the organizations for agriculture and urban planning will be required as well as a clear understanding of the balance of power, gaps, overlaps and ambiguities within all these sectors.

THE REVERSE WATER-CHAIN DESIGN APPROACH

Huibers and van Lier (2005), and Huibers and Raschid-Sally (2005) suggest that a water-chain approach to link upstream and downstream needs and issues is a helpful platform for negotiating and distributing responsibilities of various stakeholders along the chain. Despite problems with existing governance arrangements for wastewater, there is a considerable benefit to linking the use of wastewater to the way it is handled upstream. We further suggest that for sustainability, one has to go beyond simply the wastewater chain and establish the links with the food-contamination chain as these two are intimately linked via agricultural use. In both chains, there is a series of stakeholders that in their actions use the water and influence the quality (positively or negatively) of the water or food product. In order to support decision-making and to develop best management practices, it is useful to understand the links and relationships between stakeholders and the processes they are involved in.

In the conventional wastewater system, design and management are basically top-down. Farmers are passive receivers of polluted water and are often both poorly informed on the composition of the water and left out of decisions and negotiation within the system. They consequently have no say in how the wastewater is handled. The reverse water-chain approach implies that end-users can express their preferences on volumes and quality as they relate to intended use, costs and benefits. This way, wastewater is considered a resource rather than a waste product.

A key element of this approach is flexibility. Centralized approaches are often highly rigid and are designed with little regard to the particular context. Policy frameworks frequently specify end-of-pipe quality requirements, without always considering end use. Flexibility would allow for more local government discretion in standards applied to the use of wastewater for different crops now and those envisaged in the future.

In concept, the water chain resembles a production chain comprising numerous actors. Supply-chain management theories suggest optimizing the management of a production chain by coordinating the actions of the independent actors in a unified whole (Peterson et al., 2001). Supply-chain management has the following characteristics:

- It is a systems approach that views the supply chain as a whole and manages the flow of goods from the supplier to the ultimate customer.
- It stimulates strategic choices of two or more organizations in a production process to join efforts that realize optimal use of resources and converge in generating a product.
- It has a customer focus to create unique and individualized sources of customer value, leading to customer satisfaction.

Peterson et al. (2001) describe the relationships between the different stakeholders of a supply chain and their strategic options. At one end, stakeholders can position themselves as spot market buyers or sellers in which they act independently of other stakeholders within the supply chain. The other end is described as vertical integration where stakeholders recognize a common benefit when they cooperate within the supply chain to deliver a satisfactory good to the end recipient. The continuum moves from a low to a high intensity of coordination and control. Mutual trust is necessary to increase cooperation between agencies when a shared goal is pursued (Mentzer et al., 2001).

Evers et al. (2008) suggest that, when applied to the wastewater generation and effluent use process, these principles allow consideration of the system and the governance requirements from a different perspective. In applying these principles to a case study of peri-urban use of polluted water for agriculture in Hanoi, Vietnam, one concludes that Hanoi typifies the situation in many developing cities where spontaneous use of wastewater takes place within a management system in which each actor acts in a spot market with very few linkages to the other actors (Box 14.1).

Users of an urban wastewater source should be identified in relation to their intended use and conditions should be defined for wastewater supply, such as location, storage facilities and quality assurance. This would, in a supply-chain approach, lead to a negotiation process, which includes contribution to costs by the different stakeholders. In such a system the notion of wastewater swaps can be accommodated more easily, leading to more integrated water management.

An integrated approach also creates new flexibilities, as specific problems possibly can be solved in different ways and/or at different places in the chain, either in technical design or in the envisaged operation of the system (Huibers and van Lier, 2008). At its core, the design process requires the adoption of downstream user perspectives in order to be effective. Incorporating user perspectives in wastewater management matches recent trends in service delivery to enhance the power of service recipients in other domains. For instance, citizen report cards are used in Bangalore, India, to monitor service quality, while participatory budgeting is being used in several cities as a way to manage investments (World Bank, 2004). Such examples only work where there is political will for their adoption.

Moreover, the reverse water-chain approach should be accompanied by appropriate cost-recovery mechanisms. For example, if users are to determine, design and work with local authorities on the appropriate ways to harness the wastewater, the responsible authorities (whether the utility or the local government) must be empowered by the central government to develop ways to capture revenue from those using wastewater and benefiting from these services. Without such an accommodation, user-centric design has little hope of being sustainable.

Box 14.1 Hanoi peri-urban use of
WASTEWATER FOR AGRICULTURE

Hanoi is the capital and second largest city of Vietnam, with a population of over 3 million. An important driving force behind this urbanization process was the reopening of Vietnam to the world economy in the late 1980s. This reform, locally referred to as '*doi moi*', reduced the role of the state and opened up the Vietnamese economy to foreign capital. However, the state still plays a key role through a four-level governmental structure (state, municipal, district and communal). Each level has its own 'people's committee'. Institutions at lower levels have to refer their problems to higher levels which then give decisions downwards for implementation. This is a time-consuming process. Luan and Minh (2005) note that the system lacks synchronized coordination between, on the one hand, agencies that make decisions (higher level departments) and, on the other, agencies that are responsible for implementation (lower level departments). There is also a spatial separation on governance responsibilities of different departments in the so-called urban districts and the peri-urban districts of Hanoi municipality respectively. In addition, responsibilities concerning the water and food chains are divided among different departments (Evers, 2006).

Most urban residents of Hanoi have a flush toilet with a connection to the sewerage system where wastewater drains into water bodies within and around the city. A minority has functioning septic tanks from which the effluent (septic) is discharged into sewer lines and semi-open drainage canals. There is no other treatment of wastewater; therefore Hanoi has serious pollution of its ponds, lakes and rivers that serve agriculture. With regard to wastewater management, responsibilities are scattered among different departments: no department is fully responsible for urban wastewater management (see also Raschid-Sally et al., 2004).

Though the physical reality is that agriculture and urban wastewater are linked, the institutional reality is that they are strictly separated. Agriculture and irrigation officials acknowledge the existence of a physical wastewater chain when they are confronted with it. However, when asked directly if wastewater is used for irrigation most of them say no. This is understandable as in their view the river is the source of irrigation water. That this river water is in fact often diluted wastewater is usually not realized or fitting their institutional accountability. Department officials in Hanoi hardly knew about the policies and responsibilities of other departments that are recognized as stakeholders of urban wastewater management and agriculture (Luan and Minh, 2005). Farmers were also hardly able to name the responsible authorities of the urban wastewater chain.

DECENTRALIZATION OF WASTEWATER SERVICE PROVISION

Much of the argument in favour of decentralization in the management of wastewater stems from the evidence that:

- Centralized systems in developing cities are prone to mismanagement and malfunctioning, leading to eventual breakdown.

- Centralized conveyance and treatment are very expensive (UN-Habitat, 2006; World Bank, 2004).
- It is very difficult to provide adequate sanitation infrastructure and administrative coverage to peri-urban areas of developing cities due to their rapid expansion (UN-Habitat, 2006).

Above and beyond these arguments, a policy to maximize agricultural use of wastewater would further favour decentralized systems. While in a conventional design of a wastewater treatment plant its location is based on its (topographical) position vis-à-vis the wastewater producers (generally the lowest possible position is chosen to guarantee maximum gravitational inflow), its optimal location in an effluent use perspective would be at a higher level to maximize the irrigation command area downstream of the treatment plant. It can consequently be expected that optimum use of irrigable area would lead to the decision to site decentralized systems. This would also allow selection of locations best suited to control the wastewater inflow qualities and to exclude toxic-waste streams in the sewerage.

Small towns and peri-urban areas are often excluded from centralized services due to decreasing cost-efficiency and reasons of administrative/fiscal boundary. At the same time they are sufficiently 'rural' to accommodate or support agricultural activities. It is here that decentralized service provision that allows for water and nutrient resource recovery can have the maximum impact.

There have been numerous pilot efforts to decentralize the physical infrastructure for wastewater, often with the objective of increasing water recovery (Bakir, 2001; Brooks, 2002; Choguill, 1999). Collective biological treatment systems, household wastewater treatment, constructed wetlands and even larger systems such as waste stabilization ponds are low-tech solutions that offer promise, both from the standpoint of improved water quality and, eventually, reduced health risks for food. In relative terms, these systems are quite simple in design and function; as a result they present operational, financial and managerial advantages.

The 1990s saw a rapid increase in proponents of decentralization of management and operational responsibility and power to lower-level authorities. The main consideration was to increase the responsiveness of these authorities and 'democratize' governance by increasing public participation (Tannerfeldt and Ljung, 2006). A well planned and executed decentralization policy can provide a less expensive and better service, and improve water quality in the long term. There is broad agreement that decentralization is good practice (e.g. Bahri, 1999; Coombes and Kuczera, 2003; Maher, 2003). Argentina and Chile have had qualified successes by delegating some operations and management to user associations and the private sector. In Mexico, irrigation systems managed by user associations have increased cost recovery from 30 per cent to 80 per cent (Litvack and Seddon, 1999). In Ghana, the Community Water and Sanitation Project allows communities to own and operate their own water and sanitation systems. According to the agency responsible for the project, 78 per cent of the target groups respond that their water services have improved (Agodzo and Huibers, 2002) while most decentralised wastewater treatment facilities fell into disrepair. There are also other examples where decentralization of service provision has not been accompanied by appropriate capacity-building, budgeting or fiscal reforms that allow for local tariff setting and tax revenue collection (Tannerfeldt and Ljung, 2006).

There is often confusion about who is responsible and who pays for those services (World Bank, 2004). In some cases, municipal authorities have been delegated responsibility without the capacity to manage or legal ability to generate revenue. This has often led to a collapse in trust between local authorities and their constituents and a lack of accountability. One way to mitigate this problem is to enhance citizen engagement in decision-making in the context of decentralization (Pahl-Wostl, 2005). For instance, participatory budgeting, which is being practised in a growing number of cities, allows for a level of citizen decision-making over service delivery. Other solutions can be found in better policy coordination between the different levels of government at national, state and local levels.

POLICY COHERENCE AND COORDINATION FOR LINKING SECTORS, ATTRIBUTES AND COSTS

Given these broad challenges, for user-centric wastewater management to be effective a necessary first step is to provide the appropriate legal backing for local governments to manage services such as wastewater provision. This would replace the driving force of current policy (based on health fears) with a more rational approach to how risks can be minimized and wastewater user benefits amplified. By negotiating the conditions of wastewater use, a change is possible in how project financing and costs are allocated.

Segregated budgets that allocate financing for specific projects are an important tool as opposed to trying to fund multiple activities with a common pool of funding (the latter option being open to political manipulation and ad hoc spending). Such an arrangement would allow utilities to collect fees from different polluters and end-users for the specific purpose of covering costs for services provided. The 'polluter pays' principle is widely accepted in most OECD countries, for example in Brussels, where 30 per cent of the costs of services are paid for through pollution charges associated with waste (OECD, 1998). Mexico charges for wastewater discharge permits that are effective in raising revenue to cover service costs (Bruns et al., 2005). Other mechanisms, such as the widely used increasing block tariff, encourage progressive financing where there are different cost-recovery mechanisms for high-income domestic households producing large amounts of wastewater versus low-income, or for large-scale industry versus small-scale commercial. In Tunisia, reclaimed water is currently used on 8000ha to irrigate vineyards, citrus and other fruit trees (olives, peaches, pears, apples and pomegranates), fodder crops (alfalfa, sorghum and berseem) and cereals. The regulations allow the use of secondary treated effluent for specific crops and the regional agricultural departments supervise the water reuse decree and collection of charges. Farmers pay about $0.01 per m^3 for the reclaimed water irrigation. In Drarga, Morocco, a public participation programme led to the development of an institutional partnership between the local water-management stakeholders, the urban water users and the farmers' water-user group (USEPA/USAID, 2004). To increase sustainability of the new facilities, an additional fee for domestic water supply was levied and other cost-recovery mechanisms were under consideration.

Another challenge for user-centred wastewater management is that due to its sensitive nature and its status as a public good, water is most often legislated at the national level in terms of planning and rights, while municipal and public utilities are left to operate infrastructure services and carry out local planning. Two governance prerequisites are needed if the 2006 WHO Guidelines are to be implemented effectively. First is the immediate need to coordinate vertically between levels of government and horizontally across sectors, and second to link water quality with food quality.

Many national governments have created a multitude of institutions with different roles and responsibilities related to water and they often lack effective coordination (UN-Habitat, 2006). At the national level, ministries responsible for water, agriculture, environment, natural resources, urban development and health usually have some responsibility for water. National agencies (with varying degrees of separation from the government) will sometimes be charged with coordinating legislation, planning and management of the resource. To complicate things further, the administration of basic services is often divided amongst three levels of government: national, state (or provincial) and local (or municipal). An independent regulatory authority is often charged with ensuring appropriate pricing and compliance with environmental standards. This complex chain of actors might work well when properly funded and with access to the necessary expertise; however, in practice these conditions are rarely met. In such situations a first-level solution would be to set up a coordination body amongst responsible institutions which links across levels and sectors (agriculture, public health, urban water and sanitation, environment, economy, etc.).

Historically, the agriculture and sanitation sectors were always separate. This reflects the dichotomy between urban (wastewater disposal) and rural (agriculture) practices and management domains. In the new paradigm, governance for drinking water and sanitation must better coordinate with governance for agriculture; it is imperative to understand what incentives are needed for this partnership to work. As an example, the urban–rural link can also be epitomized in wastewater swaps, where water diverted from agriculture for urban use is returned to agriculture as wastewater (Scott et al., 2007). Such a system requires an appropriate legal and management framework that would facilitate negotiation between different user groups.

Integrated approaches are sometimes discouraged because regulatory responsibility for water management can be contradictory or split across different agencies. These agencies sometimes even work at cross-purposes from one another. With the multiple-barrier approach advocated by the WHO (2006) for wastewater use in agriculture, there is the further need to establish a bridge between water quality and food safety. Two different sets of institutions are thus involved. Water quality may be the prerogative of the environmental authority or the water authority or even sometimes the irrigation authority. Food quality is the responsibility of the public-health authorities, who may not necessarily be reporting to the ministry of health but rather to a local authority if there has been devolution of power.

At the national level there is a need for ministries and agencies responsible for agriculture, urban development, water, health and environment to accept that wastewater and pollution management require a cross-sectoral approach. However, it is also critical that vertical cohesion between national, state and municipal levels of governance be developed.

STAKEHOLDER INVOLVEMENT

The pre-existing conditions for a change in paradigm are that a large and diffuse group of stakeholders is involved, and that no single organization or person has the capacity to implement and upscale the 'technology' required for sustainable wastewater use. The stakeholders differ, depending on whether wastewater use is spontaneous or planned, but involve in general: water users, farmers, consumers (of food grown with wastewater), national and local level authorities (responsible for agriculture, irrigation, sanitation, public health and environment), local level planning authorities where the technology will be put in place and various other actors with a stake, depending on the context of adoption.

Increasing recognition of the need for better stakeholder engagement requires that water service providers (water providers, wastewater agencies, irrigation agencies) consider participatory planning, shifting the attention from public acceptance of predetermined technological options towards ways in which that public participation can be successfully institutionalized. Participatory institutions encourage the development of shared values amongst diverse stakeholder groups and lead to innovative solutions for dealing with water management (see Chapter 18).

Examples of efforts to close the accountability gap between citizens and those that make policy are plentiful, with some notable successes. In Porto Alegre, Brazil, participatory budgets have allowed citizens to directly influence spending on services (World Bank, 2004). Such direct influence over how money is spent increases accountability and builds trust between local governments and their citizens. In Ghana, a new initiative by the World Bank involves civil society umbrella organizations in monitoring water and sanitation projects. Specifically the National Coalition of NGOs in Waste Management (NACONWAM) will monitor the Second Urban Environmental Sanitation Project, and the Coalition of NGOs in Water and Sanitation (CONIWAS) will monitor the Urban Water Project. This can be seen as a major step in institutionalizing participation.

DISCUSSION

Surmounting the governance challenges that have so far impeded the effective devolution of wastewater management is a tall order. It will require political will on the part of elected officials and recognition of the inherent value of wastewater as a resource. Not least, it will require serious attention to accountability and ensuring that those using wastewater services are represented in the planning and design phases of solutions. The integration of users in the design and management of wastewater collection, treatment and use is the most effective way to improve accountability of designers and planners. Furthermore, with direct user engagement, planners and engineers would have the information required to develop systems that are far more responsive than current ones.

Good governance of wastewater requires stakeholder engagement at and across all the levels of the wastewater chain, although in practice this can be difficult. Municipalities are often in charge of basic service provision and play an operational role, while water and agriculture often fall under the jurisdiction of the state and various ministries. Consistently, it is the ministry of health that demonstrates the most reluctance to accept 'progressive' standards seeing any relaxation from international guidelines as substandard. This also partly explains the reluctance of national governments to delegate the appropriate authority to lower levels. Given these institutional barriers and the list of failed investments in conventional sanitation, the WHO (2006) suggested global health-based targets but gives countries flexibility in achieving them according to their possibilities and constraints using a step-wise approach (see Chapter 2). This opens the doors for central governments to set clear intermediate goals in order for local solutions to be implemented.

The advantage of using the combined water- and food-chain approach to manage risk is therefore consistent with the 2006 revision to the WHO Guidelines, which allows for progressive improvements in sanitation and risk management in the absence of full treatment. The model of decentralized systems, which presents its own set of challenges particularly in the promise to democratize service delivery, is nevertheless proving itself to be a useful solution in an increasing range of conditions. It should be at the centre of the new paradigm to manage risks to health associated with wastewater use.

CONCLUSIONS

The transfer of purely waterborne risks from the wastewater disposal system to the food chain through the use of wastewater in agriculture requires a paradigm shift in how we approach risk. Furthermore, it requires a fundamental rethinking of which viable governance mechanisms can be used to improve risk assessment and management approaches.

The combined water- and food-chain approach that we advocate needs to be accompanied by effective decentralization of financial and operational control as well as technical planning and management. Local governance reform, aid that stipulates clear guidelines associated with its expenditure and budgetary reform that requires increased stakeholder engagement will be needed. Municipalities could thus be seen as enablers and facilitators and not only as implementers.

A further implication is the strong urban–rural linkage that such use establishes, which can be addressed through the application of supply-chain management theories which try to optimize the management of a production chain by coordinating the actions of the independent actors into a unified whole. It follows that policy coherence among different sectors and different levels of government would be a central requirement for better wastewater management.

Planners can use the reverse water-chain approach to identify the intended uses of wastewater followed by better understanding of the needs, opportunities and constraints they face, leading to better engagement of users in improved wastewater management. Recognizing users and the role that they can play in monitoring for effective service delivery and financial accountability paves the way for flexible yet durable institutional frameworks.

REFERENCES

Agodzo, S. and F. P. Huibers (2002) 'Some estimates of wastewater irrigation potential in urban Ghana', unpublished paper presented at the Hyderabad Experts Meeting on Wastewater Use in Agriculture, Hyderabad, India, November 2002

Bahri, A. (1999) 'Agricultural reuse of wastewater and global water management', *Water Science and Technology*, vol 40, nos 4–5, pp339–46

Bakir, H. A. (2001) 'Sustainable wastewater management for small communities in the Middle East and North Africa', *Journal of Environmental Management*, vol 61, no 4, pp319–28

Brooks, D. B. (2002) *Water: Local-Level Management*, IDRC Books, Ottawa

Bruns, B., Ringler, R. C. and Meinzen-Dick, R. S. (2005) *Water Rights Reform*, International Food Policy Research Institute, Washington, DC

Choguill, C. (1999) 'Community infrastructure for low-income cities: The potential for progressive improvement', *Habitat International*, vol 23, no 2, pp289–301

Coombes, P. J. and Kuczera, G. (2003) 'Integrated urban water cycle management:

Moving towards systems understanding', 2nd National Conference on Water Sensitive Urban Design, Brisbane, 2–4 September 2002

Davis, M. (2006) *Planet of Slums*, Verso Books, London, p228

Evers, J. G. (2006) 'Everybody's business is nobody's business: A study on the use of wastewater in (peri-)urban irrigated agriculture in Hanoi, Vietnam', unpublished MSc thesis, Irrigation and Water Engineering Group, Environmental Policy Group, Wageningen University, Wageningen, The Netherlands

Evers, J. G., Huibers, F. P. and van Vliet, B. J. M. (2008) 'Institutional aspects of integrating irrigation into urban wastewater management: The case of Hanoi', *Irrigation and Drainage*, 29 December 2008, published online, doi: 10.1002/ird.466

Huibers, F. P. and Raschid-Sally, L. (2005) 'Design in domestic wastewater irrigation', *Irrigation and Drainage*, vol 54, no S1, ppS113–S118

Huibers F. P. and van Lier, J. B. (2005) 'Use of wastewater in agriculture: The water chain approach', *Irrigation and Drainage*, vol 54, no S1, ppS3–S10

Huibers F. P. and van Lier, J. B. (2008) 'Design of irrigation systems for the use of treated domestic wastewater', *Proceedings International Commission on Irrigation and Drainage, 20th Congress on Irrigation and Drainage, Participatory Integrated Water Resources Management: From Concepts to Actions, Lahore, 13–18 October, 2008*, Wageningen University, Wageningen, The Netherlands, pp112–14

Keremane, G. B. and McKay, J. (2007) 'Successful wastewater reuse scheme and sustainable development: A case study in Adelaide', *Water and Environment Journal*, vol 21, pp83–91

Litvack, J. and Seddon, J. (1999) *Decentralization Briefing Notes*, World Bank Institute (WBI) Working Papers, World Bank, Washington, DC

Luan T. D. and Minh, N. H. (2005) 'Institutional aspects of agriculture management in Hanoi peri-urban area', SEARUSYN, EU 5th Framework INCO2 funded research project

Maher, M. (2003) 'Sustainable water cycle design for urban areas', *Water Science and Technology*, vol 47, nos 7–8, pp25–31

Mentzer, J. T., DeWitt, W., Keebler, J. S., Soonhong, M., Nix, N. W., Smith, C. D. and Zacharia, Z. G. (2001) 'Defining supplychain management', *Journal of Business Logistics*, vol 22, no 2, p18

Nancarrow, B. E., Leviston, Z., Po, M., Porter, N. B. and Tucker, D. I. (2008) 'What drives communities' decisions and behaviours in the reuse of wastewater', *Water Science and Technology*, vol 57, no 4, pp485–92

OECD (1998) *Environmental Performance Reviews*, OECD Publishing, Paris

Pahl-Wostl, C. (2005) 'Information, public empowerment, and the management of urban watersheds', *Environment Modelling and Software*, vol 20, pp457–67

Peterson, H. C., Wysocki, A. and Harsh, S. B. (2001) 'Strategic choice along the vertical coordination continuum', *International Food and Agribusiness Management Review*, vol 4, pp149–66

Raschid-Sally, L., Doan, D. T. and Abayawardana, S. (2004) 'National assessments on wastewater use in agriculture and an emerging typology: The Vietnam case study', in C. A. Scott, N. I. Faruqui and L. Raschid-Sally (eds) *Wastewater Use in Irrigated Agriculture. Confronting the Livelihood and Environmental Realities*, CABI Publishing, Wallingford, UK, p206

Raschid-Sally, L. and Jayakody, P. (2008) 'Drivers and characteristics of wastewater agriculture in developing countries: Results from a global assessment, Colombo, Sri Lanka', *IWMI Research Report 127*, International Water Management Institute, Colombo

Scott, C. A., Faruqui, N. I. and Raschid-Sally, L. (eds) (2004) *Wastewater Use in Irrigated Agriculture: Confronting the Livelihood and Environmental Realities*, CABI Publishing, Wallingford, UK

Scott, C. A., Flores-López, F. and Gastélum, J. R. (2007) 'Appropriation of Río San Juan water by Monterrey city, Mexico: Implications for agriculture and basin water sharing', in 'Transfer of water from irrigation to urban uses: Lessons from case studies', special issue, *Paddy and Water Environment*, vol 5, no 4, pp253–62

Serageldin, I. (1994) *Water Supply, Sanitation and Environmental Sustainability: The Financing Challenge*, World Bank, Washington, DC

Stenekes, N., Colebatch, H. K., Waite, T. D. and Ashbolt, N. J. (2006) 'Risk and governance in water recycling public acceptance revisited', *Science, Technology and Human Values*, vol 31, no 2, pp107–34

Tannerfeldt, G. and Ljung, P. (2006) *More Urban, Less Poor*, Earthscan, London

Tsagarakis, K. P. and Georgantzís, N. (2003) 'The role of information on farmers' willingness to use recycled water for irrigation', *Water Science and Technology: Water Supply*, vol 3, no 4, pp105–13

Ujang, Z. and Henze, M. (eds) (2006) *Municipal Wastewater Management in Developing Countries. Principles and Engineering*, IWA Publishing, London, p352

UN-Habitat (2006) *Meeting Development Goals in Small Urban Centres: Water and Sanitation in the World's Cities, 2006*, United Nations Human Settlements Programme, Nairobi

USEPA/USAID (2004) *Guideline for Water Reuse*, US Environmental Protection Agency and US Agency for International Development, Washington, DC

WHO (2006) *Guidelines for the Safe Use of Wastewater, Excreta and Greywater*, vols 1–4, World Health Organization, Geneva

World Bank (2004) *World Development Report 2004: Making Services Work for Poor People*, World Bank, Washington, DC

15

Designing Reuse-Oriented Sanitation Infrastructure: The Design for Service Planning Approach

Ashley Murray and Chris Buckley

In any field of human endeavour, policy-makers and practitioners are accustomed by training and experience to thinking within familiar sets of parameters, and while aware of the shortcomings associated with these parameters, find it difficult to step outside them. In principle, radical new thinking is always desired but is rarely produced. When produced, it often meets with resistance even from those who sought it simply because it steps outside those parameters – 'outside the box' – of preset assumptions, experience and capacity. (SANDEC, 2000, p2)

ABSTRACT

The reuse or utilization of wastewater, faecal sludge and its embodied resources is widely acknowledged in the field of sanitation as a key component of complete sanitation. Reuse, for agriculture and other applications, is conventionally considered a means of mitigating water shortage or abating water pollution. We contend that reuse-oriented sanitation can also be leveraged to improve the long-term efficacy of a treatment scheme by providing tangible and quantifiable incentives for sound operation and maintenance that exceed those associated with running a disposal facility. The standards that need to be met for agricultural reuse are different from those required for discharge to the aquatic environment. This difference requires a change in the design philosophy and can lead to cost savings in the type of treatment process, the energy demand and the skills needed for operation. So, rather than a more complex system, wastewater treatment designed for agricultural reuse can result in a more appropriate plant for developing countries striving to enhance access to improved sanitation.

To facilitate a culture of designing site-specific and reuse-oriented systems from the outset of the planning process, this chapter introduces a five-step planning tool, Design for Service (DFS). DFS defines wastewater as a resource and choices about its reuse inform the infrastructure design including site and technology selection, and plant scale. We highlight reuse schemes at various stages of implementation in South Africa to exemplify difficulties faced in the absence of accessible planning frameworks. To demonstrate how DFS can be used for rehabilitating schemes that have fallen into disrepair and for the design of new reuse-oriented sanitation systems, we describe projects that are currently underway in Ghana and China, respectively.

INTRODUCTION

The productive use of wastewater, faecal sludge and its embodied resources is increasingly considered integral to comprehensive sanitation, the primary goals of which are to protect public health and the environment (IWA Sanitation 21 Task Force, 2007; UN Millennium Project, 2005). In many regions of the world, reuse is driven by scarcity, where a shortage of water and landfill space incites non-disposal end-use options. In other cases, reuse or capture of embodied resources is practised more for environmental reasons. For example, sludge may be applied to farmland to replace or complement the use of chemical fertilizers, or anaerobic digestion and capture of biogas may be employed to reduce demand for non-renewable energy sources at a treatment plant. While these aforementioned drivers of reuse are not only rational but valid, in our view, reuse should not only be conceived as an option that comes on the heels of wastewater treatment, but as a means of achieving the primary goals of comprehensive sanitation.

Conventional approaches to sanitation and waste disposal see wastewater and faecal sludge as environmental and public-health problems; thus, management solutions comprise costly means of preparing them for unproductive disposal – a fate that will occur regardless of what, if any, treatment they receive. It is no wonder that resource-constrained governments seldom rank sanitation high on their agendas (Stockholm International Water Institute et al., 2008). However, as Jiménez et al. have clearly articulated in Chapter 8, the consequences of inadequate sanitation are dire. In the face of the daunting task of improving global access to improved sanitation, particularly with the legacy and ongoing record of failed waste-disposal schemes, reuse has potential to be leveraged to stimulate robust sanitation solutions that reliably protect public health and the environment.

A reuse-oriented approach effectively shifts the goal of sanitation from being solely the safe disposal of waste to maximizing the extent to which embodied resources are safely captured and allocated. Recognizing wastewater and faecal sludge as resources is the first step towards reuse-oriented sanitation, but implementing this philosophy remains a challenge, as most engineers and planners have been trained to 'design for disposal'. That is, they are trained to design schemes that convey sewage to a centralized treatment plant – often as far from human settlements as land availability permits – where it undergoes mechanical, biological and sometimes chemical purification before discharge to an ocean outfall or surface water. To the extent that reuse is incorporated into a treatment scheme, it is often an afterthought in the planning process. While there are examples of planned reuse occurring around the world, designing for reuse at the outset of a waste-management planning process is often seen as a burden and unnecessary complication from both technical and institutional perspectives (Bahri, 1999; Jenkins and Sugden, 2006; Lazarova et al., 2001). When reuse projects fail it is often because they were conceived without due consideration of the local institutions, market demand and supply chains necessary for them to thrive; planning for reuse from the outset can make the system more sustainable.

Another drawback of conventional waste-disposal schemes is that they represent an enormous financial and skills burden, hence the absence or failure of adequate sanitation in many developing cities (UN Millennium Project, 2005). In addition, popular technologies such as activated sludge have large environmental externalities associated with the energy used to treat the wastewater and with the solids produced, which themselves must then be treated and disposed of. When designing a treatment scheme for reuse in agriculture, on the other hand, it becomes desirable to maintain the embodied nutrients in the water, a factor that can significantly reduce the capital and operational costs of a treatment system in comparison to those required for direct discharge to the aquatic environment.

This chapter takes the position that treatment schemes designed for reuse are more environmentally and economically sustainable as a result of resource recovery. Reuse-oriented waste-management systems are able to deliver the public and environmental health benefits associated with adequate sanitation, while also contributing productively to the local economy and livelihoods. To that end, the chapter endeavours to equip the reader (i.e. engineer, planner, local stakeholder) with a systematic means of implementing sanitation schemes that utilize the resources embodied in waste in ways that are optimized for the local context.

Design for Service is a five-step planning approach for rehabilitating or designing new schemes for reuse, which is intended to facilitate a shift from the design-for-disposal to design-for-reuse paradigm. We utilize case studies from South Africa to show the types of complications faced by projects that retrospectively incorporate reuse and to argue that these difficulties are exacerbated by the lack of planning tools for reuse-oriented sanitation design. We contend that DFS can be used to foster a coherent and deliberate decision-making process, and demonstrate through cases in Ghana and China how one can apply the tool in the context of rehabilitating existing wastewater treatment plants (WWTPs) and designing new ones.

CHALLENGES ENCOUNTERED IN REUSE-ORIENTED SANITATION PLANNING

We use three examples of initiatives to implement reuse-oriented sanitation schemes in the eThekwini Municipality, South Africa, to demonstrate the challenges associated with designing for retrospective reuse in the absence of systematic planning approaches. Like many regions of the developing world where population growth has outpaced deliberate planning processes, eThekwini finds itself with a diverse array of sanitation systems to manage. To be certain, the eThekwini Municipality has a very progressive approach to sanitation both in terms of the technologies that the authorities have implemented (e.g. urine-diverting toilets) and their pursuit of productive end uses for locally produced faecal sludge. Thus, we consider projects that have achieved varying degrees of success to show that even where local decision-makers are motivated to implement reuse-oriented sanitation, practitioners are not equipped with the planning tools to help ensure successful project outcomes.

The first case concerns the emptying of 60,000 ventilated improved pit latrines (VIPs) and the efforts underway to identify an effective means of disposing of or utilizing the faecal sludge. The pits must be emptied every five years and the costs of doing so can be very high, an economic burden that is borne by the municipality (Bhagwan et al., 2008; Gounden et al., 2006). Action-based research best characterizes the municipality's approach to adequate disposal or utilization. In more sparsely populated areas, authorities have arrived at a policy of burying the pit contents on site. However, in dense settlements there is insufficient land for burial and the sludge must be moved off site. Upon determining that discharge into the sewer networks (when available in the vicinity) was too disruptive to the wastewater treatment plants, the municipality has gone on to experiment with several other disposal routes, including trials using chemical or bio-additives to enhance the degradation of the pit contents, mixing with lime and limited discharge in a domestic landfill (Couderc et al., 2008; Foxon et al., 2009). The most feasible method to date appears to be deep trenching with trees being planted in the trenches. Trials are currently in progress to assess the risk of groundwater pollution, the ability of different types of trees and plants to harvest nutrients from the VIP sludge, plant growth rates and pathogen die-off rates (including that of *Ascaris*). The whole pit emptying and disposal process has been designed to create jobs, employing teams from within the served communities, and most of the cost to the municipality for the emptying of the pits is recycled within the user community.

On the one hand, it is encouraging that local authorities are invested in finding a sound alternative to the indiscriminate disposal of the VIP contents. On the other hand, a systematic planning procedure for designing locally tailored reuse schemes would improve the coherence of the design process; it would also provide a protocol for including a broader set of local stakeholders in this process. Currently, decisions about faecal sludge end use in eThekwini are made independently of the region's larger planning agenda and vice versa. For example, there is a parallel city-wide initiative underway to promote woodlots on vacant land to provide livelihoods for local people. Some of the intended uses of the trees include paper-making, fuel, input into medicinal and natural products, and orchards. Ideally, these woodlots would be co-designed for faecal sludge land application and the ultimate end-users of the faecal sludge would be involved in those decisions as primary woodlot stakeholders. However, there is a lack of precedent for such integrated planning and only after the woodlots have been implemented and proven successful without faecal sludge will the possibility of applying the faecal sludge to these trees be explored.

The second case study involves wastewater from a sewered area in Mnini, a district of the eThekwini Municipality, which was treated in a pond system prior to discharge to the Ngane River. The degree of treatment was insufficient, resulting in the degradation of the natural ecology with negative impacts on the river's users. In 2002, two proposals were considered, including one to use the outflow from the ponds for irrigation. By January 2003, an irrigation system was designed by a consultant and was installed. A total of 10,000 banana plants were purchased and 75 per cent had been planted by 2005 on 2ha of land. Mango plantations are planned for over 2ha and two plots (0.6ha in total but extendable to 2ha) have been prepared for vegetables and cash crops. Despite the technical viability of this reuse project, the system has never been commissioned due to institutional barriers. For example, the irrigation system had been installed prior to obtaining permission from all the role-players and stakeholders. The drivers of the reuse project did not get permission from the local traditional leader to use the land; they did not get permission from local households to install an irrigation system and utilize the land for agriculture; they did not get permission from the Department of Agriculture to break virgin ground; and they did not secure the necessary permits from the Department of Trade and Industry or the Department of Water Affairs and Forestry.

Though well intentioned, the ad hoc and top-down procedure of designing and implementing the Mnini reuse scheme is arguably responsible for its failure. Mnini is another testament to the need for a systematic planning approach that guides practitioners through a process of asking the appropriate questions and engaging the appropriate stakeholders – both institutional and individual – to avert failed outcomes. Beyond being technically feasible, a reuse scheme must also be socially, economically and institutionally robust if it is to be sustained, not to mention if it is to incentivize appropriate operation and maintenance of the sanitation scheme itself. The complexity and delays that these additional dimensions add to the planning process is enough to deter most practitioners from designing for reuse at the outset of a sanitation project. Our third case study is an example of exactly this tendency.

Because of the cost and difficulties associated with the servicing of the VIPs already described, the eThekwini Municipality has opted to install dual vault urine-diverting (UD) toilets in the rural areas where there is at least 250m^2 of empty land available for sole use by the householder. The introduction of this sanitation option to the previously unserved includes the provision of a free toilet, free water supply (9kl/household/month) and hygiene education; the householder is responsible for the maintenance of the system (Gounden et al., 2006). Currently, the reuse of the faecal solids and urine is not officially encouraged (Mnkeni and Austin, 2009). It was thought that the introduction of urine diversion is sufficiently different from normal practice that simultaneously incorporating reuse of the urine and solids would distract too much from the goals of improving sanitation and preventing open defecation. It was also considered by the municipality that this sanitation system would be more sustainable than any of the other choices (Flores et al., 2009).

One problem that has emerged since dissemination began is a social stigma attached to the use of UD toilets at the interface of a sewered area and a UD-toilet-serviced area. From the perspective of the rural householders, their UD toilets serve the same single purpose as the waterborne toilets connected to the sewer network: containment of human waste. However, UD toilets are almost unilaterally perceived by users as less modern and of lower status than the waterborne equivalent. The social reluctance to accept UD toilets could have been eased had profitable and productive reuse been incorporated into the project from the start. Let us work through a thought exercise.

What if instead of disseminating UD toilets in the name of sanitation, the effort was alternatively promoted to create new earning opportunities for rural households? With this conceptualization, improved sanitation would be an outcome of the project but not the ultimate goal, and UD toilets would be a means for households to profitably exploit the resource value of human waste. Introducing the UD toilets as new and improved sanitation inevitably sets the technology up for comparison to every other sanitation technology in the vicinity – leading, often, to the negative perceptions described above. Conversely, if economic incentives were used as the centrepiece of the project (e.g. a scheme could be implemented that enables households to sell urine concentrate for phosphate recovery), UD toilets may not be perceived by households as inferior, but as completely different systems with different purposes. The importance of harnessing the economic and agricultural benefits of reuse-oriented sanitation on a large scale has recently gained attention as a key element of simultaneously improving food security and access to adequate sanitation (Bonzi, 2008; World Agroforestry Centre, 2008). Again, taking an end-use and profit-oriented approach to what is traditionally the overt goal of improving hygiene and sanitation requires a shift in the mindset and planning strategies of practitioners. The concept must also be effectively and convincingly communicated to end-users and institutional stakeholders.

The eThekwini Municipality is a leading innovator of sustainable sanitation. Their aggressive search for solutions is a necessary response to the health and environmental problems that have emerged from the vast number of unserved communities. However, from the cases discussed here, we have identified three key issues that an effective planning tool could and must address in order to promote a culture of reuse-oriented sanitation in other regions of the world, and to ease the implementation of reuse in regions where it is already on the agenda. A useful planning framework will:

- foster a process for systematically considering and eliminating an exhaustive list of reuse options as rapidly and efficiently as possible as a coordinated effort among all agencies potentially involved in the reuse project;
- foster an inclusive planning process where outcomes are tailored to the end-users of the waste and treatment by-products, and acceptable to all other stakeholders;
- be accessible to practitioners and quell reluctance to incorporate reuse at the outset of a sanitation project.

THE DFS FRAMEWORK

In light of the illustrative case examples just presented, we introduce DFS to facilitate a coherent and deliberate decision-making process that fosters a culture of designing locally optimized reuse-oriented sanitation systems. DFS is an iterative framework (see Figure 15.1) that consists of the following five steps:

1 Generation of a list of all of the potential 'services' (e.g. irrigation, fertilizer, energy-generation) that wastewater, faecal sludge and treatment by-products can provide.
2 Assessment of the demand for those services in and around the city of interest.
3 Assessment of the business-as-usual performance of the provision of those services according to economic, social and environmental indicators.
4 Design of sanitation infrastructure for the provision of that service where it can have the greatest marginal impact.
5 Assessment of the intrinsic environmental and cost characteristics of the technology options available for rendering the wastewater/faecal sludge/treatment by-products suitable for the service of choice.

The last two steps include a life-cycle analysis (LCA) to quantify possible trade-offs among treatment options.

A unique feature of DFS is its grounding in the user-centred design philosophy (Norman, 1990), where sewage and sludge are conceptualized as a product and attention to the needs and limitations of its end-user(s) drives the design of the handling scheme. If reuse is to incentivize and motivate robust sanitation, wastewater and faecal sludge handling schemes must respond to local market demand for the embodied resources, and be sensitive to social norms surrounding their use.

The intended reuses of sewage and its embodied resources inform technology selection, site selection and scale, such that the scheme is tailored to the needs of the end-user while also meeting the needs of households and other stakeholders. To that end, DFS contains many of the characteristics that the sanitation community has deemed critical for a useful sanitation planning tool: it is technology-neutral, it fosters inclusion of multiple stakeholders in the city (e.g. households, entrepreneurs, government officials) and it is demand-driven (IWA, 2008; IWA Sanitation 21 Task Force, 2007; SuSanA, 2008).

Application of DFS for rehabilitation of sanitation schemes: Ghana case study

Though it is ideal to design treatment plants for reuse at the outset of the planning process, DFS can be used for retrofitting existing plants for reuse and for rehabilitating facilities that have fallen into disrepair. One drawback of retrofitting an

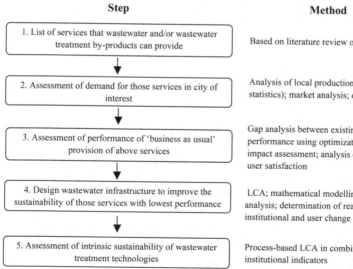

Figure 15.1 *Schematic of Design for Service (DFS) sewage treatment planning framework and corresponding methods*

existing facility is that it may be harder to find a productive end use for all of the effluent or treatment by-products – even with storage – due to circumstances of the plant's location and scale. Applying the DFS approach will help reveal reuse opportunities that take maximum advantage of the waste and the remainder will have to be adequately treated to meet the local requirements for environmental discharge.

Ghana is one location where we believe using DFS to rehabilitate treatment plants has great potential for improving the country's sanitation outlook. In fact, Ghana is not unique; the features that characterize the sanitation sector are similar for many cities of the developing world as highlighted above for the cases in South Africa. Many of the existing sanitation facilities in Ghana are in disrepair and only 10 per cent of the approximately 70 wastewater and faecal sludge treatment plants function as planned (Murray and Drechsel, 2009). Much of the failure can be traced back to limited institutional and financial capacity, but we argue that insufficient support for operation and maintenance persist due to the lack of easy-to-quantify and tangible benefits associated with treatment.

We are using the DFS approach to evaluate the market potential of wastewater, faecal sludge and treatment by-products, and to design sanitation schemes that foster linkages with the private sector and/or other beneficiary groups. The market demand for effluent and by-products, which can be harnessed via payment or in-kind exchange (see Box 15.1), should provide incentives for robust operation and maintenance of waste treatment and handling systems that far exceed the incentives associated with running a facility that is dedicated strictly to disposal.

Box 15.1 DFS APPLICATION FOR REHABILITATING THE FAILED WASTEWATER TREATMENT PLANT AT PRESBYTERIAN BOYS SENIOR SECONDARY SCHOOL, ACCRA, GHANA

Background: the treatment plant at the Presbyterian Boys Senior Secondary School (Presec) was built in 1976 and serves a population of approximately 2000 students and faculty members who live at the school. The flow is approximately 100m^3/day.

What are the services that wastewater and treatment by-products can provide?

The services that have the most practical application in Ghana include:

- biogas generation for cooking fuel;
- effluent for urban irrigation (and to offset commercial fertilizer);
- land application of treated (e.g. digested, dried or composted) sludge as a fertilizer and soil conditioner in urban agriculture;
- use of sludge as an alternative fuel in industrial processes

What is the local demand for the services that wastewater and sludge can provide?

Since the treatment plant already exists on the Presec campus, the geographic scope of our demand assessment is necessarily narrowed to the close proximity of the facility. Based on a site visit and conversations with the school's headmaster, we estimate that there are 8ha of cultivated land on the school property and adjacent to the treatment plant. To calculate the irrigation demand of this parcel under profit-maximizing conditions, we built a quadratic optimization model using water demand estimates from the FAO's CROPWAT programme, which are tailored to the local climate and soil conditions (Water Resources Development and Management Unit, 1992). According to the results of the model, the annual water requirement to maximize profit is approximately 31,000m^3.

In addition to assessing the irrigation capacity of the surrounding land as a proxy for demand, it is also critical to assess the social and economic demand for the service, as this will reveal the extent to which designing the plant for irrigation can incentivize effective operation and maintenance of the treatment plant. With respect to existing financing, the plant is owned and operated by Presec and serves strictly the school's population; no user fees are collected. The farmer who cultivates the land is the head of the agriculture department at Presec and he expressed a strong desire for access to water for irrigation, noting that his yields were severely crippled without it. He remarked that he would have several potential customers for his surplus crops and believed that the access to irrigation would also support current efforts to engage students in farming. The revenues from surplus crop sales could potentially be put towards the operation and maintenance of the treatment plant.

What is the status of irrigation on this parcel?

While the land is currently cultivated, it is entirely rain-fed because the farmer has no access to water for irrigation. According to our model, gross profit (i.e. excluding any additional labour costs or other inputs) could increase by up to 130 per cent if the full demand for irrigation water was met.

How can we redesign the existing treatment plant to optimally irrigate the adjacent farmland?

Since effluent flows at a fairly steady rate year-round and irrigation requirements will fluctuate, storage reservoirs will need to be built. According to the results of our optimization model, which is built for ease of use by sanitation planners, the maximum accumulation of effluent should be approximately 16,000m^3 per year; a more in-depth analysis of the daily wastewater flow and its temporal fluctuations, as well as discussion with the farmer regarding his intended cropping patterns, will also be used to inform the storage needs.

The layout and size of the storage reservoir(s) will depend on the land topography and availability, the needs of the cultivators and the crops that will be irrigated in light of meeting WHO water-quality standards. For ease of irrigation, it may make most sense to have several reservoirs connected by small overflow pipes scattered throughout the farmland. Crops planted around the last reservoir in the series could be those that require higher effluent quality standards (e.g. crops eaten raw) because that water would have the longest retention time (and thus pathogen reduction), while crops planted around the reservoirs at the beginning of the series (i.e. with a high pathogen concentration) could be ones with less stringent standards (e.g. wheat and maize, that are not eaten raw).

What are the trade-offs among different technology options for rendering the effluent safe for irrigation?

According to the plant's design, wastewater at Presec should flow through a primary settling tank after which the flow should split between two trains in parallel, each consisting of an aeration tank and a final settling tank. The flow should then converge for chlorination prior to discharge to a small stream and underground pipe. Sludge should be discharged to two sludge drying beds. Although wastewater is currently flowing through the facility, the plant has little to no operational capacity. One train is not in use and the remaining aeration tank has gone anaerobic since the aerators were stolen. The water is not being chlorinated and the sludge must be manually removed from the tanks. For our initial analysis, we have narrowed our consideration of different treatment technologies to those that could be incorporated into the existing infrastructure scheme.

To improve the economic and environmental sustainability of the system, re-implementing aerobic treatment is not indicated because of its high operational cost and indirect greenhouse gas emissions. As a rule, tanks that are designed to be aerobic are too small to be converted to anaerobic tanks that achieve the same treatment performance. It will be necessary to monitor the daily flow and influent quality to determine how much larger the tanks must be to effectively operate anaerobically, if at all. Chlorination is also undesirable for effluent used in agriculture; however, adequate pathogen removal is critical. Pathogen removal will be achieved with the installation of a maturation pond, on-farm holding reservoirs and/or a low-cost ultraviolet disinfection system; the logistical and economic trade-offs between these options will inform the final decision.

APPLICATION OF DFS FOR DESIGN OF NEW SANITATION SCHEMES: CHINA CASE STUDY

The full potential of DFS is best realized when it is applied to guide the planning and design process of a new treatment plant. Experiences from a number of reuse projects show that outcomes are far superior when collection, treatment and reuse are integrated into a single planning process (Lazarova et al., 2001). Where DFS is applied at the outset, a treatment plant's precise location and scale (i.e. the decision to build one centralized plant or several smaller plants) can be optimized for the intended end uses of the effluent and treatment by-products. Although designing for reuse adds additional variables to the conventional design for the disposal planning approach, and these are likely to require more time and resources to address, DFS is intended to help stakeholders navigate the more complicated planning and design process. We believe that the long-term benefits of a reuse-oriented design will far outweigh the upfront costs. Box 15.2 provides an example of an application of DFS in China to design an irrigation-oriented wastewater treatment scheme for the peri-urban district of Pixian. Local planners and decision-makers could similarly use the tool and results to tailor their wastewater treatment schemes to suit social, environmental and economic priorities.

Box 15.2 DFS application for designing a reuse-oriented wastewater treatment scheme for an unserved region of the peri-urban district, Pixian, Chengdu, China

Background: the peri-urban district of Pixian, with a population of almost 500,000, is located in the Chengdu municipality, Sichuan Province, China. Pixian is in an environmentally sensitive location, sandwiched between the urban core of Chengdu to the southeast and Dujiangyan to the northwest, which is the source of the municipality's water; thus, 80 per cent of Chengdu's water passes through Pixian. Of the approximately 25,000m³/d urban wastewater generated, about 30 per cent is treated and the remainder is discharged to surface waters. Expanding wastewater treatment is a local priority, though one that is hindered by limited financial resources.

What are the services that wastewater and treatment by-products can provide in and around Chengdu?

The services that have the most practical application in Chengdu include:

- biogas generation for cooking fuel or conversion to electricity at larger-scale plants;
- wastewater effluent for peri-urban irrigation (and to offset commercial fertilizer), urban landscape, toilet-flushing and industrial cooling;
- land application of treated (e.g. digested, dried or composted) sludge as a fertilizer and soil conditioner in urban agriculture;
- use of sludge as an alternative fuel in industrial processes, particularly cement manufacturing where the non-combustible material is incorporated into the clinker.

What is the local demand for the services that wastewater and sludge can provide?

Urban settlements are growing rapidly in Pixian, yet the population is still 75 per cent rural and more than half of the residents depend on farming for their livelihoods. There are 21,000ha of irrigated farmland in Pixian and cultivated crops include a variety of grains, vegetables, fruits, ornamental flowers and herbs used in traditional Chinese medicine. Reuse of treated effluent for local agriculture is a logical means of managing urban nutrients and bridging urban and rural settlements for mutually beneficial ends.

With respect to the productive end use of sludge, two options appear promising based on local market demands: end use as a fertilizer or end use as an alternative fuel in cement manufacturing. According to government statistics, farmers in the district apply approximately 900 tons of nitrogen (as N) and 300 tons of phosphorus (as P) as fertilizer each year. The nutrient content of sludge generated by WWTPs in the region averages 30kg of nitrogen and 10kg of phosphorus per dry ton, thus local demand for fertilizer is not a limiting factor. Alternatively, the sludge could be delivered to the Lafarge cement plant in Dujiangyan, which has the capacity and willingness to accept up to 140 wet tons (at 20 per cent dry solids) of sludge and a substantially larger volume of dry sludge (≥90 per cent dry solids) per day for use in their cement kilns. Based on the sludge-generation rates for existing WWTPs in Chengdu, Lafarge could accommodate a WWTP with a daily capacity of about 200,000m³.

What is the business-as-usual performance of irrigation in Pixian?

A performance assessment was developed to evaluate irrigation based on economic indicators, spatial equity, farmer satisfaction and the extent to which the irrigation scheme serves or hinders regional water-management goals and objectives. We built a quadratic simulation and optimization model, similar to that for Ghana, to measure agricultural profitability and equity; surveyed farmers throughout the district to assess their perceptions of the quantity and quality of their irrigation water; and conducted policy analysis and key informant interviews to understand regional water-management goals and objectives. Based on the results of the model, a location effect is evident, where farmers at the tail of the canal have lower yields per area of cropland than those at the head because of more limited access to water. There is up to an 18 per cent lower maximum profit between the head and tail of the irrigation systems. Supporting this finding, insufficient water quantity was reported by over 70 per cent of the surveyed farmers for the months between November and March. Colour, foul smell and turbidity were reported as problems by a large percentage of survey respondents across all irrigation systems: 58 per cent reported mild to severe colour (n = 39), 45 per cent reported mild to severe odour (n = 38) and 68 per cent reported mild to severe turbidity (n = 39). Farmers' dissatisfaction with irrigation water quality should enhance the appeal of using treated effluent for irrigation.

Despite farmers attesting to inadequate water quantity, it was determined that the existing irrigation scheme puts a heavy burden on surface-water ecosystems due to its water intensity. One priority of the Chengdu government is to improve surface-water quality in Chengdu from Class V to Class III on the Chinese water quality scale by 2010, and modelling done by a third party consulting firm has shown that this will require increasing the flow of water in the rivers (Beijing Ecosimulation Technology Company, 2004).

How can we design wastewater treatment in Pixian to optimally contribute to irrigation and also contribute to a broader set of local priorities?

The model was used to conduct a comparative analysis between yields under the existing irrigation scheme and those that could be expected by either supplementing or replacing the current irrigation-water supply with treated wastewater. The designs of the alternative scenarios were informed by the volume of wastewater generated by urban settlements in the immediate vicinity. According to the results of the analyses, there are opportunities to use effluent to improve the equity of irrigation; effluent could be released into the lower reaches of an irrigation system to increase the volume of water available to those farmers. Alternatively, effluent could be used to replace surface-water diversion as a source of irrigation.

For each scenario, we quantified the impact on farmer profits compared to the base case; characterized likely changes in cropping patterns under profit-maximizing conditions; and, where effluent was used to replace existing irrigation, we quantified the volume of surface water that could be conserved. Wastewater generated in towns along the irrigation canals could be used to offset upwards of 50 per cent of the current surface-water diversion for an individual canal, at a loss ranging from 1–10 per cent in farmer profits. Alternatively, wastewater could be used to supplement the irrigation water in this system in order to halve the location effect between farmers at the head and tail of the canal, and to increase profits earned by downstream farmers by nearly 20 per cent. The results of these simulations reveal several attractive options for local decision-makers, whether their priority is improving the economic well-being of farmers or mitigating the burden of water diversion on aquatic ecosystems.

What are the trade-offs among different technology options for rendering the effluent safe for irrigation?

Medium- to large-scale wastewater treatment plants that use activated sludge are becoming the norm in China; in the Chengdu municipality there are more than 20 such treatment plants. With respect to sludge treatment, one plant is equipped with anaerobic sludge digesters and the biogas is flared; the remaining facilities dewater the sludge before disposal at a landfill site. Life-cycle analysis was used to present the environmental and economic costs and benefits of an array of technology options, including conventional and natural systems. For conventional systems treating wastewater for irrigation, designing schemes to minimize nutrient removal can lower the capital and operating cost of a system that is designed for disposal. Furthermore, adding anaerobic sludge-digestion to a conventional process and capturing the biogas for on-site use can lead to substantial long-term cost savings and reductions in emissions. We calculated the payback time for a boiler to convert biogas to electricity at an existing plant in Chengdu to be less than one year. Waste stabilization ponds are an attractive option from an economic and environmental prospective but in urbanizing areas the land requirement can be prohibitive.

CONCLUSIONS

This chapter has argued that reuse-oriented sanitation can provide greater environmental and economic benefits than conventional, disposal-oriented wastewater/faecal sludge management. However, effectively planning and implementing such systems is often difficult given local-level expertise, norms and institutional constraints. In particular, the three cases from South Africa demonstrated that in spite of the urgency to solve some of these problems first, a reuse approach was adopted. This was made even more difficult due to a lack of systematic design processes for implementing wastewater/faecal sludge management schemes that incorporate reuse for agriculture. Properly managed, however, such schemes can provide both employment and revenues associated with the productive use of the treated waste. The success of these schemes depends on close understanding and collaboration between urban planners, sanitation experts and agricultural extension workers from the beginning of the planning process. Simply relying on assumptions about market demand and cost sensitivity for new materials may not provide sufficiently accurate information for the feasibility assessment and design of a reuse scheme.

The DFS planning approach was introduced as an accessible and logical planning framework for facilitating the design and implementation of reuse-oriented systems. Working through DFS should yield a plan for urban wastewater and faecal sludge management that contributes to local sustainability by not only mitigating public and environmental health risks associated with indiscriminate discharge, but by utilizing the resource potential of human waste in ways that have the greatest local benefit. Among other potential institutional and financial barriers to employing DFS, the absence of incentives or platforms for multi-stakeholder communication and cooperation and one-size-fits-all effluent standards may hinder its effective use.

When these challenges are overcome, the example applications of DFS in Ghana and China show the approach can applied for the rehabilitation of existing facilities or for the design of new treatment plants. However, to maximize the efficiency and benefits of reuse, decision-makers are encouraged to incorporate reuse at the outset of a planning process whenever possible.

REFERENCES

Bahri, A. (1999) 'Agricultural reuse of wastewater and global water management', *Water Science and Technology*, vol 40, no 4, pp339–46

Beijing Ecosimulation Technology Company (2004) *Flow Requirements to Achieve Water Quality Standards in Chengdu*, Beijing Ecosimulation Technology Company, Sichuan Province, Beijing

Bhagwan, J., Still, D., Buckley, C. and Foxon, K. (2008) 'Challenges with up-scaling dry sanitation technologies', *Water Science and Technology*, vol 58, no 1, pp21–7

Bonzi, M. (2008) 'Experiences and opportunities for human excreta fertilizers in improving small scale agriculture', World Water Week, Stockholm, 17–23 August 2008

Couderc, A. A. L., Buckley, C. A., Foxon, K., Nwaneri, C. F., Bakare, B. F., Gounden, T. and Battimelli, A. (2008) 'The effect of moisture content and alkalinity on the anaerobic biodegradation of VIP contents', *Water Science and Technology*, vol 58, no 2, pp473–7

Flores, A., Buckley, C. and Fenner, R. (2009) 'Selecting wastewater systems for sustainability in developing countries', *Water Science and Technology*, in press

Foxon, K. M., Mkhize, S., Reddy, M. and Buckley, C. (2009) 'Laboratory protocols for testing the efficacy of commercial pit latrine additives', *Water SA*, vol 35, no 2, pp228–35

Gounden, T., Pfaff, B., Macleod, N. and Buckley, C. (2006) 'Provision of free sustainable basic sanitation: the Durban experience', 32nd WEDC International Conference, Sustainable Development of Water Resources, Water Supply and Environmental Sanitation, Colombo

IWA (2008) 'The Vienna Charter on Urban Sanitation, International Water Association', International Water Association, London

IWA Sanitation 21 Task Force (2007), *Simple Approaches to Complex Sanitation: A Draft Framework for Analysis*, International Water Association, London

Jenkins, M. and Sugden, S. (2006) 'Rethinking sanitation: Lessons and innovation for sustainability and success in the new millennium', in *Human Development Report 2006*, United Nations Development Programme, New York, p37

Lazarova, V., Levine, B., Sack, J., Cirelli, G., Jeffrey, P., Muntau, H., Salgot, M. and Brissaud, F. (2001) 'Role of water reuse for enhancing integrated water management in Europe and Mediterranean countries', *Water Science and Technology*, vol 43, no 10, pp25–33

Mnkeni, P. N. and Austin, L. M. (2009) 'Fertilizer value of human manure from pilot urine-diversion toilets', *Water SA*, vol 35, no 1, pp133–8

Murray, A. and Drechsel, P. (2009) 'Positive deviance in the sanitation sector in Ghana: Why do some wastewater treatment facilities work when the majority fail?', unpublished manuscript

Norman, D. (1990) *The Design of Everyday Things*, Doubleday, New York

SANDEC (2000) *Summary Report of Bellagio Expert Consultation on Environmental Sanitation in the 21st Century: 1–4 February 2000*, Water Supply and Sanitation Collaborative Council, Dübendorf, Switzerland

Stockholm International Water Institute, UN-Habitat, Asian Development Bank, Swedish International Development Cooperation Agency (2008) 'Water and sanitation for developing clean and healthy cities: Seminar report', World Urban Forum 4, Nanjing, China, www.siwi.org/documents/Resources/Events/seminars/WUF4SeminarReport.pdf

SuSanA (2008) *Planning for Sustainable Sanitation: Fact Sheet*, Sustainable Sanitation Alliance, Eschborn, Germany, p8, www.susana.org

UN Millennium Project Task Force on Water and Sanitation (2005) *Health, Dignity, and Development: What Will It Take?*, Earthscan, London

Water Resources Development and Management Unit (1992) 'CROPWAT version 5.7', FAO, Rome

World Agroforestry Centre (2008) 'Achieving food security and sanitation coverage through water harvesting and conservation technologies: Case examples from sub-Saharan Africa', World Water Week, Stockholm, 17–23 August 2008

16

Facilitating the Adoption of Food-Safety Interventions in the Street-Food Sector and on Farms

Hanna Karg, Pay Drechsel, Philip Amoah and Regina Jeitler

ABSTRACT

This chapter discusses the implementation challenges of the WHO Guidelines on safe wastewater use pertaining to the adoption of the so-called 'post-treatment' or 'non-treatment' options, like safer irrigation practices or appropriate vegetable-washing in kitchens. Due to limited risk awareness and immediate benefits of wastewater irrigation, it is unlikely that a broad adoption of recommended practices will automatically follow revised policies or any educational campaign and training. Most of the recommended practices do not only require behaviour-change but might also increase operational costs. In such a situation, significant efforts are required to explore how conventional and/or social marketing can support the desired behaviour-change towards the adoption of safety practices. This will require new strategic partnerships and a new section in the WHO Guidelines. This chapter outlines the necessary steps and considerations for increasing the adoption probability, and suggests a framework which is based on a combination of social marketing, incentive systems, awareness creation/education and application of regulations. An important conclusion is that these steps require serious accompanying research of the target group, strongly involving social sciences, which should not be underestimated in related projects.

INTRODUCTION

As African cities experience urbanization and globalization, they face development challenges coupled with cultural changes. Eating patterns, for example, tend to shift from traditional dishes towards fast food, often consisting of rice, poultry and salad, which is supplied by a booming but largely informal street-food sector providing employment and inexpensive food for urban dwellers (Maxwell et al., 2000; Nicolas et al., 2007; WHO, 2004).

The development challenges relate to the slow pace of urban infrastructure expansion, such as sanitation facilities, which results in widespread environmental pollution (Raschid-Sally and Jayakody, 2008). The street-food sector is especially affected, not only by the unsanitary operating conditions, but also by the quality of vegetables that are produced with highly contaminated surface water (Obuobie et al., 2006). The development of the sanitation sector in developing countries still faces a variety of challenges, hence time is needed before farmers and consumers can fully rely on wastewater treatment to safeguard water quality. As an interim measure, the WHO (2006) recognized that other options aside from or in addition to treatment of wastewater, such as on-farm water treatment, safer irrigation practices or careful vegetable-washing, can significantly contribute to health-risk reduction.

This focus on additional non- or post-treatment options can actually increase security through more diversified health-risk reduction control points (the 'multiple-barrier approach'). Farmers using polluted water, traders buying and selling contaminated crops and the private or commercial kitchens preparing raw salads play key roles in this system, which is based on the principles of hazard analysis and critical control points (HACCP) (Box 16.1). The challenge of the system is its successful application in a low-income, low-resource and low-education context, as typically found in sub-Saharan Africa, which shows the largest discrepancy between what is needed and what is experienced.

The main challenge in the food-safety sector is bridging the gap between theoretical approaches and their applicability on the field. Two basic areas of intervention are usually required: the first one is the provision of appropriate infrastructure (such as sanitary facilities in markets) and the second is behavioural change among the stakeholders of the critical control points identified for health-risk reduction. Whereas the provision of infrastructure offers a promising intervention area, the behavioural change of farmers, traders and consumers still constitutes a pristine research field in the context of 'wastewater irrigation', despite the fact that behaviour-change concepts are largely developed and have increasingly been applied in the sanitation and hygiene sector.

This chapter tries to outline a possible pathway to facilitate behaviour-change towards safer irrigation and food-handling practices, mostly drawing on the example of studies carried out by the International Water Management Institute (IWMI) with its partners in Ghana (see also Chapters 10, 12, 13 and 17). Methods

---

Box 16.1 Hazard analysis and critical control point system

The management of microbiological hazards in the street-food sector builds on the use of tools such as quantitative microbial risk assessment (QMRA) and the HACCP system. Sound microbiological risk assessment provides an understanding of the nature of the hazard and is a tool to set priorities for targeted interventions at critical control points along the value chain of, for example, vegetables eaten raw.

Related strategies for improving street-food safety should be based upon studies of the local street-food system and may include consideration of:

- policy, regulation, registration and licenses;
- infrastructure, services and vending-unit design and construction;
- training of food-handlers;
- education of consumers.

Source: WHO (1996, 2002)

---

used to analyse options for triggering a behaviour-change include literature surveys, expert interviews, street surveys, focus group discussions, observations, training sessions and a variety of knowledge sharing activities (Amoah et al., 2009; Karg, 2008; Keraita et al., 2008).

The approach used was highly iterative between empirical and conceptual perspectives. The groups targeted for behaviour-change in Ghana were: farmers (who induce most crop contamination through the use of highly polluted water); and restaurants, in particular street-food restaurants, where more than 90 per cent of the wastewater-irrigated salad crops are served (Amoah et al., 2007a, 2007b).

CHANGING APPROACHES TO UNDERSTAND BEHAVIOUR-CHANGE

In the past, many health-promotion campaigns were based on educating people about the threat of disease in order to change their behaviours (Nutbeam and Harris, 2004). However, there is little evidence that approaches based on health education have had the anticipated impact, in particular in developing countries (Burgers and Boot, 1988; Scott et al., 2007). Some programme evaluations show that knowledge has indeed increased but without resulting in behaviour-change (Favin et al., 2004). The reasons might be many, including that 'old habits die hard', especially if the benefits are not immediately visible or if they are only of indirect concern. In addition, the manner of conveying an educational message can steer its success or failure, especially if it does not match local perceptions and (risk) knowledge (Martinsen, 2008). For example, food-safety posters developed in the USA used symbols for bacteria and slogans, like 'fight bac' which the focus groups under study in Ghana did not understand.

New knowledge does not instantly result in new practices as they might be too difficult, too expensive, too time-consuming, or be opposed by other people (UNICEF and LSHTM, 1999). For interventions to be successful, and this extends also to the promotion of interventions, it is important to investigate the target groups' knowledge and perceptions beforehand.

PERCEPTIONS OF CLEAN, SAFE AND DIRTY

Curtis (1988) has underlined the importance of recognizing the strong social dimensions of hygiene in developing countries. Hygiene and related risk assessment are thus approached as social phenomena based upon culturally determined ideas. Dirt-avoidance was a desirable behaviour long before the discovery of bacterial disease transmission, thus hygiene is not only about the removal of germs (Curtis, 1988). Similar findings are documented in the work of van der Geest (1998), an anthropologist who found that, in Ghana, dirt is seen as much more than a potential health risk and can be equally perceived as physical and moral decay, whereas cleanliness stands for physical and moral attractiveness – in Ghanaian English cleanliness is often referred to as 'neatness', a term indeed often appearing in local street-food surveys.

Perception studies in Ghana targeted farmers and staff of street restaurants to gain a better understanding of opportunities and constraints for behaviour-change (Box 16.2) (Karg, 2008; Keraita et al., 2008; Rheinländer et al., 2008). Such participatory studies with the target group (see also Chapter 17) are an important step to understanding what could facilitate the adoption of innovations (Chambers et al., 1989).

BOX 16.2 PERCEPTIONS OF STREET-FOOD SAFETY IN URBAN KUMASI, GHANA

Although both vendors and consumers demonstrated basic knowledge of food safety, the food-quality (including safety) criteria used by the two groups did not emphasize basic hygiene practices such as handwashing, cleaning of utensils, washing of raw vegetables and efficacy of disinfectants. Instead, the main food-selection criteria related to: aesthetic appearance of the food and food stand; appearance of the food vendor; interpersonal trust in the vendor; and price and accessibility of food (Probst, 2008; Rheinländer et al., 2008). However, it was also observed that pressure on vendors to improve the clean appearance of vegetables can result in a prompt response (Drechsel et al., 2000).

TRIGGERING BEHAVIOUR-CHANGE

If behaviour-change, i.e. the adoption of recommended practices, is the target, one must understand which internal or external factors in the local context might trigger or hinder it. A supporting internal factor can be increased awareness about health risks. A supporting external factor can be a credit programme or enforced regulations and controls. The fact that it is hard to shed old habits certainly poses a significant internal barrier. Other barriers are the investments required or potential losses. Some safer irrigation practices, like furrow or drip irrigation, might reduce cropping density and yields. Similarly, the cessation of irrigation, even if only for two or three days, can reduce yields as the hot weather in Ghana calls for daily watering (Drechsel et al., 2008). Also more effective vegetable-washing in kitchens would require some investments in, for instance, bleach or chlorine tablets, so there may be a cost restraint.

In short, several of the recommended non-treatment or post-treatment practices to increase the safety of wastewater-irrigated vegetables require extra efforts or inputs without a tangible direct benefit unless consumers pay more for safe produce. However, although there is a general demand for safe food, the risk awareness is too low to stimulate any significant willingness to pay (Box 16.3).

BOX 16.3 WILLINGNESS TO PAY FOR SAFER VEGETABLES

In an accompanying FAO-IWMI-supported study in Ghana's major cities of Accra and Kumasi, the willingness to pay (WTP) for safer vegetables was explored, based on a sample of 300 individual consumers purchasing food with green salads or green salad alone from roadside food vendors and restaurants.

The results indicate a monthly average income of about US$280 of which US$5.50 is spent on the salad component. About 95 per cent of the sampled consumers are willing to pay for safer salads. However, the additional amounts are low. Extrapolated for the month, the consumer is willing to pay about US$0.40 more, a figure which varied to some extent with age, income and related educational level, and is slightly lower than the 10 per cent increase reported from a similar study in Vietnam (Simmons and Scott, 2007).

Source: Yahaya and Kinane (2009)

In such a situation, social marketing options should be explored to catalyse behaviour-change. While commercial marketing ultimately seeks to generate profit for a private interest, social marketing seeks to influence a target audience to voluntarily accept, modify or abandon behaviour for the benefit of individuals, groups or society as a whole. The social marketing approach applies commercial

Product	Price
The social product can either represent an idea, a practice or a concrete object which should be marketed. The idea can be: - a belief ('handwashing will protect my children'), - an attitude ('planned babies are better cared for than babies from accidental pregnancies') - a value ('all humans have equal rights'). The practice can be an act (immunization, building latrines) and the repeated act turns into behaviour (washing vegetables, using the latrine, washing hands, using a condom). The tangible product required could be chlorine tablets, a latrine, condom, soap, etc.	Price is measured in both monetary and non-monetary terms. Time, effort, change in life style, etc., all affect true cost. The monetary price serves several functions to determine the product's accessibility, discourage or encourage demand and attribute product value. In social marketing, non-monetary costs like time and perceived risk are often more critical than product price.

MARKETING MIX

Place	Promotion
The social marketing placement/distribution objective has to make sure access to the product is as convenient as possible for the target group. This could include more and closer locations, extended hours, improving the appearance of the location, and making the performing of the desired behaviour more appealing.	Communication and promotion involve persuasion to influence attitudes and/or behaviour. In order to persuade the target person or group, one must capture their attention from other competing sources. The traditional promotional tools in marketing include advertising, personal selling, publicity and sales promotion.

Figure 16.1 *Description of the four 'Ps' when used in social marketing*

Source: Martinsen (2008)

marketing principles and techniques, such as customer orientation, marketing research, and the use of the marketing mix (Figure 16.1). The concept has been tested in the sanitation sector as well as in public health (Grier and Bryant, 2005; Martinsen, 2008; Siegel and Doner Lotenberg, 2007).

Marketing approaches in general are considered a promising alternative to traditional (educational) approaches to change people's behaviours, i.e. instead of being supply driven (providing knowledge and materials), marketing approaches support a demand-driven change, thus are more consumer-oriented.

In the Ghana case, farmers might eventually change their behaviour for other, also intangible incentives, like less pressure from authorities and the media that their current practices are bad for public health (Box 16.4). Also greater tenure security could facilitate, for example, investments in on-farm treatment ponds.

**BOX 16.4 INCENTIVE OPTIONS DISCUSSED
IN THE GHANA STUDY**

- Awards and public recognition might be possible incentives for behaviour-change, especially where farmers are harassed by media and officials about wastewater use. Farmers with safe produce could get recognition during 'Best Farmer' celebrations. Fast-food stands adopting an integrated safe-food concept might get recognized in tourist guides.
- Incentives from government agencies for farmers participating in safety schemes could be the provision of extra training, support of more dedicated extension services trained in food safety, loans (micro-credit), subsidies for pumps, and/or tenure security, which farmers ranked very high (see Chapter 17).
- A market incentive could be a certification programme (Goewie, 2002) for 'safer crops' combined with dedicated marketing channels to hotels, restaurants and supermarkets, accessible at least to customers with a higher willingness to pay for safer produce. Ideally, this should also support independent monitoring of the quality standard. To bring this to the advantage of the wider public requires more awareness creation to increase the general demand for safer crops.

In Vietnam, farmers could apply for financial support if they were interested in growing safe vegetables. They were asked to pay 80 per cent back when they returned a profit (Simmons and Scott, 2007).

In many cases, supporting a desired behaviour-change alone is not enough because at the same time the current alternative to the suggested practice needs to be fought. Thus, the most effective approach might be a mix of incentives and disincentives.

NEED FOR APPLIED RESEARCH

The important part of both commercial marketing and social marketing is to identify the conditions that can make one and/or the other work. In the case of wastewater and food safety, this means analysing:

- whether safer practices would directly pay off by either improving production or reducing production costs;
- whether safer practices would eventually pay off due to an increased willingness-to-pay by consumers and traders;
- whether there are other triggers and incentives which could change behaviour and how best to instigate and build on them, while avoiding change barriers.

While the first two studies require conventional economic analysis (farm cost–benefit analysis, contingent valuation), the third study stretches most projects even further out of their comfort zone. It requires substantial social analysis of the constraints and opportunities of the target group, their perceptions, wants and attitudes (Andreasen, 1995). The reasons for a person not to change his/her practice can be numerous and of different weight, linked to tradition, family pressure, community norms, time pressure, inconvenience and so on: the reason is not always necessarily a lack of awareness of the social or health benefits of adopting the practice promoted. This analysis requires good listening skills and should be based on participatory research principles.

Aside from understanding the reasons that might limit behaviour-change, it will require a different effort to analyse what might trigger it. Trigger studies will have to consider distinct population subgroups and the social and cultural environments in which the people act. This information is used to make strategic marketing decisions about segments of the target group in terms of what benefits to offer and about how to price, place and promote products (Grier and Bryant, 2005).

The planning process based on findings delivered by applied research can be outlined in the following steps:

- Assess current food handling behaviours related to the problem(s) of concern.
- Identify feasible options for change which reduce health risks.
- Identify barriers and enabling factors (external and internal triggers) for a related behaviour-change and verify them with the target group(s).
- Study appropriate communication channels and (form of) outreach messages.
- Carefully consider which stakeholders and policy-makers will be crucial in developing, promoting and implementing effective change strategies.

Although, ideally, all aspects of food safety and hygiene should be promoted, it is recognized that hygiene-promotion programmes work best if they focus on a small number of activities and easy-to-recall messages. However, it must be borne in mind that by promoting a single practice, such as vegetable-washing, people might assume that this practice alone can prevent the spread of infection leading to an 'illusion of risk-control' (Bloomfield, 2003; Knox, 2000). Moreover, if the emphasis is placed on effective vegetable-washing alone, and handwashing or cross-contamination are ignored, it is questionable whether a campaign can achieve any significant or measurable health impact. Ideally, both effective vegetable-washing and other basic food-safety practices should be part of an integrated behaviour-change campaign.[1] Even if not all components of a 'package' will be adopted, the costs of promoting a package of maybe two to three good practices might only be marginally higher than for one practice, while multiplying its potential impact. To find the most appropriate break-even point considering cost-effectiveness and message absorption capacity of the target group, is certainly a challenge.[2]

The street-food survey in Ghana revealed a number of external and internal behaviour determinants towards adoption of better food-safety practices. Following the example from Favin et al. (2004), barriers and enabling factors were sorted according to different categories to help in formulating possible intervention strategies (Tables 16.1, 16.2).

CAMPAIGN FRAMEWORK

The study conducted in Ghana led to the development of a framework for implementing a (so far not funded) national campaign on food safety with special emphasis on wastewater-irrigated vegetables (IWMI, 2009). The framework combined different elements or strategies considered as important for changing behaviour in the street-food sector and among farmers. It draws on Tables 16.1 and 16.2 and the 'Receptivity Model' described by Jeffrey and Seaton (2004) and emphasizes the equal importance of different measures to facilitate behaviour changes and increase food safety. The framework also considers the benefit of simultaneously using incentives (for behaviour-change) and disincentives (for maintaining the old behaviour), for example via enforced regulations and fees. The elements of the framework are:

- education (given the low educational level);
- social marketing (given the low commercial incentive for changing behaviour);
- incentives (transforming needs of the target group into opportunities);
- regulations (to address bad practices and institutionalize good ones).

Education

Education or knowledge transfer by themselves might not change behaviour, as mentioned above, but remain crucial components of any multi-strategy approach, especially if they avoid top-down lecturing. When considering knowledge as a driver for behavioural change (or lack of knowledge as a barrier to change), it is important to recognize that there are two types of knowledge. The first – practical or logistical knowledge – is essential for adapting new behaviours (e.g. how to prepare the correct chlorine solution for disinfecting vegetables). The second type of knowledge, the scientific explanation of the reasons why the behaviour-change is important (e.g. how the chlorine works), may not be essential to achieve behaviour-change as experienced in the Ghana hand-wash campaign (Box 16.5).

Social marketing

Social marketing is an important tool where economic arguments do not work. Even if health considerations are not valued highly in the target group, social

Table 16.1 *External behaviour determinants and possible intervention strategies in Ghana's informal street restaurant sector*

Category	Barriers (-)	Enabling factors (+)	Possible response strategy
Input supply	Effective disinfectants are generally not known, although available. Thus vegetable-washing is not effectively reducing pathogens.	Vegetable-washing to remove dirt is done by over 90% of stakeholders; this is an excellent starting point for effective pathogen removal.	Promote available disinfectants (bleach, chlorine tablets, potassium permanganate) suitable for different classes of restaurants.
Socio-economic conditions	Vendors are concerned about costs of required inputs or training.	Public and private sector offer free training. Some ingredients (bleach) are very cheap.	Make options known. Engage private sector for promotion and subsidies. Training certificates might increase sales.
Education	In catering schools practical food safety does not get much attention.	Teaching materials are being provided/revised based on current project results.	Establish early link with educational sector to facilitate adoption of results in curricula.
Environmental conditions	The environment of street restaurants is in general unsafe; water and toilets might be missing.		Interventions have to consider local possibilities and limitations and aim at step-wise improvements.
Institutional settings	Regulating authorities are under-resourced, which might facilitate corruption.	Authorities are in place.	Interventions cannot rely on enforcement or control catalysing behaviour-change. Institutional capacity building component required.
Social groupings	Few members in catering associations due to internal problems. Most associations have weak governance and funding.	Social clubs, church groups and professional associations are common and can be used as possible communication channels. In general, vendors like to join associations and networks.	Associations should be strengthened and memberships promoted. Allow loan schemes/credit for safer behaviour.
Vendor/ customer interaction	Customers are more concerned about price, neatness and quantity of the food, rather than food safety.	Customers have much influence over the vendor. Vendors are willing to learn to please customers.	Customers' awareness about food-safety issues has to be increased.
Neatness as part of cultural norms	Neatness is important but does not necessarily include cleanliness and safe food.	Controllers, vendors and customers are very concerned about neatness which is closely associated with trust and respect.	The term neatness has to be extended to visible and invisible cleanliness; or positively linked to disinfectants.
Cultural norms	Customers are reluctant to make direct inquiries about food origin related to safety which is considered disrespectful.	Food origin can be a 'brand'; e.g. carrots from Togo are preferred to Ghanaian ones.	Safer production sites could get a brand name associated with accepted norms, such as 'clean' and 'tasty'.

Table 16.2 *Internal behaviour determinants and possible intervention strategies in Ghana's informal street restaurant sector*

Category	Barriers (-)	Enabling factors (+)	Possible response strategy
Risk awareness	Vendors do not perceive any elevated risk and consider current washing practices to be appropriate.	Vendors are to different degrees aware of health risks related to raw vegetables.	Risks should be explained. Invisible risks should be made 'visible' (see e.g. Amoah et al., 2009).
Scientific knowledge	Very little awareness of invisible risks (micro-organisms) and pathogen pathways.	High awareness of visible risks like insects and knowledge of the term 'germs'.	Risks should be explained. Invisible risks should be made 'visible' (see e.g. Amoah et al., 2009).
Practical knowledge	Few attended formal catering education in schools. Effective vegetable-washing methods are in most cases not known.	Vendors have basic knowledge of food safety through post-school training provided by projects or private sector.	Promotion of effective methods in workshops, through associations and private-sector training.
Emotions and reactions	Promotional materials and campaigns as used in other cultures do not appeal necessarily and might even be misleading if unknown symbols or vocabulary are used.	Perception studies point at positive and negative motivational factors which drive hygiene behaviour.	Strategy should be based on local knowledge and perceptions.
Intention		In general, vendors are very willing to learn about clean food preparation.	Training workshops can be combined with cooking courses or private-sector product promotions

marketing studies can help to identify related benefits that are valued, including indirect business advantages, improved self-esteem, a feeling of comfort or respect for others. Studies thus have to look for 'positive (core) values' that the primary target audience associates or could associate with the innovation (Siegel and Doner Lotenberg, 2007). For example, if using a drip kit for safer irrigation is valued for reasons of feeling 'technologically advanced', then the social marketing messages and communication strategies should reinforce this existing positive association.

Incentives

Incentives are important when the benefits are not direct, such as when individual action (safer irrigation practices) serves society (public health) more than the actor. In the hand-washing case (Box 16.5), the benefit was for the person and for the family, i.e. a much closer association than for a farmer who is not the consumer

---

Box 16.5 Social marketing studies in the West African context

'Health in your hands'

A marketing approach was applied in a nationwide hand-washing campaign in Ghana ('Health in your hands').[3] This approach involved the use of professional marketing techniques facilitated through a private–public partnership to promote 'socially useful products' (in this case, hand-washing with soap) through generation of demand. The underlying research revealed two main drivers for hand-washing with soap: disgust of dirt (yuck factor) and caring for a child, whereas protection from disease was not regarded as a key motivator. The communication campaign was thus designed in such a way as to evoke the feeling of disgust without mentioning health reasons or sickness. The campaign was fairly successful: soap use after toilet use increased by 13 per cent and soap use before eating went up 41 per cent (Curtis, 2002; Duhigg, 2008; Scott et al., 2007).

'A wanted latrine is a used latrine'

In Benin the social marketing approach was applied to improve sanitation. Previous sanitation projects in developing countries often failed because they relied only on subsidized latrine construction and health education without generating demand; and the target community did not change established habits (like open defecation), thus the latrines remained unused. In the Benin case, research was conducted to find out what triggers people to invest in a latrine and to use it. Health benefits did not appear in the top ten triggers whereas safety, dignity and prestige were among the top five (Martinsen, 2008).

---

of his/her crops. In the case of the farmer, the need for extra incentives is likely (Box 16.4). Customer–vendor interactions have been identified as an important element influencing food-safety issues, both as an impedimental factor upholding the current situation (low risk awareness) and as a potential source of improvement (if awareness has been created) (see Box 16.2).

Regulations

Regulations are required to institutionalize new food-safety recommendations. When enforced these provide the legal framework for both incentives, such as certificates, and disincentives, like fees. New rules usually also require capacity building. In order to integrate improved food-handling practices into institutional structures, inspection forms can be updated, inspectors/extension officers can be trained and pressure can be applied to caterers in the form of punitive fees and, in the extreme case, business closure. However, regulations should not be based

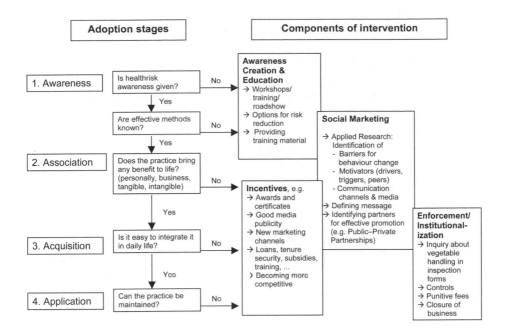

Figure 16.2 *Suggested multi-strategy campaign framework for the adoption of non-treatment interventions, on farm and off farm, for the reduction of health risks from wastewater irrigation in urban Ghana*

Source: After Roma and Jeffrey (2008), modified by Karg (2008)

on imported (theoretical) standards but locally feasible standards as otherwise they have no practical application value and can facilitate corruption. In this way, regulation and institutionalization may contribute to ensuring the long-term sustainability of behaviour-change whereas promotional and educational activities are usually limited to a specific time frame.

Application

According to different individual stages of behaviour-change from the initial awareness to association, acquisition and finally application (Figure 16.2), some components of the campaign might be more suitable for some individuals or groups than others, while in general they complement each other. An analysis assuming different adoption rates showed the potential of the suggested campaign framework, and also its cost-effectiveness (see Chapter 13). Whether the framework has advantages compared to other possible strategies for behaviour-change towards increased food safety remains to be studied.

CONCLUSIONS

The WHO Guidelines (2006) for safe wastewater irrigation recommend inter-sectoral collaboration, policy dialogue and policy formulation as key elements for their implementation. This is indeed necessary but not sufficient where safeguarding health cannot rely just on wastewater treatment. Implementing the guidelines in this situation means first of all that certain actors along the pathogen pathway have to change their behaviour. Improved policies and related education might be milestones but often do not trigger behaviour-change. This situation calls for a stronger integration of social science research in the strongholds of engineering and epidemiology to address key adoption barriers, such as:

- Recommended practices for increased food safety do not in most cases provide direct profit or reduce production costs (they may even be more expensive).
- Educational levels in developing countries are too low to understand public-health risks and related responsibility.
- Safety regulations are often too theoretical and do not fit local capacities or context.

In addition to educational and regulatory efforts, conventional and social marketing can play a significant role in understanding and facilitating behaviour-change although neither concept is without challenges (Biran and Hagard, 2003; Cave and Curtis, 1999). To be successful, social marketing requires applied research to understand the needs, aspirations, values and everyday lives of the target audiences, and their perceptions of factors which might motivate or discourage them from adopting recommended technologies. This research will greatly help in designing a well-targeted food-safety campaign under any policy supporting the WHO Guidelines in the farm and post-harvest sectors.

NOTES

1   There can be large differences between countries and cultures. In Francophone West Africa, very effective (e.g. bleach-based) vegetable-washing practices are common, while in Ghana this is not the case (Amoah et al., 2007b).
2   The size of the package or length of the message also has implications on the media to be used as TV spots, for example, are rather expensive and thus only allow short messages.
3   This campaign was developed by the 'Global Public Private Partnership on Handwashing' (www.globalhandwashing.org).

REFERENCES

Amoah, P., Drechsel, P., Abaidoo, R. C. and Henseler, M. (2007a) 'Irrigated urban vegetable production in Ghana: Microbiological contamination in farms and markets and associated consumer risk groups', *Journal of Water and Health*, vol 5, no 3, pp455–66

Amoah, P., Drechsel, P., Abaidoo, R. and Klutse, A. (2007b) 'Effectiveness of common and improved sanitary washing methods in West Africa for the reduction of *coli* bacteria and helminth eggs on vegetables', *Tropical Medicine and International Health*, vol 12, suppl. 2, pp40–50

Amoah, P., Schuetz, T., Kranjac-Berisavjevic, G., Manning-Thomas, N. and Drechsel, P. (2009) 'From world cafés to road shows: Using a mix of knowledge sharing approaches to improve wastewater use in urban agriculture', *Knowledge Management for Development Journal*, December 2009 (in press)

Andreasen, A. L. (1995) *Marketing Social Change: Changing Behavior to Promote Health, Social Development, and the Environment*, Jossey Bass, San Francisco, CA

Biran, A. and Hagard, S. (2003) 'Hygiene promotion: Evidence and practice', London School of Hygiene and Tropical Medicine, London, www.worldbank.org/html/fpd/water/rwsstoolkit/material/lsmtm_inception_310703.pdf

Bloomfield, S. F. (2003) 'Focus on home hygiene in developing countries', *International Scientific Forum on Home Hygiene*, London School of Hygiene and Tropical Medicine, London

Burgers, L. and Boot, M. C. (1988) *Hygiene Education in Water Supply and Sanitation Programmes*, International Water and Sanitation Centre (IRC), The Hague

Cave, B. and Curtis, V. (1999) *Effectiveness of Promotional Techniques in Environmental Health*, Task no 165, WELL Study, London School of Hygiene and Tropical Medicine, London / Loughborough University, Loughborough

Chambers, R., Pacey, A. and Thrupp, L. A. (eds) (1989) *Farmer First: Farmer Innovation and Agricultural Research*, Intermediate Technology Publications, London, p218

Curtis, V. (1988) 'The dangers of dirt. Household, hygiene and health', PhD thesis, Wageningen University, Wageningen, The Netherlands

Curtis, V. (2002) *Health in Your Hands: Lessons from Building Public–Private Partnerships for Washing Hands with Soap*, WSP, LSHTM, World Bank, AED, BNWP, UNICEF, Washington, DC, www.globalhandwashing.org/Publications/Attachments/WSP_H_Lessons_07Oct02.pdf

Drechsel, P., Abaidoo, R. C., Amoah, P. and Cofie, O. O. (2000) 'Increasing use of poultry manure in and around Kumasi, Ghana: Is farmers' race consumers' fate?', *Urban Agricultural Magazine*, vol 2, pp25–7

Duhigg, C. (2008) 'Changing the world, one lather at a time: "Yuck factor" boosts handwashing habits in Ghana campaign', *New York Times*, 20 July

Favin, M., Naimoli, G. and Sherburne, L. (2004) *Improving Health through Behavior Change. A Process Guide on Hygiene Promotion*, Joint Publication 7, Environmental Health Project, Washington, DC

Geest, S. van der (1998) 'Akan shit: Getting rid of dirt in Ghana', *Anthropology Today*, vol 14, no 3, pp8–12

Goewie, E. A. (2002) 'Organic Production, what is it? Certification', *Urban Agriculture Magazine*, no 6, April, pp5–8, 17

Grier, S. and Bryant, C. A. (2005) 'Social marketing in public health', *Annual Review of Public Health*, vol 26, pp319–39

IWMI (2009) 'Wastewater irrigation and public health: From research to impact – A road map for Ghana', report for Google.org prepared by IWMI, Accra, Ghana

Jeffrey, P. and Seaton, R. A. F. (2004) 'A conceptual model of "Receptivity" applied to the design and deployment of water policy mechanisms', *Journal of Integrative Environmental Sciences*, vol 1, no 3, pp277–300

Karg, H. (2008) 'From food contamination to food safety. Analysing options for behaviour change in urban Ghana', thesis, Institute of Geography, University of Freiburg, Germany, p73

Keraita, B., Drechsel, P. and Konradsen, F. (2008) 'Perceptions of farmers on health risks and risk mitigation measures in wastewater-irrigated urban vegetable farming in Ghana', *Journal of Risk Research*, vol 11, no 8, pp1047–61

Knox, B. (2000) 'Consumer perceptions and understandings of risk from food', *British Medical Bulletin*, vol 56, no 1, pp97–109

Martinsen, C. (2008) 'Social marketing in sanitation – More than selling toilets', *Stockholm Water Front*, no 1, pp14–16

Maxwell, D., Levin, C., Armar-Klemesu, M. R., Ruel, M., Morris, S. and Ahiadeke, C. (2000) 'Urban livelihood and food and nutrition security in greater Accra, Ghana', *International Food Policy Research Institute, Report 112*, IFPRI, Washington, DC

Nicolas, B., Razack, B. A., Yollande, I., Aly, S., Tidiane, O. C. A., Philippe, N. A., Colman, D. S. and Sababénédjo, T. A. (2007) 'Street-vended foods improvement: Contamination mechanisms and application of Food Safety Objective Strategy: Critical review', *Pakistan Journal of Nutrition*, vol 6, no 1, pp1–10

Nutbeam, D. and Harris, E. (2004) *Theory in a Nutshell. A Practical Guide to Health Promotion Theories*, 2nd edition, McGraw-Hill, Sydney

Obuobie, E., Keraita, B., Amoah, P., Cofie, O. O., Raschid-Sally, L. and Drechsel, P. (2006) *Irrigated Urban Vegetable Production in Ghana: Characteristics, Benefits and Risks*, IWMI-RUAF-CPWF, IWMI, Accra, Ghana

Probst, L. (2008) 'Vegetable safety in urban Ghana. A case-study analysis of consumer preferences', MSc thesis, University of Vienna, Vienna, p171

Raschid-Sally, L. and Jayakody, P. (2008) 'Drivers and characteristics of wastewater agriculture in developing countries: Results from a global assessment, Colombo, Sri Lanka', *IWMI Research Report 127*, International Water Management Institute, Colombo, p35

Rheinländer, T., Olsen, M., Bakang, J. A., Takyi, H., Konradsen, F. and Samuelsen, H. (2008) 'Keeping up appearances: Perceptions of street food safety in urban Kumasi, Ghana', *Journal of Urban Health*, vol 85, no 6, pp952–64

Roma, E. and Jeffrey, P. (2008) 'Multidimensional gap analysis to diagnose innovation adoption in the sanitation sector of LDCs', paper presented at the International Conference on New Sanitation Concepts and Models of Governance, Wageningen, The Netherlands, 19–21 May 2008

Scott, B., Curtis, V., Rabie, T. and Garbrah-Aidoo, N. (2007) 'Health in our hands, but not in our heads: Understanding hygiene motivation in Ghana', *Health Policy and Planning*, vol 22, no 4, pp225–33

Siegel, M. and Doner Lotenberg, L. (2007) *Marketing Public Health: Strategies to Promote Social Change*, 2nd edition, Jones & Bartlett Publishers, Boston, MA

Simmons, L. and Scott, S. (2007) 'Health concerns drive safe vegetable production in Vietnam', *LEISA*, vol 9, no 3, pp15–16

UNICEF and LSHTM (1999) *Towards Better Programming. A Manual on Hygiene Promotion*, Water, Environment and Sanitation Technical Guidelines Series, no 6, UNICEF and LSHTM, New York

WHO (1996) *Essential Safety Requirements for Street-Vended Foods*, revised edition, Food Safety Unit, Division of Food and Nutrition, World Health Organization, Geneva, pp36

WHO (2002) *WHO Global Strategy for Food Safety: Safer Food for Better Health*, World Health Organization, Geneva, www.who.int/foodsafety/publications/general/en/strategy_en.pdf

WHO (2004) 'Fact sheet 3: The informal food trade', World Health Organization, Geneva, www.afro.who.int/des/fos/afro_codex-fact-sheets/fact3_street-foods.pdf

WHO (2006) *Guidelines for the Safe Use of Wastewater, Excreta and Greywater, Volume 2: Wastewater Use in Agriculture*, World Health Organization, Geneva

Yahaya, I. and M. Kinane (2009) Willingness to pay study supported by IWMI and FAO Ghana (unpublished data)

17

Harnessing Farmers' Knowledge and Perceptions for Health-Risk Reduction in Wastewater-Irrigated Agriculture

Bernard Keraita, Pay Drechsel, Razak Seidu, Priyanie Amerasinghe, Olufunke O. Cofie and Flemming Konradsen

ABSTRACT

This chapter addresses the importance of understanding farmers' knowledge and perceptions on health-risk and risk-reduction measures for the development of mutually acceptable risk-management strategies. Drawing on studies from different countries, the chapter shows that it is not realistic to expect high risk awareness. In cases where farmers are aware of health risks, they assess mitigation measures in view of their overall impact on work efficiency and crop yield rather than only the potential health benefits to be gained. The chapter asserts that for on-farm risk-reduction measures to be successful, it is pertinent that farmers' needs and constraints are incorporated into the formulation of recommended practices. This might happen through indigenous processes but can be supported through farm-based participatory approaches where farmers and scientists work together in developing risk reduction measures. An important first step is the identification of mutually accepted problem indicators. Where health benefits for farmers and consumers are not sufficient reasons for the adoption of safer practices, other triggers have to be identified as well as appropriate communication channels for effective outreach.

INTRODUCTION

A wide range of measures exists for reducing health risks from wastewater and human excreta use in agriculture. Aside from conventional wastewater treatment, farmers can play a significant role in a multiple-barrier approach. Some of the on-farm measures for health-risk reduction are presented in Chapter 10 of this book. To achieve broad adoption and comprehensive health protection for farmers and consumers, it is necessary that farmers see the risks. Without risk awareness it will be very difficult to promote a behaviour-change towards safer practices. In addition, incentives might be necessary, especially in the fields of health risks where short-term benefits might not be visible, while recommended measures might even require additional resources or reduce crop yields to some extent (see Chapter 16). Soil conservation projects usually face similar challenges (Sanders et al., 1999).

Existing 'standard' recommendations for farm-based risk-management measures can seldom be transferred straight into the farmer's field. Neither drip kits nor recommended cessation periods will automatically fit local conditions, such as cropping density, wastewater quality or crop water requirements. Several technologies require analytical monitoring and evaluation tools far beyond the technical and financial capacities of most farmers, particularly in developing countries. Therefore, it is essential that the development of risk assessments and risk-mitigation measures seeks to involve farmers actively in the process. Ideally, risk-reduction methods and performance assessment should go hand-in-hand so that farmers can see the benefits. This can be best achieved, for example, through mutually agreed indicators. Many studies have shown that farm-based interventions have largely failed due to lack of farmer participation, especially in resource-poor countries (Collinson, 2000; Drechsel and Gyiele, 1998).

Knowledge and awareness of risks strongly influence how risks are perceived and managed (Peres et al., 2006; Stewart-Taylor and Cherries, 1998). Awareness can be based on practical experience, but farmers also incorporate new information and concepts from colleague farmers, agricultural extension officers, field schools, input suppliers, the media, development workers and others into their knowledge base. This chapter reviews knowledge and perceptions of farmers towards wastewater- and human excreta-related health risks from different case studies, with more emphasis on Ghana. It also discusses how this knowledge can be used to influence behaviour-change towards the adoption of health-risk reduction measures.

HEALTH RISKS: FARMERS' PERCEPTIONS
AND SCIENTIFIC EVIDENCE

Wastewater use

There is overwhelming epidemiological evidence that wastewater and excreta use pose significant health risks if undertaken without effective risk-management practices. Several studies show that the greatest risk for farm workers in wastewater-irrigated agriculture derives from intestinal nematode infections and for produce consumers, from bacterial disease infections (Blumenthal and Peasey, 2002; Shuval et al., 1986). However, perception studies show that farmers generally are satisfied with their wastewater sources and do not perceive that wastewater irrigation poses a significant health risk.

Typically, a range of other farming constraints are ranked higher than any health issue and perceived health threats are dominated by ones unrelated to wastewater (Bayrau et al., 2009; Obuobie et al., 2006; Ouedraogo, 2002). Thus, there are often no significant differences in risk perception between farmers using different water qualities as shown in Accra and Ouagadougou (Gbewonyo, 2007; Gerstl, 2001) even where quantitative microbial risk assessments (QMRA) predict gross differences (Seidu et al., 2008). Those farmers who are aware of the potential health risks from using polluted water sources appear to perceive such risks to be low and seem willing to accept these risks because of the economic benefits gained from using polluted water and the unavailability of other water sources (Gbewonyo, 2007; Obuobie et al., 2006). Also, potential risks for consumers are usually questioned although it is difficult to get unbiased answers. Compared with the consumption of wastewater-irrigated food, occupational risks affecting farmers' work performance are ranked higher by farmers (Keraita et al., 2008a, Knudsen et al., 2008).[1] This awareness, however, seldom translates into the adoption of protective measures (Keraita, 2002; Obuobie et al., 2006). Protective clothing is in most cases perceived to be unsuitable in hot conditions and also not necessary given the low level of perceived risk (Bayrau et al., 2009).

An interesting study was presented by Bayrau et al. (2009), who compared perceived risk between urban farmers using wastewater and rural farmers using clean water. The results showed exactly the opposite of what was expected, and in this way reveals the challenges such perception studies are facing (Table 17.1). The reason in this case, like in many others, is the need to see the farmer in his or her context. The wastewater irrigators were more urban-based, appeared better educated, showed a higher level of hygiene and their housing situation was better

Table 17.1 *Prevalence of perceived illness among farmers working on irrigation farms within and around Addis Ababa*

Perceived illness	Prevalence (%)[a]	
	Wastewater area (n = 240)	Freshwater area (n = 175)
Intestinal pain	18	51
Diarrhoea	6	49
Skin infection	0.5	4

[a]All differences between both groups were significant at <1%.
Source: Bayrau et al. (2009)

in terms of access to piped water, sanitation facilities and number of persons per room (Bayrau et al., 2009).

Studies from Nairobi showed that wastewater farmers were concerned about the quality of their water and its potential to cause disease (Kilelu, 2004). However, farmers' perceptions of the link between wastewater use and enteric diseases were diverse. Some farmers rejected the possibility of negative health consequences due to handling of wastewater or through consuming crops grown with the wastewater and pointed at other food-safety measures, such as cooking. In addition, most farmers indicated that they usually washed their produce before consumption; but the observation by researchers in the field was that produce was consumed without washing. Some felt that they had developed immunity through years of exposure. The farmers' view of enteric disease was that the occurrence of enteric diseases was normal and not necessarily related to their use of wastewater. It is significant that around 80 per cent of the farmers surveyed did not perceive wastewater use to be making them more vulnerable to enteric diseases but enquiry into specific diseases found that the primary health concern for most farmers was skin irritation. Even though farmers were aware of possible negative effects of wastewater on health, they continued to use it as there was no other water available for agriculture.

In Pikine, Senegal, farmers reported malaria, parasitic infection, dermatitis and fatigue as the top four illnesses they had experienced in the previous year. About 70 per cent of the farmers said that they personally had not suffered any illnesses related to wastewater (Chaudhuri, 2008). In comparison, district health statistics in Pikine listed malaria, dermatitis, parasitic infections, arterial hypertension, diarrhoea and anaemia as the top six diseases for all ages. Interestingly, diarrhoea was not cited among the farmers as a health problem, perhaps because of its greater incidence and severity among children. Under-reporting of diarrhoeal episodes may also occur due to cultural taboos because as a loose stool might no longer be perceived as noteworthy.

An earlier study by Niang (2002) found a significantly higher prevalence of *Ascaris* among wastewater farmers (75 per cent) than farmers using shallow groundwater (21 per cent), while approximately the same number in both groups (46–48 per cent) did not see a relationship with wastewater use. This suggests that many of these farmers may have been infected with parasites without knowing it.

Although this situation draws a pessimistic picture in view of risk awareness, it can change. In the case of Ghana, for example, a number of projects on wastewater and related risk mitigation significantly influenced farmers' knowledge, while different media alerted policy-makers to take action (Obuobie et al., 2006). With or without their own-risk perception, farmers felt the pressure to respond, at least to avoid confrontation and risk losing their business.

The invisibility of pathogens and the lack of connection made between symptoms of potential illnesses and exposure shows the need for mutually agreed risk indicators. While most of the research has been focused on helminth infections and diarrhoeal diseases as occupational health risks in wastewater agriculture, more investigation is needed to link skin infections to particular water pollutants (Trang et al., 2007). Studies in Nepal, Cambodia, India, Pakistan and Vietnam have strongly associated skin diseases to contact with untreated wastewater (Keraita et al., 2008b).

Human excreta use

Perceptions from farmers using fresh human excreta in southern Ghana are presented in Table 17.2. Farmers asked septic truck drivers to dump their loads on the fields (Cofie et al., 2009). Most farmers associated excreta use with increased agricultural productivity. Bad odour from excreta was mentioned as a major problem by users and also the main reason why non-users were reluctant to use excreta on their lands. Users of excreta perceived that it did not contaminate food as indicated by the high negative index value of −0.93 for users (Table 17.2), which is significantly different from the weighted average index of −0.26 for non-users. However, farmers had good reason for their assessment as, in the study location, excreta is used mainly for maize and not vegetables. After exposure to the sun, dried excreta is ploughed into the soil prior to planting. Nevertheless, out of 11 defined variables that possibly affect farmers' decision to use excreta, only health risk and loss of income emerged as negative influences on the probability of excreta use.

In northern Ghana, where excreta use has a longer tradition, farmers using human excreta associated it with skin infections, diarrhoea, foot rot and vomiting (Seidu et al., 2009). Farmers related vomiting episodes to the strong odour from raw excreta and skin infection to the handling of relatively wet sludge. Dried excreta (cake) and odourless sludge, irrespective of the treatment duration, were on the other hand considered by farmers to pose no health risk. There was no objection to handling these cakes with bare hands including those only dried for a short time. A QMRA of such 'cake sludge' across 40 faecal sludge drying sites in Tamale revealed

Table 17.2 *Farmers' perception on the use of human excreta in agriculture*

Factors	WAI[a] of Users	WAI of Non-Users	T-test	P-value
Excreta is good for soil structure	1.47	0.63	3.99	0.000
Excreta is an important source of nutrients	1.40	0.76	3.50	0.001
Excreta causes odour problems	1.50	1.60	1.04	0.302
Excreta poses health risks	0.50	0.70	0.20	0.839
Excreta is unfriendly to the environment	0.60	0.77	0.99	0.322
Excreta causes food contamination	−0.93	−0.26	2.49	0.042
Excreta deposited on farms has low quality (as perceived through visual appearance)	0.33	0.90	3.64	0.001

[a]WAI = Weighted Average Index.
Source: Cofie et al. (2009)

high *Ascaris* and viral infections risk for farmers above the WHO tolerable infection risk of 1 infection per 10,000 persons per year (Seidu et al., 2009).

FACTORS INFLUENCING FARMERS' HEALTH-RISK PERCEPTION

It is widely expected and accepted that farmers and public health risk experts perceive risks differently (Lazo et al., 2000). Understanding these differences is an important step in the development and promotion of best practices and technologies. What causes these differences and how can they be minimized to enhance adoption of safe practices? In risk-perception studies conducted in Ghana, a number of reasons, including process-related ones, were identified:

Experience of farmers in waste reuse

Studies show that knowledge and perceptions of farmers on health risks can be influenced by the duration farmers had been involved in their business. In northern Ghana, farmers with a long experience in human excreta application more easily identified diseases to be associated with poorly treated human excreta than those with little experience in its use (Seidu et al., 2009). In Kumasi and Accra, where farmers who had longer experience in wastewater farming generally rated risks lower than those who had been farming for less than two years (Keraita et al., 2008a).

Level of knowledge on risk

Given the standard educational level among farming communities, most of the farmers did not have deep knowledge about the causes of health problems and health-risk factors. This deficit applies in particular to 'invisible' health risks like pathogens. Training on health risks from wastewater irrigation has not been incorporated in education curricula including those of agricultural extension officers due to the informal nature of this practice and its relatively low national importance. Nevertheless, an increase in knowledge, awareness and interest in health-risk issues and risk mitigation was noticed where farmers were exposed to the issue, mostly through research projects.

Source of knowledge

Perceptions depend on how people obtain their knowledge. In view of health risks, there are different sources possible, and not all are appropriate. In Ghana, the media has been one of the main sources of knowledge for farmers, which has also shaped a lot of their perceptions on the risk. As observed in other studies, the media can build complex messages about risks but can also amplify or attenuate risks (Boholm, 1998); the Ghanaian media, for example, basically condemned the practices and amplified the risks (Obuobie et al., 2006). While complex messages and amplifying risks should be discouraged, risky practices should not be encouraged either. In essence, there should be a balance on presenting risk messages to farmers to ensure that they are rated appropriately to instigate change to safer practices that are necessary for health protection.

Living standards of farmers

Many farmers live in poor settlement areas under unsanitary conditions, often with limited access to safe drinking water. In such circumstances, the immediate environment influences perceptions forming attitudes and standards with which they live on a day-to-day basis, as also shown in the case reported from Ethiopia (Bayrau et al., 2009). Under these circumstances wastewater irrigation might not receive particular attention. Common standards equally influence researchers, who might have been brought up under different sanitary standards and are now challenged to perform unbiased interviews. Moreover, being exposed to different levels of sanitary standards, both scientists and farmers might have problems in agreeing on common indicators for diseases to be associated with the wastewater or excreta exposure on farm. Detailed epidemiological studies will be necessary to show the fraction attributed to different risk factors.

Defensive strategies

Interview results might be biased if farmers feel the need to develop defensive strategies to show that their practices are safe so that their business is not jeopardized or so that they are not seen as propagators of public-health risks within the community. Negative perceptions by the interviewer, the public, or harassment from authorities and media, can drive farmers to develop defensive strategies to consciously underestimate health risks associated with their practice. Similar findings have been reported among pesticide users in Brazil (Peres et al., 2006). Such denial and defensive strategies can greatly hinder risk communication and are difficult to separate from low-risk perception associated with living conditions that are unsanitary. It is therefore crucial to build trust among community members and vendors for any risk-factor communication (Siegrist, 2000). This was also shown in a related study done for street-food vending where purchase of street food was mainly based on trust in the vendor, since no reliable indicator existed for actually evaluating food safety. Therefore, trust also becomes a necessity, where no other evaluation parameter is available (Rheinländer et al., 2008).

The opposite of a defensive strategy also occurs where farmers expect external assistance and therefore exaggerate their problems.

FARMERS' KNOWLEDGE AND PERCEPTIONS OF
HEALTH-RISK REDUCTION MEASURES

Assessing farmer perceptions requires listening skills and unbiased methods. These have to be carefully worked out in different social and cultural settings, by understanding the environment and the access to information that farmers may have. Understanding farmers' knowledge and perceptions on risk-reduction measures, particularly the factors that they use to assess whether technologies are appropriate for them, is very important. This assessment of whether a measure is appropriate does not necessarily consist of an absolute 'yes' or 'no' answer. It usually consists of a ranking of the measures from more appropriate to less appropriate, based on different criteria. Knowing how to garner these perceptions, translate them into criteria for evaluating risk-reduction measures and ranking them against alternative measures is a skill that the researcher has to develop.

In Ghana, wastewater farmers were involved in identifying their own suitable risk-reduction measures (Keraita et al., 2008a), which are presented in Table 17.3. These measures were very different from those suggested in the WHO Guidelines (2006), such as conventional wastewater treatment, crop restrictions, conducting health programmes and human-exposure control. The reason for this was that while WHO's proposed measures are based only on health targets, i.e. the effectiveness of reducing levels of pathogens in irrigation water or on crops, farmers were more concerned with business-related risk factors like loss of yields or income, level of investment (capital, labour, land) needed and land-tenure issues. Generally, farmers preferred only slight changes in their current practices or those which required low investments. Similar findings have been reported in other studies done in resource-poor communities (Avila and Jabbar, 1992; Marenya and Barrett, 2007) and from participatory on-farm trials in general (Drechsel and Gyiele, 1998; Drechsel et al., 2005). Scientists therefore should address particular risk factors from an integrated multi-risk perspective to be in tune with the farmers' decision-making.

Another important dimension in risk perception studies was highlighted by Knudsen et al. (2008) in a study in Hanoi. The authors showed that the use of protective clothing was gender dependent. More women were found to be wearing protective gloves and boots and with more consistency than men. The differences were mainly attributed to the gender-specific work separation on farm, with men walking around the farms much more than women. Nevertheless, both groups felt that protective clothing constrained their work. These observations have also been made in studies conducted in Ethiopia and Ghana among farmers using wastewater (Bayrau et al., 2009; Obuobie et al., 2006) or human excreta (Seidu et al., 2009). In the Ghana study, which involved 138 vegetable farmers in Accra using wastewater, only 19 per cent wore protective clothing, mainly boots and gloves, while irrigating (Obuobie et al., 2006). In some cases, farmers were found to be wearing protective clothing not because of health risks, but to protect them from cold and physical injuries (Knudsen et al., 2008).

Table 17.3 *Measures identified by farmers to reduce health risks in wastewater irrigation*

Measures identified by farmers only	Measures identified following discussions with scientists
• Provision of safer irrigation water like shallow groundwater. • Protection of water sources. • Treating water with chemicals. • Filtration of irrigation water. • Using boots when stepping in water sources. • Treat soils against pathogens.	• Leaving water in irrigation sources to settle and not stepping inside. • Applying water to roots not on leaves. • Using right amounts of water. • Reducing splashing of soils on vegetables. • Using well-composted manure at the right time. • Using gloves when applying manure. • Stopping irrigation days before harvesting.

HEALTH-RISK MANAGEMENT MEASURES USED BY FARMERS

In general, farmers experiment on their own, responding to perceived production risks like pest attacks, water scarcity or reduced (fertile) land and labour availability (Mutsaers et al., 1997). Among the perceived drivers for change, health risks are not prominent which is not surprising given the low health-risk awareness. Despite this, health-risk reduction measures can become adopted if they are 'sold' well (see Chapter 16, on social marketing) or address more than health concerns; an example is the provision of water-saving drip kits which also avoid pathogen exposure of farmers and crops.

However, low water quality can be a concern to farmers, even if its health-affecting components are not perceived. This can be wastewater salinity affecting crop performance, high amounts of organic debris and waste blocking tubes, pumps and watering cans, or simply bad odour. Thus, in many cases, farmers have been found to be developing strategies and innovations to adapt to deteriorating water quality in order to maintain or increase yields and reduce other negative trade-offs including health problems. Of particular interest are those innovations which aim at reducing inputs, such as labour while also reducing health risks, like furrow irrigation compared to overhead irrigation with watering cans. This offers an entry point of mutual benefit. The following are a few other examples of farmers' wastewater management practices, in part with direct or indirect impact on health risks:

Hyderabad, India

Farmers alternate the use of groundwater with wastewater depending on the stage of plant growth. This was found to increase yields and decrease pest attacks on crops and infections among farm workers. Farmers were also found to be shifting to more wastewater-tolerant crops, gradually replacing paddy rice with fodder crops that are more tolerant to high salinity levels induced by the wastewater, and still have a high market value.

Dakar, Senegal

In areas where untreated wastewater has low salinity compared to other water sources in the area, such as on farming sites along coasts, farmers use wastewater to dilute the salinity concentrations in larger depressions and dugouts filled with saline groundwater. This has the simultaneous benefit of diluting other contaminants in the wastewater. This measure, as observed in Pikine, one of the largest urban vegetable farming sites in Dakar, transformed two unsuitable resources into a valuable asset.

Accra, Ghana

Farmers blocked wastewater channels with a series of sandbags to create ponds from where they could more easily fetch water with cans or pump, simultaneously creating a cascade of worm egg traps and sedimentation ponds, with an obvious impact on pathogen levels (IWMI, 2008).

Dakar, Senegal, and Lomé, Togo

Farmers fixed mosquito nets over the intake holes of their watering cans to keep debris out. This concomitantly reduced the intake of pathogens attached to floating organic matter, including excreta.

Northern Ghana

Two sun-drying methods, random spot spreading and pit composting, are used to process raw faecal sludge into odourless 'cake' by farmers. Timing of treatment (drying) is mainly in the dry season when temperatures are high to enhance dewatering of sludge. This is accompanied by the destruction of pathogenic organisms. The duration of drying ranges from a few weeks to several months. In southern Ghana, crops are also irrigated with fresh sludge, i.e. without drying. However, in both cases, the crops are mostly cereals which are cooked before eating.

IMPLEMENTATION PROCESS TO ENHANCE ADOPTION OF RISK-REDUCTION MEASURES

Participatory research approaches have shown great potential for facilitating the adoption of innovative risk-reduction measures (Chambers and Ghildyal, 1985; Drechsel and Gyiele, 1998). Participatory research allows for a mutual diagnosis of farmers' constraints and the identification of appropriate solutions within a holistic interdisciplinary framework, rather than a narrow technological or crop focus (Martin and Sherington, 1997). Technology development is based on mutual learning loops and modifications (Figure 17.1). This is particularly important in view of safer irrigation practices, like drip irrigation, furrow irrigation or cessation of water application which can significantly reduce crop yields if not well adapted to local possibilities and constraints (Keraita et al., 2007a,b). The challenge, though, is to find the best compromise between maximum risk mitigation and lowest discomfort for the farmer to minimize possible adoption constraints (Collinson, 2000).

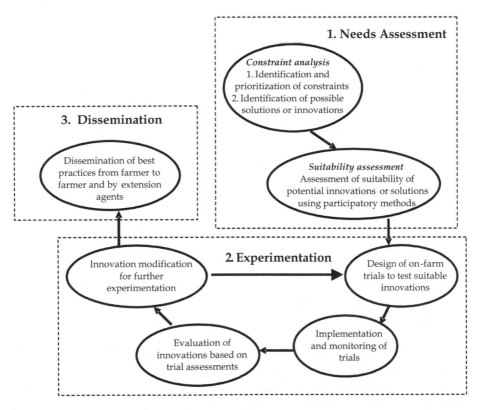

Figure 17.1 *Diagrammatic representation of the on-farm research process*

Source: Dorward et al. (2003)

THE CHALLENGE OF VISUALIZING INVISIBLE RISKS

One of the greatest challenges in safe waste reuse is getting farmers to understand health risks stemming from 'invisible' contamination such as from parasites or chemicals in water and soil. It is also a challenge to get farmers to monitor the effect of reducing invisible risks. As mentioned in Chapter 16, the Ghana hand-washing campaign faced a similar challenge but was ultimately very successful. The campaign decided not to provide any information on health risk associated with contaminated hands, but based its message on 'disgust' which appeared to be a sufficiently powerful trigger to protect the family.

Facilitating behaviour-change among farmers, on the other hand, is less straightforward because the main health risks are for consumers far down the market chain. Complaints about the food hardly reach the farmers. There are only very few cases where the farm family also consumes the vegetables that they produce, as exotic vegetables, which are actually those eaten raw, are not common in traditional diets. It is therefore important to study other possible indicators to increase awareness on water pollution and related health risk among farmers.

Low-cost test kits for water-quality monitoring could help to visualize invisible risk, as tested for example in Sri Lanka (Shingles and Saltori, 2008) and Ghana (McGregor et al., 2001). Another possible indicator of pollution could be the lack of certain indicator species such as frogs, toads or insects only known in clean water. Skin rashes might be an indicator of how bad water affects human health. Usually, farmers rely on such physical and sensuous indicators, such as colour, odour and occurrence of solid materials, to ascertain the level of contamination in water. For example, in Kano, Nigeria, some of the farmers, using untreated industrial effluents from breweries and tanneries, use colour, smell and the formation of foam to determine unfavourable or undesirable conditions (Binns et al., 2003). An example of a farmer's statement was:

> *There are three bad colours [of water] that come at different times. The oily red one and the green one will kill the crops, and when we see these colours in the channel, we turn off our pumps immediately. The bluish water is corrosive and causes a red rash when it comes in contact with the skin. We always wash our hands after we come in contact with the blue water.*

Knudsen et al. (2008) similarly illustrated how farmers in peri-urban Hanoi, Vietnam, use locally adapted indicators to characterize wastewater. When the water had pink bubbles, farmers called it 'soap detergent water' and considered it the worst type of water because it had a high content of chemical waste, such as from soap detergent factories. They also described wastewater as 'organic fertilizer water' if the water was black and smelly and associated this water primarily with toilets that discharged directly to the river.

Participatory on-farm research will allow scientists to verify how far farmers' physical indicators correspond with microbiological reality. For example, studies have shown that although shallow wells used in irrigation had clear water and no bad odour, and were therefore thought to be 'physically clean', they actually contained high levels of coliform bacteria just like water from neighbouring streams that were perceived to be 'physically dirty' (Keraita et al., 2008a). In Tamale, dried 'cake' sludge, considered by farmers to pose no health risk, still had thermotolerant coliform bacteria and *Ascaris* concentrations above the WHO monitoring guideline for faecal sludge application but, indeed, much lower bacteria levels than fresh sludge (Seidu et al., 2009).

Aside from the agreement on a risk indicator for the water or sludge, the next challenge is to explain to farmers that the recommended (alternative) practices will have a positive impact along the food chain, where other indicators are required to visualize the reduced health risk. An innovative 'germ' indicator, like the Glitterbug™ gel (www.glitterbug.com), might help to trigger a lasting visual experience which can be applied along the whole farm to fork pathway.

Whatever the indicators might be, they should increase risk awareness and help farmers and scientists to communicate. Increased awareness alone, however, in many cases will not be sufficient to trigger behaviour-change. Additional incentives are needed, such as economic incentives, access to credit or tenure security, and positive media support (Chapter 16). Figure 17.2 shows a comparative assessment of possible triggers mentioned by farmers in Kumasi and Accra versus the ranking of local experts who suggested that farmers might have downplayed their interests in subsidies while overstating their concerns for consumers' health.

COMMUNICATION CHANNELS

Participatory approaches among scientists and farmers involved in a project can help with communication, building capacity and finding mutually acceptable solutions. To reach out to even more farmers it is important to know to whom farmers listen and how best to connect with them. A pilot social marketing study in Ghana showed that it is more likely that innovations spread from farmer to farmer through social networks than through any external facilitation (Figure 17.3) and that farmers preferred field demonstration and/or learning by doing (Figure 17.4).

This also verifies the importance of encouraging farmers' own experimentation because it promotes knowledge generation and self-monitoring and evaluation. However, it is pertinent for the implementation process to recognize the wider system within which farmers operate. This system, made up of institutions, regulatory bodies and in- and output markets, can have a significant positive or negative influence on farmers' decision-making, but might be neglected by scientists.

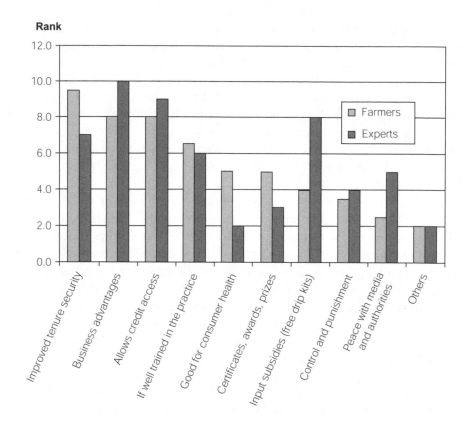

Figure 17.2 *Comparing expert opinion with farmer expressed motivation for a possible behaviour change in southern Ghana*

Source: IWMI (2008), unpublished

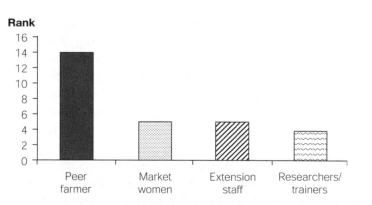

Figure 17.3 *Farmers' preferences for which 'person' to follow in teaching innovations in agriculture*

Source: IWMI (2008), unpublished

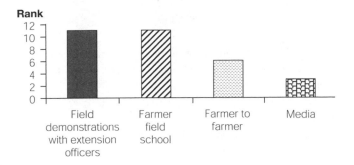

Figure 17.4 *Farmers' preferences for the method of learning new practices*

Source: IWMI (2008), unpublished

CONCLUSIONS

Farmers using wastewater and human excreta are in general not aware of the type of risks they are facing, or do not rank the risk highly. In order to find common ground and to use knowledge to change perceptions and behaviour, farmers and scientists need to work together. The lack of tools and indicators suitable for farmers to assess and monitor health risks is, however, problematic, as the physical indicators used by farmers to assess wastewater and human excreta for reuse do not necessarily correspond to laboratory assessments. It might still be appropriate for researchers to broaden their indicators to include those identified by farmers. These might include problem indicators (poor water quality) and certainly in- and output indicators which cover labour, capital and land inputs, and, most of all, the resulting crop yields.

Recommended practices might have to undergo adjustments to keep efforts low and outputs high. These may not necessarily be the most effective measures in reducing health risks but are probably more sustainable. It is therefore important to encourage farmers to look for solutions on their own, and several indigenous solutions actually reduce health risks even if it is inadvertent (IWMI, 2008).

ACKNOWLEDGEMENT

Authors wish to thank Line Gram Knudsen and Thilde Rheinländer, both of the Department of International Health, University of Copenhagen, for their contributions towards this paper.

NOTE

1   Where exotic vegetables are produced for the market, farmers generally do not consume them and may not be aware of possible health implications from own experience (Drechsel et al., 2006).

REFERENCES

Avila, M. and Jabbar, M. A. (1992) 'Socio-economic assessment of alley farming', in B. R. Tripathi and P. J. Psychas (eds) *The AFNETA Alley Farming Training Manual – Volume 1: Core Course in Alley Farming*, Alley Farming Network for Tropical Africa, www.fao.org/Wairdocs/ILRI/x5545E/x5545e09.htm

Bayrau, A., Boelee, E., Drechsel, P. and Dabbert, S. (2009) 'Wastewater use in crop production in peri-urban areas of Addis Ababa: Impacts on health in farm household', *Environment and Development Economics* (in press)

Binns, J. A., Maconachie, R. A. and Tanko, A. I. (2003) 'Water, land and health in urban and peri-urban food production: The case of Kano, Nigeria', www.cityfarmer.org/WaterLandHealthKano.rtf

Blumenthal, U. J. and Peasey, A. (2002) 'Critical review of epidemiological evidence of the health effects of wastewater and excreta use in agriculture', unpublished document prepared for World Health Organization, Geneva, www.who.int/water_sanitation_health/wastewater/whocriticalrev.pdf

Boholm, A. (1998) 'Comparative studies of risk perception: A review of twenty years of research', *Journal of Risk Research*, vol 1, no 2, pp135–63

Chambers, R. and Ghildyal, B. P. (1985) 'Agricultural research for resource poor farmers: The farmer-first-and-last model', *Agricultural Administration*, vol 20, pp1–30

Chaudhuri, N. (2008) 'Using participatory education and action research for health risk reduction amongst farmers in Dakar, Senegal', in M. Redwood (ed) *Agriculture in Urban Planning: Generating Livelihoods and Food Security*, Earthscan/IDRC, London, www.idrc.ca/en/ev-135178-201-1-DO_TOPIC.html

Cofie, O. O., Adeoti, A., Nkansah-Boadu, F. and Awuah, E. (2009) 'Adoption and impacts of excreta use for crop production in southern Ghana', *Journal of Environmental Management* (under review)

Collinson, M. (2000) 'Evolving typologies for agricultural research and development', in M. Collinson (ed) *A History of Farming Systems Research*, CABI/FAO, Wallingford, UK, pp 51–8

Dorward, P., Galpin, M. and Shepherd, D. (2003) 'Participatory Farm Management methods for assessing the suitability of potential innovations: A case study on green manuring options for tomato producers in Ghana', *Agricultural Systems*, vol 75, pp97–117

Drechsel, P. S., Graefe, M., Sonou, O. and Cofie, O. (2006) *Informal Irrigation in Urban West Africa: An Overview*, Research Report 102, IWMI, Colombo, www.iwmi.cgiar.org/Publications/IWMI_Research_Reports/PDF/pub102/RR102.pdf

Drechsel, P. and Gyiele, L. (eds) (1998) 'On-farm research on sustainable land management in sub-Saharan Africa: Approaches, experiences, and lessons', *IBSRAM Proceedings 19*, Bangkok, p254

Drechsel, P., Olaleye, A., Adeoti, A., Thiombiano, L., Barry, B. and Vohland, K. (2005) *Adoption Driver and Constraints of Resource Conservation Technologies in sub-Saharan Africa*, FAO, Humboldt, IWMI University, Accra, Ghana, www.iwmi.cgiar.org/africa/West/pdf/AdoptionConstraints-Overview.pdf

Gbewonyo, K. (2007) 'Wastewater irrigation and the farmer: Investigating the relation between irrigation water source, farming practices, and farmer health in Accra, Ghana', unpublished thesis, Harvard College, Cambridge, MA

Gerstl, S. (2001) 'The economic costs and impact of home gardening in Ouagadougou, Burkina Faso', PhD dissertation, University of Basel, Basel, Switzerland

IWMI (2008) 'Health risk reduction in a wastewater irrigation system in urban Accra, Ghana', www.youtube.com/watch?v=f_EnUGa_GdM

Keraita, B. (2002) 'Wastewater use in urban and peri-urban vegetable farming in Kumasi, Ghana', unpublished MSc thesis, Wageningen University, Wageningen, The Netherlands

Keraita, B., Drechsel, P. and Konradsen, F. (2008a) 'Perceptions of farmers on health risks and risk reduction measures in wastewater-irrigated urban vegetable farming in Ghana', *Journal of Risk Research*, vol 11, no 8, pp1047–61

Keraita, B., Jiménez, B. and Drechsel, P. (2008b) 'Extent and implications of agricultural reuse of untreated, partly treated, and diluted wastewater in developing countries', *CAB Reviews: Perspectives in Agriculture, Veterinary Science, Nutrition and Natural Resources*, CABI Publishing, Wallingford, UK

Keraita, B., Konradsen, F., Drechsel, P. and Abaidoo, R. C. (2007a) 'Effect of low-cost irrigation methods on microbial contamination of lettuce', *Tropical Medicine and International Health*, vol 12, suppl. 2, pp15–22

Keraita, B., Konradsen, F., Drechsel, P. and Abaidoo, R. C. (2007b) 'Reducing microbial contamination on lettuce by cessation of irrigation before harvesting', *Tropical Medicine and International Health*, vol 12, suppl. 2, pp8–14

Kilelu, C. (2004) 'Wastewater irrigation and farmer's perception of health risks and institutional perspectives: A case study from Maili Saba, Nairobi', *CFP Report 38*, IDRC, Ottawa

Knudsen, L. G., Phuc, P. D., Hiep, N. T., Samuelson, H., Jensen, P. K., Dalsgaard, A., Raschid-Sally, L. and Konradsen, F. (2008) 'The fear of awful smell: risk perceptions among farmers in Vietnam using wastewater and human excreta in agriculture', *Southeast Asian Journal of Tropical Medicine and Public Health*, vol 39, no 2, pp341–52

Lazo, J. K., Kinnell, J. C. and Fisher, A. (2000) 'Expert and lay person perceptions of ecosystem risks', *Risk Analysis*, vol 20, pp179–93

Marenya, P. P. and Barrett, C. B (2007) 'Household-level determinants of adoption of improved natural resources management practices among smallholder farmers in western Kenya', *Food Policy*, vol 32, pp515–36

Martin, A. and Sherington, J. (1997) 'Participatory research methods – Implementation, effectiveness and institutional context', *Agricultural Systems*, vol 55, no 2, pp195–216

McGregor, D. A., Thompson, D., Kotei, N., Poku, O. and Simon, D. (2001) 'Testing a method of environmental self-monitoring: Water quality test kit project, peri-urban Kumasi', *CEDAR/IRNR Kumasi Paper 2*, DFID Peri-urban Interface Production Systems Research Project R7330

Mutsaers, H. J. W., Weber, G. K., Walker, P. and Fischer, N. M. (1997) *A Field Guide for On-Farm Experimentation*, IITA, Ibadan, Nigeria, p235

Niang, S. (2002) 'Maitrise des risques dans la valorisation des eaux usées en agriculture urbaine', in O. O. Akinbamijo, S. T. Fall and O. B. Smith (eds) *Advances in Crop–Livestock Integration in West African Cities*, International Trypanotolerance Centre, ISRA, IDRC, Ottawa

Obuobie, E., Keraita, B., Danso, G., Amoah, P., Cofie, O., Raschid-Sally, L. and Drechsel, P. (2006) *Irrigated Urban Vegetable Production in Ghana: Characteristics, Benefits and Risks*, IWMI-RUAF-CPWF, IWMI, Accra, Ghana

Ouedraogo, B. (2002) 'Perceptions of Ouagadougou market gardeners on water, hygiene and disease', *Urban Agriculture Magazine*, vol 8, pp24–5

Peres, F., Moreira, C. J., Rodrigues, M. and Claudio, L. (2006) 'Risk perception and communication regarding pesticide use in rural work: A case study of Rio de Janeiro State, Brazil', *International Journal of Occupational and Environmental Health*, vol 12, pp400–407

Rheinländer, T., Olsen, M., Bakang, J. A., Takyi, H., Konradsen, F. and Samuelson, H. (2008) 'Keeping up appearances: Perceptions of street food safety in urban Kumasi, Ghana', *Journal of Urban Health*, vol 85, no 6, pp952–64

Sanders, D. W., Huszar, P. C., Sombatpanit, S. and Enters, T. (1999) *Incentives in Soil Conservation, From Theory to Practice*, Oxford & IBH Publishing, New Delhi

Seidu, R., Drechsel, P. and Stenström, T.-A. (2009) 'Occupational risk associated with the "cake" sludge application in northern Ghana: Comparative assessment of perceived and probabilistic health risk', in preparation

Seidu, R., Heistad, A., Jenssen, P. D., Drechsel, P. and Stenström, T.-A. (2008) 'Quantification of the health risks associated with wastewater reuse in Accra, Ghana: A contribution toward local guidelines', *Journal of Water and Health*, vol 6, no 4, pp461–71

Shingles, K. and Saltori, R. (2008) 'Community use of H_2S (hydrogen sulphide) as a verification tool for water safety plans', in H. Jones (ed) *Access to Sanitation and Safe Water: Global Partnerships and Local Actions*, 33rd WEDC International Conference, Accra, Ghana

Shuval, H. I., Adin, A., Fattal, B., Rawitz, E. and Yekutiel, P. (1986) *Wastewater Irrigation in Developing Countries: Health Effects and Technical Solutions*, World Bank Technical Paper no 51, World Bank, Washington, DC

Siegrist, M. (2000) 'The influence of trust and perceptions of risks and benefits on the acceptance of gene technology', *Risk Analysis*, vol 20, pp195–204

Slovic, P. (1987) 'Perception of risk', *Science*, vol 236, pp280–85

Stewart-Taylor, A. J. and Cherries, J. W. (1998) 'Does risk perception affect behavior and exposure? A pilot study amongst asbestos workers', *Annals of Occupational Hygiene*, vol 42, pp565–9

Trang, D. T., van der Hoek, W., Tuan, N. D., Cam, P. C., Viet, V. H., Luu, D. D., Konradsen, F. and Dalsgaard, A. (2007) 'Skin disease among farmers using wastewater in rice cultivation in Nam Dinh, Vietnam', *Tropical Medicine and International Health*, vol 12, no 2, pp51–8

WHO (2006) *Guidelines for the Safe Use of Wastewater, Excreta and Greywater, Volume 2: Wastewater Use in Agriculture*, World Health Organization, Geneva

18

Multi-Stakeholder Processes for Managing Wastewater Use in Agriculture

*Alexandra E. V. Evans, Liqa Raschid-Sally and
Olufunke O. Cofie*

ABSTRACT

Wastewater use in agriculture is a complex phenomenon since it transcends typical sectoral and geographical policy and planning boundaries, and is influenced by opinions and perceptions. Planning for wastewater use typically requires the involvement of a number of government agencies covering health, water, sanitation, agriculture and irrigation, as well as researchers, community groups and the private sector. Where wastewater use is already taking place spontaneously and unofficially, how can these stakeholders come together to improve the management of the system to maximize the livelihoods benefits while minimizing impacts on health and the environment? One option is the formation of multi-stakeholder platforms, which provide a space for stakeholders to share opinions and seek negotiated solutions in an open and 'level' environment. How effective these are, what outcomes can be expected, and how they can be improved are all questions that are still being asked. This chapter presents three case studies in which multi-stakeholder processes were used to improve wastewater management for urban agriculture. Although differences were observed, there were several cross-cutting lessons. A critical factor is the starting point, including an agreed definition of the problem to be addressed, negotiated goals and a management structure that is acceptable to all stakeholders. When multi-stakeholder processes are externally initiated, as with those reviewed here, it is essential that project priorities are commensurate with local priorities. Finding an institutional home and anchor agency can improve long-term sustainability but care must be taken in considering how this impacts on existing power structures. Participation and representation greatly influence the effectiveness of the process and much may need to be done to support this, for example by strengthening local community groups. A factor that appears to significantly improve participation and engagement is having tangible outputs, which demonstrate to stakeholders the potential of multi-stakeholder platforms.

INTRODUCTION

Multi-stakeholder platforms and processes have a number of definitions and even a variety of names, but a well-accepted definition is that of 'a decision-making body (voluntary or statutory) comprising different stakeholders who perceive the same resource management problem, realize their interdependence for solving it, and come together to agree on actions for solving the problem' (Steins and Edwards, 1998). This definition may be disputed by those who have been involved, both from the research community and those in the locations where multi-stakeholder processes take place. It is perhaps more accurate to say that this definition is the ideal to which multi-stakeholder processes should aspire. To facilitate this aspiration it is necessary to critically evaluate existing multi-stakeholder processes, including self-evaluation by the researchers involved (Sanginga et al., 2007).

This chapter reviews the application of multi-stakeholder platforms to manage wastewater for use in agriculture. Such applications are not new, but one must distinguish between two distinct circumstances of agricultural use of wastewater which influence the objectives of these platforms. The first is reuse that takes place in countries where wastewater is treated before being used to cultivate food crops. In this case the key concerns are cost, farmer willingness to pay (Neubert, 2004), farmer and public concern about impacts on crops and health, and resistance because of the 'yuck factor' (Dingfelder, 2004; Russell and Lux, 2006). Multi-stakeholder processes are implemented to gain acceptance from users, build trust and reciprocity (Po et al., 2003, Stenekes et al., 2006), and to provide the right climate for negotiation and conflict resolution.

The second circumstance is when untreated wastewater is used in an unplanned or spontaneous manner for irrigation. In this case, farmers already value it as a resource but there are health concerns (Ensink et al., 2004, 2008), which they may not take into consideration. Such situations usually occur in low-income countries where, for economic and institutional reasons, poor sanitation and wastewater-management practices prevail; they require innovative solutions to reduce water pollution and risks. In this case multi-stakeholder processes have to work towards making incremental improvements on an existing situation, including both policy changes and applying simple, innovative solutions to risk reduction that include farmers and consumers. Innovation and learning need to be integral parts of such platforms.

Obtaining acceptance for planned reuse through stakeholder involvement is covered reasonably well in the literature (Hamilton et al., 2007), but less has been written on spontaneous reuse and the role of multi-stakeholder processes in these situations. This chapter presents three cases in which multi-stakeholder processes have been applied in several countries, predominantly to address this second scenario. The projects reviewed are:

- The Wastewater Agriculture and Sanitation for Poverty Alleviation (WASPA) project;
- Sustainable Water Management Improves Tomorrow's Cities' Health (SWITCH);
- The Cities Farming for the Future Programme of the Resource Centres on Urban Agriculture and Food Security (RUAF).

These multi-stakeholder processes have been initiated to address the challenges of various aspects of wastewater management in urban areas, and urban and peri-urban agriculture, where a key concern is the health risk associated with contamination from wastewater. The focus of each is slightly different, as explained later in the chapter, with WASPA addressing the continuum from wastewater production to use in agriculture, RUAF predominantly working to improve urban and peri-urban agriculture, of which wastewater use is a part, and SWITCH addressing integrated urban water management, which in some cities includes reuse. The processes were all externally initiated but have achieved varying degrees of success and acceptance, with some having lasting impact on policy. All processes improved knowledge and motivated the stakeholders to build common visions and action plans.

These multi-stakeholder processes are analysed here to understand their potential to improve wastewater management and reuse, leading to overall improved irrigation-water quality, livelihoods benefits and public health. How stakeholders have been and can be involved to address all of these, the successes and failures and the way forward are also discussed.

BACKGROUND

Participation and multi-stakeholder processes

Partnerships and participation have been part of development practice for decades, emerging from activist participatory research and applied anthropology (Chambers, 1994) and progressing through many stages. This is traced by Reed (2008) as going from awareness-raising in the 1960s; to incorporating local perspectives in data collection and planning in the 1970s; to the development of techniques that recognize local knowledge and 'put the last first', such as farming systems research, and rapid and participatory rural appraisal in the 1980s; to the increasing use of participation as a norm in the sustainable development agenda of the 1990s (e.g. UNCED, 1992). The subsequent critique of participation, and disillusionment over its limitations and failings, resulted in a growing 'post-participation' consensus over good practice with important lessons learned from the mistakes and successes of this long history. These developments have taken place in parallel geographical and disciplinary contexts. They have been an integral part of the developments in the management of natural resources and common pool resources, for example, community forestry and integrated catchment management, and later extending to the water and sanitation sector as well as more recently the agriculture and irrigation sectors.

Stakeholder[1] involvement in problem definition and action planning developed in response to the growing expectation and demand from the public and civil society to be included in a meaningful way and not to simply accept 'expert' judgment or initiatives by government agencies (Warner, 2006). Greater stakeholder involvement also arose due to an increasing awareness that problems are multifaceted and impacts cut across many disciplines and administrative boundaries, making it necessary to find approaches that addressed this complexity (Mitchell, 1997; Stenekes et al., 2006). More specifically relating to wastewater reuse, the issue is about how the different frames of reference about risk and sustainable natural-resources management can be better understood by the stakeholders (Stenekes et al., 2006). Sustainability in this case relates to resource recovery, reduced health risks and livelihood benefits.

The partnerships of the 1990s have evolved into the multi-stakeholder processes of the present, which recognize that accommodating multiple interests in resources management is unavoidable (Ramírez, 2001) and that interaction and negotiation are necessary not just among the local community and the state agencies but all actors with a stake. This is particularly relevant in the context of wastewater agriculture in resource-poor countries, where inadequate infrastructure and the institutional vacuum (reflected in the lack of clear planning processes) make it imperative that actors consult, interact, learn from each other, attempt to consider all viewpoints and apply innovative solutions. Existing institutional systems and traditional conceptions are unable to cope with the collaboration and consensus needed to achieve sustainability. For the success of such platforms it is critical to consider the fundamental purpose for engaging stakeholders and to define clear objectives and outcomes.

Multi-stakeholder processes and platforms come in many forms and are usually perceived as incorporating several components that allow for shared learning, collaborative planning and interventions, but not all of them can be said to achieve real mutual planning and action. Understanding the broad types and what appears to constitute a 'good' and 'effective' multi-stakeholder process will assist in their replication and improvement. In this context it is useful to consider

Table 18.1 *Classification of partnerships and multi-stakeholder platforms according to relative power exerted by stakeholders*

Scale of participation and power-sharing	Rungs on the ladder of citizen participation[a]	Typology of multi-stakeholder processes according to their degree of powersharing[b]
Non-participation: limited or no power-sharing, groups operate outside 'the system'; they may have some influence through pressure and financial strength.	Manipulation – rubber-stamp committees. Therapy – power holders educate or cure citizens.	Social networks: a group of people working in different organizations that enthusiastically pursue social change but have weak links to their constituents. They struggle to have influence. Service organizations: raise money for joint projects. They take advantage of the breadth of the network to generate financial support.
Degrees of tokenism: no power-sharing but those in power may respond to concerns if it suits their purpose.	Informing: citizens' rights and options are identified. Consultation: citizens are heard but not necessarily heeded. Placation: advice is received from citizens but not acted upon	Focus or visioning groups: interested citizens and organizations giving feedback to proposals, providing information, voicing concerns and needs at the invitation of the government, only indirectly influencing the decision. Crisis management organizations: the platform tackles difficult political issues or crisis coordination in a non-threatening environment.
Degrees of citizen power: may operate outside the system but gain an element of power through cooperation; may also achieve aims by force.	Partnership: trade-offs are negotiated Delegated power: citizens are given management for selected or all parts of programmes Citizen control: full partnerships.	Social movement: an alliance for protesting about a project. It can negotiate better amenities or changes in the project when they manage to cooperate with their adversary. Management or co-management organizations: devolve decisions and management tasks to stakeholders.

Source: [a]Arnstein (1969); [b]Warner (2006)

the classifications of Arnstein (1969) according to relative power exerted by stakeholders and Warner (2006) based on the level of power-sharing (Table 18.1). It should be noted that Arnstein's categories are more clearly differentiated while Warner's range along a scale between the categories given in the table and should really be seen to be overlapping.

The plethora of multi-stakeholder platforms in the literature has led Warner (2007) to describe them as a 'multi-legged beast, often mentioned in tales, but as yet rarely spotted in broad daylight' and he considers it necessary to understand: why multi-stakeholder platforms are promoted; whether they actually emerge; and how they function. Continuing with Warner's metaphor, several of us have spotted multi-stakeholder processes and platforms but we are not always sure exactly what 'species' they are and whether they are another (less social and cooperative) beast in disguise. We may not need to know the exact species but it is useful to know how they exist and what they do so that we can try to breed good traits, for example, in terms of power-sharing and equity.

Learning Alliances and various forms of Participatory Action Planning (PAP) can be considered sub-species of multi-stakeholder processes. These were used in the cases reviewed in this chapter (either in combination or separately) and are briefly described here to give an introduction to the case studies. As stated, however, the lessons from the processes are applicable to many forms of multi-stakeholder processes and platforms and will help in identifying the traits that should be reproduced or suppressed.

Learning Alliances and Participatory Action Planning

Learning Alliances are innovative participatory processes that aim to maximize the impact of research on policy and outcomes. The term has been in use in the business world since the 1980s and is derived from work on innovation systems, where innovation is associated with the commercialization of ideas, hardware and practices, with a focus on adapting existing knowledge rather than creating new knowledge (Arnold and Bell, 2001, quoted in Verhagen et al., 2008). In development literature, Lundy et al. (2005) describe a Learning Alliance as a:

> process undertaken jointly by research organizations, donor and development agencies, policy-makers and the private sector through which good practices, in both research and development, are identified, shared, adapted and used to strengthen capacities, improve practices, generate and document development outcomes, identify future research needs and potential areas for collaboration and inform both public and private policy decisions.

Other definitions include the notions of identification, development and scaling out and up of innovations through interconnected multi-stakeholder platforms at various levels, such as community, district and national (Smits et al., 2007). The methodology has taken off in recent years, championed by the International Water and Sanitation Centre (IRC) in the water, sanitation and hygiene (WASH) sector (Moriarty et al., 2005b; Morris, 2006) and more recently as part of a holistic approach to urban water management.

Participatory action planning and the multi-stakeholder process for policy formulation and action planning (MPAP) have been used in various ways in all three of the examples, with WASPA and SWITCH drawing on the planning cycles of 'Participatory Action Plan Development' (Barr, 2001; Bunting, 2005) and the Euro-Med Participatory Water Resources Scenarios project (EMPOWERS, www. project.empowers.info). Both took the form of several iterative steps: situation and stakeholder analysis, participatory planning, visioning, assessing, consensus building, strategizing, reviewing, reflecting, disseminating and implementing (Barr, 2001; Bunting, 2005; Moriarty et al., 2005a). Central to the process is that stakeholders are given the opportunity to identify constraints, propose appropriate solutions, develop plans of action and embark upon the process of implementing preliminary development activities to address some of the most pressing and widely felt problems. Similarly, the MPAP approach used in RUAF requires a high level of participation by the parties involved. It brings all major stakeholders in urban agriculture together into a new form of communication and information exchange, dialogue, joint situation analysis, action planning, decision-making, gender-sensitive implementation, and monitoring and evaluation.

EXAMPLES OF MULTI-STAKEHOLDER PROCESSES IN WASTEWATER USE

The three examples drawn on in this chapter are distinct but have some common features, for instance:

- All three were initiated as part of donor-funded projects.
- As such, although there may have been initial stakeholder consultation to ensure that the projects and the multi-stakeholder platforms were needed or acceptable to the stakeholders, the convening agencies were in all cases external.
- All are facilitated by a lead organization that is convinced, and can persuade others that more appropriate and demand-driven research, interventions and policies will arise from multi-stakeholder processes.
- All involved the participation of both government and non-governmental stakeholders in joint situation analysis, identification and prioritization of policy issues in a manner as open and transparent as possible.
- All use similar approaches.

The findings presented here come from a combination of internal evaluations, the authors' first-hand experiences, interviews and literature reviews. The inferences about WASPA, for example, draw on a combination of experience by the authors and on findings from an internal review and process monitoring. The SWITCH findings are based primarily on literature but also on the experience of the authors in one of the SWITCH project cities (Accra). Similarly, RUAF is based on the experience of the authors in West Africa and on synthesis documents about the programme as a whole.

Wastewater Agriculture and Sanitation for Poverty Alleviation Project

The WASPA project was implemented in Rajshahi, Bangladesh, and Kurunegala, Sri Lanka, with funding from the EU Asia Pro Eco II Programme from 2005–2008 by a consortium of national and international partners. The context for the project was the use of untreated wastewater in agriculture resulting from poor waste disposal and sanitation conditions upstream. To address this a team of researchers felt that an approach which made the wastewater producers, managers and end-users part of the process, and applied holistic and sustainable wastewater-management principles, through interventions in the whole wastewater continuum, would make agricultural wastewater use more sustainable. Stakeholder involvement to develop and implement PAP was central to the project. Its objectives were therefore to:

- find innovative local solutions through joint learning;
- foster dialogue between local government, NGOs and the community;
- ensure buy-in from all stakeholders for sustainability;
- scale-up solutions to other locations.

The project proceeded through several overlapping and iterative steps (Figure 18.1), most of which were determined and driven by the convening agency (the project team):

- Initial identification of stakeholders – to answer questions about who the main stakeholders are, their roles, concerns, relationships and conflicts.
- Establishing Learning Alliances – by informing all stakeholders about the project though individual meetings at various organizations and community level meetings; and encourage them to come together to discuss wastewater management.
- Assessment, knowledge sharing and consensus building – a rapid appraisal of the existing situation, of which key components were undertaken with stakeholders, in order to create an informed basis for discussion.
- Visioning and prioritizing – once the problems were defined by the stakeholders, they were able to envisage the future desired situation, write a vision statement and define strategies to achieve them. The strategies were prioritized and action plans developed.
- Planning and implementation – by the WASPA team with working groups selected by the Learning Alliance. Specific decisions relating to the activities set out in the action plan were approved by a core group of three to four members elected by the Learning Alliance, in order to expedite their implementation.

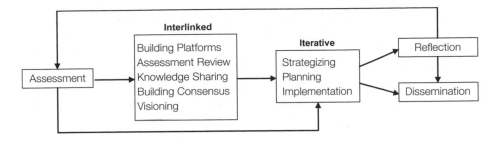

Figure 18.1 *The WASPA project process*

Source: Evans and Varma, 2009

Any amendments to the strategies or decisions about prioritizing the strategies were taken back to the full Learning Alliance.

- Monitoring and evaluation – reflection, documentation and participatory analysis with stakeholders to see whether the desired results were being achieved (Smits et al., 2009).

Achievements and challenges

Analysis of the process revealed that there were a number of successes and some challenges. Initially, the engagement of the stakeholders and development of the Learning Alliance was slow. Verhagen et al. (2008) attribute this to the lack of financial resources, which meant that it was not possible to hire a facilitator or to increase the visits by international partners. Closer examination reveals that many other factors were at least as, if not more, important, for example: inadequate training of local project staff by international partners, which would have enabled them to facilitate the process more effectively; the narrow view stakeholders held of the impacts of poor wastewater management (many saw problems that affected them in isolation, not as part of a system); political processes outside the project (such as suspension of the Bangladesh government); perceived costs in time of involvement in the Learning Alliance; potential for relinquishment of power to others within the Alliance; and insufficient legitimacy of the project team.

The process documentation and analysis identified these problems while the multi-stakeholder process was ongoing, and the project team used the findings to try to correct some of them. In both Bangladesh and Sri Lanka, team members were assigned to liaise with stakeholders; external facilitators were hired for meetings; Learning Alliance members were encouraged to share experiences, which enabled them to define a common problem and seek solutions; and structures were agreed by the Alliance, which gave greater working flexibility and resulted in more activity. The real breakthrough came when the plans began to be implemented and Alliance members saw tangible outcomes. They realized that this was not simply another 'talk shop' and they became more interested in supporting further activities.

An achievement directly attributable to the project is joint action by the government and community for improving sanitation and waste disposal in communities and thereby potentially improving water quality and public health (though these were not measured), which did not occur prior to the project. Perhaps more fundamentally, the inter-connectivity of the systems, which Huibers and van Lier (2005) describe as the water chain, was previously not part of the thinking of the Kurunegala Municipal Council or Rajshahi City Corporation, much less part of their planning. By expanding the views of the stakeholders there is the potential for wastewater agriculture issues to be addressed, or at least not ignored, in the future, and although the prospects are not certain, the stakeholders would like to keep the platform going in some form.

Sustainable Water Management Improves Tomorrow's Cities' Health

SWITCH is a large-scale research project comprising of 33 consortium partners representing academics, urban planners, water utilities and consultants, with research and demonstration activities in ten cities. The project is funded by the Sixth Framework Programme of the European Union and its goal is the development of sustainable and effective water-management systems for the 'city of the future'. The project aims to improve the scientific basis for the development and management of urban water systems, and to ensure that they are robust, flexible and adaptable to a range of future pressures. It focuses on closing the cycle through promoting the treatment and reuse of wastewater, demand management, decentralized approaches to service delivery and related innovations. The Learning Alliance approach was identified as the vehicle to drive this paradigm shift (Butterworth and Morris, 2007), with two main objectives of the Learning Alliances being to: break down barriers to horizontal (stakeholders responsible for the various components of the urban water system) and vertical (various levels of government) information sharing and learning; and speed up process identification, development and uptake of solutions.

The Learning Alliance process is required not only to understand the priorities of potential users, but also to take account of the prevailing institutional context, to undertake research in partnership with implementers and other key stakeholders, and to communicate results and emerging innovations effectively (SWITCH, 2008). Through the visioning and scenario analysis, city stakeholders have been encouraged to think about and assess the impact of the decisions that they take today on a range of possible futures, and to examine the barriers to the uptake of science in policy.

One component of the project focuses specifically on identifying and integrating appropriate productive reuse of urban water for agriculture into the policy, legislative, regulatory, urban planning and decision-making frameworks of cities. This component is being implemented in Accra, Beijing and Lima, and linkages have been developed with Hamburg (van Veenhuizen et al., 2007).

Achievements and challenges

An example of success is the Learning Alliance in Hamburg, Germany, where water has been put at the centre of development in an area of future urban expansion (SWITCH, 2008). The Learning Alliance clearly articulated that there were several problems that had to be solved and, through such conversations, trust and a sense of ownership in the Learning Alliance and its objectives were built up. The Learning Alliance now forms the basis for joint research, planning and action among four groups that were not previously well connected: the city administration, local citizens, urban water managers and planners, and researchers.

As with WASPA, the SWITCH Learning Alliances were externally initiated and not fully demand-driven, and are, so far, externally funded and not yet institutionalized. Furthermore, projects and activities related to integrated urban water management at city level were not clearly defined at the start because they were meant to be developed through the process, but this limited the possibility of attributing project funding to the activity. A similar problem was experienced in WASPA with the project funding agency insisting on detailed activities and budgets before the project had even started. It is, however, vital that in these processes multi-stakeholder platforms identify objectives quickly and start some joint activities, otherwise the energy of such platforms will diminish (Butterworth et al., 2008).

In the three cities where wastewater agriculture was the focus, van Veenhuizen et al. (2007) noted that there were both common and specific challenges. They reported that the process of developing joint action within a multi-stakeholder context requires time and needs to be adapted to the particular institutional arrangements and research and planning cultures of the different countries. Furthermore, for innovations to be scaled out and up, it is essential that there is effective process documentation, monitoring and evaluation (M&E), preferably in participatory mode, using tools such as outcome mapping, the use of micro-scenarios and knowledge management.

Resource Centres on Urban Agriculture and Food Security

RUAF seeks to develop the capacities of stakeholders, strengthen collaboration and networking among them and facilitate access to information and the sharing of experiences. Through its 'Cities farming for the future' programme, it has established multi-stakeholder platforms in 20 pilot cities around the world in order to improve the productivity of urban and peri-urban agriculture, and to increase official recognition and support for the practice, which is an important source of perishable food crops to cities in less developed countries and a source of livelihoods to urban poor. A particular problem that has to be addressed is that water resources are often contaminated with wastewater, the use of which is not officially sanctioned. Furthermore, farming is marginalized in municipal planning, with no legal framework to protect farmers, who often work without any formal structures such as farmers' organizations. As a result, it was perceived that a multi-stakeholder participatory approach should be applied (Drechsel et al., 2008) to address all these issues.

The MPAP approach, as conceived for West Africa at the onset of programme implementation, is schematically presented in Figure 18.2. It shows in particular how the policy change process could be integrated into the MPAP process to support policy outcomes which mainstream gender. The process pathway was modified for various cities within the region depending on the local policy environment.

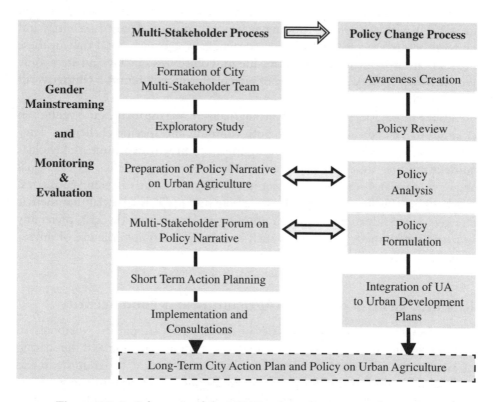

Figure 18.2 *Schematic of the MPAP approach in RUAF, West Africa*

Source: Cofie et al., 2005.

Achievements and challenges

RUAF in West Africa has had many achievements as well as broader successes associated with institutionalizing the process. It has:

- Informed policy-makers at the national ministerial level, urban agriculture stakeholders and the general public in Accra, Freetown, and Ibadan. The process has resulted in reasonable levels of commitment to promote urban agriculture, with recognition of the significance of wastewater irrigation and the need for safer practices.
- Increased capacities of local stakeholders in urban agriculture to appreciate the water-quality challenges and reduce the risks.
- Incorporated urban agriculture and informal irrigation into national irrigation and agriculture policies of Sierra Leone and Ghana with mention of the need to address water-quality issues pragmatically.
- Reviewed by-laws on urban agriculture which address safe use of wastewater through improved irrigation and agricultural practices.
- Developed guidelines for urban agriculture in Ghana, which cover how to achieve water-quality improvements on farm, applying safer irrigation and agriculture practices, and improving food safety.
- Institutionalized the National Best Urban Agriculture Farmers award in Ghana after 22 years of annual celebration and the next step is to use the adoption of safer practices as a criteria for selection.
- Secured funds for urban agriculture activities in Sierra Leone, demonstrating donor interest.
- Prompted curriculum development on urban agriculture, addressing safer irrigation practices in urban agriculture at the university level.

There were, of course, a number of significant challenges, including personal commitment versus institutional interest, which was also evident in WASPA. For instance, in some cities in the RUAF project, an institution with great power to initiate a necessary course of action did not have representation on the platform by an individual with commensurate commitment and position to effect institutional change. In other cases, the most committed individuals were from less powerful institutions. The level of capacity of stakeholders, including convening agencies, was an issue and sometimes there were conflicting interests within the platform.

DISCUSSION

One key element that has a powerful influence over the effectiveness of multi-stakeholder processes in this area is the degree to which powers of decision-making and the management of financial resources have been devolved to the administrative level at which the platform is constructed. All three processes took place at the city municipality/metropolitan level. As such the key stakeholders had some degree of autonomy over implementing decisions and the use of resources. However, in many instances devolution of responsibilities is not uniform for all the sectors interacting on wastewater agriculture. For instance, in the case of Accra, Ghana, wastewater service provision has been decentralized to the city-authority level, but this is not the case for water supply. Both agriculture and public health are represented at the city level via municipal departments, but policy and strategy decisions are still centralized. Thus, in the case of wastewater agriculture, decisions on wastewater management and the use of land and water resources for agriculture can be made at the city level for some scenarios of use, but certain sources of water are under the jurisdiction of the water or power utility, or under the water resources commission, all of which have centralized and sometimes autonomous functions outside of the administrative boundaries. Decisions on their use cannot be made if the stakeholder platform operates at the city level, unless there is vertical representation as well. This non-uniform devolution of responsibilities complicates the functioning of such platforms and processes, and overcoming the constraints requires a thorough knowledge of the governance framework under which wastewater agriculture functions.

A number of other factors critical to the success of multi-stakeholder platforms have been identified through analysis of the three case studies and other related processes (Dubbeling and de Zeeuw, 2007; Mitchell, 1997; Warner, 2006, 2007). These are listed below:

- The issues addressed must be pertinent to stakeholders.
- Institutionalization has to be built in from the outset.
- The process should be well planned with clarity about the aims, expected results, roles, responsibilities and time frame.
- Selecting the stakeholders and understanding their needs and positions is important, particularly those of less powerful groups.
- Early implementation of activities that produce concrete outputs will help to reinforce commitment and participation.
- Benefits must be widely understood and accepted to facilitate the paradigm shift needed in most multi-stakeholder processes.
- Monitoring and (self-)evaluation throughout the process by all stakeholders will result in improved learning and better outcomes.
- Regular formal and informal communication that creates transparency is critical to the process.
- Facilitation and conflict mediation skills are vital.
- Ideas and plans that deviate from current modes must be accommodated.
- Willingness to adapt to changing circumstances and uncertainty must be recognized.

- Trust, mutual respect and patience, especially in the face of frustration and slow progress, are key ingredients.

In addition, a lesson articulated by the SWITCH project, but evident in all three of the examples, was that there are critical questions that must be asked early in the process to ensure success (Box 18.1).

Several of these factors and questions have been amalgamated and are discussed in more detail below. Critical issues identified by the case studies centre around: the priorities of the stakeholders and those initiating the process; institutionalization; clarity on goals and management; stakeholder selection, involvement and representation; outputs and outcomes; and communication.

Box 18.1 QUESTIONS TO BE CONSIDERED AT AN EARLY STAGE OF MULTI-STAKEHOLDER PROCESSES

- How is the process to be funded, and costs and benefits shared?
- How will communication take place between stakeholders?
- How will capacity and training requirements be assessed and addressed?
- How will the problems around which the multi-stakeholder process is built be assessed?
- How will learning be assured both within and outside the platform?
- How will engagement with influential stakeholders outside the platform take place?
- How will the platform monitor and evaluate its performance?
- How will the process be documented to ensure that lessons are learnt and processes optimized in future?

External initiation and priorities

All three multi-stakeholder processes were initiated by 'outsiders' (although it should be noted that they, too, are stakeholders) to address needs as they perceived them; whilst these issues were undoubtedly real they did not necessarily address the most pressing needs of all the local stakeholders (Drechsel et al., 2008). The salience of an issue is one of the key factors in the desire of a stakeholder to be part of a planning process; the absence of this may result in late entry or self-exclusion, not least because involvement takes time (Warner, 2006). It could be argued that any multi-stakeholder process that attempts to address issues that are not pertinent to all stakeholders should not take place, but this fails to recognize the fact that not all stakeholders have the same experiences and thus some may be concerned while others are not. Furthermore, the problem may not currently seem urgent but it may be prudent to initiate research and planning – for example, wastewater management in a city may be manageable at present but as cities grow the sheer volume of waste will increase the difficulty.

The purpose of a multi-stakeholder process is to overcome this and to change attitudes. However, even if stakeholders do have an interest in the issue they may not be convinced that a multi-stakeholder process is the most appropriate way to resolve it. Therefore, good facilitation is essential and a level of awareness-raising is likely to be necessary.

Institutionalization

The initiating and anchor agencies, and the processes they follow, influence the level of institutionalization that can be achieved. Success and long-term sustainability are helped by building on existing processes and depend on the anchor institution. Ramírez (2001) suggested that before initiating the process, platform convenors must analyse their own roles and objectives in terms of power, legitimacy and urgency. The issue of urgency relates to the perceived salience of the issue as discussed above. In RUAF, the main convenor at the city level was an international research organization (the International Water Management Institute, IWMI) and in WASPA it was IWMI and national non-governmental organizations. These organizations had limited power, which influenced the willingness of stakeholders to come to the table and their level of involvement. In WASPA, legitimacy could have been enhanced if the project had received the formal approval of central government departments, which emphasizes the importance of interlinked multi-level platforms as advocated in the Learning Alliance approach. With SWITCH, the level of commitment and progress varied depending on the institution that facilitated the process: where a local authority embraced the project, more progress and real impact was seen. The advantage of an independent research organization leading the process is that it is not perceived to be supporting existing power structures.

In emerging economies where civil society and the private sector still play only a minimal or marginal role, and government has a majority say in decisions, there is a need for the right government institution to be convinced of the usefulness and to be the anchor for the process. However, an external skilled facilitator is also required as they are perceived to be more neutral.

Clarity on goals and good management

All multi-stakeholder processes, especially when externally initiated as projects, start with a set of goals. Ideally, as the SWITCH project highlighted, there is a need for establishing shared goals early on, but it is difficult to initiate the process without some predetermined goals. This may not be incompatible with participatory goal-setting provided the goals work at different levels and are not mutually exclusive. For example, the project goal may be 'to encourage multiple stakeholders to engage in knowledge sharing and collaborative planning for improved wastewater management', while the multi-stakeholder platform goal may be vision-based (e.g. to improve the quality of water reaching farms by reducing inputs from hospitals). If goals cannot be agreed upon, then there is a fundamental problem that would suggest that the platform has either been created around an inappropriate issue or that additional preliminary work needed to be done to share opinions and to identify the appropriate challenge. In some such cases, conflict resolution and negotiation skills are likely to be needed, but such situations are rare and stakeholders are usually willing to discuss and seek pragmatic solutions. The WASPA project team realized that even more awareness-raising and joint activities to understand the issues around wastewater agriculture at the outset would have made the visioning, planning and implementation far smoother.

The goals need to be achievable to avoid disappointment if expectations are raised too high (Warner, 2006). In the projects reviewed, expectations tended to be high, aiming for policy changes, demand-led research and implementation of action plans. Only some of these expectations were met but in all cases stakeholders commented that the multi-stakeholder platforms had contributed to their knowledge and capacity, an outcome which should not be underestimated. They also brought together individuals and organizations who had rarely or ever met in the past. Of course, this can be seen as a form of tokenism, as observed by Arnstein (1969), but not if it is part of a legitimate process to stimulate understanding, capacity and ultimately collaboration, in which case it is a necessary first step.

Goals must be time-bound and supported by a negotiated framework of roles and responsibilities that will result in their realization. The RUAF project found that the results of the process can be disappointing if there is poor management, inadequate planning and insufficient transparency. There is, however, a balance to be struck between being 'well organized' and 'overly prescriptive', which can make the process very slow and resource-intensive, and may alienate stakeholders because they feel that everything has already been decided and they are just pawns in the process to legitimize predetermined concepts and activities. The optimal situation is one in which a minimum set of criteria are provided for the platform or process that ensure that it goes beyond rhetoric and tokenism. The specific structure, mandate, and terms and conditions should be one of the first things decided by the stakeholders themselves.

Stakeholder involvement and representation

The importance of stakeholder selection, analysis and inclusion are naturally central to an effective multi-stakeholder process. All three projects were concerned with how to ensure that as many stakeholders as possible were represented but inevitably some will be overlooked and others will exclude themselves. One approach is to encourage stakeholders to play an active role but it may be more productive to work with those who perceive the benefits and want to engage. The danger is that stakeholder groups who are normally excluded from decision-making processes, but who are highly affected by decisions, may exclude themselves for various reasons, and special measures might be need to overcome this (Verhagen et al., 2008).

Even where the platform appears to be representative it is not always certain that the delegate is adequately representing his or her constituency. As the RUAF project found, it is sometimes difficult to differentiate between the involvement of the individual and the organization, likewise it is hard to determine whose views they represent without meeting the entire group. Multi-stakeholder platforms therefore have a tendency to 'federate' often competing local interests and do not provide a clear understanding of individual motivations. This is especially true when there is no mechanism to select representatives and provide exchanges between the stakeholder group and their spokesperson. There are means to overcome this, such as establishing or revitalizing local-level groups (farmers' groups, village committees, water-user associations), as was attempted in WASPA, but this will only go some way to addressing the challenges inherent in representation as a mode of decision-making. The facilitator could also facilitate platforms at lower levels, but this may not be sustainable if these agents are external (i.e. project based), and if they are internal (i.e. other stakeholders) it may not overcome the existing power imbalances.

Tangible outputs, outcomes and good communication

The purpose of multi-stakeholder platforms is to reach consensus about problem definitions and solutions. Although this initial stage may be slow and frustrating, because developing a commonly shared vision, agreeing on objectives and establishing effective communication between members takes time and effort, it should not be rushed as it is central to the ultimate fairness, transparency and efficacy of the platform (Verhagen et al., 2008). However, that does not mean that outputs should be suspended until all aspects of the platform structure have been defined and a full plan written. Many convenors of multi-stakeholder platforms have found that stakeholders more readily converge around tangible outputs which they perceive to be real benefits. It is suggested that such physical outputs should be planned for at the outset (although the specifics should be decided with the stakeholders) to give impetus to the process by demonstrating the benefits (Evans and Varma, 2009). The crux is how fast to proceed to demonstrate results while at the same time proceeding slowly enough to have true (or acceptable) participation in setting the objectives. Lessons from WASPA suggest that the ideal is to create an initial vision and plan early on (which was not done in this instance) and to select 'quick wins' that are unlikely to negatively impact on any stakeholder or other component of the plan, but which demonstrate commitment to the process.

Attaining an optimal mix and timing is therefore critical to demonstrate valid results that have the support of all the stakeholders, especially those with the least influence. The degree of true participation is affected by how the platform perceives the initiator's attitude towards it. Equally, it is time related, especially on platforms where there is wide diversity in experience and influence of stakeholders, who need time to acclimatize and feel comfortable.

Maintaining interest can also be achieved with targeted and appropriate communication. All multi-stakeholder processes require adequate knowledge sharing and transparency, which can be supported by the early establishment of a communications strategy. This should include a variety of components to appeal to the different stakeholders, including newsletters, working papers, policy briefs, posters, calendars, drama, newspaper articles, presentations, websites and exposure visits.

Scaling-up

Scaling-up has so far proven to be one of the most difficult components for the Learning Alliances to achieve. The causes of this need more detailed analysis but at a superficial level some limiting factors can be articulated. Firstly, investment in Learning Alliances is high, mainly in terms of time but also financial, which limits them. In the cases presented here, all three projects were also engaged in participatory action planning which can be resource (time) intensive and although resulting in positive local outcomes this may be to the detriment of wider impacts. The second reason that scaling-up did not take place was that the innovations were simply not captivating enough. Thirdly, it is possible that there was a failure to engage adequately at higher political levels. This was definitely the case in WASPA but much less so in RUAF, which resulted in some policy changes. The reasons for this are complex but relate again to time, resources, political clout within the project, decentralization and the need to work closely with local government, especially on the action plans, as wastewater reuse is not a priority at national level.

Implications for wastewater irrigation

Many of these points may be equally applicable to a multi-stakeholder process around any issue. What can these case studies add to our knowledge about how to improve wastewater management for productive use in agriculture? Reviewing why multi-stakeholder processes for wastewater irrigation are different helps in this:

- Wastewater irrigation cuts across typical sectoral and geographical policy and planning boundaries.

- Stakeholders may have radically different viewpoints, not just in opinions on wastewater use but also in understanding and awareness of current practices and potential health and environmental risks and benefits.
- For some stakeholders, concerns over health and environmental risks make even discussing the issue untenable, especially where it is actually illegal.

These characteristics serve to heighten the relevance of the findings, because they create conditions that require negotiation, discussion, shared learning and mutual solution finding, more so than in many other sectors. For example, the second and third points reiterate the fact that initiation may need to be external as there is unlikely to be sufficient impetus locally because of differing opinions, but also that good facilitation, representation and communication can result in shared goals and significant outcomes.

In addition, as explained above, it must be remembered that the degree of decentralization and devolution of governance systems, especially when this is non-uniform across sectors, have particular implications for wastewater irrigation which necessitates inter-sectoral integration.

CONCLUSIONS

Wastewater management and reuse in less developed countries is spontaneous and often occurs in an institutional vacuum with poor planning processes. Under these conditions multi-stakeholder platforms play the role of convening various actors to solicit their inputs in the belief that such joint action and commitment are necessary ingredients for improving specific wastewater challenges.

Stakeholders' views on wastewater management and reuse are variously influenced by their perceptions of its risks and benefits as a resource. Thus, it is imperative that all voices are heard, for which purpose multi-stakeholder platforms are crucial. There is, however, no blueprint for the optimal functioning of a multi-stakeholder platform or process; it is dependent on the local socio-economic and cultural contexts, and the platform has to be woven into the existing institutional fabric if it is to have impact (Drechsel et al., 2008).

Understanding the metaphorical 'beast' to which Warner (2007) likens multi-stakeholder processes, and breeding its good traits, will ensure that future multi-stakeholder processes have maximum effect and do not simply become the rhetoric of projects and programmes wishing to justify their actions. Within the wastewater-agriculture sector, multi-stakeholder processes have not yet been extensively used. In the three case studies described here (WASPA, RUAF and SWITCH), some successes are recognized, but practitioners need to learn how to effectively operationalize and sustain such platforms, in particular, making them less time-consuming and resource-intensive, realistic in their goals, and inclusive. Solutions will be more easily identified and effectively implemented if such platforms can capture and make use of the knowledge, experience and desires of all relevant stakeholders.

NOTE

1   Individuals, groups or institutions that are concerned with, or have an interest in, a particular issue or systems, at any level in society and of any size, organized or disorganized (Grimble and Wellard, 1997).

REFERENCES

Arnold, E. and Bell, M. (2001) 'Some new ideas about research for development', in Danish Ministry of Foreign Affairs, *Partnerships at the Leading Edge: A Danish Vision for Knowledge, Research and Development*, Danish Ministry of Foreign Affairs, Copenhagen, www.um.dk/NR/rdonlyres/7CD8C2BC-9E5B-4920-929C-D7AA978FEEB7/0/CMI_New_Ideas_R_for_D.pdf

Arnstein, S. (1969) 'A ladder of citizen participation', *Journal of the American Institute of Planners*, vol 35, no 4, pp 216–24

Barr, J. J. F. (2001) 'Methods for consensus building for management of common property resources, R7562', DFID Strategy for Research on Renewable Natural Resources, Natural Resources Systems Programme, Final Technical Report, Centre for Land Use and Water Resources Research, University of Newcastle, Newcastle, UK

Bunting, S. (2005) 'Evaluation action planning for enhanced NR management in PU Kolkata, R8365', Natural Resources Systems Programme, Final Technical Report, Institute of Aquaculture, University of Sterling, Sterling, UK

Butterworth, J. and Morris, M. (2007) *Developing Processes for Delivering Demand-Led Research in Urban Water Management*, SWITCH, Delft, The Netherlands, www.switchurbanwater.eu/outputs/results.php

Butterworth, J. A., Sutherland, A., Manning, N., Darteh, B., Dziegielewska-Geitz, M., Eckart, J., Batchelor, C., Moriarty, P., Schouten, T., da Silva, C., Verhagen, J. and Bury, P. J. (2008) *Building More Effective Partnerships for Innovation in Urban Water Management*, SWITCH, Delft, The Netherlands, www.switchurbanwater.eu/outputs/results.php

Chambers, R. (1994) 'The origins and practice of participatory rural appraisal', *World Development*, vol 22, no 7, pp953–69

Cofie, O., Abraham, E., Danso, G. and Drechsel, P. (2005) 'Past, present and future scenarios of urban agriculture in West Africa', paper presented at the Regional Strategic Workshop on Urban Agriculture in West Africa, Banjul, Gambia

Dingfelder, S. F. (2004) 'From toilet to tap: Psychologists lend their expertise to overcoming the public's aversion to reclaimed water', *American Psychological Association Monitor Online*, vol 35, no 8

Drechsel, P., Cofie, O. O., van Veenhuizen, R. and Larbi, T. O. (2008) 'Linking research, capacity building, and policy dialogue in support of informal irrigation in urban West Africa', *Irrigation and Drainage*, vol 57, pp 268–78

Dubbeling, M. and de Zeeuw, H. (2007) *WP 1 Multi-Stakeholder Policy Formulation and Action Planning for Sustainable Urban Agriculture Development*, Working Paper Series 1, ETC Urban Agriculture / RUAF Foundation, Leusden, The Netherlands

Ensink, J. H. J., Simmons, R. W. and van der Hoek, W. (2004) 'Wastewater use in Pakistan: The cases of Haroonabad and Faisalabad', in C. A. Scott, N. I. Faruqui and L. Raschid-Sally (eds) *Wastewater Irrigated Agriculture: Confronting Livelihood and Environmental Realities*, CABI Publishing, Wallingford, UK

Ensink, J. H. J., Simmons, R. W. and van der Hoek, W. (2008) 'Livelihoods from wastewater: Water reuse in Faisalabad, Pakistan', in B. Jiménez and T. Asano (eds) *International Survey on Water Reuse*, IWA Publishing, London

Evans, A. E. V. and Varma, S. (2009) 'Practicalities of participation in urban IWRM: Perspectives of wastewater management in two cities in Sri Lanka and Bangladesh', *Natural Resources Forum*, vol 33, pp.19–28

Grimble, R. and Wellard, K. (1997) 'Stakeholder methodologies in natural resource management: A review of principles, contexts, experiences and opportunities', *Agricultural Systems*, vol 55, no 2, pp173–93

Hamilton, A. J., Stagnitti, F., Xiong, X., Kreidl, S. L., Benke, K. K. and Maher, P. (2007) 'Wastewater irrigation: The state of play', *Vadose Zone Journal*, vol 6, pp823–40

Huibers, F. P. and van Lier, J. B. (2005) 'Use of wastewater in agriculture: The water chain approach', *Irrigation and Drainage*, vol 54, ppS3–S9

Lundy, M., Gottret, M. V. and Ashby, J. (2005) *Learning Alliances: An Approach for Building Multi-Stakeholder Innovation Systems*, ILAC Brief No 8, Intuitional Learning and Change, Rome, www.cgiar-ilac.org/files/publications/briefs/ILAC_Brief08_alliances.pdf

Mitchell, B. (1997) *Resource and Environmental Management*, Longman, Edinburgh

Moriarty, P., Batchelor, C. and Laban, P. (2005a) *The EMPOWERS Participatory Planning Cycle for Integrated Water Resources Management*, EMPOWERS, Amman, Jordan

Moriarty, P., Fonseca, C., Smits, S. and Schouten T. (2005b) *Background Paper for the Symposium: Learning Alliances for Scaling Up Innovative Approaches in the Water and Sanitation Sector*, IRC International Water and Sanitation Centre, Delft, The Netherlands

Morris, M. (2006) *Learning Alliance Briefing Note No 1: An Introduction to Learning Alliances*, SWITCH, Delft, The Netherlands

Neubert, S. (2004) 'Is reuse of treated wastewater a promising strategy for water scarce countries? A stakeholder analysis in Tunisia', report prepared for the German Development Institute, Bonn

Po, M., Kaercher, J. D. and Nancarrow, B. E. (2003) *Australian Water Conservation and Reuse Program: Literature Review of Factors Influencing Public Perceptions of Wastewater Reuse*, CSIRO Land and Water Technical Report 54/03, CSIRO Publishing, Collingwood, Australia

Ramírez, R. (2001) 'Understanding the approaches for accommodating multiple stakeholders interests', *International Journal of Agricultural Resources, Governance and Ecology*, vol 1, nos 3–4, pp 264–85

Reed, M. S. (2008) 'Stakeholder participation for environmental management: A literature review', *Biological Conservation*, vol 141, pp2417–31

Russell, S. and Lux, C. (2006) *Getting over Yuck: Moving from Psychological to Cultural Analyses of Responses to Water Recycling. Methodologies for Public Acceptance Studies and Consultation*, Working Paper 2, University of Wollongong, NSW, Australia

Sanginga, P. C., Chitsike, C. A., Njuki, J., Kaaria, S. and Kanzikwera, R. (2007) 'Enhanced learning from multi-stakeholder partnerships: Lessons from the Enabling Rural Innovation in Africa Programme', *Natural Resources Forum*, vol 31, pp273–85

Smits, S., Moriarty, P., Fonsea, C. and Schouten, T. (2007) 'Scaling up innovations through Learning Alliances: An introduction to the approach', in S. Smits, P. Moriarty and C. Sijbesma (eds) *Learning Alliances: Scaling Up Innovations in Water, Sanitation and Hygiene*, Technical Paper Series 47, IRC, Delft, The Netherlands, pp3–17

Smits, S., da Silva, C. and Evans, A. E. V. (2009) *Integrated Planning for Sanitation and Reuse of Wastewater: Experiences from Two Cities in Bangladesh and Sri Lanka*, IRC Working Paper, Delft, The Netherlands, in press

Steins, N. A. and Edwards, V. M. (1998) 'Platforms for collective action in multiple-use CPRs', paper presented at Crossing Boundaries, the Seventh Annual Conference of the International Association for the Study of Common Property, Vancouver, British Columbia, Canada, 10–14 June, available at www.indiana.du/~iascp/abstracts/612.html

Stenekes, N., Colebatch, H. K., Waite, T. D. and Ashbold, N. J. (2006) 'Risk and governance in water recycling: Public acceptance revisited', *Science, Technology and Human Values*, vol 31, no 2, pp107–34

SWITCH (2008) *Sustainable Water Management in the City of the Future: A Mid-Term Review of Integration in SWITCH*, SWITCH, Delft, The Netherlands

United Nations Conference on Environment and Development (UNCED) (1992), World Summit on Sustainable Development (WSSD), Johannesburg, 26 August–September 4, 2002, www.worldsummit2002.org/index.htm

Veenhuizen, R. van, Cofie, O., Martin, A., Jianming, C., Merzthal, G. and Verhagen, J. (2007) 'Multiple sources of water for multifunctional urban agriculture. 2nd SWITCH Scientific Meeting', SWITCH, Delft, The Netherlands

Verhagen, J., Butterworth, J. and Morris, M. (2008) 'Learning alliances for integrated and sustainable innovations in urban water management', *Waterlines*, vol 27, no 2, pp 116–24

Warner, J. (2006) 'More sustainable participation? Multi-stakeholder platforms for integrated catchment management', *Water Resources Development*, vol 22, no 1, pp15–35

Warner, J. (2007) 'The beauty of the beast: Multi-stakeholder participation for integrated catchment management', in J. Warner (ed) *Multi-Stakeholder Platforms for Integrated Catchment Management*, Ashgate, Aldershot, UK

Part 5

Conclusions and Outlook

19

Wastewater Irrigation and Health: Challenges and Outlook for Mitigating Risks in Low-Income Countries

Christopher A. Scott, Pay Drechsel, Liqa Raschid-Sally,
Akiça Bahri, Duncan Mara, Mark Redwood and Blanca Jiménez

ABSTRACT

Wastewater irrigation is a widespread and growing phenomenon that carries varying degrees of risk. Whether spontaneously practised in urban and peri-urban agriculture or planned as part of water reuse programmes, food and fodder production using untreated sewage or treated effluent can have serious human health implications for farmers and consumers, and can irreversibly degrade the environment. In low-income countries water pollution is often the result of inadequate wastewater collection and treatment, and unplanned release to receiving water bodies. Making wastewater irrigation safer depends on a location-specific combination of different pathogen barriers including, where possible, appropriate wastewater treatment. Ensuring that these strategies work in an integrated, mutually supportive manner requires a multi-sectoral paradigm shift in the common approach of wastewater management for disposal. Additionally, it is crucial to continue research (especially in developing countries) on the types and severity of risk, locally feasible mitigation options, the cost-effectiveness of safer wastewater irrigation practices compared to other interventions against diarrhoea and facilitating the adoption of 'non-' or 'post-treatment' options. This concluding chapter presents an outlook for wastewater irrigation by integrating the major findings of the present volume, synthesizing key elements of the current global status and challenges of sanitation and wastewater irrigation with emphasis on the WHO Guidelines. It also highlights wastewater-governance opportunities with the greatest potential to support safe wastewater irrigation that simultaneously address the combined challenges deriving from the global sanitation, water and food crises.

INTRODUCTION

With the water and sanitation crises being main drivers of planned and unplanned wastewater irrigation, respectively, the recent rise in food prices renewed public interest in safe food production in and around cities. All three challenges (water, sanitation and safe food) are increasing as cities grow (Figure 19.1). According to the Comprehensive Assessment of Water Management in Agriculture, urban and peri-urban agriculture suffer most from poor water quality: already today urban farmers must rely on polluted water sources for irrigation in four out of five cities in the developing world (Raschid-Sally and Jayakody, 2008).

Over the past ten years growing interest in understanding untreated wastewater use for irrigation has produced a large array of publications and reports on the livelihood and food-supply benefits. It has also been made abundantly clear that the approach of banning this largely informal practice will not work (Scott et al., 2004). The key challenge is to maximize the benefits of wastewater use while

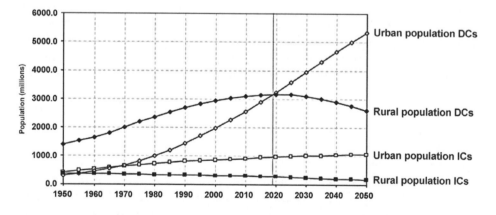

Figure 19.1 *World population from 1950, projected to 2050*

DCs = developing countries; ICs = industrialized countries.

Source: United Nations (2008)

protecting public health and the environment, i.e. making wastewater use safe while enhancing its value as a resource to address physical or economic water shortage (see the 2002 Hyderabad Declaration on Wastewater Use in Agriculture, www.iwmi.cgiar.org/health/wastew/Hyderabad_declaration.htm).

Urban and peri-urban agriculture flourishes in low-income countries as rural migrants move to cities where open plots and waste resources allow them to capitalize on the urban demands for traditional as well as non-traditional cash crops, like irrigated exotic vegetables consumed as salad. These demographic and production shifts on the food-supply side are coupled with the rising purchasing power of the urban middle class and proliferating urban markets on the demand side. The net result is an expansion of health-risk transmission pathways that may ensue from water pollution and wastewater irrigation.

Compared with rural populations, common pathways might differ. While in rural areas, exotic vegetables and raw salads might be unknown and safe drinking water is still a major challenge, the situation can be very different for urban dwellers. Although urban populations might benefit from improved diet and access to water and health care, distress-migration, increased numbers of immuno-compromised individuals (not least as a product of the AIDS pandemic), increasing street-food consumption and rising population densities of urban slum inhabitants without access to adequate sanitation constitute a new set of risk factors, 'hotspots' and possible pathways of epidemics.

The global hotspots for wastewater-irrigation-related health risks, and other health risks linked to inadequate sanitation and waste disposal, are: specifically those countries and regions where wastewater treatment, namely investing in and operating treatment plants, remains beyond the capacity of governments; and where diffuse exposure pathways exist both for wastewater irrigators (urban agriculture labourers) and especially consumers along the food chain. In such situations, it is essential to provide local governance with information on the variety of existing and possible options to minimize health risks.

In this final chapter, we summarize current understanding of wastewater irrigation by drawing heavily on other chapters in this volume, which are not cited directly here. The reader is encouraged to consult the contents of the entire volume, designed to develop the case for safe wastewater irrigation by laying out the current context, providing detail on risk assessment and mitigation, and finally considering governance and policy challenges and responses. We aim to provide an integrated outlook on wastewater irrigation and the mitigation of associated health risks in developing countries.

To characterize the multifaceted nature of the practice, we refer to the definitions in Chapter 1, but to capture for the reader the two most common but fundamentally different situations of wastewater use in terms of their geographic significance, drivers and challenges (Table 19.1), two types are highlighted here and referred to throughout this chapter:

1   Unplanned use of wastewater in agriculture is a very common and widespread practice in and around urban centres in the developing world, resulting primarily from inadequate sanitation and widespread pollution of surface-water bodies. This results in crops being irrigated with highly polluted water which might be untreated, partially treated or – in most cases – diluted wastewater. Such use occurs in humid and arid regions alike, and will continue to expand as long as investments in wastewater management do not keep pace with population growth and urbanization, leading to uncontrolled pollution of water sources.

2   Planned wastewater use is more common in drier regions where wastewater streams are generally channelled, after at least partial treatment, for controlled reuse in agriculture to offset water shortage. This practice is increasingly gaining ground given the prevailing water scarcity context.

The global extent of planned wastewater irrigation we estimate as an order of magnitude less than the former (see Figure 19.2).

In contrast to the common perception that the key challenge of wastewater irrigation is more a question of designing and implementing safe wastewater irrigation schemes, the common reality of unplanned wastewater irrigation puts authorities in need of immediate action to address the possible risks accruing from informal plots throughout urban and peri-urban spaces. Even if this might only result in 'damage control' (Drechsel and Raschid-Sally, 2009), it requires a framework for risk assessment and risk mitigation to prioritize and implement well-targeted and locally appropriate risk-management responses. This concept is based on the World Health Organization's 2006 *Guidelines for the Safe Use of Wastewater, Excreta and Greywater in Agriculture* (WHO, 2006) which put significant emphasis on unplanned wastewater use.

This emphasis was indeed necessary. In many developing countries authorities are hardly equipped to address point pollution, and are increasingly lost in view of diffuse hazards. Risk-assessment methods have never been used; data for risk quantification is missing; and there is no local information on the effect of available mitigation measures in terms of safety, risk-reduction potential, and economic and cultural acceptability. The WHO Guidelines distinguish between those situations/countries where treatment alone will be able to break the pathogen cycle and those lower on the 'sanitation ladder', where only alternative approaches or a combination of treatment and non- (or post-) treatment practices will achieve acceptable risk reduction. This does not imply that there should be different standards for different countries. On the contrary, following the philosophy of the WHO Guidelines, all countries should aim at the same tolerable disease burden per person per year. However, how fast this target can be achieved will depend on the country's current situation, context, and managerial and human resource capacity to progress. A step-wise approach is recommended as each risk reduction is better than none, while being aware that the way chosen via different combinations of treatment and

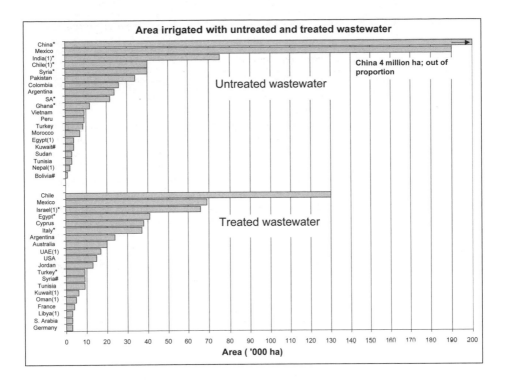

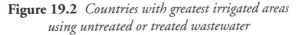

Figure 19.2 *Countries with greatest irrigated areas using untreated or treated wastewater*

* Data uncertain
(1) Area probably underestimated
Practice reported (incl. forestry), data missing

Sources: Jiménez and Asano (2008), modified; for China: Xianjun et al. (2003)

post-treatment options might change as the country develops from more human to technically based options.

RISK ASSESSMENT, MITIGATION AND THE WHO GUIDELINES

The most important 'at risk' groups are, on the one hand, farmers or fieldworkers and their families, and, on the other, food consumers, especially where irrigated vegetables are eaten raw (e.g. lettuce, tomatoes). A third group sometimes mentioned is made up of those communities living close to wastewater irrigation areas (both planned and unplanned), where accidental contamination can take place. In most cases, these groups have differing levels of knowledge about the hazards they might face – when farmers know of occupational health risks they often accept them as part of their business, whereas consumers usually do not know about the source/treatment of their food and, if they did, they would prefer another source.

Table 19.1 *Characteristics of two principal wastewater irrigation types*

	Unplanned (indirect) use	Planned (direct) use
Management status	Unplanned activities along streams in/near urban centres	Planned use at a particular location
Climates	All climates, mostly driven by poor sanitation	Mostly arid, but also driven by economic water scarcity
Physical locations	Diffuse area	Specific sites near actual or potential treatment plants, or channelled to agriculture sites
Official recognition	Often informal sector	Formal sector
Water quality	Varies largely from untreated to partially treated to seasonally or generally diluted wastewater	Treated, partially treated, or also raw wastewater
Health-risk mitigation focus	Safer irrigation and post-harvest measures mostly for unrestricted irrigation	Treatment for reuse; crop restrictions possible
Existing institutional capacity	Low to moderate	Moderate to high
Main policy challenge	Balancing benefits against risks; pollution control	Wastewater governance for safe and productive reuse
Risk-mitigation challenge	Incentives to support adoption of risk-mitigation measures	Maintenance of treatment plants and control of post-treatment measures
Position on sanitation ladder	Lower ⟶	Higher

Also, in many developing countries consumers' educational status is low in view of 'germs' and their transmission.

WHO's change of focus from water-quality thresholds, i.e. critical pathogen levels in irrigation water, to health-based targets acknowledges the needs of developing countries still unable to afford the costs of large-scale wastewater management systems. While effluent-quality thresholds might work for particular treatment plants and related wastewater-reuse schemes, they can hardly be achieved in the much more common case of unplanned wastewater use along generally polluted streams. The new focus on health-based targets and multiple pathogen barriers provides local health-risk managers with the needed flexibility to address the situation of unplanned use. The new Guidelines therefore try to respond equally to the whole range of countries from low on the sanitation ladder (developing countries) to high (industrialized countries).

For the same health-based target, unplanned use and planned use of wastewater require however different risk-management approaches and corresponding guidelines (Table 19.1). This poses the question of whether the WHO Guidelines should better distinguish between different scenarios which could make them easier to read for stakeholders in different groups. The current global nature of the WHO Guidelines makes them unnecessarily complex, which is affecting their readability especially for policy makers and adoption. However, the number of practical examples as those presented in this book is increasing, showing that the new WHO Guidelines are feasible but as the approach is new more capacity building on their local adaptation is required.

With the target being healthy fieldworkers and consumers, local risk reduction can draw on a variety of measures, which can include not only wastewater treatment but also post-treatment options such as post-harvest pathogen die-off and safer methods of wastewater fetching, application and produce processing. Instead of a single measure providing the desired effect, the combination of such measures are together able to reduce the additional burden of disease from wastewater use in agriculture to acceptable levels.

The 2006 WHO Guidelines suggest a combination of quantitative microbial risk assessment and Monte Carlo simulations (QMRA-MC) to determine the possible risk level, or in other words the required pathogen reduction via a locally appropriate combination of health-protection control measures. However, even where the available data do not allow the application of QMRA, it is perfectly reasonable to stay on the safe side and aim at pathogen reduction of 5–6 log units on the irrigated produce, which can be achieved to safeguard consumers by different combinations of treatment and post-treatment options, depending on their availability and implementation potential which must be locally ascertained. A possible combination might be 2 log units through treatment, 3 log units from safer irrigation and pathogen die-off, and 1 log unit by produce-washing in clean water. This example only requires the laboratory capacity to analyse, for example, *E. coli* as the most common pathogen indicator, without stringent need to understand the theory of the Guidelines, QMRA and the concept of disability-adjusted life years (DALYs). However, the advantage of the QMRA would become obvious if the actual risk is lower and less effort (and related costs) is required to safeguard health.

There are still a large number of key issues to be addressed (Box 19.1).

Box 19.1 Key technical and socio-institutional challenges

Health-risk assessment

The WHO Guidelines are based on models which were largely developed and verified in developed countries. This raises the need for studies in developing countries to fine-tune or improve the existing risk-assessment approaches (actual exposure, dose-response estimates, immunity, etc.) and to improve our understanding of the match between easily collected and analysed indicator organisms and actual pathogens of local relevance, and eventually the results of the QMRA analysis. Another challenge is that risk assessment and (post-treatment) mitigation measures by and large only address pathogen-based threats while, especially in emerging economies, the inflow of industrial (or chemically polluted) wastewater requires increasing attention. There is a need to build on the work of Chang et al. (1995) to further develop quantitative chemical risk assessments (QCRA) tools, including computer-based applications similar to those for QMRA.

WHO Guidelines application

While the previous, simple, water-quality thresholds still look appealing, even if they are often unrealistic, the new more flexible approach – with many options, formula-based risk assessment needs and health-based targets expressed in DALYs – is understandably complex and requires significant interpretation for different situations if it is to implemented. So far, a common reaction of agencies, officials and others charged with managing wastewater, particularly indirect use, is that the Guidelines are simply too complex to understand and use. Meanwhile, to those planning direct wastewater use they are too general and miss the 'good old' conventional water-quality thresholds. In situations of planned reuse, however, the Guidelines support strict water-quality standards, if these can be maintained, and only recommend additional post-treatment measures if treatment alone cannot achieve the log reduction needed for the intended restricted or unrestricted irrigation. As summarized above, where institutions face the widespread challenge of indirect use and low internal management capacities, in practice it is not necessary to perform QMRA in order to apply the Guidelines, especially in situations where few, if any, local data are available. However, it will still require significant awareness creation to explain the options that the Guidelines offer in these and other settings.

Protecting fieldworkers

While most examples above refer to consumers, fieldworkers are best protected through wastewater treatment. However, because this might only contribute 2 log units of pathogen reduction, additional interventions may be required. A tolerable pathogen level can be assumed provided the workers and farmers are informed of their risks and accept risk-reducing measures, e.g. wearing protective clothing, avoiding water contact while fetching water (pumping instead of immersion) and applying water (furrows instead of overhead watering using cans), or via personal hygiene and/or regular anti-helminthic treatment. However, in practice, farmers' awareness of risks is often low or the perceived problems are considered part of the business.

Rethinking wastewater management

Where countries are moving towards planned direct use key challenges can be manifold, including legislation for wastewater use and pollution control, public-health engineering (locally implementable technologies for pathogen removal), economics (costs and benefits of the treatment and non-treatment options), and institutional capacities and linkages. In particular, the latter is required to constructively strengthen links between the sanitation and agricultural sectors, e.g. via multi-stakeholder platforms. What is most required is a paradigm shift to design treatment facilities, not for waste disposal, but to enhance conservation of resources with an economic value, through forward-linking 'Design for Service' concepts. This approach, which requires capacity building across conventional disciplinary boundaries, can work both ways by bringing treated wastewater on farm or bringing the principles of wastewater treatment to farmers. Indeed, there are many options for wastewater treatment at various scales that are simple in application, effective for pathogen removal and support reuse by maintaining crop nutrients.

Social acceptability

Social challenges related to safe wastewater irrigation have so far been viewed in terms of culturally rooted discomfort with reusing human waste, which is actually less frequent among farmers than anticipated. Much larger challenges concern the ability of individuals and farm communities to adopt and sustain post-treatment risk-mitigation options. This is important as the cost-effectiveness of these options is lost if they are not sustained after initial implementation; in other words, a lasting adoption is crucial. While the safety of direct use is predicated on functioning treatment plants, risk reduction in the informal sector will be largely based on the acceptance of safer irrigation or vegetable-washing practices. As farmers or traders might not see direct benefits in changing their behaviour, studies are needed to understand local knowledge and perceptions to suggest possible positive or negative incentives and social marketing approaches to promote recommended practices with the highest potential for local adoption. These challenges and options are not addressed in the current WHO Guidelines.

Integrated and comparative risks assessment beyond wastewater use

A key challenge is to think out of the wastewater box. There is a large variety of faecal–oral contamination pathways leading to diarrhoeal diseases (Fewtrell et al., 2007) of which this volume addresses just a few. Decision-makers, however, are looking at the larger picture of all the contributory risk factors. For them the key question should be 'Which risk factors and pathways in my city are likely to cause a diarrhoeal outbreak and public-health crisis?' To address this, it is necessary to compare the risk contribution from different sources and identify target-oriented mitigation measures, and then to evaluate those which most cost-effectively prevent diarrhoea, given prevailing resource constraints. The consumption of wastewater-irrigated vegetables might not be the most important hazard in this regard and, while this might be good news for the wastewater sector, it does not diminish the importance of the sanitation crisis.

POLICY AND GOVERNANCE IMPLICATIONS

It is clear from the legacy of failed and costly sanitation strategies that the 'one size fits all' risk-mitigation approach is no longer appropriate for many countries. Based on this experience, which is reflected in the assessments included in this volume, WHO encourages a step-by-step incremental approach to the beneficial and safe use of wastewater whereby each step not only reduces risk but also builds the capacity of institutions to be able to methodically move forward to the next phase of wastewater and associated risk management. The incremental achievement of health-based targets can become visible through the gradual physical expansion of a sewer system, but equally through increasing political will for continuous investments in the health and sanitation sector.

However, to date the return on investment in wastewater treatment has had limited impact in the face of rapidly changing urban demographics and poverty. Investments in technologically complex treatment processes and policies have failed due to ill-planned, badly operated and badly managed facilities, under-resourced institutions, limited human-resource capacity and severe financial challenges. For example, a review of almost 200 wastewater treatment plants in Brazil – a relatively well-developed economy – has found that most are unreliable and prone to failure (Oliviera and von Sperling, 2008). The situation in sub-Saharan Africa is more severe. In Ghana, only 10 per cent of the approximately 70 wastewater and faecal-sludge treatment plants identified in the country still worked as planned and, even if all were working, less than 10 per cent of the urban wastewater would be treated (IWMI, unpublished). It is also clear that the lack of appropriate sanitation has health and cost implications. The Water and Sanitation Program of the World Bank has produced research illustrating that in the Philippines, Vietnam, Cambodia and Indonesia, US$9 billion are lost annually due to inadequate sanitation. This amounts to 2 per cent of their combined gross domestic product (Water and Sanitation Program, 2007).

As already noted in the context of beneficial wastewater management and use, health-risk reduction will require a combination of treatment and post-treatment options. Treatment, where feasible, is the ideal option but requires adequate planning and the selection of appropriate technology options. There are examples of middle-income countries, such as Mexico, Jordan and Tunisia, that have embarked on planned reuse, based on treatment. However, the pace is ultimately, if inadvertently, set by the case of intensive, commercially based agricultural economies such as California, which has invested huge amounts of funding in building, operating and maintaining a network of wastewater treatment plants. Furthermore, it is estimated that over the next 20 years, US$20 billion will be required to fund that state's planned infrastructure capital costs and maintain the existing network – 210 times the amount currently budgeted for the purpose (Food and Water Watch, 2008). It is worth adding that water infrastructure and treatment is among the least financially autonomous of all infrastructures when compared to telecoms, electricity, etc. (Serageldin, 1994), although financial studies have yet to be undertaken on the full benefits of water and wastewater infrastructure. Calls to fund and expand treatment in low-income countries must be matched with the ground reality and precious resources must be invested wisely to maximize the benefits to public health. Effective risk management requires a more graduated, methodical approach that integrates new actors in the wastewater-management process from the treatment plant to the farm and the consumer. The right combination of wastewater-treatment process and risk-management strategies remains the target.

We recognize that the situation of high sewerage coverage and related wastewater treatment is – at least in the short term – difficult to achieve in many resource-stressed countries, but it should remain the goal unless alternative approaches, such as water-saving ecological sanitation technologies, become implementable at a larger scale and reduce the general need for sewerage and pressure on treatment.

This would have multiple benefits as the troubling economic reality in the global economy is likely to exacerbate an already problematic situation when it comes to pollution control in low-income countries. The reduction of credit for bank lending for capital investment, an unstable bond market for governments and the anticipated decline in donor funds available will increase stress on the management of wastewater in fast-growing cities worldwide. We also recognize that the cost for sanitation, estimated by the UN Development Programme for low-income countries to range from 3–15 per cent of gross national product (United Nations, 2005) as a result of using a conventional approach, is very high and in many cases it will simply not be achievable. Under these circumstances, the most cost-effective way to significantly reduce the risks from wastewater irrigation remains the application of an integrated multiple-barrier risk-reduction approach such as presented in the WHO Guidelines and further developed in this volume.

Another advancement in thinking on wastewater management is that key actors in the management of wastewater also include farmers, traders, food caterers and consumers. For this added human contribution to be effective, behaviour-change will be required at all stages. While emerging research on the value of wastewater will broaden our knowledge of how economic incentives can modify behaviour, it is a fact that, to adopt safer practices, some along the 'wastewater chain' will need to do so without any obvious personal or business advantage. From a national planning perspective, this may be more difficult to implement and sustain than to have wastewater treatment as the principal strategy to mitigate health risk in this area. The challenge lies in effective awareness creation, and use of incentives and regulations. This implies the continued need for additional research on risk perceptions and drivers of appropriate technology adoption (see Box 19.1).

The options outlined in this volume – such as modifying irrigation practices, produce-washing and other forms of behavioural change – require concerted effort, but are less expensive than a complex treatment infrastructure and do result in considerable risk mitigation. For these reasons, the incremental approach suggested by the WHO Guidelines is of critical importance and post-treatment options will be of continued value.

Needless to say, a graduated approach to improving risk management will require significant investments in building capacity. A minimum commonsense requirement – and one that is rare given the numerous jurisdictional overlaps commonly seen – is that one agency or ministry be placed solely in charge of regulating wastewater management, coordinating reuse operations with the other concerned departments or ministries and directing investments in the sector. Given the lack of suitable governance responses at the moment, one should not overestimate the ability of national and local governments to respond to the WHO Guidelines in low-income countries. A renewed effort to tie the WHO

Guidelines to practice and existing wastewater governance systems will be a critical requirement in the coming years of development in this field.

Our collective understanding of wastewater use in agriculture has never been greater or more nuanced than it is now. The Accra Consensus (Box 19.2) demonstrates the growing understanding of the importance of a multifaceted response to address the complexities of water pollution and its impacts on food production and consumption. A combination of biophysical science, social, economic and policy analysis, and good politics and governance are required in order to reduce the impacts of wastewater-related health risks in the most effective way and to obtain win–win solutions from the sanitation, water and food crises triangle.

Box 19.2 The Accra Consensus:
AN AGENDA FOR RESEARCH, CAPACITY BUILDING AND ACTION ON THE SAFE USE OF WASTEWATER AND EXCRETA IN AGRICULTURE

To address key research challenges concerning health-risk assessment, risk mitigation and wastewater governance in developing countries, an expert consultation was held on 6–9 October 2008 in Accra, Ghana. The event was hosted by the International Water Management Institute, the International Development Research Centre and the World Health Organization as a follow-up to the consultation resulting in the Hyderabad Declaration (see above). The meeting brought together over 50 researchers, practitioners, agency staff and decision-makers and concluded with the following statement:

Rapidly expanding cities, escalating water scarcity, food supply and livelihood needs, particularly in low-income regions, are all driving the increasing demand for untreated and treated wastewater and excreta for agriculture. Although much progress has been made in our understanding of these issues since the 'Hyderabad Declaration' of 2002, significant challenges remain to make the use of wastewater and excreta in agriculture safe, economically productive, and sustainable.

We – an expert group from 30 international, regional, and national research institutes, multilateral and bilateral bodies, and universities based in 17 countries – emphasize the need to support policy-makers around the world to make informed decisions that lead to cost-effective interventions that improve public health, promote sustainable sanitation, protect the environment, and support food security and economic development.

Achieving this goal requires consolidation of information on the science and practice of wastewater and excreta use, and well-targeted research to address gaps in the evidence base needed to support informed decision-making. Therefore, we propose the following multidisciplinary agenda for action:

1 *Integrate health and economic impact assessments to determine the actual contribution of wastewater and excreta use to the burden of disease, particularly in low-income settings, and to prioritize interventions to improve health and livelihood outcomes.*

2 *Facilitate the adoption of the 2006 World Health Organization guidelines for the safe use of wastewater, excreta and greywater in low-income settings through the development and application of appropriate local practices and standards that take into account local capacities and resources. Specifically:*

- *Fill data gaps on levels, transmission, persistence, and reduction of key pathogens along the environmental pathways from faecal origin to human exposure, and measure disease incidence among those exposed.*

- *Rigorously evaluate – in multiple geographical contexts – a range of wastewater and excreta treatment approaches and other risk-mitigation strategies for their cost-effectiveness and impacts on health, livelihood and the environment.*

- *Increase human, institutional and technical capacities in low-income settings to:*
  - *Detect important pathogens in human and environmental samples*
  - *Design and operate wastewater and excreta treatment systems that can be maintained in their ecological and economic context, and thereby support the safe and productive use of wastewater and excreta in agriculture*
  - *Develop and support effective participatory governance mechanisms for sustainable sanitation design and operation and safe and productive wastewater and excreta use.*

4 *Facilitate the exchange of information on best practices, including successful risk assessment and mitigation strategies, among partners around the globe through national and regional knowledge hubs and web-based data banks.*

Accra, 9 October 2008

Source: www.iwmi.cgiar.org/Research_Impacts/Research_Themes/Theme_3/Accra_Consensus.aspx

REFERENCES

Chang, A. C., Page, A.L. and Asano, T. (1995) *Developing Human Health-Related Chemical Guidelines for Reclaimed Wastewater and Sewage Sludge Applications in Agriculture*, WHO/EOS/95.20 report, World Health Organization, Geneva

Drechsel, P. and Raschid-Sally, L. (2009) 'Making an asset out of wastewater', *Words into Action Delegate Publication for the 5th World Water Forum, Istanbul 2009*, Fairmount Media Group, Turkey, pp106–110

Fewtrell, L., Prüss-Ustün, A., Bos, R., Gore, F. and Bartram, J. (2007) *Water, Sanitation and Hygiene: Quantifying the Health Impact at National and Local Levels in Countries with Incomplete Water Supply and Sanitation Coverage*, WHO Environmental Burden of Disease Series no 15, World Health Organization, Geneva, http://whqlibdoc.who. int/publications/2007/9789241595759_eng.pdf

Food and Water Watch (2008) 'State Data. Cited on May 15th, 2009', www.foodand waterwatch.org/water/trust-fund/clearwaters/state-data

Jiménez, B. and Asano, T. (2008) 'Water reclamation and reuse around the world', in B. Jiménez and T. Asano (eds) *Water Reuse: An International Survey of Current Practice, Issues and Needs*, IWA Publishing, London, pp 648

Oliveira, S. C. and von Sperling, M. (2008) 'Reliability analysis of wastewater treatment plants', *Water Research*, vol 42, nos 4–5, pp1182–94

Raschid-Sally, L. and Jayakody, P. (2008) 'Drivers and characteristics of wastewater agriculture in developing countries: Results from a global assessment, Colombo, Sri Lanka', *IWMI Research Report 127*, International Water Management Institute, Colombo

Scott, C. A., Faruqui, N. I. and Raschid-Sally, L. (eds) (2004) *Wastewater Use in Irrigated Agriculture: Confronting the Livelihood and Environmental Realities*, CABI Publishing, Wallingford, UK

Serageldin, I. (1994) *Water Supply, Sanitation and Environmental Sustainability: The Financing Challenge*, World Bank, Washington, DC

United Nations, Millennium Project Task Force on Water and Sanitation (2005) *Health Dignity and Development: What Will It Take?*, Earthscan, London

United Nations, Department of Economic and Social Affairs, Population Division (2008) *World Urbanization Prospects: The 2007 Revision – Highlights,* United Nations, New York, www.un.org/esa/population/publications/wup2007/2007WUP_Highlights_ web.pdf

Water and Sanitation Program (2007) *Economic Impacts of Sanitation in South-East Asia*, World Bank, Washington, DC, www.wsp.org/index.cfm?page=page_ disp&pid=13392

WHO (2006) *Guidelines for the Safe Use of Wastewater, Excreta and Greywater, Volume 2: Wastewater Use in Agriculture*, World Health Organization, Geneva

Xianjun C, Zhanyi G, Jayawardane N, Blackwell J, Biswas T. (2003) Filter Technology: Integrated wastewater irrigation and treatment: A way of water scarcity alleviation, pollution elimination and health risks prevention. UNESCAP Water Resources Journal (Dec. 2003): 79-87; www.unescap.org/esd/water/publications/water/wrj215/215-5. pdf, consulted on 28 October 2009

Index